Edward Meyrick Goulburn

Thoughts on personal Religion

Being a Treatise on the Christian Life

Edward Meyrick Goulburn

Thoughts on personal Religion
Being a Treatise on the Christian Life

ISBN/EAN: 9783337054830

Printed in Europe, USA, Canada, Australia, Japan

Cover: Foto ©Lupo / pixelio.de

More available books at **www.hansebooks.com**

THOUGHTS

ON

PERSONAL RELIGION;

BEING

A Treatise on the Christian Life

IN ITS TWO CHIEF ELEMENTS,

DEVOTION AND PRACTICE.

BY

EDWARD MEYRICK GOULBURN, D.D.

DEAN OF NORWICH.

NEW EDITION.

RIVINGTONS,

London, Oxford, and Cambridge.

1869.

LONDON:
GILBERT AND RIVINGTON, PRINTERS,
ST. JOHN'S SQUARE.

TO

WILLIAM GIBBS, ESQ.,

OF TYNTESFIELD,

THE KIND FRIEND OF THE POOR,

THE MUNIFICENT PATRON OF ALL GOOD WORKS,

AND

A LOYAL SON OF THE ENGLISH CHURCH,

THESE PAGES ARE INSCRIBED

WITH REVERENCE, GRATITUDE, AND AFFECTION.

21, Sussex Gardens, Hyde Park,
October 17, 1861.

MY DEAR MR. GIBBS,

You have kindly permitted me to inscribe to you this little treatise on the Christian Life. Most heartily do I wish that I had some worthier tribute of respect and affection for one, who has shown me such unceasing kindness, and has been the instrument of such incalculable blessings to my flock. But I know you will believe that my acknowledgment of all that I owe to you is, if not of any great value, at any rate sincere.

We have laboured much and happily together in the cause of the New Church, which your munificence has enabled us to complete and to endow. Perhaps this little book may serve as a memorial of the happy hours so spent in one another's company,—hours which, I can assure you, have been some of the pleasantest of my life.

The leading thoughts of my treatise are so well expressed by a passage from a work which you gave me, that I should like to adopt it as my motto:

"The oftener I read Jeremy Taylor, the more I am satisfied of the excellence of his method of recommending holiness to the heart and imagination, as well as to the understanding of frail man by dwelling on the infinite love and condescension of our gracious Father in taking so much *pains to make it attainable, if not easy; and by mixing it up with every act and duty of ordinary life, so as to make every hour spent in the world, as well as in the closet, when sanctified by its motive, an act of religion and obedience.* I have often wished to hear Christianity inculcated from the pulpit on this principle."—*Sir John Richardson, as quoted in the Life of Mr. Joshua Watson. Vol. ii. p.* 10.

You will, I think, see that these three thoughts,—the power of attaining, under God's grace, a real, though gradual, growth in sanctity; the possibility of making the homeliest acts of common life contribute to this growth; and the expediency of giving to such topics as these much more room than they generally occupy in Christian Teaching, have been more or less present to my mind throughout my argument. I have to thank you for giving me the opportunity of here stating the fundamental principles of my little book so tersely and clearly.

There is one point connected with this treatise on which an explanation seems necessary. By those who know what an all-important position the Holy Scriptures hold in the Economy of Grace, it will be remarked as a grievous omission, that in that part of the work, which professedly treats of Devotional Exercises, there should not be a chapter devoted to the study of Scripture. My answer is, that a single chapter could not do justice to a subject so wide and important, and that I have already published a small volume upon it, which has met with a fair circulation and a kind reception. I do not wish to repeat myself in print.

It only remains to add, by way of explaining some peculiarities of the style, that these pages, before they were thrown into the shape of a treatise, have been orally delivered, some of them in your own hearing, in the form of Sermons; but that the subject of them has been upon my mind for seven or eight years, and in the course of that period most of the chapters have been reconsidered and written afresh. Faults, no doubt, many will be found in them; but I trust that on topics of such transcendent importance I have not allowed myself to put forth any crude or precipitate views.

You will join with me, my dear Mr. Gibbs, in the prayer that, so far as it exhibits His Truth, God's Blessing may rest upon this little work, and that what is erroneous in it may be forgiven to me, and neutralized to the reader, through the Grace of Our Lord Jesus Christ.

I remain, my dear Mr. Gibbs,

Your affectionate friend,

EDWARD MEYRICK GOULBURN.

William Gibbs, Esq.
&c. &c. &c.

PREFACE TO THE FOURTH EDITION.

I HAVE taken the opportunity offered by the call for a fourth edition of this little work to add two Chapters to it. The substance of the first of these (Chap. III. of Part I.) is indeed contained already in Chap. I. of Part III.; but it seemed to me to require further expansion and development than I there had space to give it. The treatise in general is an enlarged commentary on the words, " Work out your own Salvation ;" and I thought it therefore desirable to give great prominence to the other (and equally important) side of Truth, that " it is God who worketh in us both to will and to do of His good pleasure."

The line of thought taken in the other new Chapter (Chap. IV. of Part III.) has been helpful and consolatory to myself in a busy life, and I have thought therefore that it might be so to others similarly circumstanced. The leading idea of it is very beautifully and delicately traced in " Les Adieux d'Adolphe Monod (XVI. Le secret d'une vie sainte, active, et paisible)," of which address my Chapter is little more than an expansion.   E. M. G.

ADVERTISEMENT TO THE EIGHTH EDITION.

Two other Chapters (one on Fasting, and another on Almsgiving) are added in this Edition, which it is hoped will make the work somewhat more complete.

                   E. M. G.

CONTENTS.

Part I.

Introductory.

CHAPTER I.

ON THE LOW STANDARD OF PERSONAL RELIGION NOW PREVALENT, AND THE CAUSES OF IT.

"*A certain man drew a bow at a venture, and smote the king of Israel between the joints of the harness.*"—1 KINGS xii. 34.

PAGE

Religion widely diffused, but of a low type in individuals—the immense motive powers of Christianity should secure larger results—Analogy between knowledge and piety in respect of their diffusion over a wide area and their shallowness in individuals—Is there any defect in the means employed, which may account for this result?—The Ministry the great means of forming in man the saintly character—The *guidance* of the conscience (as distinct from its awakening) too often neglected in our Ministry—our aim to make good impressions, but not to follow them up by systematic teaching—Popular Lectures as a means of diffusing knowledge compared with popular Sermons as a means of diffusing Religion—Neglect of ministerial guidance of the conscience due (1) to a reaction from the confessional, (2) to a reaction from the dry moral sermons of half a century ago—Earnest desire of holiness the state of mind contemplated in the reader—This desire is the rudiment out of which the spiritual creation may be, step by step, built up 1

CHAPTER II.

ON THE CHIEF CHARACTERISTIC OF PERSONAL RELIGION.

"*Grow in Grace.*"—2 PET. iii. 18.

PAGE

Accurate notion of the nature of Personal Religion, desirable in the outset—It involves, as its chief characteristic, growth in grace—the essential connexion between growth and life in Nature—no spiritual life without growth in grace—the distinction between spiritual life and spiritual impulses illustrated by the difference between the operations of life and those of galvanism—individualizing scrutiny of the character at the Day of Judgment—the question of our Religion being personal will resolve itself into the question, Is it a growing Religion?—this (and no other) the critical question for each of us—Is growth consistent with relapses? Yes, if the fall have been one of infirmity—the occasional strong impulse of penitent love—the Christian's progress, like that of the tide, is movement *upon the whole*—Growth in Grace, as in Nature, is by many fresh starts—all healthy growth gradual—no comfort in these reflections for the indolent and formal—if we are not advancing, we must be falling back—formation of the character, either for good or evil, continually in progress 10

CHAPTER III.

OF THE ENTIRE DEPENDENCE OF SANCTITY ON CHRIST, AND OF THE RELATION WHICH THE MEANS OF GRACE HOLD TO HIM.

"*Abide in Me, and I in you. As the branch cannot bear fruit of itself, except it abide in the vine; no more can ye, except ye abide in Me.*"

"*I am the vine, ye are the branches: he that abideth in Me, and I in him, the same bringeth forth much fruit: for without Me ye can do nothing.*"—JOHN xv. 4, 5.

A clear notion of the nature of Christian Holiness essential—The difference of meaning between "Without Me" and "Apart from Me"—the fruits of the Spirit enumerated in detail in Gal. v. 22, 23—Dependence of Justification on Christ generally recognized—Sanctification not an accumulation of righteous acts and ordinances, but a momentary receiving out of the fulness of Christ—the circulating sap, which is the life of the vine-branch, not *from* the branch, but from the Stock—all graces inhere in Christ, as colours in the Sunlight; and independently of Christ, the heart has no grace, even as, independently of the Sun, a landscape has no colour—the

Contents. xi

PAGE

secret of sanctity, then, is mutual indwelling of the Christian in Christ, of Christ in the Christian—We abide in Him by faith in Him, as being made to us Sanctification—Could we doubt His willingness to sanctify us, even if we had no promise to that effect?—May not our very struggles to be holy be, in a certain sense, a token of want of faith?—yet He will not (and cannot) sanctify us, unless we yield up the soul into His hands—and this implies yielding up the *will*—Christ abides in the Christian by Ordinance, and specially by the Holy Communion—how the allegory before us implies that even this Sacrament will be profitless without faith—Ordinances are merely channels by which the Virtue of Christ is conveyed into the souls of faithful recipients—illustration from the story of the woman of Samaria—Christ the Well; the Ordinance, the Pitcher; Faith, the muscular action, which lifts the pitcher 19

CHAPTER IV.

PERSONAL RELIGION BOTH ACTIVE AND CONTEMPLATIVE.

"*In the year that King Uzziah died I saw also the Lord sitting upon a throne, high and lifted up, and His train filled the temple.*
"*Above it stood the Seraphims: each one had six wings: with twain he covered his face, and with twain he covered his feet, and with twain he did fly.*"—ISA. vi. 1, 2.

The subject falls into two great divisions—The angelic life the model of the Christian—Adoration and Service the elements of the angelic life—Monasticism discards the latter of these elements—the active services of holy Angels—necessity for work in the constitution of our nature—each of us has a stewardship, and a work annexed to it, in the great social system—the "business" of the child and of the slave—the two chief scenes, in which angels are seen engaged in Worship—the barrenness and weariness of activity, if not fed from the springs of devotion—defective devotion the snare of these busy times—The angelic life has been led upon earth, under the pressure of physical infirmities, by Christ—His persistent activity and unwearied devotion—Service and Prayer must interpenetrate one another—prayer the spot of God's children —are we men of prayer? 30

Part II.
The Contemplative Life.

CHAPTER I.

OF THE MAGNIFICENCE OF PRAYER, AND THE PRACTICAL DEDUCTIONS FROM THAT DOCTRINE.

"*He that cometh to God.*"—HEB. xi. 6.

               PAGE

An effort necessary to grasp the idea of prayer—Gradual ascent as necessary to the mind in reaching a great idea as to the body in reaching a great height—Prayer a coming to God—we will seek to realize the grandeur of this idea—supposed privilege of consulting in our difficulties the wisest and best man upon earth—of consulting a departed parent or friend—of consulting our guardian-angel—proof that such intercourse between this world and another would be largely practised, if it were feasible—these hypotheses help us to realize the idea of coming to God, which however must always transcend our powers—God permits, invites, commands our approach—But may not the consciousness of our guilt debar us from access?—were it not for Christ, it must be so—the symbolism of the surplice—difficulty of rescuing prayer from formality—design of this Chapter to help us in such difficulties—the exercise however demands time—which might perhaps be gained by self-discipline—a little well done better than much done superficially—the end of stated Prayers (as well as the entrance into them) should be made the subject of attention—we must watch against subsequent levity 41

CHAPTER II.

OF THE TWOFOLD ASPECT OF PRAYER, AND THE NECESSITY OF PRACTISING IT IN BOTH ASPECTS.

"*Let my prayer be set forth before Thee as incense; and the lifting up of my hands as the evening sacrifice.*"—PSALM cxli. 2.

Prayer introduced in two different connexions in the Sermon on the Mount—Prayer a means of supplying our wants and also an act of homage to God—the Christian a priest—his sacrifice of the body—his sacrifice of alms—his sacrifice of prayer—incense a type of prayer—the Altar on which these sacrifices must be made—prayer as a tax upon our time compared to alms as a tax upon our substance—think of yourself as a priest when you offer prayer—how these thoughts may help us against the temptation to leave off, when prayer promises to be dry and barren—we pray for God's honour, not exclusively for our own comfort—when you cannot pray as you would, pray as you can—perseverance in prayer under discouragements the most acceptable offering—an illustration of this from the writings of St. François de Sales—necessity of redeeming our Prayers from selfishness, by (1) mixing intercession with them—(2) and by mixing praise with them—Praise often quickens a torpid heart 50

CHAPTER III.

THE SECRET OF SUCCESS IN PRAYER.

"*And in the morning, as they passed by, they saw the fig-tree dried up from the roots. And Peter calling to remembrance saith unto Him, Master, behold, the fig-tree which Thou cursedst is withered away. And Jesus answering saith unto them, Have faith in God. For verily I say unto you, That whosoever shall say unto this mountain, Be thou removed, and be thou cast into the sea; and shall not doubt in his heart, but shall believe that those things which he saith shall come to pass; he shall have whatsoever he saith.*"—MARK xi. 20—23.

Our Lord's comments on incidents which pass before Him not always what we should have anticipated—the lesson He draws from the blighted fig-tree not what we should have expected—the withering of the tree led St. Peter to reflect on the power of his Master's words—Our Lord replies that His followers should say words of power like His, if only they will pray in faith and love—the small effect of the prayers of religious persons—may it not be due to their not expecting an answer?—would they not be surprised if an answer should come?—Our despondency as regards any fruits of sanctity in ourselves—necessity of honouring God while we pray, by believing that He will be true to His promise—ask for definite graces, and expect definite results—A promise to prayer which contemplates in the petitioner nothing but asking—sublimity and freedom of this promise 59

CHAPTER IV.

SELF-EXAMINATION.

"*And the Lord sent Nathan unto David. And he came unto him, and said unto him, There were two men in one city; the one rich, and the other poor. The rich man had exceeding many flocks and herds: but the poor man had nothing, save one little ewe lamb, which he had bought and nourished up: and it grew up together with him, and with his children: it did eat*

*of his own meat, and drank of his own cup, and lay in his
bosom, and was unto him as a daughter. And there came a
traveller unto the rich man, and he spared to take of his own
flock, and of his own herd, to dress for the wayfaring man that
was come unto him; but took the poor man's lamb, and dressed
it for the man that was come to him. And David's anger was
greatly kindled against the man: and he said to Nathan, As
the Lord liveth, the man that hath done this thing shall surely
die: and he shall restore the lamb fourfold, because he did this
thing, and because he had no pity. And Nathan said to
David, Thou art the man."*—2 SAM. xii. 1—7.

PAGE

David in disguise brought before his own judgment-seat—We
never judge ourselves as severely as we judge an abstract case—
evil never admitted by the will without some palliation—it is self-
examination which makes religion a personal thing—special necessity of pressing it on members of the reformed churches—prone-
ness of self-examination to lapse into formality—necessity of it
arises from the deceitfulness of the heart—Warm characters like
David and St. Peter specially liable to self-deception, and why—
dangerousness of trusting to some fair-spoken but dishonest man in
a great mercantile speculation—the trust which we naturally place
in our own hearts—self-love conspires to make dupes of us—
Means to be used in counteracting the deceitfulness of the heart
—As we cannot ourselves give a fair judgment on our own sins,
might we not sometimes call in another to judge them?—or ask
ourselves how such an one would regard it, if we communicated
it to him?—the better as well as the worse parts of our conduct
need self-examination—suspect your own motives—part of our
religion due to custom—part of it a homage to public opinion—part
of it due to the love of keeping up appearances—part to natural
activity of mind—difference between an innocent, and a gracious
motive—secret prayer more or less a test of personal religion—
dissatisfaction with ourselves of no avail unless it leads to satisfaction with Christ 68

CHAPTER V.

OF INTERCESSORY PRAYER.

*" They made the breastplate: . . . . . and they set in it four rows
of stones: . . . . And the stones were according to the names
of the children of Israel, twelve, according to their names,
like the engravings of a signet, every one with his name, according to the twelve tribes."*—EXOD. xxxix. 9, 10. 14.

The symbolism of the High Priest's breastplate—the Christian
as a priest must offer intercession—intercession and self-examination necessary to keep one another in check—instances of intercessory prayer in Scripture—how intercession is woven into the
texture of the Lord's Prayer—testimony of the Prayer Book to

this duty—grounds of the duty—we are members one of another, and our interests bound up with those of other men—the interest we have in the rulers of our country—systematic neglect of intercession for any but the members of our own family—grounds of the disinclination to it—(1) it appears presumptuous—answer to this—(2) supposed impotency of intercessory prayer—reflect that in offering it we co-operate with the whole Church—(3) want of. interest in others—selfishness hinders the success of our prayers—the ground of this explained—hints as to the particular blessings which we may ask for our friends 79

CHAPTER VI.

OF DEVOTIONAL READING.

"And Elisha died, and they buried him. And the bands of the Moabites invaded the land at the coming in of the year.
"And it came to pass, as they were burying a man, that, behold, they spied a band of men; and they cast the man into the sepulchre of Elisha: and when the man was let down, and touched the bones of Elisha, he revived, and stood up on his feet."—2 KINGS xiii. 20, 21.

In what sense Protestants may believe in relics—advantage of association with the wise and good—in society circumstances may nullify this advantage—the best mind of an author mirrored in his devotional works—bad books a powerful agency for evil—spiritual reading has to a certain extent taken the place of preaching, and therefore ought to be regarded in the light of a Divine ordinance — particular writers serviceable to particular minds—great variety of the inspired literature — corresponding variety in Devotional works—select what suits you—caution as to correctness of taste in the choice of devotional works—do not eschew the dry—read as a devotional exercise—thinking of the author (if deceased) as a Saint in Paradise—avoid dissipation in reading—recourse to the favourite spiritual author will often revive our own hearts in a period of deadness 88

CHAPTER VII.

OF FASTING.

"I keep under my body, and bring it into subjection."—1 COR. ix. 27.

Some counsels on Fasting likely to meet the state of mind contemplated in the reader of this Book—Fasting never literally prescribed, but the principle of it insisted upon—commended to us, not commanded—Analogies between it and the observance of Sunday—Division of the subject—Principle of Fasting gathered from the words of St. Paul—The imagery employed in these words, the occasion of these words, and their connexion with the argument—the principle of not indulging to the uttermost in innocent gratifications illustrated—Let there be a broad margin between you and danger—the principle applied to amusement—In amusements, however lawful, we must lay restrictions on ourselves—The principle applied to food—Certain class of sins, for the extirpation of which Fasting is absolutely necessary—Unbridled indulgence unsafe under any circumstances—how self-restraint is the highest freedom—how easily we may deceive ourselves in judging of our attachment to comforts and luxuries—Stated seasons for Fasting—the value and necessity of such seasons—The duty of habitual temperance no more supersedes the stated fast, than the duty of Prayer without ceasing supersedes the observance of the Fourth Commandment—Fasting to be spiritualized by its connexion with Prayer and Almsgiving, as the Fourth Commandment must be spiritualized by acts of Piety and Charity—Luxury and over-refinement the evils of the time on which we are fallen—how the devout observance of Fasting would apply a corrective to these evils 97

CHAPTER VIII.

ON ALMSGIVING.

"*Thy prayers and thine alms are come up for a memorial before God.*"—ACTS x. 4.

The two features of the religious life of Cornelius—Prayer and Almsgiving co-ordinate—Prayer a fulfilment of the first, Almsgiving of the second Table of the Law—both spoken of as having a sacrificial fragrance—neither have a justifying efficacy; yet both are acceptable when offered in faith—Alms often given grudgingly as Prayers are offered formally—What spirit in giving will make our alms come up as a memorial before God?—their being offered on principle and not on impulse—the obvious danger which there would be in abandoning stated Prayer, and leaving Prayer to good impulse—Viewed as an act of homage to Almighty God, Prayer must be offered *methodically*—Modern almsgiving seldom systematic, usually impulsive—How the system of things has adjusted itself to this practice—questionable methods of appeal to our sensibilities—A charity sermon defined and considered—even the charity sermon not the best way of obtaining supplies—the Apostolic precept inculcating periodical almsgiving, and the principle of it—how the Primitive Christians acted on the letter of it—The offertory of the Early Church—How the principle of the Apostolic precept may be now acted upon—Settle the proportion of your income or earnings which is due to GOD for works of Piety and Charity—Open an account of charitable expenditure, and examine periodically whether this proportion has been given—if not, make up the deficit—from the adoption of this plan by *every one*, would accrue (1) abundant supply for all deserving charities; (2) peace of conscience; (3) a growing spirit of liberality; (4) cheerfulness

Contents. xvii

in giving—Summary of what has been said—The inspiriting thought that we may have memorials in Heaven—no remembrance there without a requital—The fourfold recompense of the prayers and alms of Cornelius 112

CHAPTER IX.

OF FREQUENTING THE HOLY COMMUNION.

"*Whether therefore ye eat, or drink, or whatsoever ye do, do all to the glory of God.*"—1 COR. x. 31.

Modern convictions on the desirableness of frequent Communion—Necessity hence arising for a change in the manuals of preparation—Rare Communion would be desirable if the Eucharist were merely a commemorative Rite—but it is also the highest means of grace—and seems from the Acts of the Apostles to have been of equally frequent occurrence with other means—difference between liveliness of feeling, and strengthening of principle—it is the latter, not the former, we should seek in the means of grace—Old-fashioned feeling in favour of rare Communion analyzed—its good element—and its bad—to make frequent Communion available our lives must be conformed to the ordinance—this conformity stands in sanctifying our common and necessary actions, by supernatural motives—how this sanctification of common actions is expressed in the ordinance—objection arising from the desirableness of having stated periods for a solemn self-scrutiny—why should not the three great Communions be reserved for this special scrutiny?—frequent Communion not Popish—Adolphe Monod's death-bed testimony to the expediency of frequent Communion . 122

CHAPTER X.

OF THE PUBLIC SERVICE OF THE CHURCH.

"*If two of you shall agree on earth as touching any thing that they shall ask, it shall be done for them of My Father which is in heaven.*"—MATT. xviii. 19.

The Charter of Public Worship contained in Matt. xviii. 19—functions of Public Worship devolved both by Dissenters and Romanists on the Clergy—Public Prayer in the Church of Rome resolves itself into a number of private prayers said in public—Private prayer and public essentially different—their respective charters examined—cordial agreement as to what should be asked an essential of public prayer—difficulty of securing this agreement without a Liturgy—defective practice of our Church while her theory is perfect—coldness of the service notwithstanding the beauty of the Liturgy—way to remedy this coldness—study the Services with a view of understanding them—specially the Psalms—set yourself against the tendency to think of nothing but your own wants in public worship—great importance of making the responses audibly and heartily—strive to realize the presence of the Incarnate God, which is covenanted in the Charter of Public Worship . 132

CHAPTER XI.

ON SELF-RECOLLECTEDNESS AND EJACULATORY PRAYER.

"*Pray without ceasing.*"—1 Thess. v. 17.

How we are to reconcile St. Luke's notice of Our Lord's having ceased to pray with St. Paul's precept, Pray without ceasing—Prayer the Christian's breath of life—consists in (1) recollecting the mind, and (2) aspiring towards God—God ever present in the depth of our spirits—the refreshment of drawing ourselves into His presence from outward things—ejaculatory prayer, why called ejaculatory—illustration of the subject from the arrow which fetches down a bird—instance of the success of ejaculatory prayer in the history of Nehemiah—recognition of ejaculatory prayer in our Liturgy—Materials for ejaculatory prayer on ordinary occasions—our daily portion of Scripture—the Psalms—stated prayer cannot be dispensed with, even where ejaculatory is practised—this shown from the example of Our Lord, and from the comparison of prayers to respiration—encouragement, at the close of the second part, for those who are striving after a life of Sanctity and conscious of failure 142

Part III.

The Practical Life.

CHAPTER I.

WHAT HOLDS US BACK.

"*Work out your own salvation with fear and trembling. For it is God which worketh in you both to will and to do of His good pleasure.*"—PHIL. ii. 12, 13.

PAGE

Practical character of the work—the Reader interrogated as to his progress—What holds us back—necessity of recognizing the agency of the human will in the work of salvation—necessity of recognizing that sanctification is by grace—illustration from the probable causes of continued illness under a competent physician—two conditions which might defeat the progress of a rowing boat—necessity both of self-surrender and of trust in Christ—true faith embraces God's commands with obedience—this shown from the history of Abraham—impossibility of sanctifying ourselves as great as that of justifying ourselves—means of Grace will disappoint us if we regard them as sources of Grace—in what sense the righteousness of sanctification is inherent in us, and in what sense not—illustration of the doctrine of this Chapter from the Baptismal Covenant—vow of self-surrender in Baptism—the free gift in Baptism 151

CHAPTER II.

DO ALL FOR GOD.

"*And whatsoever ye do, do it heartily, as to the Lord, and not unto men.*"—COL. iii. 23.

The Christian's practical life comprises three elements, working, acting, and suffering—how to work devoutly—destiny of man, as an immortal being, contrasted with the earthliness of his pursuits—apparent inconsistency between secular pursuits and a heavenly calling—how monasticism arose from the feeling of this inconsistency—how the idea of this inconsistency is often insinuated in conversation, and at religious meetings—hypothesis of its being God's will that all Christians should have a directly spiritual pursuit—absurdity to which the assumption leads—the only other alternative—abide with God in your calling—how this is to be done—intention gives a moral character to actions—various intentions in secular pursuits enumerated—livelihood—distinction—natural distastefulness of a want of occupation—motive of duty—mechanical activity—the supernatural motive, Do it heartily as to the Lord—original reference of this precept to the duties of slaves—wisdom of this particular reference—inference from it—thoughts to be entertained before entering upon our daily work—renewal of our good intention at intervals—our lesser actions to be brought under the control of Christian principle—yet without indulging scruples of conscience—religious considerations which give elasticity of mind 162

CHAPTER III.

ON MAINTAINING THE CONSCIOUSNESS OF GOD'S PRESENCE IN THE WORKS OF OUR CALLING.

"The Lord appeared to Abram, and said unto him, I am the Almighty God: walk before Me, and be thou perfect."—GEN. xvii. 1.

Realization of the Divine Presence, the nucleus round which the spiritual character forms itself—how may God's presence be retained on the mind when our work itself is mental?—undivided attention necessary to do any work well—proof that the consciousness of God's Presence need not interfere with active mental work—the mind actively engaged in an extempore address—yet in such an address the Speaker is never unconscious of the presence of his audience—means of cultivating a consciousness of the Divine Presence—Secret prayer at intervals during the day—three different conceptions under which God's Presence will present itself to different minds—habit of cultivating this consciousness gradually formed—quotation from St. François de Sales—helps to realizing God's presence in a rural walk—why nature impresses us so slightly—how thoughts of God's Presence may be realized in the city—how the Incarnation connects the thoughts of God with human Society—lesson to be learnt from the original pursuit of St. Matthew 172

CHAPTER IV.

OF INTERRUPTIONS IN OUR WORK, AND THE WAY TO DEAL WITH THEM.

"We are created in Christ Jesus unto good works, which God hath before ordained that we should walk in them."—EPH. ii. 10.

The doing work earnestly for God and in God will make interruptions very harassing—subject of the Chapter proposed—when troubled by interruptions, we must copy the mind of Christ, as it transpires (1) in His discourses—which are not set and formal, but take their rise from some object of nature or incident which He comes across—the contexture of Our Lord's discourses not systematic in the usual sense of the word—the intellectual method and the method of charity—(2) in His life—apparent want of plan in it —this illustrated from Matthew ix.—God has a plan of life for each one of us, and occasions of doing or receiving good mapped out for each in His Eternal Counsels—little incidents, as well as great crises of life, are under the control of God's Providence—Events have a voice for us, if we will listen to it—Let us view our interruptions as part of God's plan for us—We may receive good, even where we cannot do good—It is self-will which weds us so to our own plans, and makes us resent interference with them—the true notion of God's Providence illustrated—Let us endeavour to subserve His designs for us 181

CHAPTER V.

FIGHT WISELY.

"*So fight I, not as one that beateth the air.*"—1 COR. ix. 26.

Second element in the Christian's practical life, his resistance to temptations—Satan's policy must be opposed by policy—want of definite aim in resisting temptations a cause of failure—the besetting sin and its deceitfulness—Vanity masked by an affected humility—under honourable emulation—Indolence masked under some more superficial sin—usual sensitiveness of men on the weak points of their moral character—in strong characters the ruling passion is more obvious—hints for discovering besetting sin—in what direction do the results of self-examination point?—What occurrences give us pain and pleasure?—having found the besetting sin, bend the whole strength of your will against it—the noiseless current of the bosom sin is always setting on a shoal—A glimpse of God's love and grace necessary to counteract the depression which results from self-knowledge 191

CHAPTER VI.

ON THE NATURE OF TEMPTATION.

"*Then was Jesus . . . . tempted of the devil.*"—MATT. iv. 1.

Brightness and cheerfulness of mind necessary to spiritual conquests—depression under temptation often arises from misapprehension of its nature—the eagle training her young to fly, an emblem of the way in which God disciplines His children—typical character of Israel's pilgrimage in the wilderness—the beginner in religion baffled by a host of temptations—special temptation which besets prayer—and Holy Communion—our non-abandonment of the struggle an augury that God has not forsaken us—discomfort arising from mistakes on the nature of temptation—temptation cannot become sin till the will consents to it—nor is it always a sign of a sinful nature—this proved by Our Lord's temptation—and by the trial of Abraham's faith—guilt arising from the corruption of our nature removed by Baptism—the doctrine of this Chapter applied to temptations in prayer—honour put by Christ upon prayer under discouragement—heaviness resulting from the consciousness of many sinful inclinations—the blessedness and dignity of manifold temptations—God offers to a soul beset by them an eminence in the Divine Life 200

CHAPTER VII.

FIGHT WITH DISTRUST IN SELF AND TRUST IN CHRIST.

"*And in the fourth watch of the night Jesus went unto them, walking on the sea. And when the disciples saw Him walking on the sea, they were troubled, saying, It is a spirit; and they cried out for fear. But straightway Jesus spake unto them, saying, Be of good cheer; It is I; be not afraid. And Peter answered Him and said, Lord, if it be Thou, bid me come unto Thee on the water. And He said, Come. And when Peter was come down out of the ship, he walked on the water to go to Jesus. But when he saw the wind boisterous, he was afraid; and beginning to sink, he cried saying, Lord, save me. And immediately Jesus stretched forth His hand, and caught him, and said unto him, O thou of little faith, wherefore didst thou doubt?*"—MATT. xiv. 25—31.

Harmony of Scripture characters with themselves, and argument thence arising in favour of their authenticity—Rehearsal beforehand of St. Peter's trial and fall—critical temptations occur but seldom—small ones not to be despised, as being a previous rehearsal of great ones—little temptations an excellent discipline of humility—instances in which great Saints have broken down in their characteristic grace, and the moral discipline of humility likely to be brought out of such failures—self-trust a certain source of failure—it often lurks under disgust with self—how the abnegation of self-trust is connected with elasticity of mind in the spiritual combat—how trust in Christ is taught in the narrative before us—never look temptations full in the face—look away from them to Christ, who is to conquer in you—weaken the affection for sin by filling the mind with the thought, and the heart with the love, of Christ—Satan's strongest assault possibly reserved for the last—terrors of the last conflict parallel with those of the disciples in the boat—let us nerve ourselves by faithfulness in lesser trials for this last conflict 209

CHAPTER VIII.

FIGHT WATCHFULLY.

"Keep thy heart with all diligence; for out of it are the issues of life."—Prov. iv. 23.

PAGE

The great force of the expression, Keep thy heart *above all keeping*—necessity for keeping the heart, arising from the fact that it is the key of the spiritual position—the traitors within the fortress—the immense fertility of our thoughts and feelings a reason for watchfulness—variety of emotions in conversation—solitude offers as many temptations as company—let us pause at intervals, and make our thoughts give up their passport—what must be done when derangements of the heart are discovered—spiritual life carried on by many fresh starts—The necessity of resisting evil when first presented to the Imagination—prayer must be mixed with watchfulness in order to success—prayer the expression of our entire dependence upon God—great difficulty of keeping the heart should teach us this dependence—the peace which results from Christ's indwelling in the heart—The peace in the stable of the inn of Bethlehem 218

CHAPTER IX.

THE HIGH PREROGATIVE OF SUFFERING.

"Verily, verily, I say unto thee, When thou wast young, thou girdedst thyself, and walkedst whither thou wouldest: but when thou shalt be old, thou shalt stretch forth thy hands, and another shall gird thee, and carry thee whither thou wouldest not. This spake He signifying by what death he should glorify God. And when He had spoken this, He saith unto him, Follow Me."—John xxi. 18, 19.

Our Lord's prediction of the manner of St. Peter's death—how the words may be applied generally as a parable of human life in youth and old age—suffering the third element in the practical life of the Christian—regard suffering as a vocation—even when plans of religious usefulness are disconcerted by it—illustration from a wise general's conduct of a campaign—what has been said applies to the little plans of daily life as well as to our prospects on a large scale—trial of interruptions—example of Our Lord when interrupted—suffering the highest of all vocations, as being (usually) the last—St. Peter's death the time when he specially glorified God—death the climax of sufferings—Even in natural character trial brings out unsuspected graces—Suffering conforms us to Christ—His virtues emphatically the passive ones—death of Christ expresses more of His Divine Character than His life—In what sense He was made perfect through sufferings—Christ's call to us to follow Him—the meaning of the words, "*Take up* the Cross"—Do not despise little daily crosses 227

CHAPTER X.

OF RECREATION.

"*Whether therefore ye eat, or drink, or whatsoever ye do, do all to the glory of God.*"—1 Cor. x. 31.

An anecdote of St. John the Evangelist—every true representation of life must embrace its lighter as well as its more sombre passages—religion designed to leaven our *whole* life—analogy between Recreation and Sleep—we cannot afford to lose a single waking moment of our time—no waking moment morally indifferent—admission that recreation must be an unbending—recreation may be, and must be, directed by our minds to the glory of God—a passage of Scripture which implies this—What should be our intention in taking recreation, expressed in words—As to their form, Recreations must be innocent (not necessarily useful)—and innocent *to us*—experimental knowledge of our own moral temperament—amusements should be amusing—burdensomeness of many (so-called) amusements—ordinary dulness of conversation—what remedies can be applied?—every mind has an interest somewhere—occasional toilsomeness of foreign travel—and its cause—even in variety we should seek a unity of plan—a good education should comprise some lighter subjects of study—refreshment to the mind of even a slight knowledge of Nature—"Consider the lilies of the field"—avoid excess in recreations—long periods of leisure should pay the tax of additional devotion—general importance of the subject of recreation, from its influence on the mind 237

Part IV.

Supplemental.

CHAPTER I.

ON THE WISDOM AND COMFORT OF LOOKING NO FURTHER THAN THE PRESENT DAY IN OUR SERVICE OF GOD.

"*He that is faithful in that which is least, is faithful also in much.*"—LUKE xvi. 10.

PAGE

Wisdom of limiting the field of research in the pursuit of knowledge—wisdom of beginning from one centre in the practical life of the Christian—the general principle applied to our time—the natural divisions of time—the day the least of them—the day a miniature of the whole life—illustration from a convex mirror—passages of Scripture implying that the day is the rudiment of the life—our provisions meted out by the day—our anxieties to be limited by the day—forethought allowed within the horizon of the day—our purposes to be limited by the same horizon—difficulty of so limiting them—the morning a miniature of youth—how much depends upon the way in which the morning hour is spent—entrance upon the business of the day compared to entrance upon the business of life—little crosses of the day compared to the great trials of life—consolatory prospect of the evening hour of devotion, if we maintain patience and watchfulness—Resemblance of Sleep to Death—and of rising to Resurrection—Look to it that the days be well spent; for they make up our life—But if we have thrown away (for all spiritual purposes) many days, still there is a possibility of redeeming the time—how this may be done—let to-morrow begin a new era with us 247

CHAPTER II.

OF UNITY OF EFFORT IN THE SERVICE OF GOD.

"*Thou art careful and troubled about many things: but one thing is needful.*"—LUKE x. 41, 42.

Simplicity and depth of the words of Our Lord illustrated by the depth of a pellucid stream—necessity of peace in endeavour, as well as of peace in the consciousness of acceptance—desirableness of having one single principle at the foundation of our spiritual character—how is this to be reconciled with the obligation of fulfilling *all* God's commandments?—the way in which Christian virtues hang together—prominence of a particular feature in all natural characters, and of a particular grace in all spiritual characters—growth in Nature proceeds from one nucleus—application of the principle—bend your efforts to the eradication of the bosom sin—other graces will form themselves while this process goes on—Choose one maxim as the foundation of the spiritual character—"Hallowed be thy Name"—what God's Name includes—"Blessed are the poor in spirit"—the principle chosen should not be too narrow, so as to give rare scope for acting upon it—nor too broad, so as to include (virtually) many principles—it should lie in a line of thought to which we are naturally drawn—Cultivate quietness of mind as a great secret of success in spiritual endeavour—how this quietness may be had even under the consciousness of falls . 257

CHAPTER III.

OF THE WAY IN WHICH WE SHOULD SEEK TO EDIFY OTHERS.

"*Let your light so shine before men, that they may see your good works, and glorify your Father which is in heaven.*" —MATT. v. 16.

A desire to do good to others is the very spot of God's children—this desire often directed in wrong channels—the history of schism—misdirected desire to edify—its mischievous results—fundamental passage on which the duty of Edification is built—Sermon on the Mount a perfect code of Christian duty—danger of applying indiscriminately words spoken to the Apostles, or to individuals under peculiar circumstances—"Let your light shine before men" explained from the context—do nothing to hide your Christian profession—Our Lord speaks of edification by example—and does not recommend even this *for the sake of edification*—every light must shine unless you cover it up—danger of indiscriminate religious admonition—as an assumption (which may be groundless) of religious superiority—as being most often a failure in point of result—as being a display of spiritual feeling, which may be mischievous to this delicate plant—How we may edify others—Live close to God, and strive to do all actions as unto Him—never lower your principles to the world's standard—aim at appearing just what you are, neither better, nor worse—eschew affectation in every form 266

CHAPTER IV.

IN WHAT THE SPIRITUAL LIFE CONSISTS.

"*And He opened His mouth, and taught them, saying, Blessed are the poor in spirit: for their's is the kingdom of heaven.*"

Blessed are they that mourn: for they shall be comforted. Blessed are the meek: for they shall inherit the earth. Blessed are they which do hunger and thirst after righteousness: for they shall be filled. Blessed are the merciful: for they shall obtain mercy. Blessed are the pure in heart: for they shall see God. Blessed are the peacemakers: for they shall be called the children of God. Blessed are they which are persecuted for righieousness' sake. for their's is the kingdom of heaven."—MATT. v. 2—10.

PAGE

The author's excuse for introducing this subject at so late a period of the work—In what the Spiritual Life does *not* consist—Not in ordinances—ordinances the means of kindling the flame or of feeding it, but not the flame—the gardener's tools not the life of the tree—our unhappy tendency to confound means with ends—Monasticism assumes that the Spiritual Life consists in ordinances—Scripture, where it touches on the vitals of religion, omits all mention of ordinance—the Spiritual life does not consist of actions—the fruit is not the life—View of religion as mere usefulness congenial to the English mind—Spiritual life does not consist in activities—religious activity of the present day—we all catch the spirit of it—our natural zest for work quickened by the disgust of young and earnest minds with the controversial extravagances of the day—the mischievous tendency of this result—Christian practice supposed to be separable from Christian doctrine—in what the Spiritual life *does* consist—answers from Scripture—it is *internal*—not even private prayer *is* the spiritual life, independently of the mind with which it is offered—it is *supernatural*—the application of this term justified—it *is developed amid trial and opposition*—this illustrated by the beatitudes of meekness and mercy—the first beatitude gives the fundamental grace of the Christian character—application of these various criteria in self-examination . . . 274

CHAPTER V.

THAT OUR STUDY OF GOD'S TRUTH MUST BE WITH THE HEART.

"*But even unto this day, when Moses is read, the vail is upon their heart. Nevertheless when it shall turn to the Lord, the vail shall be taken away.*"—2 COR. iii. 15, 16.

Jewish blindness resulted from a predisposition not to believe—In what form the truth is recognized that a man's judgment is liable to be prejudiced by his inclinations—non-recognition of this truth in the attempt of heathen philosophers to persuade men to virtue—the method of Socrates—historically Christianity began with an appeal to the affections—the doctrine of the Gospel makes the same appeal—Moral effect which the story of Christ's death is likely to produce—justifying faith shown to be an operation of the heart—every forward step in the spiritual life must be made with the heart—the necessity of "*unction*" to effective preaching—study of Scripture too often drops into a mere intellectual exercise—snare of the interest which attaches to Scripture in a literary point of view—the saving truths are the simplest—study chiefly Christ crucified, who is the centre of God's revelation 284

CHAPTER VI.

ON LIVING BY RULE.

"*Upon the first day of the week let every one of you lay by him in store, as God hath prospered him, that there be no gatherings when I come.*"—1 Cor. xvi. 2.

Discrepancy between the general tone of New Testament precept, and the passage at the head of the Chapter—wisdom of St. Paul's rule on the subject of almsgiving—impossibility of adapting the rule to all circumstances—general dearth of rules in the New Testament pointed out, and accounted for—morning and evening private prayer, and public worship on Sunday regarded as a sort of law of conscience—nature furnishes materials for all the arts of life—as Scripture furnishes principles for all rules of holy living—this analogy worked out—each Christian to frame rules for himself—grave responsibility of keeping the soul—and the necessity thence arising for a wise rule and method of life—rules must be adapted to our temperament and circumstances—rules urgently required in the matter of almsgiving—specific resolutions recommended, framed on a foresight of the trials of the day—rules should be made a help, not a penance 294

CHAPTER VII.

OF THE MISCHIEF AND DANGER OF EXAGGERATIONS IN RELIGION.

"*Let us prophesy according to the proportion of faith.*"
Rom. xii. 6.

A comparison from the writings of Lord Bacon—morbid tendency of the human mind to caricature the truths presented to it—all heresy a caricature of truth—this instanced in the erroneous views of the Quaker—and in those of some modern divines, who magnify God's Justice at the expense of His Love—spiritual writers often put a strain upon favourite precepts of the Gospel—an instance in which a holy man caricatured the grace of resignation—naturalness of character in the scriptural Saints—traces of it in St. Paul—in order to keep the mind free from exaggerations, read Scripture copiously—candidly—and giving full weight to those parts which do not naturally attract you—imbue the mind with it 304

CHAPTER VIII.

OF THE GREAT VARIETY OF MEN'S CHARACTERS IN THE CHURCH OF CHRIST.

"As the body is one, and hath many members, and all the members of that one body, being many, are one body: so also is Christ."—1 COR. xii. 12.

PAGE

The various extraordinary gifts of the early Church came from the same author, and work together to the same end—variety in unity the law of nature—agency of the same laws of nature in distinct spheres—great variety in Holy Scripture—the unity of Holy Scripture traced from its earlier to its later books—same feature of variety in unity to be expected in the Church of Christ—the supernatural gifts have most of them some natural endowment which corresponds with them—difference of character and endowments in St. Peter, St. Paul, St. John, and other Scriptural Saints—religious experience of different Christians widely different—conversions of a wholly different kind recorded on the same page of Scripture—our method of serving God will differ with our capacities and position—lesson of charity towards those who take a different line of religious thought from ourselves—each Christian designed to be an original specimen of redeeming love and grace . 312

CHAPTER IX.

OF THE IDEA OF SACRIFICE, AS PERVADING THE CHRISTIAN'S LIFE.

"An holy priesthood, to offer up spiritual sacrifices, acceptable to God by Jesus Christ."—1 PET. ii. 5.

All forms of religion have involved the idea of sacrifice—this perhaps traceable to the lingering tradition of Noah's sacrifice after the flood—instinct of the human heart which instigates men to sacrifice analyzed—hold which the idea has of the mind, shown by the system of Romanism—the sacrifice of Christ, which is the central doctrine of our religion, comprehends the sweet-savour offering of His Life, and the sin-offering of His Death—fundamental difference of these two offerings explained—Christ our altar—God still requires from Christians the sweet-savour though not the sin-offering—the offering of the body as a living sacrifice—of praise—of alms—how all these three offerings are recognized in the Communion Service—possibility of offering an acceptable sacrifice an encouraging thought—privilege of being allowed to please God by an acceptable tribute—self-oblation should form part of our morning's devotion, and the spirit of it should pervade our common actions—materials of an acceptable offering always at hand—but no offering can be acceptable independently of the mediation and intercession of Christ, Who is the true altar 322

CHAPTER X.

OF ALLOWING IN OUR MINDS A PREPONDERANCE TO TRIFLES.

" Woe unto you, Scribes and Pharisees, hypocrites! for ye pay tithe of mint and anise and cummin, and have omitted the weightier matters of the law, judgment, mercy, and faith: these ought ye to have done, and not to leave the other undone."— MATT. xxiii. 23.

PAGE

Attention to little duties continually recommended in this treatise—and why—ordinary life made up of little things—great crises occur comparatively seldom—Even duties not moral but ceremonial (such as reverent postures in prayer) have their importance—making the responses—attention to little things may degenerate into scrupulosity—case of the Pharisees—two opposite habits of mind as regards little things imported by men into their religion—punctiliousness in small matters quite consistent with the neglect of greater—the comparative insignificance of ritual and antiquarian controversies, and of the decoration of Churches—formalities often adhered to by those who profess to disregard forms—how the spirit of Religion may be allowed to evaporate, while formal regulations are observed—formal restraints as to amusement—formal observance of Sunday—While you use rules as a help, keep your eye fixed on the spirit and principle of them—Love to God and man the fulfilling of the whole Law—view all other things as they stand related to these two great objects . . . 331

CHAPTER XI.

OF IMPROVING OUR TALENTS.

" For the kingdom of heaven is as a man travelling into a far country, who called his own servants, and delivered unto them his goods. And unto one he gave five talents, to another two, and to another one; to every man according to his several ability: and straightway took his journey.

*" Then he which had received the one talent came and said, Lord, I knew thee that thou art an hard man, reaping where thou hast not sown, and gathering where thou hast not strawed: and I was afraid, and went and hid thy talent in the earth: lo, there thou hast that is thine. His Lord answered and said unto him, Thou wicked and slothful servant, thou knewest that I reap where I sowed not, and gather where I have not strawed: thou oughtest therefore to have put my money to the exchangers, and then at my coming I should have received mine own with usury."—*MATT. xxv. 14, 15. 24—27.

Contents. xxxi

PAGE

Misapprehensions which might arise from the moral of the Parable of the Virgins—how the Parable of the Talents corrects them—the character indicated by the slothful servant—shrinking from the pastoral responsibility in those qualified for it—ordination by constraint in the early Church—scantiness of endowments a plea for not improving them—the phrase "according to his ability" explained—St. Paul endowed with ten talents—his improvement of them—St. Barnabas's one talent—his improvement of it—how St. Barnabas might have acted like the slothful servant—men largely endowed are not generally slothful, and why—the majority mediocre—what motives induce the slenderly endowed to be slothful—What is the one talent entrusted to me?—conjectures as to what it may be—How may I gain from it the largest interest?—hard thoughts of God lie at the root of unfruitfulness in religion—He never calls us to a standard of duty for which He is not ready to qualify us—in proportion to the burden laid upon us He gives more grace 340

CHAPTER XII.

OF THE INTERIOR LIFE.

" Then shall the kingdom of heaven be likened unto ten virgins, which took their lamps, and went forth to meet the bridegroom. And five of them were wise, and five were foolish. They that were foolish took their lamps, and took no oil with them: but the wise took oil in their vessels with their lamps. While the bridegroom tarried, they all slumbered and slept. And at midnight there was a cry made, Behold, the bridegroom cometh; go ye out to meet him. Then all those virgins arose, and trimmed their lamps. And the foolish said unto the wise, Give us of your oil; for our lamps are gone out. But the wise answered, saying, Not so; lest there be not enough for us and you: but go ye rather to them that sell, and buy for yourselves. And while they went to buy, the bridegroom came; and they that were ready went in with him to the marriage; and the door was shut. Afterward came also the other virgins, saying, Lord, Lord, open to us. But he answered and said, Verily I say unto you, I know you not. Watch therefore, for ye know neither the day nor the hour wherein the Son of man cometh."—MATT. xxv. 1—13.

We recur in this Chapter to the fundamental idea of the treatise—the Prophecy on the Mount—solemn period of its delivery—the tetralogy of Parables, which closes the Prophecy—the Virgins are those who correspond fervently with the grace originally bestowed on them—the flame of hope and earnest expectation—what kept it burning in the early Church—delay of the Second Advent, and discrimination of character resulting therefrom—religion passes into a matter of principle—modern Christians often go on upon the stock of their early religious impressions—decay in them of the interior life of faith—how defectiveness in the Sermons of the day may contribute to such decay—conversion (not edification) regarded as the business of the pulpit—the emblems of the light and the oil explained—so much grace expended on the outward life of the Christian, just as so much oil is expended in keeping a light burning—Prayer the means of securing a reserve of oil—Yet not stated prayer, but that which mixes itself up with all our actions—how in the midst of active service we may secure fresh supplies of grace—necessity of spiritual industry in order to perseverance—our treatise a protest in favour of the interior life . 351

PART I.

INTRODUCTORY.

CHAPTER I.

ON THE LOW STANDARD OF PERSONAL RELIGION NOW PREVALENT, AND THE CAUSES OF IT.

"*A certain man drew a bow at a venture, and smote the king of Israel between the joints of the harness.*"— 1 KINGS xxii. 34.

No one, however well satisfied he may be with the intellectual and moral progress of the age in which we live, can look abroad upon the state of the Church in this country, without gathering from the survey a painful impression that the standard of Personal Religion among us is miserably low. Doubtless there is a great deal of talk upon the subject of religion. And doubtless, also, as the candid observer will not hesitate to confess, there is something better and deeper than talk,—a certain excitement of the public mind, a general sensation on the subject, which indeed is the reason of its being so much discussed. The interest of all classes is alive about religion; a delightful contrast indeed with the torpid state of things which Wesley and Whitefield found, when they were first visited with serious convictions, and from which they were God's instruments for recovering both the Church and the sects. But this general interest in the many is quite consistent with a very low standard of religious attainment in individuals,—low, I mean, in comparison of what might be expected from the motive power which the Gospel brings to bear upon the heart.

Let it be considered that God cannot be guilty of the folly of employing a stupendous machinery to achieve an insignificant result, or a result which might be achieved, and has been achieved, in another manner. And then let it be observed how stupendous the machinery is, which Christianity brings to bear upon the human heart; that the force employed to sanctify that heart is, if I may say so, the whole force of God,— the force of motive derived from the Incarnation and Resurrection, the force of principle derived from the descent of the Holy Ghost. Let it be remembered that it is the repeatedly declared design of this expenditure of power to make men meet for the inheritance of the saints in light,—in other words, to sanctify or make saints of them. And then let us turn, and look about us, and ask where are the saints? Is Christianity producing among us the fruits, which God, when He planted it in the soil of the earth, designed it to produce? To many questions respecting our moral condition, we can perhaps give a satisfactory answer. If you ask where is integrity, where is amiability, where is social worth, where is attendance upon the ordinances of religion, where are almsdeeds and charitable institutions, we can produce our instances. But be it remembered that many, if not all, of these fruits can be borne by unregenerate human nature. The annals of heathenism record numerous instances of integrity and even ascetic self-denial among the philosophers, and many others of a high moral tone and a brilliant disinterestedness among the people at large. Nay, is it not notorious that there were among the heathen, men in whom the religious instinct was strongly awakened, men of earnest minds who looked forward with vague apprehension, not however unmixed with hopes of release, to that future life, of which they caught a glimpse ever and anon from the flickering and uncertain ray of the light of Nature?

But Christian saintliness must surely go beyond this, as being the product of much higher agencies. And where is Christian saintliness among us? Without denying its existence, it may be yet said that none of the instances we can show of it are of a high caste.

Indeed, is it not the case that there is a singular analogy between the present state of knowledge and of piety,—that in this age literature and religion fare much alike? In what were called the dark ages, literature was the monopoly of the few; gross ignorance was the condition of the many. There were some monks and priests who represented all the erudition of their times, and were great luminaries of learning. And much later than the dark ages, while printing was in its childhood, and the helps to knowledge few or none, you meet with men who were great repositaries of the literature of the day, giants of intellectual resource. It is not so any longer. Every one knows a little; few know much; and fewer still know profoundly; they have drawn what they know, not from the fountain-head, but from commentaries, and abstracts, and summaries, and indices, and other books whose province is to make the attainment of knowledge cheap and easy. Is it not the same with piety? The great saints of primitive (nay of mediæval) times stand out like stars in the firmament of the Church, all the brighter for the darkness of heathenism or of superstition which surrounds them. But the tendency of modern times has been to diffuse among many the piety which was once concentrated in the few. The public are religious as a public, but in individuals the salt has lost its savour. Every body can speak volubly upon controversial subjects; but where are the men, upon whose heart the Truth, which is at stake in controversies, is making every day, by means of prayer and meditation, a deeper imprint?

If any remedy is to be applied to this state of things, it is plain that we must first set ourselves to inquire into its causes. And in conducting this inquiry, it is natural to turn our eyes in the first place to the Christian Ministry, as at present exercised in this country. If the results of the Gospel are not what they should be, it is probable that there are some defects in the instrumentality which it condescends to employ. If saints be not made by the great system, may it not be that the means of working it are out of order? Now we are distinctly told that God's great instrumentality for the sanctification and salvation of souls is the ministry of the Word; "He gave some, Apostles; and some, prophets; and some, evangelists; and some, pastors and teachers;" (for what end?) "*for the perfecting of the saints,* for the work of the ministry, *for the edifying of the body of Christ:* till we all come in the unity of the faith, and of the knowledge of the Son of God, unto *a perfect man,* unto the measure of the stature of the fulness of Christ." Stripping this passage of its beautiful inspired phraseology, and dropping its reference to those miraculous gifts which have now passed away, its gist and upshot is this, that the ministry of God's Word is the great appointed means for the perfecting of the saintly or Christ-like character in man. Is there then any flaw in our ministry, which may in some measure account for the low standard of Personal Religion, on which we have been commenting? We fear there is. We believe that the Christian Ministry having, by God's design and constitution, two arms wherewith to do its work, one of these arms has become paralyzed by inactivity. We believe that its office (as regards the Word of God) being twofold, to rouse consciences, and to guide them, we have for a long time past in the National Church (and probably it is the same with the sects) contented ourselves with rousing, while we have done scarcely any thing to guide them. The one object of all our teaching, whether in formal sermons or in books, has been to make impressions, not to give them a right direction when made. The sermon is thrown every Sunday into the midst of the people, very much as the arrow which found out King Ahab was darted into the host of Israel, to take its chance amid the thousand arrows which on that day were winging their flight to and fro. Often, no doubt, the grace and providence of God directs the shaft to the right quarter, causes it to reach some sinner's conscience, through the joints of a harness of insensibility and indifference, and to rankle there in real and abiding convictions. But the misfortune is, that where such an effect is really produced, both minister and people seem to think, judging from their conduct, that the work in that particular case has gone quite far enough. The impression having been made is thenceforth left to itself; the working power being there, it is assumed that it will work, without any further pains on our part. The minister prepares a similar stirring appeal for other consciences; and the people acquiesce in a religion of good emotions, as if these emotions were sanctity itself, and not rather something to begin and go on upon,—the primary impulse in the life-long pursuit of sanctity. And thus the good impressions are allowed to run to waste, and no real ground is gained by them.

We have said that a low standard and a wide diffusion seem to be the law to which both religion and education are subjected in the present day. And perhaps there may be, when we come to look closely, a similar defect in the instrumentality employed by both. Popular lectures are one of the great agencies employed in the spread of knowledge. It is the object of these lectures to put in a lively and attractive form so much of the subject as is agreeable and entertaining, and to hide away all the abstruse research, or the abstruse reasoning, by which the results are arrived at. The lecturer is considered to have gained his point if he has skilfully dressed a rather spare dish of knowledge with the garniture of amusement, and sent away his audience pleased and tickled with the conceit of having caught a cursory insight into the bearings of his subject. But as they have never grappled with the elements of the study, the new facts or ideas conveyed to them are forgotten almost as soon as acquired. Whatever advantages such a system may have, it is certain that no scholar was ever made by it. For even now (notwithstanding our intellectual advance) there is no royal road to knowledge; and those who would really and truly know must still submit to the condition of laborious and gradual discipline; "line upon line, precept upon precept, here a little, and there a little."

But do not the great majority even of good and useful sermons resemble in their principles and objects these popular lectures? Do not those sermons especially resemble them, which it is now the fashion to preach to the masses, and from which we expect some great results, as if they were the one religious agency of the day? If we were to define modern sermons as "popular expositions of Holy Scripture, with a warm and stirring application to men's consciences," should we go far wrong? They are designed to make, and often (under Grace) they do make, wholesome impressions of a spiritual character, and the people who are touched by them go away pleased, thinking "they have got good." And good they have got, no doubt; but then it is good which is not followed up. If the good should go in some cases as far as real conversion, or change of will, there seems to be no provision for edification, that is, for building on the foundation thus laid. They have been exhorted to religion; but they have not been instructed in it. There is in our exercise of the ministry no systematic plan on which people are taught, and brought on gradually towards "the measure of the stature of the fulness of Christ." And the results are most mischievous. Piety degenerates into a series of shallow emotions, which evaporate in the absence of stirring appeals to the conscience. The souls of our people become like Bethesda's pool. Periodically they are impregnated with an healing influence; "an angel goeth down into the pool, and troubleth the water." But, alas! the virtue of the stirring is but momentary; the dregs quickly fall again to the bottom, and the water becomes dead, stagnant, and unprofitable as before.

Thus we seem to have found that one of the causes of the low standard of Personal Religion among us, is probably the want of any definite direction of conscience, after it has been once awakened. If we carry our inquiry still further back, and ask the reasons why this part of the ministerial work has been neglected, we shall probably find that it is owing to reactions from a state of things wrong in itself. Before the Reformation, the confessional existed as a living power in the Church; it exists still in the communion of the Church of Rome. Frightful as are the evils and abuses inseparably connected with the system of regular compulsory confession, there was at least this advantage connected with it, that under such a system the minister could not forget the duty imposed upon him of directing the awakened conscience. Counsel he must perforce give, counsel practical and definite for the eradication of those sins, the avowal of which was poured weekly into his ear. The Protestant clergyman on the other hand, confined to the pulpit, is thereby, of course, thrown back to a much greater distance from the minds of his flock. He does not know, and cannot know, except in those very rare cases, where a revelation of such things is voluntarily tendered to him, what is the nature of their difficulties, or the quarter in which their trials lie. Hence arises a temptation (though surely not a necessity) to do as the certain man in the passage above referred to did, to let fly his word of counsel without any definite aim, to be general and vague both in doctrine and exhortation. And it is well if the generality and vagueness do not go so far as to become unreality, if the portraitures of the believer and unbeliever are not so overcharged as that no man really resembles either of them, and if consequently the discourse, being meant for nobody in particular, does not fare worse than the death-shaft of Ahab, and hit nobody in particular. But why, because we rightly reject the odious system of the confessional, are we to abandon the attempt to direct the human conscience from the pulpit, or from the press? The Apostles had no confessionals. And yet were not the Apostles ever making such attempts as we speak of? What is the nature of the Apostolic Epistles? Are they not all addresses to believers in Christ, whose consciences had already received the *primary* impulse of true religion, with the view of guiding them in their perplexities, confirming them in their convictions, forewarning them against their temptations, encouraging them in their troubles, explaining to them their difficulties, and generally building them up in their most holy faith? And are not the Apostolical Epistles the great model of what stated Christian teaching in a Christian country should be?— a process, be it observed, widely different from the evangelizing of the heathen, and recognized as different in the great baptismal commission given by our LORD in the last verses of St. Matthew's Gospel, where He bids His Apostles first "teach" as a *preliminary to baptism*,—teach with the view of *making* disciples,— and *subsequently to baptism* "teach" the converts so made "to observe all things, whatsoever He had commanded." Those two teachings are quite distinct. The object of the one was to arouse the conscience of the heathen; the object of the other was to direct the conscience of the Christian.

The state of things on which we have been animadverting is also probably due in part to a reaction from the hard and dry style of preaching, which was in fashion some half-century ago. Some of us can remember the time when sermons were nothing more than moral essays, setting forth some duty, or some grace of the Christian character, with little or no reference to those evangelical motives from which alone an acceptable obedience can spring, and no suggestions of any value as to the method in which the particular grace recommended might be obtained. You were told that humility, and self-denial, and contentment were excellent things, and worthy of being pursued by all men; but as to the considerations which alone can move to the pursuit, and as to any practical method of maintaining them under difficulties, you were left in ignorance. But when it pleased God to quicken the dry bones of the Church with new life, men began to see that to divorce the moral code of Christ from His constraining love, which alone can enable us to keep it, was an unhallowed act, upon which God's blessing can never rest, and that the exhortations of the Christian preacher should be something warmer, and more genial, and more persuasive than the moralizings of Seneca. Since that time, with the usual precipitancy of men to extremes, our divines have chiefly busied themselves with doctrine, and relinquished (or but feebly occupied) the ground of precept. The impression has been that people know every thing about Christian duty, and have no need to be enlightened on that head. And if by Christian duty he meant simply the moral law of God, in its outward, literal aspect, perhaps the impression is more or less correct, at least as regards the educated classes. But if by Christian duty be meant sanctity of life and character, and a growing conformity to the image of the Lord Jesus, we must be pardoned for expressing our conviction that our best and most respectable congregations have very little insight into the thing itself, and still less into the method of its attainment.

We devote these pages, then, to giving some suggestions on the nature of Personal Religion, and the method of cultivating it,—a subject for the treatment of which by the ministers of Christ it appears to us that the circumstances of the time urgently call. We address our remarks more especially to those who perceive the hollowness of a religion of merely good impressions, and who feel that, if there be vitality in the Christian principle within them, they ought, as years roll on, to be making progress. The mere earnest desire for a holier life, which is often found in such souls, is something,—nay, it is much,—it is the fruit of grace, it is the working in the inner man of the instinct which Baptism implanted. Take courage, brother! Earnest desire of holiness *is* holiness in the germ thereof.

Soon shalt thou know, if only thou wilt *follow on* to know, the Lord. But take one short and plain caution before we start. Sanctity is not the work of a day, but of a life. Growth in grace is subject to the same law of gradual and imperceptible advance as growth in nature. God's natural creation, Moses tells us, was built up step by step, out of its first rudiments. Who could have believed that the germs of all the fair objects which we behold in nature were in that void, and dark, and formless earth, over whose waters the Spirit of God spread His fostering wing? And who could have believed that in this heart of ours,—such a medley of passions, vanities, pettiness, ignorance, as now it is,— there should be the germs of every grace which can bloom in the garden of God—of child-like humility, yea, and of heroic self-sacrifice? Yet so it is. Be but true to your convictions. Do but follow the instigations of that Spirit who hovered over the waters of your Baptism. Follow Him in darkness and light, through honour and dishonour, through evil report and good report, and in due time the new creation shall dawn within thee, and the fair fabric of God's spiritual kingdom shall be built up step by step,—"righteousness, and peace, and joy in the Holy Ghost."

CHAPTER II.

ON THE CHIEF CHARACTERISTIC OF PERSONAL RELIGION.

"*Grow in grace.*"—2 PET. iii. 18.

IN our first Chapter we spoke of the low standard of Personal Religion now prevalent, and of the causes of it. We assumed that every one of our hearers would form a more or less correct idea of what was meant by Personal Religion, and thus that there was no need,—at all events at that early stage of the argument,—of any formal definition. The words spoke for themselves sufficiently to enable us to follow the line of thought, along which our minds were then travelling. We shall gain, as we proceed, a more distinct and more highly chiselled notion in connexion with them; and such a notion, we trust, the present Chapter will convey.

What *is* Personal Religion? What has been said already will have taught us that it is something more than a mere partaking in those sensations and in that general interest about religion, which are now so widely diffused among the public. We have also seen that it is something distinct from good impressions on the mind of the individual, which too often terminate upon themselves. These, however, are rather negative than positive features of it; and, having intimated what it is not, we are now inquiring what it is. One positive characteristic, then, of Personal Religion—perhaps its chief positive characteristic—is, spiritual growth—the growth of the individual soul "unto a perfect man, unto the measure of the stature of the fulness of Christ." Personal Religion involves growth in grace; so that where there is growth, there is Personal Religion; and where there is no growth, although there may be interest in religious subjects, and keenness about controversies, and a perception of the importance of Divine truth, and a warm defence of orthodoxy, there Personal Religion is unknown.

Now to say that Personal Religion is characterized by growth, is only another form of saying that the man who has it is spiritually alive. Growth in the animal and vegetable worlds is the sure sign, and the only sure sign of life. If a branch does not sprout, and put forth leaf and blossom in the spring, we know that it is a dead branch,—the sap which is the life of the tree does not reach it, is not circulating through it. If an infant lives, it grows,—increases in stature daily, while its features fill out gradually into that definite shape which they are to wear through life. But we need not restrict the remark to infants. The bodies of adults grow as really, though not as sensibly, as those of children. Particles of matter are continually flying off from our bodies, and being replaced by others; so that, according to a very old and often-quoted computation, the whole mass of the human body undergoes an entire change,—becomes, in fact, a new body,—once in every seven years. This constant discharge of old particles, and accretion of new ones, though accompanied with no change of feature or stature, is growth; and it is a sign of the vitality of the body. A dead body lacks the principle of life, by which alone nourishment can be taken in from air and food, and transmuted into the substance of the human frame.

Now we know that nature is every where a parable of grace. Its being so is the basis of all those beautiful illustrations which are called the parables of our Lord. And in the case before us, nature furnishes a most important parable of religious truth. There is no organic life without growth in nature; and there is no spiritual life without growth in grace. I say, no spiritual life,—no *continuous state of life*. Spiritual impulses there may be many. Impulses, however, are not life, though they may originate or restore life. Here again we resort to nature for an illustration. There is an agency connected with life called galvanism. You may galvanize a paralyzed limb, and by galvanism may restore the circulation, and so restore life, to it. But the galvanism is not the life; it only rouses the dormant powers of life. Galvanism is a certain development of electricity, the same mysterious agent which, in another form, darts to and fro among the clouds of heaven. The life of the limb, on the other hand, consists in its answering the purposes for which it was made, in its habitual subservience to the will, in the power of contracting and relaxing its muscles, when the will gives it notice to do so. Now the professing Christian, who is not spiritually alive, is a paralyzed member of the Body of Christ. Impulses from a heavenly agent, the Holy Ghost, are ever and anon sent through the medium of God's ordinances into this

Body of Christ, and impart a convulsive, fitful motion even to those limbs which are paralyzed. It does not, however, follow that the paralyzed limbs are restored. In some cases they may be; in some they may not. At all events, the fitful movement of the limb is one thing, its permanent vitality another. That glowing impression which you carried away from such a sermon, that seriousness which such a warning or such a bereavement left on your mind, may, after a convulsive movement of the soul—after saddening you for a week, or wringing a few tears from you—pass away for ever, and leave you still in a state of spiritual paralysis. Or it may really rouse the powers of life in your soul, may succeed in enlisting the whole machinery of the inner man,—understanding, affections, will, in Christ's service,—may act as the first impulse in a career of holiness. Do not confound God's grace, its motions, influences, instigations, inspirations, with spiritual life. It is on account of this confusion of thought that well-meaning persons often suppose all to be right with them because they are the subjects of so many good impressions. God's grace comes to us from without, in order to quicken spiritual life in us; but the life itself is something internal. The grace resembles the angel who troubled Bethesda's pool, and for a moment conveyed to it a healing virtue. The life of the water would have consisted in its being changed permanently from a stagnant pool into a living spring, which as a fact was never done.

. To resume, then, our argument at the point from which we have slightly digressed. The question whether any of us has Personal Religion, resolves itself into a question whether he has in him a principle of spiritual growth; and spiritual growth implies spiritual life. Personal Religion therefore is, in fact, one and the same thing with the spiritual life of the individual soul.—And now let us turn, at this early period of the discussion, to examine our own consciences upon the truth which we have already gained. It must, I suppose, stand to reason that nothing but a Personal Religion will stand us in stead at the last day. The individual will then be the object of the divine scrutiny; not the society in which he has moved, and whose sentiments, habits, and circumstances have perhaps reflected upon him a superficial tinge of piety. Society is made up of individuals; and the sentiments of society are ultimately formed and determined by the sentiments of individuals; and therefore God, who searches all deep things, will examine at that day microscopically the little world of the individual's mind. "And when the king came in to see the guests," says our Saviour, "he saw there a man which had not on a wedding garment." He saw there *a man;* one man,—singular;—not that there will not be found at the last day hundreds of thousands of souls in the same sad plight as this poor man; but to teach us forcibly, by the selection of a single specimen, that no one shall pass muster in the crowd, that not only all, but each must be judged,—that upon each soul in that awful crisis the full glare of Divine Omniscience must be turned in,—that the religion which alone will then abide must be personal, deep, individual. Is ours then at present a Personal Religion? Is it a growing one? Is there a principle of growth in it? Does it wax stronger against temptations, more stedfast in faith, more constant and more fervent in prayer, as years roll on? Are our views of God and of Christ gradually enlarging and clearing, and becoming more adequate? Are they more humbling to ourselves, but at the same time more inwardly satisfactory and consolatory than they used to be? Are besetting sins more resolutely and successfully mortified than they used to be? Are our souls, though sometimes stirred by spiritual emotions, like Bethesda's pool? or is the Spirit's agency in them deep, profound, eternal— "a well of water springing up into everlasting life?"

Reader, seeing that on the answer to these questions our all is suspended, it behoves us to be very careful in answering them. Is my religion a growing one? In that word "growing" the decision of the whole question is wrapped up. Mark the point, I pray you, and keep to it. The point is not whether I have very lively feelings, very warm emotions in connexion with religion (those are often constitutional and dependent on physical temperament), but whether I am growing? The point is not, whether I fulfil certain duties, social and religious, with commendable regularity (a reflection satisfactory enough as far as it goes, but not bearing on the present question), but, whether I am growing? And again the point is not (God forbid that it should be!) whether I am coming up to the standard of character and conduct, which I have set before myself? whether I am satisfied with my own life? whether I am as yet near to the mind and image of Christ? whether I am in sight of the goal of perfection?—not this, but simply, "Am I growing?" This one little word is the test, which, faithfully applied, shall reveal to us our state. But how to apply it? how to be sure that we are applying it right? Methinks I hear some reader ask whether this growth is consistent with frequent relapses, with the backslidings (some of them very serious) of which he is only too conscious? To which we answer, with some assurance, "Yes, if the fall have been one of infirmity; if the will has (so to say) picked itself up afterwards, and, though bruised and bleeding, gone manfully forward, giving its hand once again to the Lord Jesus, and consenting heartily (as before) to His guidance." There may be health and vitality in a constitution plagued with sickness; and if there be such a vitality, it will enable the constitution to throw the sickness off. We do not for a moment desire to excuse sin; but at the same time God's people should be instructed, for their comfort, that there is a wonderful economy in His Kingdom of Grace, by which He sometimes brings even out of relapses (as in the case of the fall of St. Peter) a burst of penitent love and zeal, which gives the soul a most powerful forward impulse. The Apostle had denied Christ in a moment of weakness; but he rises from the denial at once, when his Master's look recalled him to himself, and goes out and weeps bitterly. Soon afterwards we discover that he has grown in grace. We see him throwing himself into the water, and wading ashore to meet the Lord,—a mute but very touching way of saying that his affection is now more zealous than ever. As an illustration of this law in the Kingdom of Grace, consider the movement of the tide when it is coming in. It is *movement upon the whole.* The water is sure to cover that dry beach in two or three hours' time, and to float that stranded sea-weed; *but it is not a movement without relapses.* Each wave, I suppose, gains a little ground, but each wave falls back as soon as it has plashed upon the shore. Even so in the Christian life, there may be a forward movement on the whole, consistently with many relapses, though this assertion requires to be guarded by the observation that the relapses must be such as proceed from infirmity, and not from malice prepense. Deliberate, habitual sin, cannot possibly consist with spiritual growth; but the shaking of a man's stedfastness by a sudden tornado of temptation (which was St. Peter's case) may do so. The great question is whether, after every such fall, the will recovers its spring and elasticity, and makes a fresh start with new and more fervent prayer and resolve. Indeed, the making many fresh starts after relapses of infirmity is a hopeful sign of growth. In order to any great attainment in spiritual life, there must be an indomitable resolve to try and try again, and still to begin anew amidst much failure and discouragement. On warm dewy mornings in the spring vegetation makes a shoot; and when we rise, and throw open the window, we mark that the May is blossoming in the hedgerows. And those periods when a man can say, "I lost myself sadly yesterday in temper or in talk; but I know that my crucified Lord took upon Him those sins and answered for them, and to-day I will earnestly strive against them in the strength of His Spirit, invoked into my soul by earnest prayer:" these are the warm dewy mornings of the soul, when the spiritual life within us sprouts and blossoms apace.

Again, it should be remembered, lest any whom the

Lord hath not made sad should be put out of heart by the application of the test, that all real growth is very slow, and its actual progress imperceptible. The seed sown on stony ground, which *forthwith* sprang up, because it had no deepness of earth, proved a failure. Jonah's gourd, which came up in a night, perished also in a night. We never see plants actually growing; we only take notice that they have grown. He who would form a sound judgment of his spiritual progress must throw his eye over long, not short, intervals of time. He must compare the self of this year with the self of last; not the self of to-day with the self of yesterday. Enough if amid the divers and shifting experiences of the world, and the manifold internal self-communings arising thereupon, that delicate plant, spiritual life, has grappled its fibre a little deeper into the soil than it seemed to have done in an earlier stage of our pilgrimage, now fairly past.

Let those characters, for whom they are designed, take to themselves the comfort of these considerations. But let not the indolent and formal derive from them the slightest encouragement. Again we say, that the one sign of vital Personal Religion is growth. There is no growth in a life of spiritual routine, in a mechanical performance of duties, however important, or a mechanical attendance upon ordinances, however sacred. There is no growth without zeal and fervour, and that sort of enthusiastic interest in religion, with which a man must take up any thing if he wishes to succeed in it. There is no growth in the deliberate adoption of a low standard, in the attempt to keep back a moiety of the heart from Christ, in consenting to go with God thus far only, and no further. There is no growth in contenting ourselves with respectability, and declining the pursuit of holiness. There is no growth without fervent prayer, "in spirit and in truth." And, finally, there is no growth (whatever be the hopes with which we may be flattering ourselves) without continual and sincere effort.

But it is now time to conclude this chapter. And

we will do so by remarking that if an examination of conscience should show that we are not growing in grace, there is but one alternative, which is that we are falling back. An awful truth; but one as infallibly certain as any other phenomenon of our moral state. Neither in mind nor body does man ever "continue in one stay." His body, as we have seen, is constantly throwing off old particles of matter, and appropriating new ones. Every breath he breathes, every exertion of his muscles and limbs, every particle of food he swallows, makes some minute change in the bodily framework, so that it is never entirely the same. Of each individual among us it may be said with truth at any given moment, that he is either rising to, or declining from, the prime of life and the maturity of his physical powers. And the mind no less than the body is in a continual flux. It too has its moral element, the society in which it lives,—it too has its nourishment, which it is constantly imbibing,—the influences of the world and the lower nature, or those of the Spirit of God. One or other of those influences is always imperceptibly passing into the mind and effecting a gradual change. And the awful thought is, that if the change is not for the better, it must be for the worse; if the mind is not appropriating the higher, it must be appropriating the lower influences; if there is no growth in grace, there must be a growth in worldliness and sin. Strictly speaking, nothing is morally indifferent; every moral action leaves its impress upon moral character. Our fireside conversations, our thoughts as we pass along the streets to our daily work, our spirit in the transaction of business, all have some amount, small though it be, of moral value; all are tending more or less remotely to form the character; amid all, and through all, we are either making spiritual progress or falling back from the mark. With what solemnity do these thoughts invest even the most trifling incidents of life! It is impossible to pass through them and come out the same;—we are changed either for the better or for the worse. We will look to it, then, that in future at least it shall be for the better. If it have been hitherto for the worse, we will this very hour embrace that already purchased pardon, which obliterates in an instant the guilt of a whole past career of sin, and that grace proffered by Christ no less gratuitously, which renews the will unto newness of life. And tomorrow we will, in the strength of that grace, make a new beginning, taking up this anthem into our mouths; "All my fresh springs shall be in Thee."

CHAPTER III.

OF THE ENTIRE DEPENDENCE OF SANCTITY ON CHRIST, AND OF THE RELATION WHICH THE MEANS OF GRACE HOLD TO HIM.

"*Abide in Me, and I in you. As the branch cannot bear fruit of itself, except it abide in the vine; no more can ye, except ye abide in Me.*
"*I am the vine, ye are the branches; he that abideth in Me, and I in him, the same bringeth forth much fruit: for without Me ye can do nothing.*"—ST. JOHN xv. 4, 5.

THE subject of this treatise is Personal Religion, or, in other words, that "holiness, without which no man shall see the Lord." It is evident that we shall be liable to misapprehend the subject fundamentally, unless we have at the outset a clear notion of the nature of Christian holiness. It is to give the reader this clear notion that the present Chapter will be devoted.

In the passage which stands at the head of it, there is a slight inaccuracy of translation, which requires to be set right before the force of Our Lord's words can be thoroughly appreciated. "*Without Me* ye can do nothing," should rather be rendered, "*Apart from* Me," "separate from Me," "in a state of independence on

Me, ye can do nothing." "Apart from Me," by no means conveys the same idea as "Without Me." The latter would imply merely that unless Christ concurred with His people in their efforts, they could do nothing. "Apart from Me," goes beyond this. It implies that He is the alone originating Source of all sanctity in them. "Without" the concurrence and assistance of a strong person, a weak one cannot lift a heavy weight; but the dependence of the weak person on the strong in order to lift the weight, is not the dependence which the word here employed indicates. "Apart from" the soul (or principle of life) the body is motionless, and cannot stir a finger. This is the sort of dependence indicated in the passage before us. Christ is to the Christian the alone source of sanctification or spiritual life, just as the soul is to the body the alone source of natural life.

I do not know that any other prefatory observation is needed, except that "the fruit" mentioned in this passage generically is specifically, and in detail, those fruits of the Spirit which are enumerated by St. Paul in Gal. v., "Love, joy, peace, longsuffering, gentleness, goodness, faith, meekness, temperance." The fruit consists in certain holy tempers and affections of heart, the possession of which will uniformly ensure right conduct, but which are much more easily seen to be absolutely dependent upon Christ's working than right conduct itself is. If a man be commanded by God to do any *action* whatsoever, he can string up his will to do it. But when certain sentiments and dispositions are required of him, which involve a thorough change of the heart's natural propensities, that is another matter. The affections are far less under the will's control than the actions are.—That these gracious sentiments and dispositions are called by the Apostle, fruits of the Spirit, and by His Divine Master, fruit proceeding from Himself, the true Vine, need not cause any difficulty. In Christ dwelleth all the fulness of the Godhead bodily. He is the smitten rock of the wilderness, through whom alone the living waters force their passage to polluted man. His glorified humanity is the appointed receptacle of Grace, from which Grace emanates into all the moral universe. Hence the Spirit is called the Spirit of God's *Son*.

The great subject brought before us by the passage is, that THE SANCTIFICATION OF THE CHRISTIAN, LIKE HIS JUSTIFICATION, IS ENTIRELY DEPENDENT UPON OUR LORD.

As regards our Justification, this is clearly seen (at least in the Reformed Churches) and generally admitted. That Christ alone can atone for sin; that His Blood and nothing else can procure the pardon of it; that on the ground of His merit exclusively we can find acceptance with God, reinstatement in His favour, and admission to His Presence; that " all *our* righteousnesses are as filthy rags," and that therefore we must look out of ourselves for a righteousness which can stand the scrutiny of GOD's judgment, and that such a righteousness, white as the driven snow, is to be found in Christ only,—all this, whatever reception such a doctrine might have met with half a century ago, is now so thoroughly established, and has gained such a footing in the minds of religious people, that to prove it from Holy Scripture to persons of ordinary religious acquirements would be altogether superfluous.

But it is thought that, unlike Justification (which is something that passes on the sinner externally to him, a sentence of acquittal pronounced on him by God, in consideration of Our Lord's merits), Sanctification is a process within us (which no doubt is true); and hence it is erroneously inferred that it is carried on much more independently of Christ than Justification is; that human will, effort, and exertion contribute very mainly to it, and that Christ is not the all in all of it, not "our strength" in the same way and to the same extent as He is "our righteousness." And hence a false notion of holiness springs up in many minds, and finds such a lodgment that it is very difficult to dispossess it. Holiness is supposed to be an achievement mastered at length—much as a lesson is mastered—by a variety of exercises, prayers, fastings, meditations, almsdeeds, self-discipline, Sacraments; and when mastered, a sort of permanent acquisition, which goes on increasing as the stock of these spiritual exercises accumulates. It is not regarded in its true light as a momentary receiving out of Christ's fulness grace for grace, as the result of His inworking in a heart, which finds the task of self-renewal hopeless, and makes itself over to Him, to be moulded by His plastic hands, resigning, of course, its will to Him in all things, without which resignation such a surrender would be a horrible hypocrisy.

Now let us take up the illustrations of this truth; and first His own illustration, the wisest, profoundest, and most beautiful of all. "As the branch cannot bear fruit of itself, except it abide in the vine; no more can ye, except ye abide in Me;" "Apart from Me ye can do nothing." The circulating sap, which is the life of the tree, is indeed *in* the vine-branch, so long as it holds of the stem; but in no sense whatever, is it *from* the vine-branch. Cut off the branch from the stem, and it ceases instantaneously to live, for it has no independent life. Even so the fruits of the Spirit, while of course our hearts are the sphere of their manifestation, are in no sense *from* our hearts; they are not the result of the energizing of our own will; they are not a righteousness of our own, built up by a series of endeavours, or a laborious process of self-discipline, but a righteousness outflowing continually from the fulness of Grace which is in Christ.

Another illustration may perhaps help to impress the truth. When we walk abroad on a beautiful day, and survey a landscape lit up by the beams of a summer sun, our eye catches a variety of colours lying on the surface of this landscape,—there is the yellow of the golden grain, the green of the pasture-land, the dark brown of those thick-planted copses, the silver gleam of the stream which winds through them, the faint blue of distant hills seen in perspective, the more intense blue of the sky, the purple tinge of yonder sheet of water; but none of these colours reside in the landscape, they are not the properties of the material objects on which they rest. All colours are wrapped up in the sunlight, which, as is well known, may be seen resolved into its elementary colours in the prism or the rainbow. Apart from the sunlight no object has any colour; as is shown by the fact that, as soon as Light is withdrawn from the landscape, the colours fade from the robe of Nature. The difference of colour in different objects, while the sun is shining, is produced by some subtle difference of texture or superficies, which makes each object absorb certain rays, and reflect certain other rays, in different proportions. Now Christ is the Sun of Righteousness, in Whom dwelleth all the fulness of the Godhead bodily,—the fair colour of every grace and Christian virtue. When Christ is shining upon the heart, then these virtues are manifested there, by one Christian graces of one description, by another of another, according to their different receptivity and natural temperament, just as, when the sun is shining, colours are thrown upon a landscape, and reflected by the different objects in different proportions. But as no part of the landscape has any colour in the absence of the sun, nor can acquire any independently of the sun, so Christians have no grace except from Christ, nor hold any virtue independently of Him.

Let it be clearly understood, then, that the great secret of bringing forth much fruit, or, in other words, of all advance in grace and holiness, is, according to the profound teaching of our Lord Himself, a constant keeping open (and if possible, enlarging) the avenues of the soul towards Him. If a vine-branch is to sprout and throw out new suckers and shoots, the tube by which it communicates with the stock of the tree must adhere tightly to the stem, and be well open for the passage of the sap. If you desire to see the colours of furniture in this room, whose shutters are closed, throw open the shutters, and admit the full flood of sunlight. And if you desire to see the dead heart put forth the energies of spiritual life, and the dark heart illumined by the fair colours of spiritual grace, throw wide open the passage of communication between Christ and it, and allow the Life which is in Him, and the Light which is in Him, to circulate freely through it.—But how to do this? in other words, how to fulfil His own precept, "Abide in Me, and I in you?" Ah! vitally important question,—question upon which the whole of our sanctification (and thus the whole of our salvation) is suspended! Let us address ourselves to answer it, with the earnest prayer that God would guide us into all truth.

Observe that our Lord prescribes mutual indwelling, as the secret of spiritual fertility. Take heed that ye "abide in Me, and I in you." Here is not one idea only, but two; the dwelling of the Christian in Christ, as the body dwells in an atmosphere, and the dwelling of Christ in the Christian, as the soul dwells in the body.

I. Take heed, first, that "ye abide in Me." This is done by faith. As we first consciously entered into fellowship with Christ by faith (I say *consciously* entered into fellowship with Him, for when we were baptized as infants, we entered *unconsciously* into His fellowship), so there is no other way to abide in Him, than by repeated exercises of the same faith. The faith which enables the soul to abide in Christ is nothing else than an assured trust and confidence on our part, that, as He has already wrought out FOR us our acceptance with GOD, so He will work IN us every gracious disposition (be it repentance, or faith itself, or humility, or hope, or love) which is necessary to qualify us for glory. It is not enough to supplicate these graces; we must lean upon Him for them, and fix the eye of expectation upon the promise of His new Covenant; "I will put My laws into their mind, and write them in their hearts:" being well assured that He will fulfil to us the terms thereof. There is a promise, I say, that He will fulfil in us all the work of

Sanctification; and it is well that it is so, by way of making assurance doubly sure, and giving to the doubtful heart a stronger consolation. But even were there no promise, could it be a question as to whether He would form in us those tempers and frames of mind, which He Himself requires of us? Do we seriously believe that He loved us so intensely as to abdicate His throne in Heaven for our sakes, to empty Himself of all the glory which He had with the Father before the world was, to confine Himself within the limits of man's feeble faculties, and feebler body, to expose Himself to shame, and spitting, and obloquy, and a death most cruel and ignominious? If we do not believe as much as this, we are clearly no Christians. And if we do believe thus much, is it conceivable that He who has gone to the utmost verge of self-sacrifice in ransoming our souls, should be wanting to us in what will cost Him no sacrifice, but yet is necessary to complete our salvation? If the soul has the least scintillation of a desire to be holy; much more, if it is bent on being holy, as far as its power goes; still more if it is striving and struggling to be holy, and beating against the cage of its corruptions in a great longing for spiritual freedom, as a poor imprisoned bird beats, who sees outside the bright sun and the green trees, and other birds flitting to and fro in the blue ether,—is it conceivable that the Incarnate Love, the Love which bled, and agonized, and poured itself out in death for the objects on which it had fastened, should not meet that desire, that longing, that striving, and visit the soul with power? As without holiness no man shall (or can) see the Lord, must not Christ be much more earnestly anxious to make us holy, than we can be to be made so? If we do not believe in this earnest anxiety of His, do we believe in His love at all? Have we ever really apprehended it; or has it been merely a tale recited in our ears, which we do not care indeed to contradict, but which has never at all taken hold of, or touched, our hearts?

Ah! what if these struggles to be holy should themselves be in a certain sense a token of unbelief? What if the poor bird imprisoned in the cage should be thinking that, if it is ever to gain its liberty, it must be by its own exertions, and by vigorous and frequent strokes of its wings against the bars? If it did so, it would ere long fall back breathless and exhausted, faint and sore, and despairing. And the soul will have a similar experience, which thinks that Christ has indeed won pardon and acceptance for her, but that Sanctification she must win for herself, and under this delusion beats herself sore in vain efforts to correct the propensities of a heart which the Word of God pronounces to be "desperately" wicked. That heart,—you can make nothing of it yourself;—leave it to Christ, in quiet dependence upon His grace. Suffer Him to open the prison-doors for you, and then you shall fly out and hide yourself in your Lord's Bosom, and there find rest. Yield up the soul to Him, and place it in His hands, and you shall at once begin to have the delightful experience of His power in sanctifying.

"Yield up the soul," we say. And in saying so, we of course imply (though it needs to be expressed, as well as implied) that you yield up your will without reserve. There is no such thing as yielding up the soul, without yielding up the will; for the will is the chief power of the soul. Christ Himself cannot sanctify a moral agent, whose will holds persistently to his corruptions. Even a man cannot liberate a bird from its cage, which likes to stay there, refuses to move when the door is opened, and flies back when it is taken out. God has given us a free will, the exercise of which cannot indeed change our hearts, or renew our moral nature, but which *can* say "Nay" to the world, to the flesh, and the devil; which shows that it can say "Nay," by saying it sometimes, when worldly interests are concerned. And this "Nay" it must say, if the soul is to be sanctified and bring forth fruit.

II. But our blessed LORD said not only "Abide in Me," but also "Let me, or take heed that I, abide in you." He thus teaches us that Ordinance, as well as Faith, forms part of the system of His religion, and especially that Ordinance, in which indeed all others are included, by which He communicates Himself to the faithful soul. In order to the fruitfulness of the vine-branch, two conditions have to be fulfilled; the first that the branch shall adhere closely to the stem, and offer an open tube for the passage of the sap,—this is the abiding of the branch in the vine; the second, that the sap shall rise ever and anon from the vine-stock, and pass into the branch,—this is the abiding of the vine in the branch. Similarly in the case of the Christian. The first condition of his spiritual fruitfulness is that he shall adhere by a close trust to Christ, and keep open towards Him the avenues of faith, hope, and expectation. This is, "Abide in Me." The second is, that Christ shall continually send up into his heart a current of holy inspirations, new loves, good impulses, devout hopes. Or, more accurately, that He shall communicate Himself to the soul by the continual influx of the Holy Ghost. This is, "And I in you." And this communication of Himself is made specially (where that Sacrament may be had) in the Supper of the Lord; He comes at those seasons into the opened avenue of the faithful communicant's soul, comes to cement by His own passage into the inner man the union in which our faith cleaves to Him; and the result is "the strengthening and refreshing of our souls by the Body and Blood of Christ, as our bodies are by the Bread and Wine."

Thus a devout and frequent use of the Sacrament appointed for spiritual growth, and as the instrument of Christ's indwelling, is, though not literally expressed in this passage, clearly implied. And it should be observed that the Divine allegory quite precludes the supposition that without faith in the recipient the Holy Supper will avail any thing for sanctification and growth in grace. The vine-stock may push upwards its sap in strong current, at the first outburst of the genial spring; but what will that avail the branch, which does not hold closely to the tree, which is half broken off from the stem, and the fracture filled up with dust, or corroded by insects? Christ may offer Himself to us in the Lord's Supper; but, if the soul cleaves not to Him, if the avenues of the heart are not open towards Him, how can He enter?

Finally; it is particularly important in speaking of Christ's communication with us by Ordinances, to recognize the exact position which the Ordinance holds, so as not to estimate it unduly, or erect it into the place which is due only to the Lord of the Ordinance. Be it clearly understood, then, that no Ordinance (not even Holy Communion itself) is otherwise valuable than as a channel or vehicle of communication with the Church's Lord. They are all (even the highest and holiest) so many tubes, through which the sap of grace rises from the vine-stock into the branches. For which reason, in advocating the devout use of Ordinances, we do not in the slightest degree derogate from our Lord's honour, nor direct the eye of the mind to another point of sight than Him. It is not to be imagined for a moment that a man by prayers, and fastings, and meditations, and Sacraments, lays in a stock of holiness, which becomes to him so much realized spiritual gain, upon which he may draw in case a spiritual bankruptcy should threaten him at the hour of death or the day of judgment. Away with such ideas, which are a modern form of Pharisaism! These Ordinances are precious and blessed for no other reason than that they bring us into relation, by His own institution of them, with the great Head of the Church; and except we stand in such relation, and except such relation is from time to time renewed, and cemented, and strengthened, there is no life in us. Of faith itself the same remark might be made. There is no intrinsic merit in trusting to Christ, just as there is no intrinsic merit in praying and communicating; but faith is the ordained inward means, as Prayers and Sacraments are the ordained outward means, of communication with the One Source of Life and Sanctity.

An illustration may sometimes serve a good turn in

keeping truth distinctly before the mind. I therefore offer the following illustration of the mutual relations between Christ, our faith, and Christian Ordinances. A woman, like the Samaritan in the Gospel, comes with a pitcher to draw water at a well. Her object is to reach and procure the water; and she does this by letting down the pitcher into the well, and drawing it up again. It is at once understood that the pitcher is not the same thing as the muscular action, by which it is let down and drawn up. Both must contribute to the result: for without either pitcher or muscular action no water could be obtained; but the pitcher is external to the person, the muscular action a movement of the person. It is also clearly seen that neither pitcher nor muscular action are water,—that the arm might put itself forth for ever, and the pitcher be let down continually, but that if it were a dry pit into which the vessel were lowered, no refreshment could be had thereby. The figure is easy of application. Christ is the Well of the Water of Life, from Whom alone can be drawn those streams of Grace, which refresh, and quicken, and fertilize the soul. It is by faith that the soul reaches out after this living water; faith is the soul's muscular action, by which the water is drawn up and brought into use. But faith needs as an implement those means which Christ has appointed, and particularly the mean of means, which He instituted for the conveyance of Himself to faithful souls. These means are the pitcher, in which the water is conveyed. Faith is not a Christ; neither are Sacraments a Christ; but faith (under all circumstances) and Sacraments, where they may be had, are necessary to the appropriation and enjoyment of Christ.

Oh for more faith, more of the principle which cleaves closely in trust, and affiance, and self-surrender, to the Lord! It is not in the use of means, generally speaking, that religious persons are deficient; but it is in that believing use of them, which recognizes Him as the only Source of Grace and Life, and having done His will with simplicity, assures itself of the blessing.

O True Vine, let us cleave to Thee with such a faith, so that the virtue which is in Thee may pass into our souls, and that we may bring forth much fruit, to the glory of God the Father! Amen.

CHAPTER IV.

PERSONAL RELIGION BOTH ACTIVE AND CONTEMPLATIVE.

" *In the year that King Uzziah died I saw also the Lord sitting upon a throne, high and lifted up, and his train filled the temple.*
" *Above it stood the Seraphims: each one had six wings: with twain he covered his face, and with twain he covered his feet, and with twain he did fly.*"—Isa. vi. 1, 2.

WE are speaking of Personal Religion, which has been explained to be one and the same thing with the life of God in the individual soul. In this Chapter we propose to trace out the two great divisions of the subject.

We are taught by our Lord Himself to pray that God's will may be done "upon earth, as it is in heaven." The persons by whom it is done in heaven, are, of course, the holy angels. Our Lord, therefore, in bidding us offer this petition, proposes to us the angelic life as the model of the Christian life. And this throws us back upon the inquiry what the life of angels is; for manifestly we cannot form our life upon their model, unless we have some sufficient idea of their pursuits and occupations. Accordingly, the Scripture furnishes such an idea. The veil is drawn aside by the prophet Isaiah, and a glimpse is given us of the life of Seraphim, or "burning ones" (for such is the meaning of the Hebrew word), an order of angels who in all probability take their name from the fervent zeal and burning love with which they are animated. The prophet sees in a vision these shining creatures standing above the throne of Christ (for it was He, St. John informs us, whose glory Isaiah saw on this occasion); and their occupations were twofold: first, contemplative devotion; secondly, quick and active service. "Each one had six wings; with twain he covered his face, and with twain he covered his feet:"—this is the Seraphim's life of devotion. "And with twain he did fly;"—this is his life of active service. If, then, God's will is to be done by His people on earth, as it is by His angels in Heaven, there must enter into the spiritual life upon earth two great elements, devotion towards God, and work for God. We will take a general view of each of these. Subsequent Chapters will prosecute the subject in detail under these two heads.

I. The spiritual or angelic life upon earth consists not only of devotion. To suppose that the spiritual life is devotion, and nothing else, is the mistake of the recluse, the ascetic, and the monk. One round of religious service, one long peal of the organ from matins to evensong, one prayer unbroken, except by the actual necessities of the body, and by these as little as may be,—this is the idea of conventual life, though it may be an idea never realized to the full extent. And quite apart from the conventual system, wherever there are multiplied religious services (a great help, of course, if used in a certain way), and leisure and the will to attend on them, there is always a tendency, against which the devout man must be on his guard, to wrap up the whole of religion in attendance upon the means of grace. But the Seraph himself, though indeed the spirit of adoration is upon him always, is not always engaged in direct acts of praise. "With twain of his wings he doth fly,"—speed forth, like lightning, upon the errands on which God sends him. Gabriel, who stands in the presence of God, must come down to the earth, and enter beneath a humble roof in Nazareth, to salute a pure maiden as mother of the Son of God. Another angel has it in charge to descend periodically into the pool of Bethesda, and impart to the waters a healing efficacy, sufficient for one patient. Another is sent to roll back the stone from the Holy Sepulchre, and sit upon it, inspiring the Roman guard with terror, and the holy women with an assurance of the resurrection. Another must pass into St. Peter's prison-house, and lead him out through bolt, and bar, and iron grating, "to freedom and cool moonlight air." Another must shoot down, like a falling star, into the cabin of a ship tossed with the waves of the stormy Adriatic, and announce to St. Paul that, despite all the fury of the elements, he and all the crew, of which he formed a part, were safe in life and limb; while another is commissioned to salute by name a praying centurion of the Italian band, and to assure him that his prayers and his alms had come up as a memorial before God. Thus one and all of them are, not merely adoring spirits, but also "ministering spirits, sent forth to minister for those who shall be heirs of salvation." Praise is not their only occupation; they have active work to do for God.

Reader, there is a deep-seated necessity for work in the constitution of our nature. In the absence of regular and active occupation, the mind is apt to grow morbid, stagnant, and what is worse than either—selfish. One of the greatest thinkers of antiquity defined happiness to be "*an energy* of the soul." And is it not true? Only watch the avidity with which men, even in extreme old age, when one would think that the interests of this life were on the wane for them, catch at some exciting pursuit, like politics. The lesson, which as Christians we should draw from this observation, is that most unquestionably God has made man for activity, as well as for contemplation. The reason why the activity fails in numberless instances to secure happiness, is that it is separated from God, that it is not in His service and interests. This being the case, it too often engrosses, hampers, entangles, impedes,—is as a dead weight to the soul, instead of, as it might be, a wing, and a means of furtherance.

Let every one, therefore, who studies Personal Religion, seriously consider, first, in what quarter lies the work which God has given him to do; and next, how he may execute that work in a happy and a holy frame of mind. I need not say that the services on which God condescends to employ men are almost infinitely various. Each one of us has a stewardship somewhere in the great social system, and some gift qualifying him for it; and if he will but consult faithfully the intimations of God's providence, he will not be long before he discovers what it is. It may be that we are called to very humble duties, duties very low down in the social scale. Still even they are held from God, and constitute a stewardship; and the one talent which qualifies us for them will have to be accounted for as much as if it were ten talents. To regard the business attaching to any station of life as insignificant, is as unreasonable as it is unscriptural. St. Paul says of the human body, that God has "given honour to those members which lacked." The same may be said of society. Its whole fabric and framework is built up of humble duties accurately fulfilled by persons in humble stations. What would become of society, and how could its well-being and progress be secured, if all the subordinates in every department of life, all those who have to play the more mechanical parts, were to throw up their callings on the excuse that they were not sufficiently dignified? How would it fare with the plans of the architect, if the builders and masons throughout the country were to suspend their labours? But we need not reason upon the subject, where the Word of God has spoken so explicitly. The Scripture, with that wonderful penetration into the thoughts of man which characterizes its every page, has taken care to set the seal of dignity and sacredness upon those callings and employments which are lowest in the social scale. Our Blessed Lord, when learning of the doctors in the Temple, and through their instruction growing in wisdom, teaches us that to be engaged thus in childhood is to be about our Father's business. We naturally look down upon a child learning a lesson, and think that it is no great matter whether the lesson be learned or not. Christ opens a widely different view of the subject, when he connects even a child's growth in wisdom with its relation to God: "Wist ye not that I must be in the things of my Father?" (ἐν τοῖς τοῦ πατρός μου.)

But still more remarkable, perhaps, in its bearing on our present subject, is the treatment of the duties of servants in the New Testament. These servants were slaves, and mostly slaves to heathen masters. If ever duty took a degrading form, it must have done so frequently in their case. If ever of any calling one might say, "There is no divine stewardship in it," this might have been said surely of slavery among the heathens. Yet it is recognized in the strongest way, that even the slave's duties may be sanctified by importing into them a Christian motive, and that when such a motive is imported into them, the service is really done not to the human master, but (marvellous condescension!) to the great Head of the Church Himself. "Servants, obey in all things your masters according to the flesh: not with eye-service, as men-pleasers; but in singleness of heart, fearing God: and whatsoever ye do, do it heartily, as to the Lord, and not unto men; knowing that of the Lord ye shall receive the reward of the inheritance: *for ye serve the Lord Christ.*" No less truly, then, than quaintly did good George Herbert sing:

> "All may of Thee partake:
> Nothing can be so mean,
> Which with this tincture (for Thy sake)
> Will not grow bright and clean.
>
> "A servant with this clause
> Makes drudgery divine.
> Who sweeps a room, as for Thy laws,
> Makes that and the action fine."

Now if both a child's education, and a slave's drudgery find their place in the vast system of God's service, what lawful calling can we suppose to be excluded from a place in that system?

II. But we remark, secondly, that there is a contemplative element in the service of the Seraphim,—that their activity is fed from the springs of their devotion. There are two chief passages of Holy Scripture (one in the Old and one in the New Testament) in which we obtain a glimpse of angels engaged in worship. One is that before us, in which the prophet sees the Seraphim, with veiled faces and feet, crying one to another before the throne, " Holy, holy, holy, is the Lord of hosts ; the whole earth is full of His glory." This was a heavenly scene. It was enacted in the Temple, which represented Heaven. But in the New Testament we find the Seraphim domesticating themselves upon earth, in the outlying field of a village where cattle were penned. When the Lord of Heaven, laying aside the robe of light and the tiara of the rainbow, appeared among us in the form of an infant cradled in a manger, He drew an escort of the Seraphim after Him : " And suddenly there was with the angel a multitude of the heavenly host, praising God and saying, Glory to God in the highest, and on earth peace, good will toward men."

The ministry of angels then is only half their life. The other half, which indeed makes their ministry glow with zeal, is their worship. And so it must be with God's human servants.

The activity which flows from ambition, the diligence which is purely mechanical and the result of habit, is not angelic diligence and activity. To attempt to lead the spiritual life without devotion is even a greater mistake than to go apart from our duties in order to lead it. Our flying on God's errands will be an unhallowed flight, if we do not first secretly adore Him in our hearts. A prayerless day of hard work, consecrated by no holy meditation, oh, what a dull, plodding, tramping day is it ! How do we spend money in such a day for that which is not bread, and our labour for that which satisfieth not !

How does God in such a day deal with us, as with the Egyptians of old, taking off the chariot-wheels from our work, so that we drive it heavily! How, if we turn our mind to better things in the stillness of the night, does the Lord seem to stand over the bed, and reprove all that godless toil and turmoil, which in a spiritual point of view has run to waste, with this loving irony: "It is but lost labour that ye haste to rise up early, and so late take rest, and eat the bread of carefulness; for so He giveth His beloved sleep!" And in these times in this country the danger of the vast majority of men—your danger, perchance, reader —lies in this direction. Activity is now, if it ever was, the order of the day with all classes. Competition, and the cry for qualified persons in every department of industry, are driving all drones out of the social hive. No one has a moment to spare. The strain and stress of occupation frequently proves too great for feeble bodies and sensitive minds. And with those who are physically and intellectually equal to cope with the pressure of multiplied and urgent business, the mind too often burrows and is buried in its work, and scarcely ever comes out to sun itself in the light of Heaven. With a fatal facility we dispense ourselves from prayer, and meditation, and self-examination, on the ground of fatigue, or pressing avocations, or necessity of refreshment. Yet secret devotion is the source, not of strength only, but of comfort, and even of success, in any high acceptation of the word. Success is no success, if it makes not a happy mind; and the mind which is not holy cannot be happy. A good author, writing before the invention of the compass, says,—"Even when your affairs be of such importance as to require your whole attention, you should look mentally towards God from time to time, as mariners do, who, to arrive at the port for which they are bound, look more up towards Heaven than down on the sea on which they sail; thus will God work with you, in you, and for you: and all your labour shall be accompanied with consolation."

Hitherto we have been founding our remarks on a passage of Holy Scripture, which represents to us the employment of angels. And it may be thought by some that the nature of angels being probably exempt from those infirmities which beset ours, and not exposed to the pressure of weariness or the urgencies of appetite, they are in truth no suitable model for us, or at all events a model which, from the disparity of their circumstances, can only put us out of heart. But have we no instance of a life, both eminently practical and eminently devout, led in the flesh, and under the constant pressure of physical infirmities? Has man never yet attained to live the angelic life upon earth? Indeed he has done so; and the record of his having done so is in the Gospels. There was One "tempted in all points like as we are, yet without sin," who followed up days of active benevolence, in which He spent and was spent for the people, by nights of prayer. Consider only that touching passage of His history, in which, after receiving the announcement of the Baptist's death, our Lord expresses a natural desire for privacy and repose. The multitudes, however, track Him to His place of retirement, and throng around Him there with the clamour of their necessities, as heretofore. Fallen human nature could hardly have done otherwise than vent a slight irritability at having its purpose thus rudely crossed; but from the depths of that most pure and loving heart there struggled up no other feeling than that of compassion, as He looked forth upon the sea of human heads. Human misery called the Good Shepherd, and He at once responded to the call. He healed all the sick whom they had brought, and "began to teach them many things," until the day wore away. Having fed their minds with Divine truth, He proceeded to feed their bodies miraculously before He dismissed them, "lest they should faint by the way." And this being done, one might have thought that at the close of so laborious a day, He would at length have sought repose. But He does not so. The pouring out of His soul before the

Father has been delayed; but it shall not be precluded. That His solitude might be entire, He compels His disciples to get into the ship, and go before unto the other side, while He Himself upon the mountain offers His evening orison late into the night. And though, of course, no fallen creature has ever maintained the same nicely-adjusted balance between devotion and active service, which is observable in the mind and life of Christ,—though some saints have been (like St. John) characterized rather by devout contemplativeness, and others (like St. Paul) by zealous activity,—yet all His true people have preserved in different proportions the twofold character;—all have been men of service, and all have been likewise men of prayer.

We have spoken of service and prayer separately, as it is necessary to do in a disquisition. Yet we ought not to think of them as independent things, but rather as closely related and interpenetrating one another. Service and prayer are the web and woof of the Christian life, of which every part of it is composed. Both are in the groundwork of the stuff. Not even in point of time must they be too rigidly sundered from one another. Prayer at stated seasons is good and necessary; but a man aiming at sanctity in ever so low a degree, will find it impossible to confine his prayers to stated seasons. He will soon discover that prayer is literally, and not merely in a figure, "the Christian's breath of life;" and that to attempt to carry on the spiritual life without more prayer than the recital of a form on rising, and retiring to rest, is about the same absurdity as it would be for a man to open his casement morning and evening, and inhale the fresh air for a few minutes, and then say to himself on closing it, that that amount of breathing must suffice him for the rest of the day. The analogy suggested by this image is, I believe, a perfectly true one, and will hold good if examined. The air from the casement is very delicious, very healthful, very refreshing, very invigorating; it is a good thing to stand at the casement and inhale it; but there must be air in the shop, in the factory, in the office, as well as at the casement, if the man, as he works, is to survive. Under this view of it, ejaculatory prayer is seen to be even a more essential thing than stated prayer. Both are necessary to the *well-being* of the Christian life; but the momentary lifting the heart to GOD,—the momentary realization of His presence amidst business or under temptation,—is necessary to *its very being*. The life is no more, when this work is suspended. For which reason probably it is that the great apostolic prayer-precept is given with a breadth which excludes all limitations of time and place, —" Pray without ceasing." Ejaculatory prayer, however, must by-and-by form the subject of a distinct Chapter, which we will not now anticipate.

Reader, our subject assumes, as we progress with it, a more definite shape in our minds. Personal Religion, as we saw in our last Chapter, involves growth. Personal Religion, as we now see, involves prayer,—including under that term all the exercises of devotion, both public and private. Then are we men of prayer? Let the conscience take home this question and answer it faithfully. Let the conscience of men, and of men of business, take it home. It is a man's question, and a busy man's question, rather than a woman's. Women as a general rule have more leisure than men, and have certainly more of that constitutional temperament, which, when God's grace visits it, inclines to devotion. It is in a hard, busy, bustling life, a life which asks an active and unimaginative mind, and which chills all approach to sentiment,—in short, it is in the life of an Englishman of business habits that the temptation to live without prayer is felt. How then, in your case and in mine, can the searching question be met? Widely as in different ages and different countries the experiences of the children of God have differed, this has been the one universal experience, the one common characteristic without a single exception,—hoary-headed elders, and brave martyrs, and wise teachers, and weak women, and servants, and even little children, " the great multitude which no man could number, of all nations, and kindreds, and people, and tongues,"—all have been people of prayer. Prayer is the very spot of His children; and the more we know of the power of Personal Religion, the more distinctly will the spot come out, as it were, upon the surface of the skin. Is the spot upon us? Do we enter often into the closet of the dwelling, oftener still into the closet of the heart, to commune with our Father which seeth in secret? Unless this be our case, all our interest in religion is superficial, not personal, and will appear to be so, to our confusion, in the day when God shall judge the secrets of men by Jesus Christ according to the Gospel.

PART II.

THE CONTEMPLATIVE LIFE.

CHAPTER I.

OF THE MAGNIFICENCE OF PRAYER, AND THE PRACTICAL DEDUCTIONS FROM THAT DOCTRINE.

"*He that cometh to God.*"—HEB. xi. 6.

THE Christian life, as we saw in our last Chapter, branches out like the life of the Seraphim, into the two divisions of Devotion and Action. We shall speak first of Devotion, endeavouring to furnish some thoughts which may be practically useful to the reader in his efforts to maintain communion with God; and then of Active Life,—the spirit in which its duties should be fulfilled and its difficulties surmounted. And as ejaculatory prayer is, in fact, the intermingling of devotion with action,—as it is the meeting-point of prayer and service,—we shall give it a middle place between the two, and use it as a bridge, whereby to pass from the first to the second division of our subject.

First, then, to speak of Devotion, which for our present purpose may be all summed up in one word, Prayer. There would be less of formality in prayer, and far more of strength and enjoyment in it, if men did but grasp the idea of what prayer is. But simple as the idea is, it requires an effort of mind to master it; and while we are willing enough to pay mechanically our daily tribute of homage at the Throne of Grace, natural slothfulness always recalcitrates against an effort of mind. Gradual ascent is as necessary to the mind, in order to its reaching a great idea, as it is to the body, in order to its reaching a great height. We cannot ascend to a pinnacle of a cathedral, which towers aloft in air, without either steps or an inclined plane. We cannot reach the summit of a mountain without first toiling up its base, then traversing its breast, and then, successively, crossing the limits where verdure passes into crag, and crag into a wilderness of snow. Even when we have gained the highest point, we are still, it is true, at an infinite distance from the blue vault of the firmament which stretches above our heads. Still we have a better and more exalted view of what that firmament is: we have at least risen above the fogs and mists which obscure its glory; and the air which encompasses us is transparent to the eye, and invigorating to the frame. Now the law of man's bodily progress is also the law of his mental progress. Both must be gradual. No grand idea can be realized except by successive steps and stages, which the mind must use as landing-places in its ascent. But what if the mind, after all its toil, should prove unable fully to master the idea, as must be the case where the idea to be mastered is connected with God and things divine? It does not at all follow that therefore our labour has been lost. We have, at all events, risen to a higher level, where our view is more transparent, more elevating, more sublime, and where the play of the thoughts is invigorating to the inner man. And now let us apply these reflections to the subject in hand.

Prayer is nothing more or less than a "coming to God." Now the bare conception of this thing, "coming to God," is sublime and ennobling to the highest degree. But we are familiar with the idea, and our very familiarity with it—the currency of it among religious persons and in religious books—has worn off the sharp edges of it, until it has ceased to have any definite impress. Let us seek and pray that the idea may revive with some power in our minds. And this we will do

II.] *Practical Deductions from that Doctrine.* 43

by a series of hypotheses, which shall be as landing-places for the mind in its ascent.

1. Let us suppose as the first step that we enjoyed the privilege of opening our minds to, and consulting in our every difficulty and trial, the very wisest, and best, and most powerful man upon earth. Suppose that such a person resided in our immediate neighbourhood, so as to be at all times easily accessible to us. Suppose that his doors stood open day and night, and that he had left instructions with his servant never to deny him to us. Suppose that, from his repeated invitations, coupled with the well-known sincerity of his character, we were perfectly assured that he would give his whole mind to any case which we might lay before him, and consult for us to the best of his ability, and with the keenest interest in our welfare. Can there be any doubt that the doors of this wisest, and best, and most powerful of all men would be besieged with applications for admission to his presence, and that even where persons in distress were not immediately extricated by his advice, it would be a great relief to their minds to hear him say, "This is an intricate case, and will require a great deal of management; but be assured I will bear it in mind, and take such measures in it as are most for your welfare?"

2. But the judgment of even the wisest and best men, while in the body, is liable to be disturbed by many influences, which death will set aside. Mixed up inevitably with earthly interests, and looking at things more or less through the medium of public opinion, they are not now as impartial judges of truth and right as they will be, when separated altogether from the world. Let us imagine then this great separation to have taken place,—the just man to have been "made perfect," and to be now lying in Abraham's bosom, his mind stocked not only with the experiences of life, but with the thousand additional lessons which death will convey. Imagine his spirit to be accessible after death (as some foolishly and wickedly pretend that disembodied spirits are accessible) to those in

whom he felt, while living, the strongest interest. Let us suppose, to make the image more definite still, that he is a father, who has always had, during life, a word of counsel and sympathy, and a hand of succour for his children; and that it has so come to pass that death has not cut them off from this resort. Doubtless, they would avail themselves of the privilege with great eagerness; the difference between the consultations with the living and the departed parent being chiefly this, that a certain awe would rest upon their minds in the latter case, from the reflection that they had to do with the inhabitant of another world, and that the advice given would be doubly valued, coming (as, on the hypothesis, it does) from a sphere where all errors of judgment are thought to be corrected.

3. And now for another step in our ascent. The Scriptures speak largely of angels, a class of beings whose faculties transcend ours in our present state; and certain words of our Blessed Lord are upon record, which, though they cannot be said to prove, yet, certainly, favour the popular idea of the Jews, that to each person is assigned a guardian-angel. Assuming, then, for the sake of argument, that such guardian-angels exist, let us suppose that each of them feels a special loving interest in the particular soul under his guardianship, trembles for it as in the mad phrenzy of transgression it hangs upon the brink of eternal ruin, and rejoices for it, and with it, as it is plucked away from that brink by the arm of the good Shepherd, and brought back to the fold from which it had strayed. Suppose, again, in this case that we had each of us some power of access to this guardian-angel, that we could summon him to our aid,—lay our difficulties before him, unburden our minds to him, with the assurance of receiving from him both sympathy and succour. Can it be supposed that we should not avail ourselves of such a privilege, as opportunity offered? that we should never call him to our councils, or submit to him our cares?

The truth is, that both with regard to angels and

II.] *Practical Deductions from that Doctrine.* 45

to the spirits of departed saints, the very questionable notion that they are accessible to us has been greedily caught at and acted upon by the Roman Church. In defiance of Holy Scripture, which gives no intimation whatever of the possibility of such intercourse, and which, even if it were possible, would exclude it, as having a tendency to idolatry, and as being a perversion of a religious instinct, the Romanist still calls on the Virgin, the saints, the holy Apostles Peter and Paul, his own patron saint, and his own guardian-angel, to help him in his troubles. A clear proof this, that, if such intercourse between this world and the other were feasible and sanctioned, it would be abundantly practised by all men, that the wisdom and power of creatures above us in the scale of nature would be called in aid of our ignorance and feebleness at almost every hour of our existence.

4. But we have now climbed by gradual stages to the summit of the mountain, and are left to contemplate a privilege, which not only might be, but which is our own, and yet of which (partly from its very cheapness and commonness) we either do not avail ourselves at all, or avail ourselves in a formal and mechanical manner. "He that cometh to God." Inasmuch as God is the Infinite One, we can never by any reach of the mind grasp entirely the idea of coming to Him; but have we not derived some help, some clearness of view, some apprehension of the magnificence of prayer, from the train of thought which we have been pursuing? Created power, wisdom, love, all have their limits, beyond which they cannot help, counsel, or sympathize: our difficulties, our perplexities, our sins, might easily outrun them; and access to them might not be nearly of so much value as we are apt to imagine. But, "he that cometh to God"—what shall I say of this privilege? The tameness of human language is disappointing when we attempt to describe it. Throw into one great sum total all that you have ever experienced, or can conceive, of wisdom and power, the most far-sighted discernments of results, with the most

absolute control over them,—the keenest intuition into character, with every conceivable influence for moulding it,—think of a providence not of this earth, which no opposition can surprise, and no device counterplot, calmly and serenely evolving its own designs from the perverse agencies of man, and turning the very arm which is raised to defeat it into a minister of its will,—imagine a Being so wonderfully endowed that the whole keyboard of Nature, Providence, and the human heart lies under His hand, and, smitten by His mystic fingers, gives forth the harmony which pleases Him; and then invest Him in your conceptions with an intensity of love, which is not discouraged by the deepest moral degradation in its objects, and which clings to the person of the sinner with unchilled devotion even while it condemns his sin with an abhorrence no less than infinite,—imagine such a Being, and imagine Him accessible to man, and you imagine One, to whom in their hour of need all the world, unless indeed the spell of some deadly fascination were laid upon them, would be resorting continually for guidance, help, and comfort. But this is no imagination. It is a reality. God is such a Being as we have laboured to describe. He not only permits, but invites; not only invites, but commands, the approach to Him of every comer. And if there be no promise that every prayer shall be heard according to the exact tenor of its prescription, yet assuredly there is a promise to all who ask,—most simple,—most express,—most universal,—of that nourishment of grace for the human spirit, which is the alone support of spiritual life: "If ye then, being evil, know how to give good gifts unto your children, how much more shall your Father which is in Heaven give the Holy Spirit to them that ask Him?"

But might we not be reasonably barred from this access to God by a deep feeling of His purity, coupled with the consciousness of our own sin? Indeed it might most justly be so. The Scriptures, and our own hearts re-echoing the Scriptures, assure us that in God there is, by the very necessity of His nature, a deep-seated moral antipathy to evil. "He is of purer eyes than to behold iniquity." In His holiness He is a consuming fire to the unholy creature. The rays of the sun, concentrated in a burning-glass, cause any combustible material, upon which they are so brought to bear, to become sere, to shrivel, to crumple, to ignite, and finally to pulverize: Something analogous would be the fate of the sinner who, without mediation, should presume to draw upon him the full notice of the holy God by venturing into His presence. But we know well that God has provided for the removal of this barrier. We know well that the obedience of the Lord Jesus was such that the holiness of God can detect in it no flaw; that His Death and Passion were the endurance by the Righteous One of God's curse upon sin; and that the earliest message of the Gospel is, that both the obedience and the death of Christ are available for every member of the human family, who, without an attempt at self-justification, simply throws himself upon that plea. The way to come to God, and the only way to come so as not to meet with rejection, is Christ. "I am the way: no man cometh unto the Father but by Me." In other words, when the soul is to be lifted up in prayer, it must be in dependence upon His merits and blood-shedding. It was to symbolize this precious and fundamental truth, that the primitive Christians wore a white garment in divine worship (which still survives among us under the name of the surplice), thus giving a lesson, as they were fond of doing, through the eye, that no soul of man could appear before God in its native deformity; but that before we draw near to the throne of grace, we must put on the robe of righteousness, which the Lord Jesus wove, and now offers gratuitously to all who sincerely confess their spiritual nakedness and shame.

But it is now time to exhibit the bearing of these remarks upon our general argument. Prayer is the source and secret of the strength in which the Christian must cope with the duties and difficulties of life. And one most obvious danger besetting the constantly repeated prayers of persons in active life, is formality. Such persons, while too conscientious to abandon the habit of stated prayer, soon find that there is every temptation to satisfy the conscience with the attentive repetition of a form, which takes no hold of the mind, and exerts no moral or spiritual influence on the temper. Every real Christian is well aware that thus to reduce prayer to a form, is to drain away from the exercise all its virtue, until it becomes a broken vessel, empty of power and comfort. But how to prevent, even with the best disposition, its lapsing into a form? The thing is by no means easy, or to be accomplished without effort. This is just one of those struggles which beset real Personal Religion, and which baffle and often make sad the Christian who cannot acquiesce in mere respectability, and feels that God has called him to saintliness. The design of this treatise being to afford help and counsel to such persons, and to lead them gradually onward, let me recommend that special attention be paid to the beginning and end of stated prayers. "Before thou prayest," says the wise man, "prepare thyself." Let the mind, as much as may be, be solemnized, calmed, toned down, by taking in the thought of the presence of God, and the sublime idea of coming to Him. It has been our purpose in this Chapter to indicate the path along which the mind may travel with interest and profit on such an occasion. Endeavour to recall these thoughts, or such as these, with a secret aspiration that by grace you may be enabled to realize them. Lift up the mind gradually, and by stages, to some apprehension, however dim and unworthy, of the majesty, the might, the wisdom, the holiness, the love of God; and when, to use the Psalmist's expression, "the fire kindles, then speak with your tongue." The ready excuse for not complying with this advice, which springs to every lip, is, "Time; the sort of prayer you describe asks time; and my occupations drive me into a corner for time." To which the answer is twofold; first, that time might probably be gained by a very little of that self-discipline, which surely no man should grudge to bestow on the work of his salvation. Let conscience answer whether, despite all this pressure of occupation, time is not continually *made* for engagements of an agreeable nature? and if made for them, why not for more serious engagements? Secondly; that as in other things, so in prayer,—a little done well is vastly better than more done superficially. Let it be remembered, too, that both the precept and the model which Our Lord has given us, rather discountenance *long* prayers. We are expressly counselled by Him against using vain repetitions, and thinking that we shall be heard for our much speaking, while the compression of thought and brevity of the Lord's Prayer is such, as to make it desirable that the petitioner should pause a little upon each clause, and slightly expand for himself the meaning, as he goes along.

The end of stated Prayers should also be made the subject of some attention and care. It is surprising how little this principle has been recognized in books of devotion. In manuals of preparation for the Holy Communion, for example, how little emphasis is laid, as a general rule, on the regulation of the heart and conduct, *subsequently* to the Ordinance! The natural recoil from the strain which real prayer always puts upon the mind is levity. Against this levity the devout man should watch and strive. When we have withdrawn into ourselves for a while for Communion with God, the glare of the world should be let in gradually on the mind again, as an oculist opens the shutters by degrees upon his restored patient. The impression of having had an interview with the King of kings amid the ministries of Cherubim and Seraphim should not be rudely tossed off, but gently and thoughtfully cherished. And it shall be as a nosegay of fresh flowers, which a man gathers before he leaves some fair and quiet garden, a refreshment amidst the dust and turmoil of earthly pursuits.

Make experiment of this advice, remembering that in spiritual as in intellectual discipline, early efforts are for the most part clumsy failures, and that repeated trials are the uniform condition of success: and you shall find, under the blessing of God, that your prayers will grow in life and interest, and will give that bright and happy tone to the mind, without which no one ever encountered successfully the duties and temptations of active life.

CHAPTER II.

OF THE TWOFOLD ASPECT OF PRAYER, AND THE NECESSITY OF PRACTISING IT IN BOTH ASPECTS.

"Let my prayer be set forth before thee as incense; and the lifting up of my hands as the evening sacrifice."—PSALM cxli. 2.

IT is observable that our Blessed Lord, in His Sermon on the Mount, takes up the subject of prayer twice; once in the sixth, and again in a totally different connexion, in the seventh chapter of St. Matthew's Gospel. Why, it may be asked, when He was on the subject of prayer in the sixth chapter, did He not then and there exhaust all that was to be said upon it? It is possible that the answer to this question may be found in the twofold aspect of Prayer, which will form the subject of this Chapter. Prayer is a means of supplying man's necessities; this is its human aspect, its face towards man. Under this aspect our Lord regards it in the seventh chapter, where He gives the consolatory assurance that all our real wants *shall* be supplied by it: "Ask, and it shall be given you; seek, and ye shall find; knock, and it shall be opened unto you." But Prayer has another quite distinct aspect. It is an act of homage done to the Majesty of God. Accordingly it is to be performed with the utmost reverence and solemnity; there is to be no babbling in it, no familiar glibness of the tongue, no running of words to waste, but simple, grave, short, sound, well-considered speech. So had King Solomon said long centuries ago: "Be not rash with thy mouth, and let not thine heart be hasty to utter any thing before God: for God is in heaven, and thou upon earth: therefore let thy words be few." And so says One greater and wiser than Solomon, even Christ, "the Power of God, and the Wisdom of God." These are His words in the sixth chapter of St. Matthew's Gospel: "But when ye pray, use not vain repetitions, as the heathen do: for they think that they shall be heard for their much speaking." "Be not ye therefore like unto them." In the same paragraph, He says that the homage is not to be ostentatiously offered, but in the privacy of the closet. Privately as it may be paid, the Father will acknowledge it openly. Observe how the promise runs in this section of the Sermon. He says not, "The Father will give you the thing asked for;" for that was not exactly the aspect under which He was then viewing Prayer; but "He shall reward thee openly,"—acknowledge Thee as a true worshipper in the face of men and angels. The secret homage of the Saints is to be owned *at the Day of Judgment*. Their wants are to be supplied *in the present life*. Both these benefits are the crown and meed of real believing prayer. But they are entirely distinct subjects of thought.

In our last Chapter we rather looked at Prayer in the former of these two views, as a means of supplying man's wants. We regarded it as a pouring out of the heart with all its felt necessities, trials, and burdens, before God. This it is. But it is something more than this. And unless we hold before the eyes of our minds this second aspect of it, not only will our view be theoretically incomplete, (which of itself would signify little,) but practical errors will be insinuated into our minds, against which it behoves every devout man to be upon his guard.

Let us turn, then, to consider this second aspect of Prayer a little more closely. In the passage which stands at the head of this Chapter, the Psalmist very beautifully compares Prayer to the things which indeed were types of it under the Old Dispensation, Incense and Sacrifice. "Let my prayer be set forth in thy sight as incense, and the lifting up of my hands as the evening sacrifice." With this we connect the words of St. John in the Revelation,—"Jesus Christ hath made us kings and *priests* unto God and His Father." Every Christian is really and truly a priest, consecrated in Baptism and Confirmation, (not indeed to minister in the congregation, but) to offer up spiritual sacrifices, acceptable to God by Jesus Christ. If it be asked what these sacrifices are, the Scriptural answer would be,—first, our own bodies, which we are bidden by St. Paul to present as "a living sacrifice, holy, acceptable to God, which is our reasonable service:" secondly, our alms-givings, which the same Apostle declares to be "an odour of a sweet smell, a sacrifice acceptable, well-pleasing to God; and last, not least, our prayers (including under this generic term all the exercises of devotion,—confession, intercession, thanksgiving, praise, no less than direct petitions for ourselves). As the fragrant incense-cloud went up from the kindled coal in the censer; as the sweet savour went up from the burnt offering, when it was roast with the fire of the altar; so true believing Prayer, coming from a kindled heart, rises of necessity to God, and steals into His immediate presence in the Upper Sanctuary. We may complete the imagery by observing that the Altar upon which these sacrifices must be laid,—the only Altar which sanctifieth the gift, and renders it acceptable,—is our Lord Jesus Christ Himself, in the faith of whose meritorious Cross and Righteousness every prayer and spiritual oblation must be made.

Now is not the view of Prayer which we have thus sketched out very distinct, and very important in its practical bearings? Prayer is designed not only to be serviceable to man, but honourable to God. It is a tax (redounding indeed with unspeakable benefits to the tax-payer, but still it is a tax) laid upon our time; just as almsgiving is a tax laid upon our substance; and if we would render unto God the things that are

God's, the tribute-money must be faithfully and punctually paid. This indeed is the inner principle and spirit of the fourth Commandment. God says we must keep a certain portion of our time clear from secular occupations. That time is to be devoted to the observance of His ordinances, and to attendance upon His Worship. It is true we reap priceless blessings from this observance and attendance. But the blessings are not the sole point to be considered. All our time from the cradle to the grave is due to God. Every day is the gift of His mercy through Jesus Christ. Therefore one day in each week,—and, on precisely the same principle, a certain portion of our leisure each day,—must be fenced round from the intrusion of secular cares and secular business, and reserved for devotion, in acknowledgment that we hold all from Him. Upon this principle the stated private prayers of morning and evening should be offered punctually, as well as under the other view already dwelt upon, that we need something of God, and must go and ask it. Think of yourself before you kneel down, not simply as a suppliant for help, but as a priest addressing himself to offer sacrifice and to burn incense. The time of the morning or evening oblation is come; the Altar is ready; the incense is at hand; the sacerdotal robe of Christ's Righteousness waits to be put on; array thyself in it; and go into the sanctuary of thy heart, and do the priestly ministration.

Now let us consider of what practical service these reflections may be to us, in resisting those temptations, and overcoming those difficulties which beset all earnest Prayer.

Prayer, like faith (of which it is the voice and expression), is a thing perfectly simple in idea, but exceedingly difficult of execution. If you can pray aright, you have mastered the great secret of the spiritual life; but easy as it is to understand theoretically what right prayer is, it is far from easy to practise it. The difficulties, if traced to their origin, arise, no doubt, very much from the fact that our adversary the Devil is fully aware of the power of real

Prayer, and therefore sets in operation all his devices to harass, distract, and disquiet every earnest petitioner. So long as a man's prayers are dead and lifeless exercises, and act as an opiate to the conscience, without exercising any sanctifying influence on the character, of course it meets with no opposition from this quarter; but let it once pass out of the domain of form into that of real communion with God, and it is sure of disturbance in one shape or another,—sure of falling far below the mark which the petitioner sets before him. Consider what perfect trifles to the Christian even the worst trials of life would become, and with what ease the most formidable temptations would be mastered, if Prayer always opened to him the gate of Heaven, as perhaps it has seemed to do on some favoured days; as it might do always, if there were not certain disturbing influences, constantly drawing it down, as with the force of gravitation, to a lower level. One of the earliest of these disturbing influences, of which the awakened soul becomes conscious, is the temptation to leave off, when the exercise promises to be dry and barren, and when the mind is much harassed by distractions. When we fail to derive from Prayer comfort and satisfaction, we become cowards, and run away from the faldstool. We give up the attempt, because it meets with discouragement at the outset. Now this, like most other defects of practice, is traceable ultimately to an error of principle. We have forgotten that Prayer (I am now speaking of stated Prayer) is an act of homage to Almighty God; we regard it simply in its bearing on the spiritual welfare of man,— on his inward peace, light, strength, and comfort. We become utilitarians as to Prayer, and secretly think that where no sensible benefit is derived from it, it need not be pursued any further. And if Prayer were only valuable for its effect upon the mind of man,—if it had no higher significance than this,—the reasoning would be just. But if Prayer be truly a sacrificial act, an act of ministry on the part of the Christian, a homage rendered to the Majesty of Heaven, then to abandon it in disgust, because it cannot be performed with entire comfort and satisfaction to our own minds, instead of being regarded as a recognition of the spirituality of Prayer (which is the light we are apt to view it in), ought to be regarded as a dereliction of duty. It is a peevish indulgence of self, by which God is robbed of His incense.—Nay,—let the rule invariably be this; *where you cannot pray as you would, pray as you can.* It was the quaint but excellent saying of an old saint, that a man should deal with distractions in Prayer as he would deal with dogs, who run out and bark at him when he goes along the street,—walk on fast and straightforward, and take no notice of them. Persevere in presenting yourself to God during the period for which the Prayer ought to last, and would last under happier circumstances. He loves to draw out perseverance in Prayer, loves the indication thus given that, amidst all discouragements, the soul clings obstinately to Himself; and very early in the world's history He signified His approval of this temper of mind by rewarding and crowning, as He did, Jacob's struggle with the Jehovah-Angel. Something obscure and mysterious will always hang over that passage of Old Testament history. But we cannot err in regarding the Patriarch's words, "I will not let thee go, except thou bless me," as designed to teach us a lesson of perseverance and resolute determination in our intercourse with God, amidst all the difficulties by which earnest Prayer is beset.

It must be remembered that this quiet, resolute patience, even amidst the disorders and distractions of our own spirit, is probably the most acceptable offering which can be made to the Most High. It is an easy thing to pray, when our prayer soars to Heaven on the wings of a warm emotion, and when the Holy Spirit, like a favouring gale, seems to swell the sails which the mind spreads to catch His blessed influence. Prayer is then a matter of feeling rather than of principle. But when we have to woo the gale, and yet the gale comes not, when the vessel has constantly to be set on different tacks, and yet seems to make little or no way towards the shore, it is then that our fidelity in paying our homage to God is tested and approved. And let us be sure that it will not be long tested and approved, before it is rewarded. We shall not long wait on the Lord, without renewing our strength. We shall not long persevere in asking, amid repulses, before He will turn and open to us the treasury of His bounty, and say to us, as to the Syrophœnician of old, " Great is thy faith; be it unto thee even as thou wilt." Yet if the blessing come not in the shape of sensible comfort, resign thy will to God's Will, and that resignation itself shall be an acceptable sacrifice. Thou worshippest Him not for the mere comfort of worshipping Him, but because He is infinitely worthy of homage from every knee and lip. " How many courtiers be there," says an excellent writer on devotion, " that go an hundred times a year into the prince's chamber, without hope of once speaking with him, but only to be seen of him. So must we, my dear Philothea, come to the exercise of Prayer purely and merely to do our duty, and to testify our fidelity. If it please His Divine Majesty to speak, and discourse with us by His holy inspirations and interior consolations, it will be doubtless an inestimable honour to us, and a pleasure above all pleasures; but if it please Him not to do us this favour, leaving us without so much as speaking to us, as if He saw us not, or as if we were not in His Presence, we must not for all that go our way, but continue with decent and devout behaviour in the Presence of His Sovereign Goodness; and then infallibly our patience will be acceptable to Him, and He will take notice of our diligence and perseverance; so that another time, when we shall come before Him, He will favour us, and pass His time with us in heavenly consolations, and make us see the beauty of holy Prayer [1]."

We have been exhibiting Prayer under its aspect of homage,—the aspect in which it has reference to God's

---

[1] S. François de Sales; Introduction à la Vie dévote.

glory rather than man's wants. We are confident that by many excellent and devout people this aspect of it is altogether dropped out of sight. And we are sure also that this defective view leads frequently to a degenerate style of Prayer. Robbed of its character of homage, Prayer soon becomes an entirely selfish thing; and the petitioner, when engaged in it, soon comes to regard every thing as beside the mark, which has no reference to his own immediate necessities. It is very desirable to redeem Prayer from this exclusively selfish character; to give it a wider scope and a grander bearing; and the keeping in mind what has been said of it as an act of homage and priestly service will perhaps help us in achieving this desirable end. But definite practical rules may be given, which will not be long acted upon without giving a better tone to our devotions. There are parts of Prayer which *cannot* be selfish, which directly seek either the interests of others, or the glory of God;—see that these parts be not absent from *your* prayers.

First; intercede for others, and acquire the habit of interceding. Consider their wants, trials, and difficulties, and bear them upon your heart, as you bear your own, before the Throne of Grace. Intercession is a priestly service. Christ, the great High Priest, intercedes for us all above. And we, if we would prove ourselves members of God's Royal Priesthood upon earth, and perform with fidelity those spiritual sacrifices which we were consecrated in Baptism to present, must intercede for others. It is truly lamentable to think how defective in this point of view are the devotions of the best Christians,—how thoroughly well content they are that the half-hour daily spent in intercourse with God, should be devoted entirely to their own struggles, their own trials, their own wants. So little proficients are they in Charity,—and so little—so very little—can they realize the constant "our" and "us" of the Lord's Prayer,—whereby Christ teaches us, in a way more emphatic than many sermons, that we should pray as members of a family,—with the wants, sins, temptations, burdens of the whole family continually upon our hearts. Until we can in some measure do this, we do not pray after the Lord's model.

Secondly; let Praise—I say not merely thanksgiving, but Praise—always form an ingredient of thy prayers. We thank God for what He is to us; for the benefits which He confers, and the blessings with which He visits us. But we praise Him for what He is in Himself,—for His glorious excellences and perfections, independently of their bearing on the welfare of the creature. In Praise the thought of self vanishes from, and is extinguished in, the mind; and therefore to be large and fervent in Praise counteracts the natural tendency to selfishness which is found in mere Prayer.

Think not, O man, whosoever thou art, that God will dispense with this tribute of Praise from thee! Remember that, merely as man, thou art the High Priest of all creation, a little miniature of the Universe in thyself, representing the Angels in virtue of thy immortal spirit, the lower creatures in virtue of thy sensations and appetites, and matter in virtue of thy body. Thus, when thou singest Praise, all Creation (in a manner) sings in thee and with thee.

And it shall often happen that when thy heart is numb and torpid, and yields not to the action of Prayer, it shall begin to thaw, and at last burst, like streams under the breath of spring, from its icy prison, with the warm and genial exercise of Praise. The deadness, the distractions thou deplorest, shall flee away as the harp is taken down from the willow, and strung to celebrate the Divine perfections. For how much is there to kindle the heart in the very thought of Praise! Praise is the religious exercise—the one religious exercise—of Heaven. Angels are offering it ceaselessly, resting not night or day. Saints are offering it ceaselessly in Paradise. Nature in her every district is offering it ceaselessly. From the Heavens, which declare the glory of God, and the firmament, which showeth His handiwork, down to the dewdrop which sparkles with the colours of the rainbow, and the lark, who tunes her cheerful carol as she salutes the rising sun, the whole Creation sends up one grand chorus of Praise to the throne of God. Thou shalt feel that thou art not alone in offering it, that every act of true Praise is social, and, as it were, choral, though offered in solitude. "All saints far on earth, and in Paradise, feel without knowing it, the impulse of each other's adoration, and join in with it, like strings that vibrate to the same tone, without touching each other[z]." And the sense of sympathy in the exercise shall kindle life in thee, and the soul shall recover its benumbed energies, and prayer shall be no more a painful wrestling with thy own mind, but a solace, and a strength, and a light, and a healing.

CHAPTER III.

THE SECRET OF SUCCESS IN PRAYER.

"*And in the morning, as they passed by, they saw the fig-tree dried up from the roots. And Peter called to remembrance saith unto him, Master, behold, the fig-tree which thou cursedst is withered away. And Jesus answering saith unto them, Have faith in God. For verily I say unto you, That whosoever shall say unto this mountain, Be thou removed, and be thou cast into the sea; and shall not doubt in his heart, but shall believe that those things which he saith shall come to pass; he shall have whatsoever he saith.*"—
MARK xi. 20—23.

IT is very observable that the remarks which Our Blessed Lord makes on the incidents presented to Him, and His comments on the sayings which were dropped in His presence, do not at all meet our natural anticipations of what the occasion required. Merely human

---

[z] Rev. Charles Marriott. Thoughts on Private Devotion.

comments on what is said or done in society are almost always obvious; and they are so, because they are shallow, caught up rapidly from the surface of the subject, and flung abroad at random upon the apprehension of the hearers. But infinite wisdom—and our Lord is the Infinite Wisdom personified—explores the depths of every subject which is brought before it, and dives into the heart of every speaker, and answers not according to the superficial bearing of the subject, not according to the literal expression of the lips, but according to the hidden harmony, which it requires thought and prayer to bring to light, and according to the intent of the heart.

As an illustration of this, take the words which stand at the head of this Chapter, with the circumstances which gave rise to them. Our Lord on finding a fig-tree barren, which had made a great show of leaves, had pronounced on it a solemn curse. In consequence of the curse the fig-tree had withered. The disciples seeing it dried up from the roots, call the attention of their Master to the fact. And He replies, "Have faith in God,"—and so forth.

Now, the question is, What remark would a mere wise man—one wiser than his fellows, if you will; but still a mere man,—have made under such circumstances? Supposing we ourselves were great teachers of moral truth;—what comment would have risen to our lips on having our attention called to the sere and blighted tree? Possibly we might have drawn from the circumstance its obvious moral—thus: "That fig-tree is the Jewish nation. Its show of leaves is the profession which they make of godliness—'We are instructors of the foolish; lights of them that sit in darkness; guides of the blind; teachers of the babes,' &c. Its want of fruit is their spiritual barrenness,—their want of practice, while they have so much profession. Its present withered state foreshows their future doom,—which is to stand a blighted monument of wrath on God's highway." But whatever our comment on the occasion might have been, this, I think, is certain, that it would not have been, "Have faith in God." That is not obvious enough. We know that it must be exactly to the point, the precise word for the occasion,—because the Infinite Wisdom said it,—but it requires a great deal of consideration to see *how* it is to the point. Faith, and prayer, and forgiveness, are, no doubt, matters of vast importance; but what have they to do, how are they connected with, the cursing and withering of a fig-tree? On the surface we can trace no connexion whatever. And we conclude that we must dive beneath the surface by meditation, and prayer for the Light of God's Spirit, if we would catch the silver thread, on which are strung these beautiful diamonds of holy instruction.

The outline of the connexion is probably this:—

St. Peter's expression was, "Master, behold the fig-tree which thou cursedst is withered away."—That was his language. What was the thought of his heart, which spoke itself out in that language? Probably of this kind. "What words of power are thine, O Master! Thou spakest yesterday a few simple words, 'No fruit grow on thee hereafter for ever.' Thou spakest them quietly, as thou ever speakest. No immediate sign followed. The earth did not tremble at thine utterance. The vault of heaven did not echo it back in thunder. All things seemed unchanged around us. The insect hummed upon his way in the morning sun, and the waggoner trolled his song, as he drove past us with his market-stores—and we dropped the word out of our memory. But it has not fallen to the earth. Fallen to the earth! no, it was a power-word. No sooner said than done. The word sped to its accomplishment, as an arrow speeds to the mark. The imprecation yesterday;—to-day, in visible and due development, the blight!—'Behold! the fig-tree that thou *cursedst* is withered away.'" "And Jesus answering, said unto them"—possibly, as if to answer his thoughts, He fixed His wonderful eye upon the speaker, in the assurance that He explored his inmost soul—"Have faith in God." As if He had said, "My words are power-words indeed. They take effect—immediate effect. They are not spoken in the air; they achieve something. Little children, ye shall be as your Master. I will teach *you* to speak power-words like mine. Your prayers for good shall speed to their accomplishment, as surely and as fast as my prayer for evil upon the fig-tree. Ask, and ye shall have. Asking and having shall be linked together as closely as the cursing and the withering of the fig-tree,—if only ye will ask in faith,—if only, on the ground of God's promise made to prayer, you will believe, while ye ask, that you receive the object of your petitions. This and another condition—that you forgive injuries,—that you pray in love as well as in faith—this shall ensure the success of your Prayers. You, like your Heavenly Father, shall speak, and it shall be done—you, like Him, shall command, and it shall stand fast."

Such is the connexion of thought between our Lord's words, and the occasion which gave rise to them. Let us now learn from them the secret of successful prayer. Prayer is, without doubt, the great means of advance in Personal Religion and the spiritual life. But it is surprising, and most disheartening, how very little proportion the progress of religious persons bears to their prayers. Were the prayers formal,—that is, were they said without seriousness and attention, and without any corresponding effort to amend the life, of course the account of this barrenness would be obvious. But this is by no means the case. The petitioner, in the case which we are supposing, seriously and earnestly desires spiritual blessings. He gives serious and close attention to the words which he employs in prayer. He strives to realize, when he employs them, the awful Presence of God. Yet somehow or other the prayer is not so successful as it should be. It may calm his mind, quiet his spirit, spread a general sensation of happiness over his soul; these are what I may call the natural influences of Prayer; but it does not seem that he is substantially the better for it. There is a great mass of Prayer, and very little sensible improvement,—

very little growth in grace. Years roll on; and his character is still very stagnant in any spiritual view of it; excellent, upright, and devout as far as man can mark, he has not made much progress in Divine things. The many, many words of Prayer seem spoken in the air; they are sent forth into the vast world of spirits, like Noah's raven from the ark, never to return again.

Is this true as a general description, if not to the full extent, of any one who reads these lines? Then let me invite such a person to consider the secret of successful Prayer, as explained by our Lord Himself. May it not be that your words are not words of power, because they are not words of Faith? You pray rather as a duty, than in the definite expectation of any thing to be gained by it. You pray attentively, seriously, devoutly; and you go your way with a feeling of satisfaction that you have done well upon the whole, and there the matter ends. In the ancient augury by birds, as soon as the augur had made the preliminary arrangements,—covered his head, marked out the heavens with his staff, and uttered his prayer,—he stayed on the spot, watching for the first appearance of the birds,—he was on the look out for the result. But this is just what many Christians fail to do in regard of their prayers; they have no expectation of being benefited by them; they do not look for the blessing to which, in virtue of God's promise in Christ Jesus, the prayer entitles them. If, some day, after praying for the Light of God's Spirit, they were to find in the study of His Word a wonderful clearing up of things which had been dark before, and a lucid apprehension of Divine Truth, they would be inwardly surprised, from the mental habit of disconnecting Prayer with its effect, and would say, "What do I owe this to?" Now what would this surprise argue? What does the want of expectation that good will result to us from our prayers prove respecting our state of mind? Surely that we have no definite belief that the blessing will be granted,—in a word, no faith in God's promise, which connects Prayer with the answer to Prayer,—the word with the power.

The Scriptures lead us to suppose that there is no height of holiness to which, in the might of God's Spirit, we cannot attain. There is no reason why we should not be so full of love and zeal,—why our souls should not be so penetrated at all times with a sense of Christ's Love and Presence, that we should breathe habitually the element of praise, and that every meal should become a Sacrament. I say there is no reason, except such as resides in ourselves. And the difficulties which reside in ourselves, and result from our corrupt nature, hard heart, stubborn will, and so forth, the Spirit of God *has* overcome in numberless instances of saints of old, and *may* overcome in us. "Is the Lord's arm shortened, that it cannot save; or His ear heavy, that it cannot hear?" "The power that worketh in us" is, as we read, "able to do exceeding abundantly above all that we ask or think." This is admitted in theory by all. But now, when we come to pray, and to set before us this high standard of holiness as an object of ambition, a subtle unbelief rises and spreads like leaven in the heart. We have no notion (the truth had better be told candidly) that God either will or can make *us* eminent saints. Perhaps He may help us a little to overcome this evil temper, to rid ourselves of that bad habit, and may make us, very gradually indeed, fair average Christians; but as for any great progress, any high pinnacle of virtue, that is out of the question with our temptations and under our circumstances. We have not leisure enough. We have not time enough for prayer; and we cannot get time. Our passions are strong and in their heyday. The least cross turn of things in the day upsets our temper. We are men hurried with engagements, all hot with a thousand secular interests; or we have a mighty passion for human praise and the laurels of earthly distinction: you cannot make saints out of that material. It is an impossibility. You might as well advance to the brink of one of the lakes that lie embosomed in Alpine scenery, and command the enormous granite mountains that tower above you to descend and cast themselves into the sea. They would not answer you. There would be neither voice nor hearing. And the evil tempers and corrupt inclinations will not answer us, when in the might of Prayer we command them to come out. Something like this is too often the secret process of our hearts, when we kneel down to pray. Now I am not going to plead for a fanatical view of answers to Prayer. I have no great faith in sudden revulsions of feeling, or instantaneous conversions. I know full well that growth in Grace, as in Nature, may be so rapid as to be unhealthily rapid, as to indicate shallowness and want of depth. But one thing I do believe,—to disbelieve which were the most unreasonable of all follies,—to believe which is the dictate of the calmest, soberest, purest, highest reason. One thing I do believe,—more surely than the evidence of the senses, for they may be imposed upon;—more surely than those self-evident axioms, upon which mathematical truth is built, for those axioms are only spun out of the human mind, and not external to it. I do believe that GOD IS TRUE. I do believe that whenever God makes a promise, He will assuredly fulfil it. I do believe that if you or I come under the terms of the promise, He will fulfil it to us. I see that He has promised the Holy Spirit to them that ask Him: and it were blasphemous not to believe that the Holy Spirit is able to surmount any and every difficulty.

Therefore if I have ever secretly reasoned as above, if such has ever been the secret process of my heart, I stand convicted of unbelief. It is no marvel that God has withheld the blessing, if I so dishonoured Him in my heart as never seriously to believe that He could or would bestow it. And, in future, if I would meet with success, I must come to the Throne of Grace with *an undoubting mind*. Having launched my petition into the world of spirits, I must stand (like good Habakkuk) upon the watch, and set me upon the tower, and must watch to see what He will say to me. Having prayed "Show me a token for good," I must wait, like the augurs, looking up to Heaven until the token comes. I must in the depth of my inmost heart expect to receive what I ask for. And then if, besides this, my prayer be a prayer of Love,—if, while I breathe it, my heart goes forth on an errand of forgiveness towards the man who has thwarted or striven to injure me,— then *the answer cannot long tarry.* The prayer-word must in that case be a power-word. The effect must be in that case as surely linked to the petition as the blighting of the fig-tree was linked to the Saviour's malediction. "Though it tarry, wait for it; because it will surely come, it will not tarry."

Before concluding this Chapter, we will give one simple piece of advice, by way of rendering more practical what has been said.

Strive to acquire the habit of asking definitely for particular graces of which you stand in need, and of expecting a definite result. For example; what point of character was it in which you found yourself most deficient in the examination which preceded your last Communion? Until the next Communion comes round, let that particular grace, whether it was purity, or humility, or patience, or zeal, or love, be made the subject of a distinct petition in your prayers. Do not forget the petition; always have it in your mind's eye; try to expect the result,—to assure yourself, on grounds of simple reason, that, as you have sown, so you will, in due season, reap.

Some may ask, and it is well that they should have a distinct and unequivocal answer,—"Where is my warrant for believing that?" There are many warrants. We will take that which seems least capable of being evaded. It occurs in Luke xi. 13. Read it over before you make your daily petition, and remember that, whatever else may be false, this must be true.

"IF YE THEN, BEING EVIL, KNOW HOW TO GIVE GOOD GIFTS UNTO YOUR CHILDREN: HOW MUCH MORE SHALL YOUR HEAVENLY FATHER GIVE THE HOLY SPIRIT TO THEM THAT ASK HIM?"

It will be admitted that if, after saying *that*, God

were to withhold the Holy Spirit from those that ask Him, He would be raising expectations which would be disappointed,—a thing plainly abhorrent to His character. I must also call particular attention to the fact, that the one only condition which this promise contemplates, in the persons to whom it is addressed,— is the asking. If you ask, then, clearly and beyond the shadow of a doubt you are entitled to receive. You may be very sinful at present, very weak, very different in many respects from what you wish to be; that is all beside the mark. The terms of the promise under which you must come, if you desire its fulfilment, are not that you shall be holy, but *only that you shall be an asker.*

Glorious promise! so sublime! "If ye, being evil, know how to give good gifts to your children" (why, we know that the tenderness and love of human parents is proverbial): "how much more shall your heavenly Father give"—Give what? Health, and freedom from pain, and a sound mind in a sound body? Good things these; but He will give something better. What then? Long life, and many days? Ah! it might be only a grief of heart to thee;—no, something better. Large store of silver and gold, flocks and herds, and great worldly well-being?—Ah! the canker of self-indulgence might convert it all into a curse;—no, something better. Lofty distinction, high posts, crowns, and empires, and a great name,—all the kingdoms of the world and the glory of them? Nay, better, much better. "THE HOLY SPIRIT," to be the soul of thy soul, to new-create thy moral nature in the Image of God, to dwell in thee, and walk in thee, making thy heart His shrine; a present stream of joy, and strength, and consolation, springing up into everlasting life;—" how much more shall your heavenly Father give the Holy Spirit to them that ask Him?" Glorious promise! so free! Free as the air of heaven to those who will but come forth and breathe it. Free as the rivers of the earth to those who will but dip a cup in them, and slake their thirst. Then come forthwith, and claim this mighty Boon. Come with strong desire. Let the heart speak, rather than the mouth. Come in stedfast faith, fastening the whole soul upon that solemn asseveration,—" Yea, let God be true, and every man a liar!" And lo! your word is a word of power. It has unlocked Heaven. Before you call, He answers; and while you are yet speaking, He hears.

CHAPTER IV.

OF SELF-EXAMINATION.

"*And the Lord sent Nathan unto David. And he came unto him, and said unto him, There were two men in one city; the one rich, and the other poor. The rich man had exceeding many flocks and herds: but the poor man had nothing, save one little ewe lamb, which he had bought and nourished up: and it grew up together with him, and with his children: it did eat of his own meat, and drank of his own cup, and lay in his bosom, and was unto him as a daughter. And there came a traveller unto the rich man, and he spared to take of his own flock and of his own herd, to dress for the wayfaring man that was come unto him; but took the poor man's lamb, and dressed it for the man that was come to him. And David's anger was greatly kindled against the man; and he said to Nathan, As the Lord liveth, the man that hath done this thing shall surely die: and he shall restore the lamb fourfold, because he did this thing, and because he had no pity. And Nathan said to David, Thou art the man.*"—2 SAM. xii. 1—7.

IN this striking passage of Holy Scripture we see King David in disguise brought before his own judgment-seat. His judgment, as chief magistrate of his realm, is demanded upon an imaginary case of wanton and cruel oppression, the exact counterpart of that which he had himself committed. David, not recognizing himself under the disguise which the prophet had thrown over him, passes sentence of death and fourfold restitution upon the imaginary offender. No sooner had the sentence gone out of the king's mouth than the prophet unmasks the muffled and mysterious figure which stood at the bar, tears away the disguise, and shows to the astonished king himself: "Thou art the man." How came it to pass that David was so incensed with cruelty and oppression in a supposed case, though he had remained so long (since his child was born when Nathan came to him, it cannot have been much short of a year) insensible to the far more heinous cruelty and oppression of his own conduct? The reason is, of course, that we never judge of our own conduct in any affair, as we do of an abstract case in which we are not ourselves mixed up, and in which our feelings, passions, and prejudices are not interested. Moralists have questioned, and there seems every reason to question, whether a man *can* do a bad action without justifying it to his own conscience as at least excusable under the circumstances,—or, in other words, whether evil, without a certain colour, pretext, and palliation, can ever be accepted by the human will; but the colours and pretexts which serve for our own conduct are never available for that of other men. We judge *them*, as David judged the imaginary offender in the parable, nakedly, truly, and severely enough.

It is the object of these pages to give some thoughts, which may be practically useful on the subject of Personal Religion. Now the chief devotional exercise which turns Religion into a personal thing, which brings it home to men's business and bosom, is Self-examination. A man's religion cannot well be one of merely good impressions,—the staple of it cannot well be an evaporating sentiment, if he have acquired the habit of honestly and candidly looking within. The subject, therefore, which we treat to-day, has the closest bearing upon the general argument of the work.

Self-examination may be called an arraignment of ourselves at our own bar, according to that word of our Eucharistic Service: "Judge therefore yourselves, brethren, that ye be not judged of the Lord." It is an exercise most essential to our spiritual health; and the more earnestly to be pressed on all Protestants, because there exists in the Reformed Churches no security but that of right principle for its ever being practised. In the Roman Church you are aware it is otherwise. The system of the confessional, with all its evils and abominations, may at least fairly lay claim to the advantage of exacting a certain amount of introspection from those who honestly conform to it. We who have not this check, and among whom the work of probing the conscience with the Word of God is done from the pulpit, must at least see to it that we make such work personal, by applying to ourselves in Self-examination the Sermons which we hear and read.

It is easy,—fatally easy,—with Self-examination as with Prayer, to allow the exercise to be drawn down from its high moral and spiritual aim to the level of a form. A string of questions put to the conscience every evening before our evening prayer, never varying with the circumstances of the day, turning principally upon outward conduct, and answered almost mechanically—this, if the truth must be confessed, is what the Self-examination of devout and well-intentioned people too often reduces itself to. Not that we at all counsel the abandonment of such a practice, where it is done with real seriousness and attention. It is almost a principle of the spiritual life that ground is never gained, always lost, by giving up forms through a dread of formality; the way to gain ground is to quicken and vitalize the forms. Nightly examination of the conscience is any how a safeguard for the performance of the duty, and a most excellent preparative for evening prayer. But while we continue it, let us strive to throw reality and life into it by regarding the great duty on a large, comprehensive, and spiritual scale.

Consider first, the necessity for all of us, in respect

both of our sins and of our good works, of an exercise like Self-examination. This necessity arises from the fact, so distinctly stated in Scripture, that "the heart is deceitful above all things," and that "he that trusteth in his own heart,"—in its dictates respecting himself and his own spiritual condition,—"is a fool." It has pleased God to illustrate this cardinal truth by two grand examples, one in the Old and one in the New Testament. It must have been by trust in the subtle evasions and plausible shifts of his own heart, that David, after committing two of the worst crimes of which our nature is capable, so long contrived to keep his conscience quiet, but at length was convicted of the desperate folly of severely condemning in another man, the very faults, which, in an infinitely aggravated form, he had been palliating and excusing in himself. And it was by trusting in the assurances which his heart gave him of his own strong attachment to his Master, that St. Peter, secure of himself, was betrayed into the weakness and folly of denying Christ.

May we say that, while all characters are liable to the snare of self-deception, those are more particularly exposed to it, who, like St. Peter and David, are persons of keen sensibilities, warm temperaments, quick affections? Probably we may; for affectionateness of disposition readily commends itself to the conscience as a thing which cannot be wrong, and secretly whispers to one, who is conscious of possessing it, "This generous trait in you will cover and excuse many sins." An acrid, soured character cannot flatter itself that it is right with half the facility of a warm and genial character. A man, who sins by passions the reverse of malignant, is apt to thank God secretly that he is not malignant, totally forgetting that, although not malignant, he follows his own impulses as entirely, and so is as purely selfish as the malignant man.

But how shall we bring home to ourselves the dangerousness of trusting, without due examination, to the verdict of our own hearts? We will do so by supposing a parallel case in a matter, where we are all peculiarly apt to be cautious and suspicious,—the goods of this world. Suppose then (and, in a commercial country like this, the supposition has been not unfrequently realized) that the chief agent in some great speculation is a man, who, though most untrustworthy, has all the art of conciliating trust. Suppose him to be fluent, fair-spoken, prepossessing in manners and appearance, and to be especially plausible in glossing over a financial difficulty. Advance one more step in the hypothesis, and suppose him to be a private friend of many of those who are embarked with him in the same speculation; allied to some of them by marriage, and, more or less, in habits of intimacy with all. If such a person is at the head of affairs, and entrusted with the administration of the funds contributed by all, it is evident that he might impose upon the contributors to almost any extent. His artful representations would quiet their little panics, when such arose; and he would have it in his power to keep them still, while embezzling their resources, until the great crash comes, which announces to many of them, as with a clap of thunder, that they are bankrupts. Now the peril of such trust in worldly matters supplies a very fair image of the peril of a still more foolish and groundless trust in spiritual things. Our hearts are notoriously most untrustworthy informants in any case where we are ourselves interested. It is not only Scripture which assevers this. We confess it ourselves, and re-echo the verdict of Scripture, when we say of any slight matter, with which we happen to be mixed up, "I am an interested party, and therefore I had better not be a judge." But while our hearts are thus, by our own confession, untrustworthy, there is no one in whose assertions we habitually place more trust. We think we cannot be deceived respecting ourselves; we know at all events our own motives and intentions, if we know any thing. The unkind, the insincere, the ungenerous, the ungrateful, never, we think, had any affinity with our nature; for we have never, as I observed above, admitted these forms of evil, without first palliating and disguising them, and making them look respectable to our own consciences. Faults there may have been, no doubt, in our temper and our conduct;—(feelings and transactions, too) for which we feel that we are in account with God; but we leave our own heart to manage and superintend the account; and it soothes us with the assurance that we never had any very bad intention, and so the whole affair will turn out well in the end,—we need not fear the ultimate exposure. Self-love conspires with trust in our own hearts, to make dupes of us as regards our spiritual account. Proverbially, and in the verdict of all experience, love is blind; and if love be blind, self-love, being the strongest, the most subtle, the most clinging, the most ineradicable of all loves, is blinder still. Self-love will not see, as self-trust cannot see, any thing against us. With these strong partialities to self in our own heart ever operative within us, and never probably capable, even in the best men, of being entirely detached from us, to what an extent may we be imposed upon, in that which most vitally and nearly concerns us, if we do not from time to time call in and examine the accounts! What frightful arrears may we be running up, unawares to ourselves, if we do not sharply check and suspiciously watch this heart, who administers for us the account between us and God! And how may this accumulated arrears of guilt burst upon our minds with an overwhelming force when God judges the secrets of men by Jesus Christ according to the Gospel,—when the divine sentence unmasks our sin of those excuses, with which we have been palliating it, and brings it home to us with a "Thou art the man!"

The first step in real Self-examination is to be fully aware of the deceitfulness of the heart, and to pray against it, watch against it, and use every possible method of counteracting it. But what means *can* we use? We offer a few practical suggestions in answer to this question.

First; *as regards our acknowledged sins.* We must

remember that their hatefulness, and aggravations, if they were publicly confessed, might very probably be recognized by every one but ourselves, the perpetrators. There are certain loathsome diseases, which are offensive and repulsive in the highest degree to every one but the patient. And there is a close analogy between the spiritual frame of man and his natural; if the moral disease be your own,—rooted in your character, clinging to your own heart, it never can affect you with the same disgust as if it were another man's. Every step therefore must be taken to stand as clear as may be of the sin, while we sit in judgment upon it. In the first place, in the case of exceptional and grievous sins, might not another sometimes be called in to sit in judgment, and so a fairer sentence secured than we are competent to give ourselves? If there be the moral courage equal to a perfectly candid avowal,—such an avowal as keeps back no aggravating circumstance,— and if an adviser is to be had at once holy, discreet, and considerate,—why should it not be related to such an adviser, that his counsel, prayers, and sympathy may be sought? Surely the Scriptural rule has a foundation of wisdom; "Confess your sins one to another, and pray for one another, that ye may be healed." If however we are aware that such an exposure could not be made by us in our present state of moral attainment *with perfect integrity,*—that we should be casting about in it to regain by palliating touches the forfeited esteem of him, on whom we threw ourselves thus confidentially, —or, in other words, that we are not men enough to make ourselves as vile in the eyes of our fellow-creatures as we are in God's eyes,—then, until such moral courage is attained by us, (and surely we may lawfully pray for its attainment,) we must attempt to secure the same end—a fair judgment upon our sin—in another way. To stop short of the whole mischief in confession to a fellow-creature, would only be to deceive him as well as ourselves, and to entangle our consciences more effectually in the snares of hypocrisy. We must take another method, and this method will apply to the more usual and common as well as to the grosser sins, of forming an impartial estimate of the evil which is in us. Let us only *suppose*, by an effort of the imagination, that we confessed it frankly to such and such a person, known for wisdom and goodness,— how would he regard us? what is the measure of our sin in his esteem? because doubtless that should be the measure of it in ours also. Would there not be a shrinking from revealing to such an one, not merely sins of a gross or glaring character, but such as the world calls trifles,—omissions of private prayer, little acts of dishonesty in trade or in respect of an employer's property, falsehoods which have slipped from us in the ordinary intercourse of life, impure or sensual thoughts, allusions in conversation which might lead the mind of others in a wrong direction, conceit of accomplishments and abilities, not merely suggested (for no man is accountable for the suggestions which the Devil makes to him), but secretly fondled and nourished in the chamber of the heart? If we shrink from making such disclosures to a wise and good man, *why* do we shrink? Because we feel that they would lower us in his esteem, and we have such a regard of man's esteem that we cannot bear to be placed lower in it. If a person to whom we had long given credit for a blameless and pious life should come to us, and confess the very sins to which we ourselves have recently given way, should assure us with evident sincerity that, however good the character he maintained, yet he had lived for such and such days without prayer, had practised or blinked at little dishonesties, or had seriously distorted truth on such and such occasions, we might (and, no doubt, should) sympathize with the distress of mind which the confession evinced, but we could hardly help saying within ourselves, " I should never have expected this from him. I should have thought that he would be truer to principle, when the stress of trial came." Then, if this be the estimate which we should form of another, who had committed our sins, should it not be the estimate which we should form of ourselves? and is not the comparatively lenient view which we take of our own case due to that self-partiality which leavens and vitiates our whole nature? This light in which we see the sin as it exists in our neighbour, is the true light in which we shall see it at the last day; and to see it now in that light, while at the same time we believe that the Blood of Christ has entirely cancelled it, is the great end of Self-examination, and the true fulfilment of the precept: "Judge therefore yourselves, brethren, that ye be not judged of the Lord."

But the probe of Self-examination needs to be applied to the better, as well as to the worse parts of our conduct. The natural heart is an adept in flatteries, not only suggesting excuses for the evil, but also heightening the colours of the good which, by God's grace, is in us. Where conduct stands the test of Self-examination, the motives of it should be called in question. We must do in regard of ourselves what we may never do in regard of others,—suspect that an unsound motive may underlie a fair conduct. It is something to be possessed with the knowledge that our actions take their whole moral colouring from the motives which prompt them. And to apply this knowledge practically to our own good actions, and thus to discriminate what is hollow and spurious in them from what is genuine, is the second branch of the great duty of Self-examination. By way of giving some serviceable hints for this investigation of our motives, it may be briefly remarked that of the religious conduct of religious persons a good part is usually due to custom. By almost all of us, to a certain extent, the Ordinances of religion are attended mechanically, without repulsion on the one hand, but at the same time without any effort or definite aim on the other. Again; certain proprieties and regularities of behaviour, whether devotional or moral, are secured by deference to the prevailing opinions and habits of society, as is shown sometimes by the fact that, when we are in foreign parts, and no longer under this restraint, those proprieties and regularities are not so carefully maintained. Again; many good actions are done, more or less, because they are in keeping with a man's position, conciliate credit to him, gain him the praise of others. Again; works of usefulness and social (and even religious) improvement may be undertaken, more or less, from that activity of mind which is inherent in some characters, because naturally we cannot bear to be standing still, and are constitutionally unfitted for a studious, contemplative life. In a real work of benevolence a man cannot but find a very pure pleasure, and it is quite possible that this pleasure, and not any thought of Christ's service or God's glory, may be the main motive which actuates him in doing it. And perhaps some one will ask whether such pleasure is not, at all events, an innocent motive of action? To which the answer is, "Perfectly innocent; while at the same time it does not go the length of being gracious or supernatural." Nature can produce such a motive; it is no necessary mark or token of the grace of God. Gracious or supernatural motives must at the least have respect to God and Christ, and the world to come, and the welfare of the soul. The highest of them, defined according to its principle, is the love of Christ, and, according to its end, the glory of God. But it is probable, alas! that very few actions, even of the best men, are prompted exclusively by this motive, unalloyed with any sentiment of a baser kind. Nay, generally speaking, few indeed are the actions which are done from unmixed motives, whether purely good or purely bad; and our wisdom is not to be discouraged if we find, upon close Self-examination, as we shall assuredly find, that much which looks well before men is hollow and defective when tried by the touchstone of God's Word. Suffice it, if with trembling confidence we are able to make out, that we are under the lead of Grace, and following that lead. Motives more defecated from the dregs of nature, more purely and exclusively gracious, will come, if we press towards the mark, with a greater measure of spiritual attainment. If our conscience should affirm *upon the whole* the presence in us of earnest secret prayer, that is a great point for humble thankfulness; because it is hard to see how secret prayer can be prompted by any but a religious motive, or how it can fail to be due to the supernatural Grace of God.

But we must hasten to bring these thoughts to a close. And let the close of a Chapter, whose great scope has been to render the reader dissatisfied with himself, be devoted to assure him that this dissatisfaction will avail him nothing, except as it leads him to a perfect, joyful, and loving satisfaction with his Saviour. To have probed their own wounds, and pored over their own inflamed and envenomed frames, would have availed the poisoned Israelites nothing, unless, after such a survey of their misery, they had lifted their eyes to the brazen serpent. "Look unto Him," therefore, "and be ye healed." Judged by the criterion of the highest motive, nothing can be more miserably defective than the best righteousness of the best man. It flows indeed from the Holy Spirit within him; but even the influences of the Spirit derive an admixture of infirmity from flowing through the tainted channels of the human will and affections. It was not so with the Lord Jesus. The nature which He took of the pure Virgin was subject to all the physical, but none of the moral, infirmities of our nature. His heart beat always true to God's glory and man's salvation;—a magnetic needle ever pointing to that great pole, not shaken even for a moment from its stedfastness by the vacillation of lower and less perfect motives. And His singleness of aim, His piety and benevolence of conduct is ours,—God be praised,—not only to copy, but also to appropriate. Take it, Christian; it is thine. Delight in it, as God delights in it, and thou shalt be agreed with God, and shalt stand before Him at the last day in the white robe, pure as driven snow; not having thine own righteousness which is of the law, but that which is by the faith of Christ, the righteousness which is of God by faith.

CHAPTER V.

OF INTERCESSORY PRAYER.

"They made the breastplate: .... and they set it in four rows of stones: .... And the stones were according to the names of the children of Israel; twelve, according to their names, like the engravings of a signet, every one with his name, according to the twelve tribes."—EXOD. xxxix. 9, 10. 14.

THE Spouse in the Canticles, who represents the Church, cries to the heavenly Bridegroom, "Set me as a seal upon thine heart." Christ answers this prayer by interceding for each of His people in Heaven, by bearing upon his heart the wants, trials, troubles, sins, of each, and by pleading for each the merits of His most precious Death and Passion. In the seventeenth chapter of St. John's Gospel, which contains the great high-priestly prayer of Our Lord, we find Him commencing this office of Intercession. "I pray for them," says He of His disciples. The Intercession then commenced; but it has been continuing ever since; it is prolonged through all time; it embraces not the Apostles only, but every soul of the redeemed. Of this Intercession the breastplate of the Jewish high priest supplies a beautiful figure. In the breastplate there were twelve precious stones, arranged in four rows of three, upon each of which was written the name of one of the twelve tribes. The breastplate, of course, when worn, would rest upon the priest's heart,—would rise and sink with every palpitation of the breast. When he appeared before God in his full sacerdotal attire, there would be the twelve names upon his heart, indicative of his love and care for the whole people of Israel. Names! the names of those with whom we are well acquainted, how much they imply! how true to nature is that Scripture idiom, or phraseology, which makes the name stand for the whole character! Let but the name of a person familiar to us be mentioned in our hearing, and what an instantaneous rush takes place into the mind of the personality of the man,—of his temperament, manners, features, way of thinking and acting, in short of all his physical and mental peculiarities! The names upon the high-priest's breastplate betoken the individuality of Christ's Intercession for His people. Not a sparrow is forgotten before God. And not a single want or woe of a single soul is forgotten by the God-man, when He intercedes.

It was observed, in a recent Chapter, that every Christian is in a certain important sense a priest, consecrated in Baptism and Confirmation to offer up spiritual sacrifices to God. Accordingly every Christian must intercede, because Intercession is one of the priestly functions. The Intercession of the great High Priest for the whole Church is ever rising, like a cloud of fragrant incense, to the Throne of Grace. And it should be our ambition to throw, each one for himself, our little grain of incense into His censer. The prayer, which is offered by the Head in Heaven for the whole Body, should be re-echoed by the members here on earth.

The consideration of Intercessory Prayer properly follows that of Self-examination. They are at the opposite poles of the Christian's devotional exercises. Self-examination is the most interior, as Intercession is the most exterior, of those exercises. The one is a retiring into oneself and shutting out the whole world: the other is a going forth in sympathy and love towards other men,—an association of oneself with their wants, wishes, and trials. Hence these exercises are very necessary to keep one another in check. The healthy action of the mind requires that both shall continually be practised. By undue and overstrained self-inspection the mind is apt to become morbid and depressed, and to breed scruples, which tease and harass without producing any real fruit. The man becomes a valetudinarian in religion, full of himself, his symptoms, his ailments, the delicacy of his moral health; and valetudinarians are always a plague, not only to themselves, but to every body connected with them. One tonic adapted to remedy this desponding, timid, nervous state of mind, is an active sympathy, such as comes out in Intercessory Prayer, with the wants and trials of others, a sympathy based upon that precept of the holy Apostle's, " Look not every man on his own things, but every man also on the things of others."

Observe, first, the great importance attached to this duty in Holy Scripture, and in that which is a faithful uninspired echo of Holy Scripture, the Prayer Book. In the Old Testament you find Abraham winning by Intercession the preservation of the cities of the plain, on condition—a condition, alas! not fulfilled—that ten righteous were found therein. In the New Testament you find the early Church winning by Intercessory Prayer the preservation of the life of St. Peter from the sword of Herod, on which life was suspended, humanly speaking, the existence of the infant community. But let us come at once to the Lord's Prayer, as containing by implication the most striking of all precepts on the subject. If the Lord's Prayer is to be the great model of Prayer, as it surely is, how much intercession ought not our Prayers to contain! This extraordinary Prayer is so constructed, that it is impossible to use it, without praying for all other Christians as well as ourselves. Intercession, instead of being a clause added on to it, is woven into its very texture. Break off the minutest fragment you please, and you will find intercession in it. Oil and water will not coalesce; pour them together, and the one will remain on the surface of the other. But wine and water interpenetrate one another; in every drop of the mixed liquid there are both elements. When *we* pray for others, we usually add some paragraphs at the close of our ordinary prayers, distinct from them, as oil, though placed upon water, remains distinct. But in the Lord's own model

Prayer, the Intercession and the petitions for self interpenetrate one another; the petitioner, who uses it *verbatim et literatim*, never employs the singular number. A wonderful contrivance indeed, by which the Author secures a more important end than we perhaps are apt to think of. The Prayer, it must be remembered, was given as a kind of watchword for Christians, by the adoption and use of which they should be distinguished from the disciples of other Rabbis, such as John the Baptist,—" as a sign of profession, and mark of difference," to accommodate the language of our Articles to the purpose, "whereby Christian men might be discerned from others that be not christened." Now this sign or watchword must necessarily have Love woven into its very texture; for what was the appointed note, whereby the world was to know disciples of Jesus from those who were not His disciples? His own words answer that question very pointedly: "By this shall all men know that ye are my disciples, *if ye have love one to another.*" Then in the very watchword of the Disciples there must be Love. And this could not be more strikingly contrived than by drawing up the watchword in such terms that no man could use it as a prayer for himself, without at the same time interceding for his brother Christians.

Of the testimony of our Liturgy to the duty of Intercessory Prayer we need only say that, after the penitential introduction of Morning and Evening Prayer, there are, as a general rule, only three collects which supplicate blessings for the congregation then worshipping;—all that follows is Intercession. The latter and longer half of the Litany is intercessory; and the Communion Service, after the Introduction, begins with Intercession for the Sovereign, and quickly passes on to the "Prayer for the whole state of Christ's Church militant here on earth." It appears that the compilers kept carefully in view the inspired precept given for the guidance of public Prayers, "I exhort that first of all," (it may mean first in point of order, or first in point of importance, or both, but, any how, "first of all,") "supplications, prayers, intercessions, and giving of thanks, be made for all men; for kings, and for all that are in authority; that we may lead a quiet and peaceable life in all godliness and honesty."

Thus plain, then, is the duty of Intercessory Prayer. And the grounds of it are equally plain. The duty is based upon the fact that men are one body, and members one of another. Whether in Nature or in Grace, a man is essentially the member of a family. In his moral nature he has certain affections, such as benevolence and compassion, which have reference to others, and show clearly that, in the design of the Creator, he is no isolated creature. And in his spiritual nature too,—in his constitution by Grace and in Christ,—there are brotherly kindness and charity, which show that in the new creature also man is one Body. And if this be so, the weal and the woe of other men, of other Christians, must be, to a certain extent, our weal and woe,—cannot fail ultimately to reach us. The different parts of the living frame of man have a wonderful sympathy with one another: "Whether one member suffer, all the members suffer with it; or one member be honoured, all the members rejoice with it." And so, if a blow is struck at the body politic either of the State or of the Church, in some extremity of that body which is very remote from ourselves, the blow cannot fail to vibrate through the whole frame, until it reaches even us in our distant corner. Few prayers of the Liturgy are regarded with such general indifference,—few, I fear, would be more readily dispensed with by the worshippers,—than those for the Sovereign, the members of the Royal Family, and the Hierarchy; but let any reasonable person ask himself, if he desire to see the necessity of such prayers, whether he really thinks that a general abandonment of these exalted functionaries by the Providence and Grace of God would prove in the end indifferent to himself. Suppose the court and the clergy, the whole body of our rulers in Church and State, to be utterly godless, (and godless they must be without the Grace of God,) could such a state of things be of little moment to me, because I happen to be at the lower extremity of the social scale? Would not the ungodliness in high places reach me, though in a low place, through a thousand avenues? If in no other way, would not God send judgments upon the nation and the Church, for the ungodliness of their rulers? If then each of us has a real interest in the moral and spiritual welfare of the community, it must be expedient for ourselves that we should pray for the whole community, and specially for those who before God are its Representatives. But, expediency altogether apart, if a man's relations to others are, as we have shown, bound up in his own nature, he must surely bring his relations and sympathies with him, when he appears before God. Otherwise, what does he do but virtually say to God, "Thou didst create me a member of a family, to love and to care for my brethren; but here I stand before Thee in all the isolation of my own selfishness?"

And yet, though both the duty of Intercessory Prayer and the grounds of it are thus clear, there is perhaps no part of devotion which good Christians more systematically neglect. May it not be said that commonly even devout persons feel very little interest in any Intercessions, except such as touch their own immediate circle of family and friends? While perhaps there are some, who of set purpose hug a sort of spiritual selfishness, and would not hesitate to avow that for them the personal question of their own salvation is indeed the whole of religion.

Now can we analyze this feeling of disinclination to a religious exercise, at once so reasonable and so scriptural? It seems to be a mixed feeling, having in it a good and a bad element. Some, no doubt, shrink from Intercessory Prayer, under a feeling that, as coming from them, it would be presumptuous. "What am I; that I should plead the cause of others,—I, who have so much to ask for myself, and who have no native right to ask at all? Or how can I think that prayers from me, like those from righteous Abraham, can win any thing from God for my brethren?" The feeling is good, but mistaken in its application. In the first place, what God expressly commands us to do, it can never be a presumption to do. If by His holy Apostle He has taught us to make prayers and supplications, and to give thanks for all men, His command surely is enough to exempt such prayers from the charge of presumptuousness. Had He *not* commanded them, such a scruple might reasonably find place. Prayers for the dead are not commanded,—nay, they are implicitly discouraged by the suggestions made in Holy Scripture that the state of the dead admits of no change; and therefore to offer such prayers *is* presumption, because they are beyond the warrant of God's express will and Word. But prayers for the living are, as we have seen, made obligatory upon the disciples of Jesus Christ, by the very form of the model Prayer which He gave us to use.

Next, as regards the imagined feebleness and impotency of our prayers for others,—a feeling which looks humble and plausible enough on the surface,—we must inquire how far it may possibly resolve itself into a half-sceptical question as to the efficacy of Prayer altogether. And if there be in our minds no doubt on this head, we should then remember that our intercessions do not stand alone, but that in offering them, we co-operate with the whole Church, and, above all, with Christ, the Head of the Church. Do not omit to calculate the power of combination. Many very slight muscular efforts, put forth imperceptibly, will create, it is said, force enough to turn a heavy piece of furniture. The smallest contribution made by a vast number of people would soon fill a monarch's treasury. Let, then, thy feeble intercession be put forth to move the will of God to show mercy to others. Other intercessions shall meet it at the throne of grace, which shall convert it into a strong force. Yea, His shall certainly meet it, which is singly and by itself the strongest of all forces with God,—powerful at all times to bend His Will, and to impetrate from Him the highest blessings. Rhoda, the damsel who admitted St. Peter to the house of Mary the mother of Mark, was one of those who were gathered together praying for the Apostle's deliverance. Her prayer was one of those which won from God the preservation of this chief Apostle.

But in our reluctance to Intercessory Prayer we must acknowledge, if we be candid with ourselves, the presence of a bad feeling, a great want of sympathy with others,—or, in other words, a lack of love. We feel no interest in them, and therefore do not care to pray for them. Now, so far as this is the case with us, we must consider, first, that such selfishness invalidates and empties of efficacy our prayers for ourselves. Our Saviour in His comments on the cursing of the fig-tree, lays down, you will find, two great conditions of success in Prayer,—the first, that we shall pray in faith; the second, that we shall pray in love. How does he pray in love, who in his prayer looks only on his own things, and not on those of others? Can he hope to win any thing from God, while he is in a mind so different from that of God? It is a great truth, reader, that if we desire to gain any thing from the Most High, our minds must be set more or less to the same key as His. If two harps be strung to the same key, but not otherwise, when one of them is struck, the other gives a responsive sound. There must be some secret affinity in nature between the lightning of heaven and the conductor which draws it down,—between the steel and the magnet which attracts it,—between the light substances and the chafed glass or sealing-wax, towards which they leap up and cling. And in Grace there must be a secret affinity between God and the soul (this affinity itself being the effect of Grace) before the soul can lay hold of God's Will, and draw out a blessing from Him, yea, draw God Himself into it.

This affinity stands in Love. God, the great Father, loves all men. He will have all men to be saved, and to come to the knowledge of the truth. He sent His Son to save all,—Redemption being, as far as His will and intention are concerned, co-extensive with the human race. Therefore he who prays with the largest sympathy, he who embraces in his prayer the widest circle of his fellow-creatures, is most in sympathy with the mind of God when he prays, has the key of God's heart, and therefore the key of God's treasury. And as for him who prays in the total absence of this sympathy, does it not stand to reason that God must remain mute to such a man? Suppose an entire absence from a petitioner's mind of the fraternal feeling towards fellow-men and fellow-Christians; and what does it seem to imply, but an absence of filial feeling? Is not the filial feeling the correlative of the fraternal, according to that word of the Apostle: "Every one that loveth Him that begat, loveth him also that is begotten of Him?" Thus are the two first words of the Prayer of Prayers bound together in an indissoluble wedlock; and he who cannot in sympathy and love say "Our," cannot, in faith and trust, say "Father."

Then pray for others, if you have not yet done so, uniting with your prayers, where it is possible to do so and opportunity offers, that kindly interest in their concerns, which attests the sincerity of your intercessions. Pray particularly for those who have done you wrong: nothing tends more to engender that frame of mind, which is essential to success. Do not be baffled by the thought that explicitness of request is always necessary. The mention of the name, the thought of the person before the Throne of Grace, the simple commendation of him by Prayer to God's mercy and blessing, is a great point gained, and in numerous cases is all that can be done. If we much desire explicitness, and yet not know exactly into what form to throw the petition, the Holy Spirit, the Gift of gifts, which involves holiness and happiness both here and hereafter, may always be petitioned for on behalf of all. But, after all, there is much in that beautiful word of our Prayer for all Conditions of Men, "that it may please Thee to comfort and relieve them *according to their several necessities.*" God understands those necessities perfectly; and we may safely ask Him to supply them all, according to the understanding which He has of them in His Infinite Mind. You may do for your friend, or your relative, the same kind office which those interested in the poor paralytic in the Gospel did for him,—bring him in the arms of Prayer, and lay him down in his helplessness before Jesus, thus silently commending him to the pity and sympathy of the Infinite Love. You may have many thus to commend, parents, brothers, sisters, colleagues, helpmates, friends, children and godchildren, masters, servants, pastors, parishioners, and may commend them all by the simple, quiet, devout recitation of their names. Yes, thou mystical Aaron, washed for thy sacred functions in the laver of regeneration, and clothed in the Righteousness of Christ, forget not to wear thy breastplate, when thou goest in to offer up a spiritual sacrifice,—neglect not to exhibit silently before God, graven upon thy heart, the names of all thou lovest; yea, be an intercessor, as far as in thee lies, for all the people; for of what member of the human family can it be said that he has no claim whatever upon thy sympathy and kind offices?

CHAPTER VI.

OF DEVOTIONAL READING.

"*And Elisha died, and they buried him. And the bands of the Moabites invaded the land at the coming in of the year.*
"*And it came to pass, as they were burying a man, that, behold, they spied a band of men; and they cast the man into the sepulchre of Elisha: and when the man was let down, and touched the bones of Elisha, he revived, and stood up on his feet.*"—2 KINGS xiii. 20, 21.

WE Protestants do not attach virtue to relics, in the ordinary sense of that term; but there is a sense, in which we may reasonably enough do so. Relics are remains; and while we believe that no virtue resides in the *material* remains of a good man, we do not therefore exempt from efficacy his mental or spiritual remains. If he has left behind him in writing the effusions of a devout mind, we believe that these writings, by which "he being dead yet speaketh," often exercise an influence for good upon readers, long after he himself has passed away, and that thus the miracle wrought by the bones of Elisha is continually repeating itself in the experience of the Church. Souls are being quickened and edified by the instrumentality of books, which books are all that remain of their authors. A holy man, who lives in habitual communion with God, has a living influence on his generation, and also, if he be a writer, an influence on posterity. His living influence may be compared to the miracles wrought by the shadow of St. Peter, or by the handkerchiefs and aprons brought to the sick from the body of St. Paul. The influence exercised by his writings after death, may be fitly compared to the posthumous miracle recorded in the text, a miracle which stands alone in Holy Scripture, and in which it is clearly desirable to find some moral significance.

We shall speak first of the power of devotional reading, and then give some practical suggestions for the conduct of this exercise.

I. (1) The power of devotional reading may be seen from considering the effect, which constant association with the wise and good would naturally exert upon the mind. It is an axiomatic truth which has passed into an inspired proverb: "He that walketh with wise men shall be wise." Mere common intercourse with wise men, however,—the merely being thrown with them in ordinary society, might not, for various reasons, be productive of much good. The time might pass in remarks upon those trite and superficial topics, which are the necessary introduction to something deeper and better. We might not be able to get at the wise man's mind. He might be reserved in communicating his sentiments, or we might be awkward, and wanting in the tact to draw them out. Comparatively few persons have the gift, for a gift it is, of lively table-talk on subjects of secular interest. How much fewer possess such a gift on religious and spiritual topics! There are nine chances to one against your coming into contact with the mind of a devout person by merely being thrown with him in company. To see him in society is a different thing from seeing him in his closet, pursuing his meditations, and mixing Prayer with them. The nearest approach you can make to seeing him thus, and it is a very near approach indeed, is by reading his works of piety. In them is mirrored his best mind at his best moments. Words committed to the press are maturely considered and pruned of all excrescences, whereas in conversation there is necessarily much that is extemporaneous, and still more that is redundant. Suppose now that we were made privy to much of the interior life of men eminent for piety,—that they communicated to us the counsel, which was the result of their experience in religion, gave us their fresh thoughts upon the Holy Scriptures, threw out suggestions to us to help us in leading a holy life, made in our hearing remarks which had a certain heavenly savour and gave a relish for spiritual things,—suppose that they were constantly by our sides with these counsels, thoughts, suggestions, and remarks,—could we fail of deriving benefit from our association with them?—must not our minds, almost according to their natural constitution and independently of the operation of Divine Grace, insensibly take a tinge from theirs? Shall it not be that some glowing sentiment of theirs, thrown out like a hot ember from the fire of their zeal, shall light upon combustible material in our hearts, and kindle there the flame of Divine love? Often has the opposite effect been produced by tales and poems, which have had a malignant tendency to stimulate the worst passions. If bad books are a very powerful engine in the hands of the Devil, as there can be no doubt that they are, shall not good and holy books be an equally powerful agency in the Economy of Grace? No one who has really studied *personal* religion, who has cultivated the piety of the closet as distinct from that of the platform, will hesitate to acknowledge that they are so.

(2) But the power of good books may be seen from another very important consideration respecting them. Spiritual reading has to a certain extent—more entirely for some minds than for others, but to a certain extent for all minds—taken the place of preaching: this has come about in the order of God's Providence, which has ordained the diffusion of literature through the press, just as it has ordained many less important movements. Without at all denying that oral teaching has still certain great prerogatives over teaching by books, that in voice, and manner, and generally in the influences which go to make up public speaking, there is something electric and sympathetic, which no mere dead letter can ever supply,—and without denying also that the form of Christian teaching, which is closest to the primitive and Apostolic model, is more likely to have God's blessing upon it than a mere modern form,—it would yet be preposterous in the highest degree to say that we are as dependent for religious instruction upon oral teaching, as the early Church was. We see nothing derogatory to the Christian Pulpit in acknowledging that God, in modern times, causes some, though not all, of its work to be done by religious literature. Such an acknowledgment, if rightly understood, does not degrade the pulpit, but exalts the literature. And here we come across a thought, which must reappear presently in the shape of practical advice. The reading of spiritual books may be regarded, and ought to be regarded, more or less, in the light of a Divine Ordinance. That *Preaching* is an Ordinance would be generally admitted by Protestants, and indeed must be admitted by all who take the New Testament as their guide. The only error which is sometimes allowed to cloud a little the clearness of the truth so admitted, is the narrowing the meaning of the word

Preaching to a formal discourse delivered by a minister in the course of Divine worship. Instead of imposing upon the word this somewhat technical and cramped sense, take Preaching as being the communication of Divine knowledge to men through the instrumentality of men: and then Preaching is in the fullest sense an Ordinance, yea, one of the chiefest Ordinances of the Gospel. "Faith cometh by hearing, and hearing by the Word of God." It is an Ordinance for the illustration, exposition, and application of Holy Scripture to the conscience. Instruction of this kind is essential to vital religion; it is the oil of the spiritual lamp, which keeps Prayer burning. Only admit that the power of Preaching may come to some,—nay, to all, more or less,—through a written, as well as through a spoken word. Only admit that there may be a hearing in the closet with the inward, as in the Church with the outward ear. But then this admission involves the duty, which we are all so slow to fulfil, of reading, no less than hearing, with all the solemnity of a devotional exercise. If it is wrong to be otherwise than seriously attentive to Preaching in Church, where the preacher is a living man, it is equally wrong to be otherwise than seriously attentive to Preaching in the closet, where the preacher is perhaps a dead one. And we doubt not that if good Christians were persuaded that some of the power and dignity of Preaching now rests upon the reading of good books, and if accordingly they read them with the same seriousness of spirit, and desire of edification, with which they listen, or try to listen, to formal Sermons, such books would be largely blessed to quicken in them the spiritual life, and to advance the Kingdom of God in their hearts.

II. But what suggestions may be given as to the conduct of this exercise? First, a discrimination must be used in the choice of books. All good books are not equally attractive, and therefore not equally profitable, to all minds. It is with spiritual very much as it is with bodily food. A man by a little experience, by a few trials, and by a short insight into his own constitution, soon gets to know that this or that is bad for him, that this or that, on the other hand, is for him digestible and wholesome. I say, *for him*. Probably it would be a mistake in medicine to assert that, independently of the constitution, circumstances, and temperament of the patient, any particular food was digestible or the reverse. And certainly it is a grand mistake in Theology to suppose that all the productions of devout writers are equally serviceable to every class of minds. It is notoriously the reverse. In His Holy Scriptures, which are the great fontal abyss from which every work of piety and devotion must be drawn, the Lord has given us an infinite variety of Inspired Literature. What literature is there which does not find itself represented in the Holy Scripture,—poetry, history, biography, proverbs, letters, fables, allegories? There never was a book so little monotonous as the Bible, so continually changing its key,—if so be that some, at all events, may be charmed by the voice of the Heavenly Charmer. The same Spirit, who inspired the Holy Scriptures, gave great diversity of gifts to the early Christian teachers. All were not Apostles, nor all prophets, nor all teachers, nor did all speak with tongues, nor all interpret. And now that the supernatural gifts have died out of the Church, the same Spirit observes the same rule of variety in the different mental endowments, which He distributes to different teachers of Divine Truth. All men's writings have not the same power over all men's minds. Is there not a plain testimony to this in the avowal which we hear so often made; "I know I ought to like such and such a book, which all the world agrees in praising; but I cannot do it?" What the complaint really means is, that the book does not suit you, that the general strain of the author's mind has not that harmony with the general strain of yours, which will give him an influence over you for good. That being the case, leave him alone,—without however doubting or denying the power which he may have over other minds. Even in the Holy Scriptures themselves we think ourselves quite warranted in selecting those passages which are most suitable to the circumstances, intelligence, and character of the reader. No one would think of recommending a peasant to engage himself much with the Book of the Revelation, or a child to study the eighth chapter to the Romans. Much more, then, may we exercise a similar discretion with those works, which, however pious and edifying, do not come to us on the authority of Inspiration. Choose, then, those books to which, from a cursory knowledge of their contents, you find yourself most drawn. There are several which have attained the rank of standard works, from their possessing excellences of various kinds. Such are the Saint's Rest, the Pilgrim's Progress (which all know a little of, but very few have studied), the Imitation of Christ by Thomas à Kempis, Taylor's Holy Living and Dying, Cecil's Remains, the Thoughts of Adam, Pascal's Thoughts on Religion, Bishop Hall's Contemplations, Edwards on the Religious Affections, Leighton's Commentary on St. Peter, the Christian Year, and several others which will at once suggest themselves to all who have a general acquaintance with our religious literature. To these I may add Foster's Sermons, and Archer Butler's Sermons, both of which combine originality of view with piety of sentiment in an unusual degree, and also two works which are most valuable as theological compendiums, while their authors never lose sight of the edification of the heart, Griffith on the Creed, and the Bishop of Tasmania's (Nixon's) Lectures on the Catechism. There are indeed many devotional publications, especially some of recent date, which will seem more attractive than the above, and which will better meet the unhealthy craving for something new and highly flavoured, which now is so generally prevalent. But spiritual nourishment resembles natural nourishment in this respect, that the most stimulating is by no means the most wholesome or the most safe. He who honestly reads for edification must not discard a book for being dry, as if he read for diversion. In a certain temper of mind, the Holy Scriptures themselves will fall upon us as insipid; it will seem to us as if we knew them by heart, and had nothing further to learn from them, as if they could neither settle controversy nor quicken thought. But this temper of mind is one in which we are incapable of edification, however capable we may be of amusement. In a right state of mind, those books will please us most which most resemble the Holy Scriptures,—which are most weighty, most sober, most simple, most savouring of a spiritual mind. To a pure taste the manna was a more attractive food than the fleshpots of Egypt. Bear this in mind in the choice of devotional reading.

But suppose our book chosen, and chosen well and wisely. In what manner shall we read it? The answer to this question has implicitly been given already. Read it as a devotional exercise, mixing Prayer, or at least devout aspirations, with the reading. Every thing that can be said on the subject is really wrapped up in this,—that the reading shall be devotional. Yet we will expand the thought a very little.

Think of the author as now a member of the Church triumphant, one who is with Christ in Paradise, and, for aught you know, looking down upon your struggles and trials from a sphere where sin and sorrow are unknown. Regard this book as a sort of letter sent from him to you, to encourage you on your heavenward pilgrimage, and to stir in you a livelier hope of the inheritance to which he has (by Grace) attained. By degrees you shall feel attracted in a strange way, though you have never seen him, towards his mind, as it is mirrored in his writings, and shall realize something of the sentiments described in that beautiful passage of the Christian Year:—

> "Meanwhile with every son and saint of Thine,
> Along the glorious line,
> Sitting by turns beneath Thy sacred feet,
> We'll hold communion sweet,

> Know them by look and voice, and thank them all
>   For helping us in thrall,
> For words of hope, and bright ensamples given,
>   To show through moonless skies that there is light in
>   Heaven."

The recollection that you read for edification, and not for curiosity, or to serve a controversial purpose, will suggest many wholesome rules. Carefully eschew all dissipation in the method of reading. Dissipation is the great snare of all study, whether secular or religious, in the present day. There is so much to read,—such profusion of matter in every department of literature, nay, even in the public journals,—that insensibly the habit is formed of skipping the dull, and sipping the interesting, and never honouring any book with a fair and thorough perusal. We must set ourselves in opposition to this habit, if we wish to profit by devotional reading. Books must be read through from end to end, if it were only as a corrective to that discursive habit of mind, which the literature of the day fosters, and which is so particularly inimical to devotion. Generally speaking, a second book of devotion should not be taken up, till the first is finished. If the time which we can spare for such reading is short, books of thoughts, more or less sententiously expressed (such as some of those I have mentioned, and to which I may here add "Selections from the Writings of Payson"), will be found very serviceable. The eye soon runs over a few lines, which convey a weighty sentiment; and, when the sentiment is caught, the mind may recur to it at spare moments during the rest of the day.

We have already said that good and holy sentiments are the oil which feeds the lamp of Prayer. They are emphatically so. And this suggests an occasional use of good books, over and above their regular and normal use. There are seasons known to every devout person, when the vessel of the heart seems to run dry, and the flame of Prayer burns low in the socket. You may then often replenish the vessel by reading the favourite spiritual author. Pass your eye once more over that marked passage,—over those words which glow with such a fervour of devout sentiment; and the oil will flow again, drop by drop, into the vessel. Particularly may this be done with Christian poetry. Poetry is the voice of the affections; and, therefore, has a peculiar tendency to quicken the affections. The music of David's harp chased away from Saul the evil spirit of moody sullenness. Elisha's minstrel, playing with his hand, laid such a spell upon the prophet's mind, that the hand of the Lord came upon him, and he prophesied. And the minstrelsy of psalms and hymns, and spiritual songs, has often brought the Christian out of a state of mind, in which Prayer seemed a labour and a drudgery, if not an impossibility, into that calm and holy frame, in which he could again put forth spiritual energies, and has found himself able to renew his interrupted converse with God. Give the specific a trial, and you shall ere long know its virtue for yourself.

CHAPTER VII.

OF FASTING.

"*I keep under my body, and bring it into subjection.*"— 1 Cor. ix. 27.

THE passage which stands at the head of this Chapter carries our minds at once to the subject of Fasting. And it is a subject on which those who desire above all other things quiet advancement in the religious character will gladly hail counsel and direction. Fasting is a practice uncongenial to that form of piety which consists wholly in good emotions and serious impressions. But if any one is profoundly discontented with emotions and impressions which terminate on themselves, and leave no mark on the character; if any one seeks growth in grace and knowledge as the only satisfactory criterion of Spiritual Life, the subject of Fasting will seem to that person worthy at least of serious consideration, as a practice which, if discreetly and devoutly used, might at all events conduce to his advancement. By many of my readers Fasting is probably looked at so much as an obsolete exercise, and the revival of it would be regarded as so irksome, that it is necessary, in approaching the subject, to pray for an ingenuous and open mind, ready to welcome any conclusions to which God's Word may seem to lead us.

To the question whether Fasting is prescribed in Holy Scripture, it must be answered that in its literal form it is nowhere prescribed, but that its spirit and principle is strongly insisted upon. Also it may be said, that, though not commanded, it is strongly commended, both by Our Lord's assumption in the Sermon on the Mount that His followers will practise it, and by the example not only of Scriptural saints, but of holy men in modern times, to whatever Theological School they may have belonged. In both these respects it bears some resemblance to the practice of keeping Sunday, which I shall have occasion presently to draw into a further comparison with it. Keeping Sunday is nowhere literally prescribed in Holy Scripture. The Fourth Commandment, understood in the letter, prescribes the keeping holy *the seventh day*, which none but the Jews ever do keep. But the principle of setting apart a portion of our time to God, both weekly and daily, and the principle of assembling ourselves together for Public Worship, which cannot be done by the whole community unless occupations cease on a given day, is clearly recognized in several passages. And, as in the matter of the weekly rest, the Church, or Christian Society, has stepped in from the very earliest time, and prescribed that the day of Christ's Resurrection (or first day) is to be observed instead of the seventh, so somewhat analogously the Church has given a definite shape to the Scriptural principle of self-denial; and appointed certain days in her Calendar as days of Fasting and Abstinence.—Moreover, inasmuch as no religious person has ever slighted this Ordinance of the Lord's Day, or lived in habitual disregard of it, so I believe that no man eminent for piety (and here the appeal must be made to Religious Biography) has ever failed to exemplify in some measure the practice of Fasting, though doubtless the modes in which the principle has been exemplified have been very various.

In pursuance of the thoughts with which I have opened the subject, I will speak first of the principle of Fasting, as universally binding upon Christians; and, secondly, of Fasting as an observance for which special days have been set apart.

I. What is the principle of Fasting? Let us gather it from the words of St. Paul; "I keep under my body, and bring it into subjection." It should be remarked at the outset, that both the verbs by which the Apostle here denotes the discipline of the body are strong and peculiar. The first occurs only once again in the New Testament, and the second never again. The first carries on a metaphor, which the Apostle has already employed in the previous verse: "So fight I, not as one that beateth the air." The fighting here alluded to is not fighting with swords, but that pugilistic encounter with the cestus, or boxing glove, which formed one of the Greek games held in honour of the god Neptune at the Isthmus of Corinth, and which therefore the Apostle's Corinthian converts had frequently witnessed. In what follows he pursues the same image. His body he regards as his antagonist in a pugilistic encounter; and accordingly employs a peculiar word, which, literally translated, signifies, "But I cover my body with bruises." [It should perhaps be observed by the way, that the Apostle's Corinthian readers would by no means attach to the allusion those ideas of a coarse and brutalizing sport which we can hardly help connecting with it. All the games held at the Isthmus would be regarded by them not only as exercises of chivalrous gallantry, like the tournaments of the Middle Ages, but as solemn religious festivals, held in honour of the god Poseidon.] The next word, by which he denotes the discipline inflicted by him on his body, would be more exactly rendered, "I reduce it to a condition of slavery"—a stronger expression this than merely, "I bring it into subjection." The children are in subjection to the father, the wife to the husband; but this is a comparatively mild rule, which not only consults the interests of the governed, but appeals to their reason and conscience. A slave, however, according to the views of slavery current when the Apostle wrote, was simply a living piece of property, who had no rights and no claims, and who, if he were rebellious or insolent, must be chastised by blows, and coerced by being made to grind in the prison-house.

So much for the words which are now more immediately under review. But from the Apostle's style of writing, which is a style of copious digression, very few of his weighty words can be appreciated, unless we trace them back to their connexion with the general argument. They all have their roots grappled deep into that argument; and, accordingly, to isolate them and consider them apart from the context, is like rudely tearing up a flower, instead of looking at it while it waves its fair tresses upon the flower-bed;—even while we gaze, it loses its grace and freshness, and withers in our hand. What then led St. Paul to speak of this severe discipline which he inflicted upon his body? In the foregoing chapter he had been advocating certain restrictions (in reference to meats offered to idols) which the Corinthians were to observe, not at all out of conscience, but out of consideration for the prejudices of others. In the chapter before us, he thus pursues the train of ideas which had been started by that topic; "Do not murmur because a restriction is thus laid upon you in things which ye might innocently enjoy; for do not I myself lay many such restrictions upon myself? In one point especially I do so. I might—not innocently alone, but most lawfully—claim support from you to whom I preach. The Lord hath ordained that they which preach the Gospel should live of the Gospel; and

I have as good a right to stand upon this ordinance as other Apostles. If I threw myself upon you for maintenance, it would only be asserting what is my Divine prerogative, and claiming from you not a gratuity but the fulfilment of a solemn duty. But all of you know that I have never stood upon my right, nor accepted a single denarius from any of you. Why not? Partly, because I feel that this manifest disinterestedness will conduce to the great cause which I advocate, and give me influence and weight in certain quarters where I desire an influence. But I have another reason. I know that it is a hard thing to be saved. I know that my dear Master said that strait was the gate and narrow was the way that leadeth unto life, and that few there be that find it. I know that I am a highly-privileged man; but that does not make me a safe man. Rather I know that eminent privileges involve eminent dangers, even as the being placed on a lofty pinnacle creates dizziness and imperils life. In short, I know that I am unsafe if I use my Christian liberty to the full extent. I know that I cannot insist upon every thing which I might lawfully enjoy, and at the same time be secure. So I do not stand upon my right in this particular. I earn my own bread by the sweat of my brow. When I have comforted and edified my flock in the district where I happen to be, and chosen pastors for them, and laid hands upon those pastors, and dictated my Epistles to those distant Churches, with which I am present in spirit, though absent from them in body—then I grasp the hammer, the saw, and the needle, and set to work upon my tent-poles, and upon the shaggy goat's hair which forms the covering of my tents. True; it is severe labour—cruelly severe—lasting sometimes long into the night, when the day has been one of cares, and prayers, and earnest expostulations with tears. I know that the body is wearing out, and the outward man perishing beneath the stress of such labours. Well; but I feel it to be essential. It is not by exertion simply, but by straining every nerve and sinew, that your runners in the Isthmian foot-race gain the pine-garland, which is the victor's meed. It is not by empty and pretentious flourishes of their hands in the air, but by well-aimed and well-planted blows that your Isthmian pugilists overwhelm their antagonists. And so, being resolved to gain the mastery over my fleshly and animal nature, I deny it much of the rest and many of the indulgences which it might lawfully enjoy. I batter it with toils and labours, I coerce it firmly, and chastise it as being my slave. "I keep under my body, and bring it into subjection: lest that by any means, when I have preached to others, I myself should be a castaway."

Now what is the principle of Christian discipline which the Apostle is here laying down? Let me exhibit it to you in a figure,—a figure which, if not itself found in Holy Scripture, is yet only an expansion and development of one which is frequently found there. We are called, nay we *are* in virtue of our Baptism, children of God. It is upon this relationship, and the sentiments and duties flowing from it, that the Apostle builds his exhortation when he says, "Be ye therefore followers" (the literal translation is "imitators,"—the allusion being to the trick of imitating the parent which the child readily acquires) "of God, as dear children." The phrase "walking with God" may be drawn into the circle of the same imagery. The child walks by the father's side over the breezy down, holding his hand, and looking up into his face ever and anon to ask questions and obtain an explanation of difficulties. The Christian in like manner walks in affiance and trust along the thorny paths of life, guided by the Word and Providence of his Heavenly Father, and leaning on His wisdom and His grace. Now extend this imagery a little. Imagine the child leaving the father's hand for a moment, and sporting about under his eye. Partly from curiosity, and partly from that spirit of frolic which is attracted by danger and the prospect of an enterprise, the child nears a steep cliff. What does the father do? He cries, "Come away immediately." The spot where the child is may be perfectly safe, so long as he continues there; the child's weight may be so light that there could be no danger of a projecting boulder toppling over with him; the sea-breeze at the verge of the precipice may be delicious and bracing, and the turf may be enamelled with daisies and buttercups; but the stern command is repeated in a voice which the child knows he must not disobey; "Come away instantly, without a moment's delay." And reasonably so. It is not reason to venture too near danger, or to continue in its neighbourhood. Dizziness may seize the child, or he may be tempted onwards to an insecure spot. A moth, which flies so near the bright flame as just to preserve its wings from being singed, is a foolish moth and certain to come to mischief.—Now apply all this to our spiritual walk along the perilous and slippery, though sometimes flowery, path of life. "All things are lawful unto me, but all things are not expedient: all things are lawful for me, but I will not be brought under the power of any." Take the various forms of worldly amusement. So far as they are really amusements and not labour and sorrow (which in fact many of them are, dreadfully jading the body and mind, and exhausting the energies), and so far as no breach of God's moral law is involved in them, they are innocent and lawful. Nay, we go further. Amusements of an intelligent and rational character are a positive benefit; for the mind, wherewith alone we can serve God acceptably, needs relaxation as urgently as the body needs sleep. But it is one thing to say of amusements that in themselves they are innocent and lawful; quite another thing to say that Christians must lay no restrictions upon themselves as regards amusement. St. Paul, when he became an Apostle, might have lawfully parted with his whole stock in trade as a tentmaker, and might have held himself exempt from other cares and labours, save those of the Sacred Ministry. Did I say lawfully? Nay, we may go further. There was an order of the Lord for his doing so, if he pleased. But St. Paul knew that he must not use his Christian liberty to the full extent, if he would be safe. And we surely, who are not burning, shining lights like that extraordinary man, but very humble and commonplace Christians, living in the low range of commonplace trials and infirmities, and altogether unworthy to stoop down and unloose the shoe-latchet of the humblest saint of Jesus, can hardly dispense with a discipline which St. Paul considered to be essential for himself. Does any one find by experience that some worldly amusement, though innocent in itself, and very possibly innocent for others (let us remember in judging *others* on these points, that "to the pure all things are pure"), yet has a tendency to inflame his passions, to set up his vanity, and to brush rudely from his mind the thought of God's Presence? Then let there be no compromise. Let him listen to the Voice of the Everlasting Father calling him out of harm's way; "My child, come away instantly." But supposing he experiences no evil spiritual effect from the indulgence, or at least none of which he is conscious, may he abandon himself without restriction to the amusement in question, live in it, sacrifice a considerable amount of money, leisure, time to it? Surely not. To live in any amusement is to be the slave of it. And the Christian should spurn any such dependence. The tone which he takes up towards all innocent enjoyments and recreations should be just that of the Apostle, "All things are lawful for me; but I will not be brought under the power of any." Besides, the Christian *dares not* give himself full latitude in this respect. With an insidious heart, with crafty spiritual foes watching for his halting, with that awful warning respecting the straitness of the gate and the narrowness of the way ringing in his ear, it would not be safe to do so. He sports not within a very wide margin of the precipice's edge.

Now it is quite clear that the principle which we have laid down admits of an application to food, as well as to all other less essential recreations. And it is equally clear that in respect of food, as well as other recreations, the Christian must be under the guidance and government of this principle. By the bounty of Our Heavenly Father, too little thought of, because it reaches us through a train of secondary causes (such as good harvests, prosperity in the country, our own ability to buy, our own ability to get), our board is daily spread not with necessaries only, but with luxuries. We may innocently enjoy these things, if we partake of them with thanksgiving. "Every creature of God is good, and nothing to be refused, if it be received with thanksgiving: for it is sanctified by the word of God and prayer." Meats are in themselves a matter of indifference; and the Christian has nothing in common with the ascetic, who imagines that in the mere act of abstinence there is a purity and a virtue. But it is quite another thing to say that we may with safety indulge in food to satiety, and lay no restraint upon our appetite for choice viands and delicate fare. In the first place, there are, as every one knows, certain classes of sins, to which any thing approaching to soft and luxurious living would act as a direct incentive and stimulant. Fasting combined with earnest prayer must be in *reason* the meet corrective for such sins. But it is so in Scripture, as well as in reason. Commenting upon His disciples' inability to cast out the foul spirit from the lunatic child, Our Lord implied that their failure was due to their not having used the means always found necessary under those circumstances; "*This* kind can come forth by nothing but by prayer and *fasting.*"

But suppose other cases, in which the spiritual consequences of unbridled indulgence are not, as far as we can perceive, mischievous. Even then we say, "You cannot possibly be safe in using your Christian liberty to its utmost extent. Safety without self-denial is the safety of the child gambolling on the edge of the precipice, and of the moth fluttering in the ray of the candle. Some men—many more than suspect themselves to be so—are slaves of food,—peevish and fretful, if the natural craving for it be in the least stinted or thwarted. Is their Christianity cast in the mould of

St. Paul's? We doubt not that they relish his views of Christian liberty; but do they equally relish his views of Christian restriction? And yet it is in the restriction that the highest freedom of the Gospel lies. If, as regards any one innocent enjoyment, a man has not moral courage enough, or force of character enough, to abstain from it occasionally, to that enjoyment the man is a slave. And the only true freedom lies in his obtaining by Grace such force of character as to be lord paramount over the enjoyment, and to be able to say, "I could easily dispense with this or that comfort, if there were any good object for resigning it." But then this power of easily dispensing with comforts is not to be gained except by actual practice and experiment. To all the numerous blessings of daily life, wherewith a bountiful God crowns our cup, we have no idea, we can have no idea, how much we are wedded, until we are deprived of them. While in the enjoyment of them, we readily fancy that, at a moment's notice, if need arose, we could dispense with these trifles, and scarcely feel their loss; but this fancy argues very little acquaintance with the human heart. That heart, wherever it plants itself in life, throws out suckers of dependence all around it. No soil is so muddy, no root is so dry and rotten, that the heart will not grapple a sucker into it, will not twine a sucker round it; so that when torn away from the muddy soil, and the rotten root, the heart bleeds. What Religion says is, "Learn gradually, not to purify yourself by pain (that is the dream of the ascetic), not to expiate your sin by self-inflicted torture (that is abhorrent to the Christian mind, as infringing on the only meritorious Atonement of the Saviour), but to detach your affections from all things earthly and sensual, and aim at a despotic control over every appetite." That is the fundamental principle of Fasting; and it is a principle which every man must carry out in his daily life, one after this manner and another after that, if he desires to be a good soldier of Jesus Christ. No good soldier ever refused to endure hardships. What would the general say, if the soldier averred a distaste for the hard fare, the broken slumbers, and the scanty accommodation incidental to camp life?

II. But it may be said that the self-control (or in other words the temperance) which I am advocating, should run parallel with our daily life, and not be confined to stated seasons.

Most true, as far as the bare statement goes; but most false, if what is intended or implied by the statement be that stated seasons of Fasting, such as our Church appoints, are useless formalities, which had better be expunged (as they have already expunged the State Services) from the Liturgy. The "Table of the Vigils, Fasts, and Days of Abstinence, to be observed in the Year," standing (as it does) in the forefront of the Book of Common Prayer, is a solemn and valuable reminder to us that habits of self-control form an essential part of the Christian character,—a solemn, and now greatly needed protest from the book, which, next to the Holy Scriptures, we are most bound to venerate, against the luxury and softness of a degenerate age and an overwrought civilization. But more than this,—much more. It is, indeed, most true that self-control is to be the discipline of a life, not the fitfully-adopted practice of the Eve before a Saint's Day, or of an Ember week, or of a Friday, or of Lent. But those know little indeed of the human heart who do not know that a duty for which no stated seasons are set apart, more especially if it be an unpalatable duty, is apt to be altogether evaded by the conscience. That which has no time of its own, but simply may be done, and ought to be done at every time, is sure to be done never. The God who made the human heart, must know the human heart. And because He saw and knew its tendency to find loopholes of escape from observances, which have no definite season, He instituted the Sabbath in the law of the Fourth Commandment, between which and the Ecclesiastical Institution of Fasting Days there is much which is very analogous. Undoubtedly men should "pray without ceasing," and not on the Sunday only. Undoubtedly, men should surrender some portion of their daily, and not only of their weekly leisure, to prayer (private and domestic), and to the study of God's Word. Undoubtedly, men should every day withdraw into the screened sanctuary of their own hearts, and resting awhile from worldly cares, give their minds to heavenly Contemplation. But undoubtedly, also, the restrictions of the Sabbath-law are wise and useful restrictions. Judge in yourselves whether they be not so indeed. Suppose that a day of religious rest were prescribed by no authority. Suppose that, worship and meditation being pressed upon us as urgently as they are at present, the time of fulfilling these duties had been left to our own option, and that the seventh day were undistinguished by any special consecration of it. Can you suppose that, under these circumstances, there would have been one tithe of the devotion in Christendom which there is at present? Would not the result infallibly be that the Lord's tax upon our time would be altogether disregarded,—that our odious cupidity would overleap every barrier of reason and conscience,—that there would be no pause to the toils of the artisans in our factories,—no cessation in the jingle of commerce among our crowded thoroughfares,—and that, if any one were inclined for a pause or a break, or felt his heart yearn a little for the tinkling of Church bells, and the beautiful sight of Christ's flock coming to worship Him in His House of Prayer, his neighbours would say to that relenting man, "Come, and let us make a little more money to-day; and, as for God, we can think of Him at any time?" Is it not clear that, as human nature goes, the ordinance of the Fourth Commandment is a real security for a certain amount of devotion? And, although we freely admit that Fasting Days are not of Divine, but only of Ecclesiastical, appointment, yet is not the same reasoning applicable to them? In the ordinary course of things, are men likely to exercise self-control more or less, if certain days are specially set apart for the exercise? Anyhow, they are certain to exercise it little enough; but we are sure that if the ordinance of the Fasting Days were expunged from the Calendar, they would exercise it still less. Therefore it is that we bless God that we have as yet at all events retained these days; that we have not as yet surrendered them up to that spirit of license and dislike of religious restraints, which clamours in the nation at large, and finds a voice even in the Legislature; and therefore it is that we recommend Christians, not in a spirit of sour asceticism, but in the exercise of a sound and wise Christian discretion, to observe these days by some restrictions upon their liberty as to innocent comforts, enjoyments, and recreations,—the restrictions being always limited by regard to health (any interference with which would be not only sinful in itself, but a positive contradiction of the end of Fasting, which is to clear, and not to cloud the mind) and being always guarded as far as possible from the notice of others.

I cannot conclude without pointing out, that the analogy which I have suggested between the Divine Institution of the Sabbath and the Ecclesiastical Institution of Fasting Days, is one which, if carried out, would effectually rectify the abuses to which Fasting is exposed. Observe that, if any good result is to be looked for from it, the Fast Day (like the Sabbath Ordinance) must be spiritualized and Christianized,—redeemed from Judaism and the bondage of the letter, and kept in the freedom of the Spirit. The Sabbath-law, as it stands in the Ten Commandments, merely prescribes rest on the seventh day. But no Christian imagines that mere literal rest is, of itself and by itself, a sufficient fulfilment of the precept. No Christian imagines that a man who should sleep all Sunday, or loiter about in indolence all Sunday, would be observing the Sabbath-law, or indeed doing any thing but contravening it. Such an obedience would be in the letter and not in the spirit. The spirit of the precept enjoins public worship, holy thought and reading, deeds of love, and cheerful Christian intercourse. Apply the same observation to the Fasting Day. The mere omission or retrenchment of a meal is by itself nothing. It will be worse than nothing,—it will contravene the spirit of the Ordinance,—if it make us morose instead of cheerful, or disqualify us for the exercise of the mind in Prayer, Self-examination, and the study of the Scriptures. Fasting is designed as a help to Prayer; and the moment it becomes an hindrance, that moment it defeats its own end. It is designed also as a help to Almsgiving,—a retrenchment of our own superfluities to supply the needs of the poor. Now Almsgiving can only be acceptably practised in a spirit of love; and therefore to allow Fasting to interfere with those little duties of love, kindness, and consideration, which we owe to those around us, is again a counteraction of its end. For some constitutions, doubtless, the self-control required of them lies in other departments rather than in that of food. Surely there are subjects enough in which we may lay a restriction upon ourselves, comforts enough which we may spare for the good of others, superfluities enough which we may retrench. We cannot be at any real loss for a quarter in which to exercise self-denial; and so long as it is wisely and lovingly exercised, the quarter is a matter of quite secondary importance. Whatever be the form which we adopt of keeping under our body and bringing it into subjection, let us at all events take care to spiritualize it by a larger amount of Prayer and devotional retirement, by meditation upon our sins, by acts of kindness, by deeds of love.

As regarding the observance of Lent generally, so regarding the specific observance of Fast Days, we feel that it is specially demanded by the times on which we are fallen. Here again we believe, that in a faithful adherence to the system of our Church is to be found a remedy for the tremendous social evils which ever attend the progress of Civilization, when that progress becomes unhealthily rapid. The iniquity of Sodom is said to have consisted in "pride, fulness of bread, abundance of idleness," and neglect of "strengthening the hands of the poor and needy." If with "abundance of idleness" our times and country cannot be justly taxed, the other traits—haughtiness, luxury, and hard-hearted inconsiderateness — are frightfully exemplified in our rich and prosperous community. "Fulness of bread" especially. The luxuries and over-refinements of the age—all the manifold softnesses whereby art contrives to make life easy, and to soothe the little wearinesses, and minister to the little whims of the opulent,—remind the student of profane history of the degenerate effeminacy of manners under the earlier Roman Emperors,—those monsters of cruelty and of lust. While in the mind of the student of Scripture, these luxuries call up sterner and more awful associations, as he remembers what was the end of the certain rich man, at whose gate was laid Lazarus full of sores, while he himself "was clothed in purple and fine linen, and fared sumptuously every day." The flesh grows wanton and insolent ; the spirit, just kept alive in the nation by the august presence of the Gospel, and by the ministrations of a Church, whose labours are totally incommensurate to the extent of her harvest-field, pines and languishes, and is ready to die. Now the remedy for this state of things is the revival of the Fast·Day,—not in the narrowness of a mere literal observance, but in that spirit of humiliation and love and self-restraint, to which alone God has respect. It was one of Our dear Lord's last warnings to His followers : " Take heed to yourselves, lest at any time your hearts be overcharged with surfeiting, and drunkenness, and cares of this life, and so that day come upon you unawares." May this warning ring like an alarum in the ears of this soft and luxurious generation! And that it may do so, let us fall at the knees of Him who gave it, with that Prayer of our Church, which in a few short lines expresses the whole use and force and significance of Fasting :—

" O Lord, who for our sake didst fast forty days and

forty nights; Give us grace to use such abstinence, that, our flesh being subdued to the Spirit, we may ever obey Thy godly motions in righteousness and true holiness, to Thy honour and glory, who livest and reignest with the Father and the Holy Ghost, one God, world without end."

CHAPTER VIII.

ON ALMSGIVING.

"*Thy prayers and thine alms are come up for a memorial before God.*"—ACTS x. 4.

THESE are the words, in which an angel assures Cornelius that his way of life has met with God's approval. "His prayers and his alms had come up for a memorial before God." His own account of what the angel said to him notices the same two points, with a very trifling verbal discrepancy:—" A man stood before me in bright clothing, and said, Cornelius, thy prayer is heard, and thine alms are had in remembrance in the sight of God." And the sketch of the life of Cornelius, drawn by the Evangelist, has the same features. He is described as " a devout man, and one that feared God with all his house"—(so much for his general character; now for the particular exercises by which the character expressed itself)—" *who gave much alms to the people, and prayed to God alway.*"

This Chapter shall be devoted to the subject of Almsgiving; and we open it by observing the position which Almsgiving holds in the scheme of Christian duty. " Thy prayers *and* thine alms." There is a deeper meaning in the circumstance of Prayers and Alms being noticed side by side than might at first sight appear. Alms are the correlative of prayers. The two exercises are, if I may so say, branches from a common stem, which binds them together. And what is that common stem? It is the moral Law of God; that Law to which, though it be not the Covenant under which (as Christian men) we live, we must yet be conformed as a rule of life. The Law branches out, as we know, into two great precepts,—supreme and unbounded Love to God, and Love to our neighbour as to ourselves. Now the man who really and habitually prays, the man who lives in the spirit of prayer, fulfils the first great branch of duty. True spiritual prayer,—"the effectual, fervent prayer of a righteous man," such as was Cornelius, is the outcome and expression of a man's duty to God. Such prayer is called in Scripture "incense;" partly from its reaching the Throne of Grace, even as incense, when kindled, soars up to the sky; partly from its spiritual fragrance and acceptability. "Let my prayer be set forth in Thy sight *as the incense.*" And the man who gives alms, in the true spirit of almsgiving, is equally fulfilling the second great branch of duty. Devout almsgiving—such as was that of Cornelius, who "gave much alms to the people," and that of the centurion in the Gospel, who loved the Jewish nation, and built for them a synagogue—is the outcome and expression of a man's duty to his neighbour. Yet think not that the act passes no further than to our neighbour. It too, no less than prayer, comes up before God as a memorial. It too, no less than prayer, finds in the fragrant, soaring incense its Scriptural emblem and type. "I have all, and abound" (says the grateful Apostle, whose need had been supplied by his Philippian converts); "I am full, having received of Epaphroditus the things which were sent from you; *an odour of a sweet smell, a sacrifice acceptable, well-pleasing to God.*"

Thus, then, Prayer and Almsgiving are seen to be co-ordinate. This circumstance alone lends a value to Almsgiving, which perhaps we have not been apt to attach to it. Viewed side by side with Prayer, as the expression of love to our fellow-men, it assumes a position and a significance which we never hitherto gave it credit for. Nay, if truth must be said, we have been occasionally somewhat suspicious of Almsgiving. In the term itself we have fancied we heard a legal ring, as if it were not genuine Gospel coin; and some of us, it may be, have secretly regarded those happy characters, who are profuse and munificent in relieving the distress of others, as seeking to be justified by the works of the Law and not by the faith of Christ. But this correlation between Prayer and Alms puts the subject in a new light. Almsgiving need be no more a work of human merit than Prayer is. Neither Almsgiving nor Prayer can justify the sinner. No almsgiving, however profuse, and no prayer, however fervent, can wipe away a single stain of guilt from the soul. That is the special and exclusive prerogative of the Blood of Christ's Atonement. But both Prayer and Almsgiving—the one as well as the other—"come up for a memorial for God," when offered to Him in faith, even in such imperfect and inchoate faith as that of Cornelius must have been, before he heard the preaching of the Gospel from the Apostle Peter.

It must however be obvious that, as it is not every so-called Prayer, so it is not every so-called Alms, of which the great things that have been said above can with truth be predicated. We have been speaking of Prayer in its broadest sense, as embracing every form of communion with God; and of Alms also we have been speaking in the broadest sense which the term will bear; not merely as an occasional dole to the poor, but as the relief of human distress from a deep living sympathy with man's sufferings and sorrows. I have looked at Almsgiving for the moment as the genuine expression of Christian Charity, just as I have looked at Prayer for the moment as the genuine expression of Christian Piety. But this, we know, is by no means the case with every Alms and every Prayer. Both in the case of Prayers and of Alms the act has, in the sadly degenerate practice of Christians, become detached from the spirit which should animate it, and which alone can render it acceptable. Prayer is performed by multitudes (performance, alas! is the correct word) without the smallest sense of its being a privilege or a refreshment, merely because conscience or the usages of society exact a certain measure of it. And Alms, similarly, are extorted reluctantly from the majority of those who give them, with a feeling that any petition for them, whether coming from the persons in need, or from the minister of God acting in their behalf, is an importunity of which we would willingly be rid. It cannot be imagined that such Prayers or such Alms have any acceptability on high.

Let us inquire then in what spirit Alms may be so given as to come up for a memorial before GOD. And may GOD bless our reflections on this subject, not only to the enlightenment of the understanding, but to the stimulating and strengthening of our wills!

Pursuing then still the parallel between Prayers and Alms, which has been already drawn out, we remark that both these offerings to God must be made, not on casual impulse, not as the mere inspiration of a happy moment, but on principle. As regards Prayer, this is generally acknowledged, and need scarcely be pressed. No one, it may be presumed, thinks that he has acquitted himself of his duty as a Christian, unless he has offered Prayer systematically and periodically. No one probably could satisfy his conscience by lifting up his heart to God only when he found himself in a happy frame for doing so. Acceptable as such a plan might be to our natural indolence, it would scarcely approve itself to our minds as right, if we should say, "I shall abandon *stated* Prayer altogether; I shall leave Prayer for those happy moments, few and far between, like angels' visits, when the mind is released from care, made complacent by good health, good spirits, and good fortune; or when it is inclined to serious thought by a good Sermon or by a visitation of Providence." However such a plan might defend itself argumentatively as a method of avoiding formalism and unreality in Prayer, the instinct of the Christian mind would at once repudiate it as wrong. In the first place, the duty which is left for performance at a convenient season is too sure, according to the ordinary laws of human experience, to find no season which is convenient; and he who defers sailing till he has wind, weather, and tide all in his favour, is apt to end by never setting sail at all. In the second place, Prayer is not simply (or chiefly) for the edification of the individual soul (in which case there might, perhaps, be some reason in deferring it till we could perform it with sensible profit and complacency); it is also an act of homage to Almighty God, a recognition of His claim upon our time, our thoughts, and the best energies of our minds. If our Prayers are to have any significance in this latter view of them, if they are not merely to please ourselves by the indulgence of pious sentiments, but to honour God, they must be offered systematically and methodically. We must pray when we rise up; we must pray when we lie down; we must join in the prayers of the congregation on Sundays and Holy Days. All this is conceded as regards Prayer; but, as regards Almsgiving, how different is the view generally taken of the subject, and how miserably uncertain and precarious the practice which prevails! Instead of recognizing a certain portion of their earnings or income as being due to Almighty God, and as being a sacred fund, which must be spent in the course of the year on works of Piety and Charity, the modern Christian abandons himself, for the most part, to the appeals which are made to him on behalf of Philanthropic objects, and helps those objects only where his sensibilities are stirred in their favour. His beneficence is not an organized work at all; it is an occasional and irregular impulse. A Charity Sermon, which he happens to hear, awakens in him a kindly interest in the institution advocated; and he gives, if he has the money with him; if not, he determines to give; but often, in the pressure and hurry of the week's work, his ardour cools, and his resolution is forgotten. Then there are cases of distress *personally known* to him, which he relieves with more or less generosity according to the liveliness of the interest which he feels in them. But he has no idea, because he has never been at the pains to make the reckoning, what proportion his alms bear to his resources; he has never asked himself the question, or at least has never seriously prosecuted it to an answer; " Do they bear a fair proportion; a proportion which satisfies my own convictions of what is right; because, if they do not, I am quite determined they shall?"

Modern Almsgiving being, thus for the most part, the result of good impulse, rather than of principle, the system of things has adjusted itself to the sentiments of the majority. Money must be had for the various objects of benevolence; and, as it is not to be had upon principle, it must be had by an appeal to our sensibilities, or even by more questionable methods. Inducements to give are held out by the showy and exaggerated oratory of the public meeting, by the gaiety and little dissipation of the bazaar, or the luxury and social intercourse of the public dinner; these being the baits by which money may be caught even from those who never part with it from higher motives. The least objectionable form in which these appeals are made is that of the Charity Sermon. A Charity Sermon, according to the accepted definition of it, means the pathetic exposition by a preacher of some object of benevolence, designed to work upon the sensibilities of the hearers, and to draw from them assistance in the way of money. If this is done with simplicity, and without aiming at rhetorical effect, and if the special object is always subordinated to the great end of instruction in Divine Truth (the sacred province of the Christian pulpit), the proceeding is quite unobjectionable, and may be productive of good. Nor probably, in the present state of Christian sentiment, could any better method of raising funds for a good object be devised. But even the Charity Sermon is not the theoretically high and true way of obtaining supplies for a desirable object. If the standard of Christian sentiment and practice were higher, if it at all resembled what it was in early days, before Christian zeal and love cooled down, Charity Sermons would be unnecessary. The Apostolic advice on the subject of Alms runs thus (and if every Christian would act on the principle of this advice, all occasional appeals on behalf of good objects would be superseded and extinguished): "Now concerning the collection for the saints, as I have given order to the churches of Galatia, even so do ye. Upon the first day of the week let every one of you lay by him in store, as God hath prospered him, that there be no gatherings when I come," that is to say (extracting the spirit of the precept from its letter), "Periodically examine your earnings, and set apart a due and fair proportion of them for works of Piety and Charity. Let that proportion constitute a separate fund, and when objects of benevolence are brought before you, assist them out of that fund." The Primitive Church acted on the letter of this Apostolical precept; and a trace of their practice is still to be found in that part of the Office of the Holy Communion, which is called the Offertory. In the course of the Liturgy (or Service of the Communion) offerings either of money, or of food and clothing, were made by all members of the congregation, who did not lie under any Church censure. These offerings were afterward divided into four parts. The first part went to the relief of the poor; the second to the maintenance of the Bishop; the third part defrayed the expenses of the sacred fabric and its ornaments; the fourth was divided among the subordinate Clergy. Indeed, from a remarkable passage of St. Chrysostom, it would seem that the early Christians never entered the Church to pray without giving alms to the poor, some of whom were stationed at the Church-door for the purpose. So deeply was the mind of our forefathers in the faith imbued with the connexion between Prayers and Alms;

so thoroughly were they inoculated with the Scriptural view that acts of homage to God must go hand in hand with acts of love of man.

Now, without asserting that exactly the same form of Almsgiving would suit the present altered state of things, without maintaining (as nevertheless many wise and good men do) that the Offertory and the alms-chest could even now be advantageously made the medium of giving all that is given for the Service of God, and the relief of the poor, we may surely say that *the principle* of these primitive offerings is as applicable as ever, and that, if it were conscientiously applied by *every* Christian, the result would be an abundance of means for every good object, which would quite supersede these occasional appeals. The principle is, to be systematic, regular, and methodical in our Alms, instead of casual and impulsive. All that is necessary in order to this is a little time, a little trouble (very little of either), and perhaps, I should add, a little moral courage. Let us first settle with our own minds, as in the sight of God, what proportion of our income is due to works of Piety and Charity. The proportion will vary very much; for it is clear that the same proportion will be much more severely felt when subtracted from a very narrow income, than when it is the mere exuberant overflow of a very large one. No one man can lay down a rule for another in this respect; the only point of importance is, that we should satisfy not the expectations of others, but the requirements of an enlightened and a pure conscience in ourselves, or, in other words, the claims of God. The proportion having been settled, all that follows is more or less mechanical, and may be done with a very slight expenditure of time. A private account is opened, exhibiting on one side all our receipts, on the other every item of our charitable expenditure. Periodically the account is examined. If it should appear that the sum of our charitable expenditure comes up to the proportion we have determined upon, well and good; we have done our duty, and have the satisfaction of knowing that we have done it. Should it exceed the proportion, the excess may be balanced (though I think it scarcely ever will be) by a retrenchment of charity in the succeeding period. But should it fall short of the proportion, it may be made a point of conscience at once to seal up the deficit, and send it off to the best Charitable Institution we know of. If *every one* would act thus,—poor as well as rich,—and the poor are quite as much bound to give their small proportion as the rich their large one,—I believe that the resources of deserving Charities would never fail. It is because Charities are thrown upon impulse, instead of principle, for their supplies, and because impulse is so fitful and casual a thing, that the funds of most of them fall off as soon as the enthusiasm which started them subsides.—But benefits of a much higher kind would accrue from the exercise of systematic benevolence,—benefits, whose sphere is the spirit and moral being of the giver. It contributes greatly to that peace of mind, which is so essential an element of spiritual progress, to be assured that to the extent of our ability we are fulfilling our religious obligations. This assurance we can have respecting Almsgiving, only if we are giving on principle and methodically. And another happy effect of this methodical giving on the mind will be,—that the very satisfactoriness of the process is likely to lead to a further advance in the same direction. He who has conscientiously given one twentieth this year will feel urged to give a tenth the next. The appetite for Christian liberality will grow, when it is healthily indulged, instead of morbidly stimulated. And that wretched feeling that every fresh charitable appeal is an exaction, would wholly cease, when we know that a sum has been set apart for expenditure of this kind in one form or another; and our gift would have that element of alacrity and forwardness essential to its acceptability; it would be given in the spirit prescribed by the Apostle: "Let every man do according as he is disposed in his heart, not grudgingly, or of necessity; for God loveth a cheerful giver."

The whole of what has been said is an expansion of, and reduces itself to, the one idea, that Alms should be given on principle. Alms and Prayers are co-ordinate exercises of Piety; they are both of them offerings to God; and as, in the one case, we must be careful not to rob God of the time and the mental effort, so, in the other, we must be equally careful not to rob Him of the gold and silver, which are His due. A portion of our time must be fenced round from the intrusion of worldly cares and secular business, if we are to discharge God's claims upon us. And on the same principle a portion of our substance must be regarded as a sacred treasury, not to be invaded by our own necessities, much less by our self-indulgence, and love of luxury.

The offerings made to God out of this treasury,—if made with faith in His Name,—are represented in Holy Scripture as memorials of us in Heaven. How inspiring the thought that we may have such memorials, —deeds which may serve (so to speak) to embalm our names, and keep them ever fresh and fragrant in that bright and cloudless realm! The believing and beautiful action of the woman in the Gospel who anointed Our Lord's head, as He sat at meat in Simon's house, was to be rewarded,—has been rewarded,—in a similar manner. Wheresoever the Gospel has been preached in the whole world, that woman's act of faith and piety has been rehearsed, commended, echoed on from the fathers to the children. A fame more glorious than hers, a memorial more rich in its results and consequences, as being a memorial not among men, but before God, is open to all of us who hear the Gospel. Do you desire that your name should be known in Heaven,—should be whispered and carried upward by the angels,—should be graven on the heart of our great High Priest,—should be mentioned by Him to God continually? Aspire to Heaven with devout prayers and sighs. Seek Christ with devout sympathies and devout succours, in the poor, whom He has constituted His representatives. Multiply acts of faith, and acts of love. And these acts shall keep alive the remembrance of you in the Heavenly Court, where no remembrance is without a requital. Cornelius was recompensed for his prayers and alms, by the visit of an Angel, by the visit of an Apostle, by the glad tidings of the Gospel, and, to crown all, by the gift of the Holy Ghost. How striking an instance of the large and munificent scale, on which God responds to the desires and efforts which His own free Grace has prompted,—of His "giving more" (as is His wont) "than either we desire or deserve!" How wonderful a fulfilment of the promise made by Our Lord both to secret Alms and secret Prayers,—"Thy Father, which seeth in secret, Himself shall reward thee openly!"

CHAPTER IX.

ON FREQUENTING THE HOLY COMMUNION.

"*Whether therefore ye eat, or drink, or whatsoever ye do, do all to the glory of God.*"—1 Cor. x. 31.

It is curious to observe how religious ideas are continually in a state of flux and change. Not only do outward fashions alter, but habits of thought are different from what they once were. Controversies have shifted their ground; and the theological combatants have gone off to a different part of the field. Time was when many a controversial lance was broken in our Church on the question at issue between Calvinists and Arminians. The keen interest once taken in that debate has entirely collapsed; and thinking men on both sides would probably admit that there is much precious truth in both Calvinism and Arminianism,—which is only another form of saying that Holy Scripture makes statements which favour both. To pass from doctrines to practices (not that the two can ever be severed except in idea, for practice must ever be based upon doctrine), there is now in progress a revolution in our habits of thought on the subject of frequently communicating. Serious Christians are coming round gradually, it is presumed by the force of conviction, to the habit of communicating much oftener than they used to do. More frequent opportunities of receiving the holy Supper are given by the Clergy; an index in itself of a changed state of thought and feeling on the subject; for where there is no demand, there is usually no supply. And, accordingly, the old manuals of preparation for the Holy Communion, excellent as several of them are, and containing, as many of them do, much valuable material for edification, are becoming, to a great extent, obsolete. They need to be thrown into a new form, adapted to a weekly or fortnightly recurrence of the Ordinance. For that the copious meditations and self-examinations, which most of them contain and recommend, should be gone through weekly, fortnightly,—nay even monthly, —by persons engaged in the active business of life, is of course out of the question,—a simple impossibility. A volume of preparatory devotions, (and several of these manuals *are* volumes,) implies that the Ordinance recurs but rarely, at great and solemn periods.

Is the old method of rare Communion, or the new method of frequent Communion, the best? We believe the new method to be so, because it is based upon a truer view of the Ordinance. The frequency or rarity of celebration would be in itself of comparatively little moment, if it were a mere outward fashion, if there were no principle involved in it. But a principle there is, underlying, and giving rise to, the change of practice: and we rejoice to think that this principle is more freely and generally recognized than it has hitherto been.

If the Eucharist were merely, as Zwingle most erroneously thought, a commemorative rite,—if the whole design of the Ordinance were to affect us with a picture of our Saviour's Passion,—this design would doubtless be carried out more effectively by a rare than by a frequent Communion. For it is a law of the mind, from the operation of which we shall strive in vain to exempt ourselves, that the impression which is constantly repeated gradually loses its force. But the Lord's Supper is not merely a commemoration, but an actual channel or vehicle of Grace to the soul. It stands on the same footing in this respect with Prayer, reading of Scripture, public worship, and sermons; only we believe that it takes precedence of them all, as the instrument of a higher Grace, and a means of a closer communion with God. Observe that by the Word of God itself, the Eucharist is placed in the same category with the other means of Grace, and that it seems to be intimated that the early Christians were equally frequent in the observance of all of them. "And they continued stedfast *in the Apostles' doctrine and fellowship*" (they constantly attended the teaching of the Apostles, and did not forsake the assembling of themselves together with them in the name of CHRIST), "*and in breaking of bread, and in prayers.*" There is no hint here that the doctrine and the prayers were to be of frequent recurrence, but the breaking of Bread to be reserved, as I may say, for state occasions. If all are means of Grace, and if the "breaking of Bread," as being the distinctively Christian Ordinance,—yea, as communicating to the soul, not indeed by a carnal transubstantiation, but "after an heavenly and spiritual manner," the very Body and Blood of our crucified Redeemer,—is the highest means of Grace, why should not all recur with equal frequency? Do we allege that the liveliness of our feelings respecting the Lord's Supper will wear off with the frequent repetition of it? Nay; but it is not liveliness of feeling which in any Ordinance we should seek, but the strengthening of principle. The two objects are quite distinct. Feeling occasionally runs very high, when principle is at its lowest ebb. Church history supplies instances in abundance of spiritual ecstasies (mere Satanic delusions, of course), where there was no real submission of the will to God. And on the other hand, principle may be in its full strength, and faith may be really clinging to God with all the force of moral determination, while feeling seems to have ebbed away altogether out of the soul. Thus Our Lord cries out upon the cross that God has forsaken Him, while He is really tightening His hold upon the Father, and indicating this firmness of grasp by the little word expressive of so much clinging, "My," — "My God, My God, why hast Thou forsaken Me?"

If superficial liveliness of feeling were what we ought to seek in the Ordinances of religion, there could be no question that too frequent repetition in any of them would be a mistake, calculated to counteract their influence. If for the next two years we shut up our Bibles, and thus divested our minds in some measure of their glib familiarity with the phraseology of Scripture, and at the end of that period opened them at one of the more pathetic or sublime passages, that passage would stir in our minds a far more vivid emotion, than Scripture ever communicates under our present circumstances. At the first outbreak of the Reformation, when the Sacred Volume was scarce, and the people sunk in gross ignorance of its truths, men had a much keener appreciation of it, a much livelier feeling of its preciousness than now, when it lies on the shelf of every cottage, and its comparatively fresh-looking binding shows the neglect in which spiritual blessings are held, as soon as they have become cheap, and easy of access. But in order that we might again have those vivid impressions respecting God's truth which men had in those old days, when they gathered round the chained Bible in the parish church, and appointed one of their party to read it aloud to them, it would be a strange method of proceeding, and one based on a false logic, to unlearn as much of this blessed Book as we possibly could, in the hope of thus coming fresh to the perusal of it. Then why is not the same reasoning, which holds good in the case of the Holy Scriptures, to be applicable to other means of Grace? If all we sought in the Eucharist were a certain natural sensibility to the Death of Christ, which Death the

Ordinance is appointed to show forth, then indeed might we go once a year only, like the Scottish peasants, over hill and dale, to partake of the Heavenly Banquet;—then indeed might we enjoy the artlessness with which the rite is there celebrated, as being a nearer approach to the original institution *in the way of picture*. But I seek much more in the Eucharist than to look at a picture and be touched by it. I seek to be fed in that Holy Ordinance; to be spiritually nourished, through the elements of Bread and Wine, with that Flesh which is meat indeed, and that Blood which is drink indeed. And if the things of the body furnish any sufficient analogy to the things of the soul, I should fear that the receiving this Heavenly Food only once a year would be something very much resembling spiritual starvation.

Yet argue as we may, our arguments will go for nothing against instinct. And in devout minds which have been reared under the old system of things, there is an instinct adverse to very frequent Communions, which it is difficult, if not impossible, to supplant. We believe that in this instinct there is an element of reason and reverence, however false may be the conclusions to which it leads; and that at all events our forefathers had hold of a truth, for which it behoves us to find some place in the modern system. Let us endeavour to analyze the feeling of reluctance which many good persons still entertain to a frequent (say a weekly) Communion.

Unquestionably, reverence towards the Ordinance has some share in engendering the reluctance. It is felt, and very justly felt, that in order to make so frequent a Communion of real value to us, there must be a general correspondence between the Ordinance and our lives. There is something dreadful in the thought of so high an Ordinance degenerating into formality; and degenerate into formality it must, unless, contemporaneously with this frequent celebration, there should be a general raising of the tone of the recipient's character and conduct. This is all true, just, and sound,—right in feeling; right in principle. But why should we implicitly reject the other branch of the alternative? Why is there *not* to be a general raising of the tone of our character and conduct? Why should we resolve to acquiesce in respectability, and virtually decline to aim at sanctity? Ah, sluggish will, thou art in fault! Frequent Communions demand higher aspirations; and higher aspirations involve stronger efforts and harder struggles. And these efforts and struggles are a tax upon the will, which the will perhaps is not quite ready to pay. Is this the secret cause of our reluctance? I believe it is frequently one cause. For if a man be honestly bent, not merely on reaching a very fair average standard of excellence, but on "perfecting holiness in the fear of the Lord," the reluctance very soon vanishes. Frequent Communion is then willingly embraced as a help, not declined out of a false homage to the Ordinance.

But what, it may be asked, constitutes conformity of life to the Ordinance of the Holy Communion? What is that habitual state, the living in which (more or less) establishes that correspondence between us and the Ordinance, which makes a very frequent reception available? Let the text which stands at the head of this Chapter furnish us with an answer to this question.

It is a great mystery, which teaches us many valuable lessons, that God has consecrated our reception of food into the highest Ordinances of religion. What may this circumstance be designed to teach us? The lesson expressly stated in the text, "Whether therefore ye eat or drink, or whatsoever ye do, do all to the glory of God." The reception of food is a *common* action,—homely, trivial, having nothing dignified or sublime about it, as is intimated by the words, "whatsoever ye do," following upon the specification of it,—" Whether therefore ye eat, or drink, or whatsoever ye do, do all to the glory of God." And again, the reception of food is a *necessary* action,—it is what we *must* do, in order to maintain our lives. The implication of the text, then, is that in our common and trivial actions, even in those which are bound upon us by necessity, and which we cannot any how escape from doing,—there is room and scope for glorifying Almighty God. On the one hand, we may do them mechanically and in a spirit of routine, or from the low motive of the pleasure which is to be had from them, or from the wrong motive of human praise. Or, on the other hand, we may do them, or strive to do them, in a religious spirit, fixing the eye of the mind, while we do them, on the great end of God's Service and Kingdom. In one word, we may either go through common life in a common way, tying up our religion to Public Worship on Sundays, and private prayer on week-days, or we may go through common life with an uncommon motive, —the thought of God, and the desire of pleasing and serving Him in all things. Now if a man should be going through common life thus,—if he sanctifies and elevates it, or even strives, as much as he can, to sanctify and elevate it, by importing into it a Christian motive, there is between him and the Holy Communion a certain correspondence, which is easily perceived. What were the materials out of which Christ framed the highest rite of His holy Religion? Did He prescribe a costly sacrifice, such as it would be a tax upon human resources to furnish? No such thing. He blessed a common meal, and consecrated it into a Sacrament, and made it the means, by a marvellous mystery of Grace, of communicating Himself to man's soul. What did He mean by so doing? Many things of grave import, some things, possibly, beyond our reach; but this most assuredly,—that the genius of His Religion, as expressed in its highest Ordinance, is to sanctify all the actions of human life, even down to the humblest and most necessary. To do this is, if I may so say, to breathe the atmosphere of the Holy Communion, and to have such a congeniality with it, as shall never make it match ill or show unsuitably upon the general groundwork of our lives. Reader, are you and I striving thus to sanctify,—not only holy seasons and holy exercises,—but all the common actions of daily life? Then shall we feel attracted towards a frequent reception of the Holy Communion, as one great means of furthering our object.

But in the feeling of reluctance to frequent Communion, there is one decidedly good element, which we must not pass over without notice. Persons think it beneficial to have certain solemn and stated periods, at which they may look into the affairs of their souls more narrowly, wind up their spiritual accounts more at leisure, and make a fresh start, as it were, upon their Christian course. These periods have been with them hitherto their Communions; each of which has thus become a sort of era in their inner life. But, if they are now to communicate every week or every fortnight, this solemn scrutiny and preparation, if it be not an actual impossibility, will become an unreality. Special devotional exercises are good at special seasons, but the mind cannot profitably be under such a strain every week or every fortnight. Sundays are great helps to a holy life; but only one day in every seven is appointed to be a Sunday.

In all this there is great force and reason. And he who is minded to live the Devout Life must on no account abandon the excellent practice of periodically examining his conscience on every department of duty, and seeking from God in prayer, and retirement from the world, that fresh spring of holy energy which is to be found for all of us in the Blood and Grace of Jesus Christ. But why must this necessarily be done before every Communion? Why might it not be done only before the three great Communions of Christmas, Easter, and Whit-Sunday? Or if even this be found impracticable, as with persons heavily engaged will very likely be the case, why should not these special devotions be limited to one Communion in the year, that of Christmas or that of Easter? Assuredly, a thorough and sifting Self-examination, once satisfactorily performed, is better than three or four cursory inspections of the conscience: Self-examination being a matter in which to be cursory and superficial is usually to deceive oneself. Then for ordinary Communions, assuming, of course,—and I am assuming all through,—that the conscience is kept clear of wilful sin,—our usual evening retrospect of the day, with some very trifling addition to our evening prayer on Friday and Saturday, the eighty-fourth Psalm, for example, and the prayer of access in the Communion Office, "We do not presume to come to this Thy table," &c., would abundantly suffice.

Have we now reached and met in any mind the objections which are felt to a frequent Communion? Or does there remain still a lurking mistrust of such a practice, under the suspicion, perhaps, of which Englishmen are at all times so susceptible, that it is popish? Such a suspicion is, in the first place, not borne out by the facts. Romanists, as a general rule, although they constantly assist at the Mass, (that is, are present at the celebration, and follow what is being done mentally,) communicate much seldomer than English Churchmen. Their unscriptural tenet of Transubstantiation, giving as it does a false awfulness and a superstitious mysteriousness to the Ordinance, frightens them away and holds them back from frequent Communion. So much for the real state of the case among them. And as regards the *theory* of frequent Communion, by way of showing that it is by no means exclusively Romanist, let me close this Chapter with an extract from those touching and edifying addresses published under the title of the Adieux of Adolphe Monod. The speaker was a French Protestant pastor, eminent for piety and for his extraordinary abilities as a preacher. The pulpit from which he spoke,—and it is sometimes the most effective of all pulpits,—was a death-bed, around which, Sunday by Sunday, (for he lingered long,) he gathered as many members of his little flock as the sick-room would hold, and received with them the Holy Communion, and spoke to them of such subjects as the "Regrets of a Dying Man." One of these addresses is headed "Frequent Communion." While guarding myself against being understood to recommend, as he does, a *daily* Communion, I willingly quote him as an advocate of frequent celebrations. Thus he speaks to the little flock at his bed-side, the words being taken down from his lips by his children:—"My dear friends, I wish you to know that in the frequent reception of the Communion during my illness I find much comfort, and I hope also much fruit. It is a great evil that the Communion should be celebrated so rarely in our Church, an evil which people on all sides are now applying themselves to remedy. Our Reformers, in establishing this order of things, have taken care to explain that they did it only for a time, and to prevent certain very grave abuses, which had crept into the primitive Church. But what they did as a temporary precaution has remained for ages in the greater number of our churches. At length we reach the time when we may expect to have frequent Communion restored to us. Calvin says somewhere, that the Communion ought to be celebrated at least every Sunday. Remark this *at least*. If it should be every Sunday *at least*, what should it be *at most?* *At most* must be, to take it as the early Christians did, according to Calvin (and that comes out, too, clearly enough from the Acts of the Apostles), every day from house to house, at the close of the family repast. Each of you may have remarked that rare Communion gives I know not what strange and extraordinary idea of the Communion,—of the preparation which ought to precede, and of the emotions which follow it. On the contrary, frequent Communion makes us understand much better the true character of this Sacrament; and it is impossible that daily Communion should fail to put us in perfect possession of that true character; for it teaches us to connect the Communion with all that there is most simple in Christian life, just as a repast is one of the simplest things in ordinary life. But whether there should be a daily celebration or not, certainly in seeing in the Communion the simplest expression of our faith, we shall profit by it most, we shall gather from it the greatest fruit, and it is thus that it will nourish our souls most effectually with the Flesh and with the Blood of Jesus Christ."

CHAPTER X.

OF THE PUBLIC SERVICE OF THE CHURCH.

"*If two of you shall agree on earth as touching any thing that they shall ask, it shall be done for them of My Father which is in heaven.*"—MATT. xviii. 19.

IT would be well if, in considering the various Ordinances of Religion, we began by narrowly examining their charter, as it exists in God's Holy Word. How shall we ascertain their true character? how shall we know what we may expect from them, and what we may not expect? how, in short, shall we secure ourselves, against a false estimate of them, otherwise than by looking into their original constitution? The exact limits of a patent or prerogative, granted by the government of a country to any individual, can only be ascertained by consulting the terms of the patent. Let the holder abstract from the public records, and hide away the parchment on which those terms are written, and there are then no powers which he may not assume, on the general vague representation that the patent is his.

The passage which stands at the head of this Lecture contains the charter of Public Worship. The Church has given to Public Worship divers forms of its own devising; but here we have, if I may so say, the raw material, out of which all forms are manufactured. Now, from the examination of this charter, we will seek, first, to ascertain the true theory of Public Worship; and then draw from that theory some practical hints for the conduct of this devotional exercise.

It is not with any controversial object, for controversy is seldom edifying, but by way of clearly defining the idea, that we say, at the outset, that in the practice both of the Church of Rome, and of the Protestant sects in this country, we trace a degeneracy from the Scriptural theory of Public Worship. Extremes continually meet; and it is not a little remarkable that both by Romanists and Dissenters the functions of Public Worship are all devolved upon the clergy,—whether priest or officiating minister,—and the people take, I do not say no part, but no common part with him. The Mass is the chief office of the Roman Church; at which even those who do not communicate assist, as it is called, every Sunday. In what does this assistance consist? The question may be answered by examining the books of devotion recommended and used at the Mass. It will be found, on looking into such books, that the idea of the congregation's praying as one body,—using the minister as their mouthpiece, and signifying their assent to him by occasional responds,—is, if not eliminated, very much obscured. The priest is doing one act, supposed to be sacrificial, to the effectiveness of which the congregation can contribute nothing; and while he is doing it, the people are furnished with separate devotions appropriate to the several stages of it, which each person recites secretly. The priest and they are not asking the same thing at the same time; and the only agreement which there is in their petitions stands in place and time,—in the fact that they are offered in the same church at the same hour. Nay it might happen that several of the worshippers should use different books of devotions on the Mass, even as with us different members of the congregation bring with them different books of devotion on the Holy Communion; and that thus two persons, kneeling side by side, might be so far from agreeing in what they ask, as to be offering two different petitions at the same moment. If the principle were carried out to an extreme, no two members of the congregation would be praying for exactly the same thing; and Public Prayer would resolve itself into *a series of private prayers said secretly in public.* But the truth is, that Private Prayer and Public Prayer are wholly different things, separated from one another by a much deeper distinction than the mere accident that the one is offered in the chamber, the other in the face of the Church. Their Scriptural charters proclaim that they are Ordinances differently constituted. The charter of Private Prayer runs thus: " Thou, when thou prayest, enter into thy closet, and when thou hast shut thy door,"— exclusion of the world from the thoughts, if not from the place, is an essential,—" pray to thy Father which is in secret; and thy Father, which seeth in secret, shall reward thee openly." The charter of Public Prayer, on the other hand, runs thus: " If two of you shall agree on earth as touching any thing that they shall ask, it shall be done for them of My Father which is in heaven." Agreement in the petition (not necessarily, as I understand it, agreement in the place or time of offering the petition, though that is both natural and proper) is an essential of this sort of prayer, so that if you remove this agreement, the prayer ceases to be Public Prayer at all. It is not the resorting to the same House of Prayer, it is not the being side by side with one's neighbour in bodily presence, but it is the mental and cordial agreement with him as to what we shall ask, which constitutes the prayer public. Develope this idea a little further, and you will arrive at the conclusion, which is as rational as it is Scriptural, that Private Prayer touches and deals with the relations of the individual to God, those relations to which no other heart than his own is privy, his secret sins, trials, struggles, successes; whereas Public Prayer embraces his relations as a member of the Church, not only to the Head of the Church, but also to the other members. In the one, there can usually be no agreement, by reason of the diversity of characters and wants. In the other we approach God as a Society, incorporated by the royal charter of His Son, having an understanding with other members as to our wants and petitions, and framing them in language so general as to meet the necessities of all. To use an illustration, Private Prayer is the exhibition of a biography to God; Public Prayer, the exhibition of a history. A biography is a distinct thing from a history. The one presents the individual in the private sentiments which actuate him; the other in his public enterprises, as a member of the body politic. And on account of this difference of character, no collection of biographies of any period would form a history of the period, any more than the aggregate of private devotions said in public constitutes public devotion. At the same time it must be admitted that, just as biographies mention occasionally the public exploits of their subjects, and histories sometimes delineate the private characters of public men, so Public Prayer and Private Prayer will occasionally trench upon the strict provinces of one another,—as when in his closet a man intercedes for the whole Church, or as when in the congregation some passage of the Liturgy comes home to our own present wants with a peculiar force and appropriateness. Suffice it that, generally speaking, the provinces of the two are distinct. We may not press *any* distinction too hard.

Turning now to the Protestant sects; does their practice realize better the true ideal of Public Worship than that of Romanists? We hold it to be at least a nearer approach to the true ideal; for the theory of all Protestant Worship certainly is, that there shall be agreement as to the things asked for, that minister and people shall join in the same petitions. But how can such agreement be effectually secured in the absence of a Liturgy, or form previously prepared, unless the pastor and congregation should meet before Divine Service, and come to some understanding as to the substance of their petitions; a course which, if not impracticable, has probably never been attempted? In extempore prayer it is out of the question that the people can know what the minister is about to pray for: when he has uttered his petition, they may, of course, give their mental and cordial assent to it, and doubtless devout Dissenters, of which there are numbers, endeavour to do so; but before this mental process, which consists of first taking in the petition with the mind, and then assimilating it with the will, is well finished, the minister has passed on to another petition, faster than the worshipper can follow, and the latter soon finds that there is no way of really joining, but by listening, as he would to a Sermon, and giving a general assent to the contents of the prayer by means of the Amen at the end. On the other hand, a Liturgy, if seriously and intelligently used, necessarily secures exact agreement among the worshippers as to the things sued for; nay, determines even the form in which each supplication shall present itself to the minds of all. There are, we believe, many other advantages accruing to a Liturgy like ours, which are beside the purpose of the present argument. We prize our Prayer Book for its intrinsic beauty, for its chaste fervour, for its primitive simplicity, for its close harmony with Scripture, for the way in which it fences us against false doctrine; but the fundamental advantage of a Liturgy, merely as a Liturgy, is this, that it secures, far more than any extempore prayer can do, that agreement in the things asked for, which is part of the charter of Public Prayer, and so grounds the act of worship on Christ's own Word of Promise: "If two of you shall agree on earth as touching any thing that they shall ask, it shall be done for them of My Father which is in heaven."

We have canvassed freely the defective theories of Public Worship, maintained by those who are opposed to us on either side; but it is in no spirit of boastfulness that we have done so, nor with any desire to conceal our own faults, which are both patent and abundant. The truer and more Scriptural our Church's *theory* of Public Worship is, the more cause have we for humiliation, that in *practice* we so grievously fall short of it. It is true that we have every security, which mere rule and system can give us, for agreement in the substance of our petitions; but agreement is after all a matter of the mind and heart, and cannot be prescribed by rule or system. Without such cordial agreement, the most beautiful Liturgy in the world soon degenerates into a dreary and formal recitation, lacking both the reality of the Romanist's secret devotion, and the vivacity and freshness of the Dissenter's extempore prayer. We might, if we duly prized and properly used our advantages, make our churches the very gate of Heaven to every devout soul; as it is, the felt formalism of the Service in many of them, (for formalism is a thing felt by instinct,) rather chills and throws back the energies of spiritual life. Where is the remedy to be sought? In the efforts of individuals to bring about a better state of things. In vain do we declaim against the Church of our day in the abstract. The Church is composed of individual members, upon each of whom rests his own portion of the blame and responsibility; it is I, and you, Reader, who are in fault. If we are minded for the future to do justice to the system of our Church, and bring out the beauty of its theory, let us resolve first, each one for himself, to do what in us lies to contribute to such a result. And let us consider whether the following hints, all founded on the charter of Public Prayer already quoted, may not be of service to us.

1. Let us seek *to understand* the Liturgy of the Church. If agreement in our petitions is to be secured by the use of it, it is evident that the worshippers must, each one for himself, bring some considerable portion of their minds to it, before they come to Church. The Morning and Evening Prayer, indeed, are more or less familiarized to our ears by constant repetition; but then familiarity with the sound is a totally different thing (as a child's knowledge of the Catechism proves) from intelligent appreciation of the sense—nay, is probably more or less of a hindrance to that intelligent appreciation. Words got by heart are

foolishly supposed to be thoroughly mastered, whereas all that we have secured of them is the rhythm and the run of the style, and the meaning, Proteus-like, has given us the slip. How many English Churchmen have ever made the various petitions of the Morning and Evening Prayer a subject of thought,—who yet know the Service quite well enough superficially, to catch up and fling abroad certain captious popular objections to parts of it? And in the Occasional Services, the Christening, the Wedding, or the Burial, though the first of these has all the dignity and all the efficacy of a sacrament, and the two last are of a nature to enlist peculiarly our personal feelings; where is the man who seriously asks himself, before he goes to Church, what are the blessings for which he is about to sue? Yet surely we must at least ask ourselves this question, if we would avail ourselves of the opportunity of agreement which our Liturgy affords, and so avail ourselves of Our Lord's Promise to united Prayer. We must *think* about our Prayer Books, as well as about our Bibles, if we are to profit by them. The real action of a man's own mind upon the Liturgy would be worth a great deal of book learning. However, if explanation and comment be required, by those who wish to study the subject chiefly in its devotional aspect, Dean Comber supplies plentiful and wholesome matter; and for those who desire something less prolix and less expensive than the works of Comber, Shepherd on the Common Prayer may be found suitable. It would be one great point (and I mention it, because in all studies a definite and circumscribed aim is of great importance) to make the Psalms thoroughly available in Public Devotion,—to say them, or sing them, with more of understanding, as well as more of spirit, than heretofore. With persons who are only moderately acquainted with Divinity, some commentary will probably be found necessary for this purpose, and Bishop Horne's is perhaps the best that can be recommended. I may add that it is a great clue to the right devotional use of those Psalms, which manifestly refer to

Christ, to remember, while saying or singing them, that we are one with Him; and that we repeat them in Church as being identified with Him in God's sight —"members of His Body, of His Flesh, and of His Bones;" not as if we were reading mere instructive lessons.

2. Do not allow Public Worship to degenerate into a mere saying of your private prayers in Church. Set yourselves against this selfish and narrowing tendency; for it rather defeats the end of the Ordinance. Think of the many others who are around you at Public Worship, of their sins, trials, wants, wishes, mercies,— trying to throw yourself into their case. Be you praying and giving thanks for them, while they are praying and giving thanks for you; this will constitute a sweet agreement, a beautiful symphony, in the ears of the Most High. Too many Christians, good and pious in the main, go to Church with this idea working in their minds: "I go to ask for what I myself want, and to give thanks for what I myself have received, and I do not busy myself with other people." Then you might nearly as well stay at home. The closet is the place for pouring out the heart before God, and laying down the secret burdens at the Throne of Grace. The Church is the place for the intercommunion of Saints with one another, and of all with God. Hence the great comprehensiveness of the terms in which our Confession and Thanksgiving are drawn up. They are expressly framed to cover all cases.

3. Let not the outward expression of agreement be wanting; or, in other words, be careful to make in an audible voice all the responses prescribed by the Church. This may seem a slight matter in itself; but it really rests upon profounder principles than we are apt to imagine. In the first place, the audible respond is a valuable protest in favour of the undoubted Scriptural truth, that all Christians are, in virtue of their Baptism, priests, and that all therefore are bound to join and bear their part in the spiritual sacrifices which are offered to God in His Church. The practice of

Romanists and Dissenters, by which the clergy or officials recite the whole Office, obscures this precious and important truth: our practice as members of the Church of England ought to bear testimony to it. But besides this, there is in us, our nature being composite, a strange mysterious sympathy between the outward and the inward, which makes us dependent for the life and energy of our spirits upon the little outward symptoms and accidents of our position. Our bodies expand or contract according to the temperature of the atmosphere which surrounds them; and our minds in a spiritual atmosphere, which makes itself felt in just the same subtle and delicate way as the natural atmosphere, observe the same law. If persons around us in the congregation are merely silent auditors of the Service, not active participators in it: much more, if they are careless, slovenly, and indevout, our own devotion is instantaneously chilled, and, as it were, thrown inward. If, on the other hand, they have all the appearance of earnest worshippers, devotion soon stirs and wakens up in our own heart, much as a frozen snake will move, and uncoil itself, and rear its crest, when brought near the fire. Throw, then, your contribution of heart, and soul, and sympathy into the Service of the Church, by making the responses simply and sincerely, in your natural voice. Berridge seems to have understood well the great charm of congregational worship, when he thus writes respecting the mutual salutation of the priest and people, as given in his own little Church at Everton:

"When I say, 'The Lord be with you,' I love to hear their murmur of response breaking forth from all corners of the Church, 'And with thy spirit.' It reminds me of those words of the Revelation, descriptive of the worship of the redeemed at the marriage supper of the Lamb: 'I heard as it were the voice of a great multitude, and as the voice of many waters, and as the voice of many thunderings, saying, Alleluia! for the Lord God omnipotent reigneth.' The Dissenters have nothing to compare with it."

Of the Public Service of the Church.

It should be our ambition to bring the worship of the Church Militant into as close a resemblance with that of the Church Triumphant as our circumstances will admit. To this great result each one may contribute something by bringing to Church a thoughtful and prepared mind, a devout heart, and a humble voice. Let but a few worshippers do this, and oftener than we think we shall seem to intercept an echo of that sinless and perfect Worship which is ever carried on above.

We have spoken of the agreement of the members of Christ's Body as that which gives its character to Public Worship. But what are the members without the Head? Only so many bricks of an arch without a key-stone. There can be no agreement without the Head: for it is the Head which holds the members together, not in unity only, but in existence. Not therefore without a very profound connexion of thought does Our Lord thus complete the passage, upon which we have been founding our remarks: "If two of you shall agree on earth as touching any thing that they shall ask, it shall be done for them of My Father which is in Heaven. For where two or three are gathered together in My Name, there am I in the midst of them."

There is great significance in the "For." He would have us to understand that it is His Presence in the midst of the two or three gathered together in His Name, which lends all the efficacy to their petitions. The High Priest, He would say, is in the midst of the worshippers, whose functions of Atonement and Intercession are the alone procuring cause of the acceptance of their prayers. Then our last practical recommendation shall be that, as in Private Prayer our thoughts are turned to that God who seeth in secret, so in Public Worship we should seek to realize a rather more definite conception of the Presence of the Incarnate God. The human presence visibly around us in the Church is the pledge, the token, the Sacrament of His. He is among them in all the sympathies of His Humanity, in all the glories of His Divinity, in all the precious virtues of His Mediatorial Work. And it will be found useful, before the commencement of the Service, and at any of the necessary breaks which occur in the course of it, to occupy the mind with the thought of His Presence. The apprehension of it, and nothing short of the apprehension of it, will impart to Public Worship a mingled sweetness and solemnity, which will constrain us to exclaim with the Psalmist: "How amiable are Thy tabernacles, O Lord of Hosts! My soul longeth, yea, even fainteth for the courts of the Lord. Blessed are they that dwell in Thy house: they will be still praising Thee."

CHAPTER XI.

ON SELF-RECOLLECTEDNESS AND EJACULATORY PRAYER.

"*Pray without ceasing.*"—1 THESS. v. 17.

THE Apostle bids us "pray without ceasing." Yet of our Blessed Lord, the great model, as of every other virtue, so also of Prayer, it is expressly said by the Evangelist St. Luke that, "as He was praying in a certain place, *He ceased.*" The precept and the Example are capable of an easy reconciliation. When it is said that Christ ceased from prayer, it is meant that He ceased from stated prayer, from prayer offered probably upon His knees. When St. Paul exhorts us to "pray without ceasing," he means that we should maintain unbroken the soul's communion with God.

Prayer is to be regarded not only as a distinct exercise of Religion, for which its own time must be set apart, but as a process woven into the texture of the Christian's mind, and extending through the length and breadth of his life. Like the golden thread in a tissue, it frequently disappears beneath the common threads. It disappears, and is hidden from the eye; yet nevertheless, it is substantially there, like a stream running underground for a certain period of its course. Suddenly, the thread emerges into sight again on the upper surface of the tissue, and suddenly again disappears; and thus it penetrates the whole texture, although occasionally hidden. This is a very just illustration of the matter in hand. Look from without upon the Christian's life, and you will see divers occupations and employments, many of which, it may be, call for the exercise of his mind. But beneath the mind's surface there is an undercurrent, a golden thread of Prayer, always there, though often latent, and frequently rising up to view not only in stated acts of worship, but in holy ejaculations. We are now passing from the consideration of the devotional life of the Christian to that of his practical life, and we make Ejaculatory Prayer the bridge to the latter part of our great subject, because it is the exercise by which business and devotion are interlaced one with another.

Prayer has been truly called the Christian's breath of life. The image applies to Prayer in that broad sense of the word in which the Apostle bids us pray without ceasing, and we cannot gain a better insight into the meaning of the precept, than by developing it a little.

Let us consider, then, the process of natural life. It is carried on by an unintermitted series of inhalations and exhalations. The air is drawn inwards first, and fills the lungs, and then thrown out again, that fresh may be taken in.

Similarly, Mental Prayer consists of two processes; recollecting or gathering up the mind, and breathing it out towards God. The first is to enter into the closet of the heart, and shut the door upon all but God. The second is to pray to our Father, which is in secret.

1. To recollect or gather up the mind, is to summon it in from its wanderings (as a shepherd drives home to the fold a stray sheep), and to place it consciously in God's Presence. God, though present every where, has His special residence, as being a pure Spirit, in our

minds. "In Him we live, and move, and have our being." He is somewhere in the recesses of the soul, in the springs of our existence, in that mysterious, dark, cavernous region of our nature, where the wishes, feelings, thoughts, emotions, take their earliest rise. I say, it is a dark region this spirit of ours, or rather this depth of our spirit; even as the Holy of Holies, the heart of the Temple, was perfectly dark, and not lighted by a single window. Yet was there the majesty of the Divine Presence in that small dark chamber, between the outspread wings of the Cherubim. And, similarly, the mind is a sanctuary, in the centre of which the Lord sits enthroned, the lamp of the consciousness burning before Him. All this is the case with our minds, whether we turn our thoughts to it or not. That we *should* turn our thoughts to it,—that the mind should ever and anon, both amid business and recreation, be called home for a second or two to the Presence of God dwelling in its dark recesses; this is the meaning of recollectedness of spirit. In days of hard and drudging work, in days of boisterous merriment, in days of excitement and anticipation, it is wonderfully refreshing thus to recollect the mind, and place it consciously under the eye of the Divine Majesty. It is like a breath of sweet air coming across us in a foul and crowded alley; or a strain of sweet music stealing up to our window, amid the din and discord of a populous city. Pleasant it is upon the mountains to hear the horn blow, as a signal to the lowing and bleating cattle to withdraw from pasture, and be safely folded for the night. We associate repose and security with that strange wild blare of the rudely manufactured trumpet; and the association is most fascinating. And when the Good Shepherd, by the inward whispers of His Voice, calls us to come back from the wanderings of our thoughts and the excitements of our passions, into our own spirits, there to be alone with God, and consciously under His eye, can there fail of being repose and a halcyon calm in *that* call?

2. The second process in the maintenance of animal

life is *exhalation;* the throwing out of the breath which has been inhaled.

This corresponds in nature to what divines have called *Ejaculatory Prayer* in the spiritual world. Ejaculatory Prayer is Prayer darted up from the heart to God, not at stated intervals, but in the course of our daily occupations and amusements. The word "ejaculatory" is derived from the Latin word for a dart or arrow, and there is an idea in it which one would be loath indeed to forfeit. Imagine an English archer, strolling through a forest in the old times of Crecy and Agincourt, when the yeomen of this island were trained to deliver their arrows with the same unfailing precision as "a left-handed Gibeonite" discharging a stone bullet from his sling. A bird rises in the brushwood under his feet, a bird of gorgeous plumage or savoury flesh. He takes an arrow from his quiver, draws his bow to its full stretch, and sends the shaft after the bird with the speed of lightning. Scarcely an instant elapses before his prey is at his feet. It has been struck with unerring aim in the critical part, and drops on the instant. Very similar in the spiritual world is the force of what is called Ejaculatory Prayer. The Christian catches suddenly a glimpse of some blessing, deliverance, relief, a longing after which is induced by the circumstances into which he is thrown. Presently it shall be his. As the archer first draws the bow in towards himself, so the Christian retires, by a momentary act of recollection, into his own mind, and there realizes the Presence of God. Then he launches one short, fervent petition into the ear of that Awful Presence, throwing his whole soul into the request. And, lo, it is done! The blessing descends, prosecuted, overtaken, pierced, fetched down from the vault of Heaven by the winged arrow of Prayer. Do you require Scriptural proof that such immediate answers are occasionally vouchsafed, even as regards mere earthly blessings, to "the effectual fervent prayer of a righteous man?" The proof is ready to our hand. Nehemiah, the cup-bearer, stood with a sad countenance before Artaxerxes the king. The king seemed offended by his sadness, unexplained as it was by any cause with which the king could sympathize. Nehemiah knew what Solomon had written long ago, that "the king's wrath is as the roaring of a lion,"—that to offend an oriental despot is all one with having the scimitar suspended over one's head, or the bowstring slung around one's neck. So "he was very sore afraid." The king asked him expressly what would content him. This made the case worse, for Nehemiah had a large request to make, which might seem to the king extravagant and presumptuous. The cup-bearer was in a great strait. What did he do? He entered into the closet of his heart, and shut his door, and prayed to his Father which was in secret. "I prayed," says he, "to the God of heaven." To offer prayer under such circumstances evinces command of mind. Not many seconds can elapse between a question in conversation and the answer to it; and when one feels that every thing is suspended on the success of the answer, anxiety and excitement would combine to prevent the offering of prayer in that brief interval. But Nehemiah had disciplined his mind to watch and pray, and he made the most of the interval, such as it was. It is hardly conceivable that he can have said more mentally than "Lord, help me according to my need;" but then he said it with such a fervour of heart, and such an entire faith that God *would* help him, that it was as successful as if he had spent a whole night in prayer. He candidly explained his wishes, in answer to the king; and down came the blessing immediately. The king's cloudy brow cleared all of a sudden, like a storm in an April day. He took the request very graciously, and the all-important crisis for Nehemiah, and for the city of his fathers, passed off well. "So it pleased the king to send me." One short act of the mind, one strong shaft of Prayer, had won the restoration of the Holy City, the joy of the whole earth.

But Ejaculatory Prayer is to be used not simply in difficulties, and when our affairs are in a critical posture, though such circumstances most especially call for it, but from time to time, all along the course of the day. But here some difficulty will be felt by those who strive to adopt the practice.

When the mind is under the pressure of anxiety or alarm, then, of course, there is a ready supply of materials for our petitions, and the only difficulty is the attainment of sufficient presence of mind to offer them. The compilers of our Liturgy, as feeling, I suppose, that in extraordinary emergencies this presence of mind soon deserts ordinary men, and that in such a case forms might steady the mind, and help it forward in the direction in which it wished to travel, have supplied in the " Forms of Prayer to be used at Sea," certain ejaculations for individuals, under the circumstances of a sea-fight or a storm, which, like all other parts of the Liturgy, are simple and appropriate, and which should be mentioned here, because they form our Church's testimony to the value and importance of Ejaculatory Prayer; but in common and uneventful life the mind will often experience a want of topics for this sort of prayer, and without a store of such topics it will be barren, and feel no spontaneity or freedom in the exercise. A passage of Scripture, selected from our morning's reading, or some one event in the history of Our Lord, particularly in the history of His passion, may often prove serviceable in supplying this need. On turning over at leisure moments the incident or the passage in our minds, the fire will kindle, and we shall speak, if not with our tongues, yet with our hearts, to God. One great master of devotion recommends us, after our morning meditation, to select some one thought which has most pleased and interested us, and to carry it away with us for our spiritual refreshment in the intervals of business; " as a man," he says, " does not quit a pleasant garden, until he has gathered a nosegay, with the scent of which he may refresh himself during the day." It should be added that the great repertory for ejaculations, to which every servant of God has resorted for ages, sure to find something there congenial to his wants, and coming home with peculiar power to his heart, is the Psalter, or Book of Psalms. Those who are ambitious of leading the devout life should have a large portion of the Psalms at the disposal of their memory.

It may be asked, in conclusion, whether, if constant mental Prayer be faithfully maintained, stated Prayer might not be altogether dispensed with. Looking at our great Exemplar, we answer somewhat positively, No. Our Blessed Lord's human soul breathed the atmosphere of habitual Prayer. He prayed without ceasing, in the length and breadth of that precept. Yet did He not dispense with stated seasons of Prayer. Dispense with them! He continued one whole night in prayer to God. Though His human heart was with God through all the busiest day, yet at the close of that day, when He had dismissed the multitudes, He retired to the mountain-summit to engage in solitary stated prayer, afar from the hum of men and the turmoils of the earth. What does such an example prove, but that we may not exonerate ourselves from direct acts of worship, on the plea that both mind and heart have been seeking God all day long? We have said, indeed, and say again, that Prayer is the act of spiritual respiration;—that true Prayer can no more be limited to certain hours, than respiration can. Yet even the image itself does not warrant us in thinking lightly of the virtue of stated Prayer. It is true, indeed, that life can be supported even in the populous market, in the crowded street, nay, in the worst ventilated alleys, so long as respiration continues; but what a source of health and strength would the poor overwrought artisan find, if he could resort now and then to the transparent air of the open country, undefiled by smoke, to the purple-heathered down, where sweet gales fan the cheek, or to the margin of the ocean, over whose surface careers the invigorating wind! In spots like these we not only breathe, but breathe easily, freely, and spontaneously; the mere process of animal life is a delight to us, and with every breath we drink in health. Such is the effect of an hour of stated Prayer after a day busily, yet devoutly spent. That hour wonderfully recruits the energies of the soul which human infirmity has caused to flag; and if we cannot say with truth, that such an hour is absolutely necessary to spiritual *existence*, yet we can say that it is absolutely necessary to spiritual *health and well-being*.

In concluding the second part of our Thoughts on Personal Religion, which has been occupied with the devotional exercises of the Christian, we venture to express the hope that there has been a real endeavour on the part of some at least of our readers to turn these counsels into practice. We set out with the observation that modern preaching addresses itself almost exclusively to stimulate the conscience, and overlooks the humbler but equally necessary work of guiding it,—so that the quiet edification of well-disposed Christians, the bringing them on to the measure of the stature of the fulness of Christ, is often sacrificed to the conversion of evil livers. In these pages we have been attempting (in a humble way) a movement in the opposite direction. It is plain, however, that the movement must fail, unless the readers co-operate with the writer, not so much by passively submitting themselves to impressions, as by active concurrence with his advice. It has been our purpose, and we hope we have made it apparent that it is our purpose, not so much to give thoughts which may arouse, as to make recommendations which may be tried. My reader, have you tried them? And if so, are you already, it may be, dispirited by a sense of failure? Take courage, in the name of Jesus Christ, and once again assault the great task of spirituality of mind. Was any solid and grand attainment ever yet made without repeated failures? Did ever any one climb to the pinnacle of human ambition without repeated checks, and hindrances, and disappointments, and manifold changes of worldly tactics? And is it to be imagined that a man can climb the Jacob's ladder of sanctity, whereupon angels are continually passing one another on Divine errands, adding "to his faith virtue, and to virtue knowledge, and to knowledge temperance, and to temperance patience, and to patience godliness, and to godliness brotherly kindness, and to brotherly kindness charity," without a resolute energy of will, and a buoyancy of spirit which is determined to succeed? For what other purpose was the Saviour's Blood shed, and the Saviour's Grace poured forth, but to create such an energy? Forward, then, warriors of the Cross, in the courage which is ministered by that Blood and that Grace. Where the will is stedfast, and the heart is whole with God, ground is gained unconsciously to ourselves. This one thing do, "forgetting those things which are behind, and reaching forth unto those things which are before, press toward the mark for the prize of the high calling of God in Christ Jesus." And be your motto that of Gideon's wearied but undaunted troop,—"FAINT, YET PURSUING."

PART III.

THE PRACTICAL LIFE.

CHAPTER I.

WHAT HOLDS US BACK.

"*Work out your own salvation with fear and trembling. For it is God which worketh in you both to will and to do of His good pleasure.*"—PHIL. ii. 12, 13.

THE present little Treatise, upon the third part of which we are now about to enter, is occupied with giving certain practical directions to those who, not content with passively receiving religious impressions, desire to grow in grace and in the knowledge of our Lord and Saviour Jesus Christ. We are making an extended comment upon that exhortation of St. Peter: "And beside this," (beside that purifying faith in God's "exceeding great and precious promises," which lies at the root of all true religion,) "giving all diligence, add to your faith virtue; and to virtue knowledge; and to knowledge temperance; and to temperance patience; and to patience godliness; and to godliness brotherly kindness; and to brotherly kindness charity."

Anxious for the success of what is being said, and knowing that this success is entirely of a practical and experimental character, we feel disposed at intervals to turn round to our readers, and ask of them how they are progressing? And if the answer should be, as in some cases doubtless it will be, that they are making no sensible progress at all, and that their efforts in the pursuit of holiness are continually baffled, and meet with disappointment, we wish to take that confession as a symptom,—if the trial has had a fair space of time allotted to it,—that something is wrong with them, and to stop on our journey, and ask what that wrong thing is.

Let this Chapter then be devoted to the inquiry, What is it which often holds back those, who appear to be earnest in "working out their own salvation?" And may God throw upon our minds that inward light which alone can expose the error to our consciences, and bring us into the path of truth.

Now the celebrated passage to the Philippians, to which I have just referred, contains in itself the detection and exposure of the error. "Work out your own salvation," writes the Apostle, "with fear and trembling;" intimating most assuredly, whatever Calvin may say to the contrary, that the human will has a certain part to play in the matter of salvation, and that it must be played with all earnestness, yea, even with an agonizing earnestness, "with fear and trembling;" but then he immediately subjoins, "*for* it is God that worketh in you," intimating most assuredly, whatever Arminius may say to the contrary, that we cannot ourselves work in ourselves, or produce from ourselves, a single one of the dispositions that constitute holiness,—that the origin, progress, and maturity of those dispositions is all of free grace, just as entirely as the forgiveness of sins is. It is, then, on this ground we will look for our error, if so be we may find it. It is more than likely, if we are hanging back in the Christian course, either that we are not surrendering our wills honestly and unreservedly to God, to be and to do as He bids us, and virtually saying, "I will not work at all, because it is God that worketh in me;" or, secondly, that, from a mistake as to the nature of sanctification, we are really looking to our own miserable efforts to sanctify us—putting a round of ordinances, and duties, and performances, into the place of the Lord Jesus, and virtually saying, " It is I who work in myself, both to will and to do of God's good pleasure."

By way of illustrating these contrary errors more clearly, let us imagine the case of a patient placed under a physician of most eminent skill, who has closely studied similar cases, and heretofore infallibly restored them by his treatment,—making no progress. Recovery seems to be on the whole as far off as when he first consulted the physician; and even if one day there seems to be a little improvement, the next day the hopes, to which that improvement gave rise, are thrown back; if symptoms are somewhat repressed, there is every reason to believe that the malady is still there. Now, supposing the physician's skill to be abundantly competent to a radical cure, it is evident that the non-recovery must spring from the patient's never having fairly surrendered himself into the physician's hands. And this want of an entire surrender may take one of two forms. Either the patient may not implicitly follow the physician's orders ; or, not having a full trust in him, and being persuaded of the efficacy of certain other systems of medicine, he may be giving those systems a trial side by side with the course which physicians prescribe, and thereby nullifying the efficacy of that course. The not following the physician's prescriptions, or the following his own theories as well, both may equally defeat his recovery.

Another illustration, which, from the nature of it, is even clearer still.—What are the conditions, which alone could frustrate the progress upon a river of a strong man and an expert rower, placed in a good and swift boat, and furnished with oars? Such an one might either not use the oars at all, or use only one of them. And the result in each case would be practically much the same. In both cases the boat would drift with the stream; and the only difference would be, that, when one oar was vigorously applied, the boat, in addition to drifting, would move round and round in a circle, and might perhaps for a while mock the rower by the semblance of progress. In spiritual things there are those who are utterly careless and godless—dead alike to the claims of Religion, and to its hopes. These are they who, launched upon the stream of life, quietly drift down it, giving no thought to the life which is to come after, and seeking only to gather the few perishable flowers which grow upon the brink. And, among persons of more serious mind, there are those, who are willing indeed that Christ should do all for them, but have never surrendered themselves to Him to be and do all that He requires. And there are those, on the other hand, who have surrendered the will to Christ, and are making efforts to obey Him; but because they perceive not this simple truth, that they cannot sanctify themselves,—that sanctification, from first to last, like justification, must be wrought for us by Him,—are constantly met by failures and disappointments, which a simple trust in Him to do all for them can alone remedy. Both these last are they who are rowing with one oar, moving indeed, but moving in a circle, and coming round always to the same point from which they started,—deluding themselves for a while, by the very fact of their motion, with the idea that they are progressing, and often bitterly complaining, as soon as they are undeceived, that they are making no way. And finally there are those who are equally well contented to give all to Christ which they have to give, (that is, their will,) and to take all from Him which He has to give, sanctification, and wisdom, as well as righteousness,—who in one and the same act of faith have renounced both self-will and self-trust. These are they who are rowing with two oars, and so realizing a true progress towards that haven where they would be. Show me a man who is both giving to Christ all he has to give, that is, his will, and at the same time taking from Christ all Christ has to give, which is, a perfect salvation from sin's guilt, power, and conséquences; or, as the Apostle expresses it, "wisdom, and righteousness, and sanctification, and redemption;" and I will show you a man who is growing in grace, and advancing daily in meetness for the inheritance of the saints in light. And if we find ourselves not thus growing and advancing, and yet are certainly well-disposed persons of some seriousness of mind, it is, no doubt, that we are endeavouring to push the boat forward with only one of the oars, to reach that holiness without which no man shall see the Lord, with trust in Christ alone, or with self-surrender alone. Apply the other oar simultaneously, and the bark shall at once begin to cleave the water, as an arrow cleaves the air, straightforward.

What I have said reduces itself to two very simple axiomatic positions, practically, experimentally, and really consistent with one another, even if in this life we can never see their precise speculative adjustment.

1. We must give ourselves up to God, to be sanctified.

2. We can by no possibility,—by no efforts, strivings, prayers, penances, whatever,—sanctify ourselves.

1. *We must give ourselves up to God, to be sanctified.* Have we ever done this? Have we done it honestly, and without reserving a single corner of the heart? or are we keeping back part of the price of the land, like Ananias and Sapphira, and bringing only a certain part, and laying it down at the feet of our Heavenly Master, as if it were the whole? Ah! He sees through all disguises; and His eyes, which are as a flame of fire, immediately detect the insincerity of our souls. And the awful punishment will be, that He will not take us under His efficacious treatment, unless we submit ourselves to Him unreservedly; and unless the Divine Physician treats us for sin, we shall never recover of sin; and unless we recover of sin, unless the moral malady be stanched in us by the Blood and Grace of Christ,—salvation is for us out of the question. Indeed, salvation is mainly and essen-

tially from sin,—from sin itself in its guilt and power, —and only accidentally from sin's consequences.

Ah, how many are there who content themselves with lop-sided faith—trust without surrender! But the truth is, that a lop-sided faith is no faith at all. The disposition called faith embraces God's commands with obedience, as well as His promises with trust. Abraham is the great Scriptural pattern of faith; and Abraham's faith appears no less in his obeying than in his believing God. Where God's will takes the form of a precept, Abraham does it without a moment's hesitation; where it takes the form of a promise, he rests assured that there will be a fulfilment. God bids him leave his country and his kindred; he leaves them. God bids him slay his son; he would have slain his son, had not God interposed. God tells him that his seed should be as the stars of heaven, when not only had he no child, but when it was contrary to the course of nature that he should be blest with offspring; and Abraham rests assured that it will be as God says. God tells him that in Isaac shall his seed be called, and Abraham believes it, even when called to offer up Isaac, accounting (oh! grand reach of faith, under that very twilight dispensation!) that God was able to raise him up even from the dead. That is the whole-heartedness both towards precept and promise, which God so much approves, and which is called Faith. Is there, then, aught which keeps us from an unreserved putting ourselves at Christ's disposal? Is it the fear of ridicule or contempt from an irreligious circle? the fear of being accounted over-strict, methodistical, puritanical, or what not? Is the love of any sin so strong in us that we cannot fairly put ourselves in Christ's hands for treatment, saying, "Here am I, Lord, to do as regards this sin whatsoever by Thy Spirit in my conscience Thou shalt suggest?" Is the surrender of our substance a hard saying to us, as to the rich young man in the Gospel? While we are willing to do many things for Christ, and hear sermons gladly, are we strongly disinclined to relinquish our grasp upon that proportion of our income, to which an enlightened conscience tells us that Christ has a fair claim? Is indolence mingled with cowardice an obstacle to effort, as of old in the wilderness, when the people cried, "The cities are great, and walled up to heaven; and, moreover, we have seen the sons of the Anakims there?" Are we willing to have religious impressions made upon us, but not willing to gird up our loins for an earnest wrestling-match with the powers of darkness, not willing to apply our shoulders to the wheel and move it out of the old cart-rut of bad habits? Probe your consciences with these and similar questions. To surrender himself from the very ground of his heart to sanctification, is all that man can do in the matter. Have you ever done it?

2ndly, We entreat you to take with you through this whole treatise, this other axiomatic and fundamental truth, *that man can by no possibility sanctify himself*.

We devoted a Chapter to this subject (Chap. III. Part I.) in the Introductory Part of this work; but it is of such transcendent importance, and, in the active pursuit of Holiness, so liable to be dropped out of mind, that the reader must excuse us, if we here briefly recapitulate the argument of that Chapter. It was there observed that men recognize, indeed, the *Atonement* as being exclusively Christ's work, and the Forgiveness of sins as His procuring and His free gift; but they entertain a notion that, after forgiveness, they are to go and work out sanctification for themselves independently of Christ's working in them, and, in the ground of their heart, look to be sanctified by their prayers, and their communions, and their watchfulness, and their self-discipline, and their self-denials, and their cultivation of good habits, which is just as great an error as looking to be justified by these things. In short they have never understood the force of those words; "Christ Jesus of God is made unto us not righteousness only, but sanctification." We are justified or forgiven simply by throwing ourselves upon

Christ for forgiveness, renouncing all merit in ourselves, and looking to His Agony and Bloody Sweat, His Cross and Passion. And in exactly the same way we are sanctified by simple dependence upon Christ to work in us by the Spirit every grace we need, by abandoning the treatment of ourselves for sin, and looking to the good Physician out of His fulness to supply such remedies and such virtues as will effectually make us whole. It is most true indeed that heartfelt surrender of our wills to the will of God involves human effort in every shape which effort can Scripturally take; but it is equally true that human effort is no Saviour, and true also that the Saviour will not give to it, or have us give to it, that honour which is exclusively His. Blessed things are Prayer, and Sacraments, and watchfulness, and rules of life, and self-discipline, and self-denial, when they occupy their right place in the spiritual system, as means, channels, and instruments; but if they be unduly magnified, so as to cover the whole field of view; if we for a moment allow our minds to regard them as sources of Grace, and trust to them to work in us sanctity, we shall be as utterly disappointed in them, as the poor woman who had the issue of blood was with the many physicians, from whom she had suffered many things, but never brought away a cure. Mark me, reader, our sanctification is in Christ, not independent of Him, and therefore not to be had independently. Touch His sacred Person in simple faith that in Him doth all fulness dwell,—fulness of light and love, of holy tempers, holy impulses, and of all the fruits of the Spirit,—and the virtue which is in Him shall instantly begin to flow, through the channel which faith has opened, into your soul. This is His own teaching, not ours, " Abide in Me, and I in you. As the branch cannot bear fruit of itself, except it abide in the vine; no more can ye, except ye abide in Me. I am the vine, ye are the branches: he that abideth in Me, and I in him, the same bringeth forth much fruit: for without Me" (separated from Me) "ye can do nothing." "Ye can do nothing,"—not advance a step in love, joy, or peace, or in any grace which qualifies for Heaven. The righteousness of sanctification is technically said by divines to be inherent in us; and the term is useful, as serving to draw a distinction between this and the righteousness of justification, which is imputed, and outside of us,—laid to our account, without being in any sense ours; but we must not so understand the phrase as if righteousness were inherent in us independently or apart from Christ. The sap circulates through the living branch of the vine, but not independently or apart from the root and stock of the tree. Separated from the tree, the branch has no life whatever, and is unable to put forth a single bud or blossom. The sap *in* the branch is not *from* or *of* the branch, it is only derivative,—drawn from the living energies of the root and stem. And so the Christian's holiness; it is never held independently, but derived from the fountain-head of holiness, and that fountain-head is Christ. And what we have to do is to keep open continually the communication between Christ and the soul, by repeated exercises of the same simple faith (or trust) in Him, which at first was the instrument of our justification. We stretched forth the hand of faith, and received out of Christ the forgiveness which He purchased for us; we must stretch it forth again, and again, and again, to receive that meetness for glory which He gradually imparts. Without holding this fundamental truth before our eyes, without the most entire trust in Christ to work in us every grace of the Christian character, and the utter renunciation of trust in ourselves, all our efforts in the pursuit of holiness will be only an unblessed toiling and moiling, —so much work, and worry, and fruitless striving, without any appreciable result. Has your error lain in this quarter? It is so with many really devoted people, who have a character for knowledge in the things of God. Many are the followers after holiness, the secret of whose failure is all wrapped up in those few words of the Apostle, " Not holding the Head," and who need to be taken back to the first rudiments of religious knowledge, and told by the Catechist, " My good child, know this, that *thou art not able* to do these things *of thyself*, nor to walk in the commandments of God, and to serve Him, without *His special grace.*"

We cannot bring this Chapter to a close without pointing to the confirmation which the doctrine of it derives from the Baptismal Covenant.

Observe, then, that Baptism is a covenant, in which there are two contracting parties, God and the Catechumen, both pledging themselves to certain conditions, and both having a certain part of their own to perform. This is very forcibly brought out by our Formularies, both for the Baptism of Infants, and of Adults. In the first place, on the part of the Catechumen, there is self-dedication, implying complete surrender of the will, nay, of the man's whole self to God. He renounces (i. e. declares war against) all sin, from whatsoever avenue it may make its assault; he avows implicit belief, of all God says, and he puts himself entirely at God's bidding, to " keep His holy will and commandments, and walk in the same all the days of his life." It is very important to remark, that it is not simply belief, but also *a preparedness of the will*, which he, if an adult, in his own person, if an infant, by his sureties, is required to profess. The terms are by no means to be construed as a promise that he will never sin, which would be a rash and unwarrantable vow indeed ; but are exactly equivalent to an act of self-surrender, and might scripturally be represented thus : " I present my body (this body, on which the seal of Holy Baptism is now to be impressed) a living sacrifice, holy, acceptable to God, which is my reasonable service." It is the Christian offering himself as a victim at God's altar, " Lo, I come to do Thy will, O God !"

But is that the whole of Baptism? By no means, nor even the chief part of it. The victim must not only be presented, but fire must fall from Heaven upon it: there is God's part as well as man's part to be considered. There is a gift to be bestowed, as well as a vow to be made, and the candidate himself cannot possibly do God's part; it must be done for him, and upon him. No man ever heard of a person's baptizing himself; that would be indeed an absurd impossibility: he may dedicate himself to God by an act of self-surrender, which some suppose to be the whole of Baptism, but to be born of water and of the Spirit, "to be received into Christ's holy Church, and be made a lively member of the same," this is far above—out of his reach. The Church of his day, or rather Christ acting through the Church, confers upon him Baptism, with its grace and its gift, howsoever that gift may be defined. If he is an infant at the time of receiving it, as we all were, and Baptism is to be of the smallest avail to him ultimately, he must realize his Baptism experimentally, and that as to both parts of the contract: he must now by his own act and deed surrender himself utterly and unreservedly to God, which is the teaching of Confirmation, although thousands of confirmed persons have never done it; and for his sanctification, his growth in grace, his spiritual fruitfulness, his interior qualifications for glory, he must look to Christ and Christ alone, in whom by the Father's appointment "all fulness dwells," using diligently the means, of course, because Christ enjoins them, but not putting the means in Christ's place. If he will not dedicate himself, the Lord will not send down the fiery Baptism of the Holy Ghost upon him: if he will dedicate himself, and will expect from the act of dedication the gift of the Holy Ghost, he will find himself bitterly disappointed; but if he will both dedicate himself, and at the same time look to Christ's fulness for the progressive work of sanctification, as well as for the completed work of justification, then of Christ's fulness shall that man receive, and "grace for grace." Holding the Head, he shall have nourishment ministered through the joints and bands of the appointed means, and increase with the increase of God.

CHAPTER II.

DO ALL FOR GOD.

"And whatsoever ye do, do it heartily, as to the Lord, and not unto men."—COL. iii. 23.

THE practical life of the Christian, upon the consideration of which we enter in this Chapter, comprehends three distinct elements, on each of which distinct recommendations are needed, working, fighting, and suffering. We have to do the will of God in our business; this is working. We have to oppose our bosom sin and to resist temptation; this is fighting. We have, finally, to endure with cheerfulness and submission whatever cross the Lord Jesus pleases to lay upon us; this is suffering. And to be right in the practical department of the Christian life is summed up in these three things, to work devoutly, to fight manfully, and to suffer patiently.

Our present subject is, then, how we may work devoutly.

When we remember that our destiny, as immortal beings, is to live with Our Lord, and with glorified saints, and holy angels for ever; and that, in consequence, any work which does not fit us for this society must be a great impertinence, and counteract the main end of our existence, it is at first sight a very alarming and distressing thought that the great bulk of the things which most men do daily, are of the earth, earthy. For example, how many pursuits and professions, in a commercial country like this, have reference to money,—that is to say, substituting the Scripture phraseology for our common parlance, to "the gold which perisheth" and to the "Mammon of unrighteousness." But is it not true of all pursuits, regular and irregular, with the exception only of devotion, that they are of the earth, earthy? Does it not hold good even of the pastoral work, so far as that work has reference to the sin and ignorance which is in fallen man? Must not every existing pursuit be incompatible with the heavenly state, for this simple reason, that every one of them has reference to an imperfect state of things, largely alloyed with sin, ignorance, and sorrow? All professions and trades are in fact remedial, destined to supply the defects of the existing order; and therefore, when that existing order is no more, and when the order which supersedes it proves to have no defects whatever, and excludes all sin, all ignorance, and all sorrow,—the various occupations of this life must necessarily come to an end, must die a natural death. And is there not something which *seems* inappropriate, to say the least of it, in the circumstance that one, who is called by Baptism to the kingdom and glory of Almighty God, should, during his short span of threescore years and ten, be either preparing for, or engaged in, work which has no reference to or bearing upon his Eternity, and which will be swept away for ever, like so much litter, when the Kingdom of Christ is finally and for ever set up?

This inconsistency between worldly pursuits and a heavenly calling has been deeply felt at all times by the human mind.

It was just this feeling which, among other deep-seated instincts of our nature, gave rise to Monasticism. In their speculations on the eternal future, men assumed (what certainly we have no right to assume, and what probably is false, judging from what we hear of the angels) that there will be in the heavenly state no occupation save that of Prayer and Praise. Then, knowing from God's Word that the life of Heaven ought to be begun, as indeed it ought, upon earth, they concluded that the religious life upon earth (the conventual life was always called "religious") consisted in a constant round of religious services, and directly spiritual employments. Hymns, and prayers, and good reading, and deep meditation were to be the business of the day; and all else, if any thing else were attempted, (as it often was in the way of almsgiving, and writing or illuminating manuscripts,) was to be a by-work. Let us not rail at their mistake. It is by no means so certain that we stand clear of it ourselves. Have we never thrown out words on the same false assumption, that a secular pursuit is an obstacle to a heavenly mind? What remark is more commonly heard in conversation, than that such a young man, being more seriously disposed than his brothers, is the one pointed out for the Church,—meaning the Ministry? And what does such a remark imply in the mind of the person making it, but this very feeling, that nothing but a sacred occupation sits suitably on a person who contemplates with seriousness the end for which he was created? And we have heard the feeling take more foolish and unguarded shapes than this. We have heard well-meant addresses at Missionary meetings, which,—from the undoubtedly true position that the work of a Missionary, as being nearest to that of an Apostle, is the highest upon earth,—really almost infer, or, at all events, leave upon the minds of the hearers the impression, that every one should abandon his present calling, and go forth to preach the Kingdom of God in the dark places of the earth.

As the pushing a false theory to its extreme point is one way of exhibiting its fallacy, let us for a moment suppose it to be God's will that all Christians should have a directly spiritual pursuit. The system of society must in that case be brought to a dead lock; for who knows not that the system is founded upon division of labour; and upon the very simple principle that one man shall produce what his neighbour wants, and take in exchange what his neighbour produces? The fair fabric of civilization is all built upon this principle, as its fundamental law. Take away the variety of vocations, reduce all callings to those of the monk, the priest, or the missionary, and you undermine civilization, or, in other words, society lapses again into barbarism. And this assuredly cannot be the will of Him, who has implanted in the human mind those instincts which develope themselves in civilization.

But if this cannot be the will of God, if common sense, without calling in the aid of Scripture, repudiates such an hypothesis, then it must be His will (for there is no alternative) that different men should follow different pursuits, according to the station in which they are born, the gifts they possess, the circumstances in which they find themselves. Bring it down to individual cases, and the truth still holds. It is still the will of God that this man should ply a humble craft; that this other should have the duties entailed by broad acres and large property; that a third should go to the desk, and sit behind a counter all his days; that a fourth should give his time to the restoration of sick patients; that a fifth should fight the battles of his country. Now if this is God's will in each individual case, no good, but the greatest harm, would ensue from an individual's infringing that will; from his thrusting himself out of his own vocation into one which seems to be higher and more dignified. Each man's wisdom and happiness must consist in doing, as well as his faculties will admit, the work which God sets him. So thought and so wrote (both thinking and writing by immediate Inspiration) the great Apostle of the Gentiles. He did not counsel his converts to join himself and St. Barnabas in their missionary tours; but while reminding them ever and anon that the great system of Society would ere long run down and come to an end,—ringing ever and anon the great funeral knell of the world, " the fashion of this world passeth away,"—he told them distinctly and emphatically that so long as the system still worked on, each one was to retain his position in it. " Let every man abide in the same calling, wherein he was called." "Brethren, let every man, wherein he is called, therein abide with God."

Ah! " with God." Those words wrap up the secret of which we are in search, the secret by which we may do God service in our daily business, and convert the most secular occupation, so long as it be an innocent one, into fine gold of the altar.

How then may we abide with God in the work of our calling? The answer (or rather that portion of it, for which alone we can find space in this Chapter) is, by throwing into the work an holy and pure intention.

It is clear that intention is to our actions what the soul is to the body; and that, just as it is the soul and not the body which makes us moral agents, so it is the motive or intention, with which a thing is done, which gives to the action a moral character. To kill a man in wrath, of malice prepense, is murder; but to kill him accidentally by an action which we could not possibly foresee would do him harm, and which we meant to benefit him (as where one might administer poison to his friend by mistake for medicine), is so far from being murder, that it is no sin at all. Again, a good and holy work, such as Prayer, becomes hypocrisy, if done in a false Pharisaical spirit, to have praise of men.

This point then being admitted,—that it is the intention which constitutes an action good or bad,—we proceed to remark that the great bulk of work done in this busy bustling life is not done with any intention whatever of complying with the Will, or furthering the Service of Almighty God. The many who run to and fro from morning to evening in the work of their calling think nothing of subserving His designs, and are even unconscious, in many cases, of the place which they hold in His system.

The intention of some persons in their work is simply to gain a livelihood by it. To render this livelihood more abundant and more independent, they rise up early, take rest late, and eat the bread of carefulness. A perfectly innocent motive; nay, in a merely moral and social point of view, a commendable one, but not a spiritual motive, such as glorifies the work and redeems it from earthliness.

Others, in a higher class of life, labour unremittingly with the view of winning eminence in their particular pursuit or profession. The effects of work done in this spirit, if it does not meet with the success which it seeks, are very sad to witness. That elasticity of mind which is the spring and nerve of duty, is gone from a disappointed man. He is a stranger to the bright cheerfulness of mind which characterizes the Christian, who knows that no one ever sought to please our Heavenly Master without succeeding and being overabundantly recompensed.

Others work merely from what is called energy of mind. They would be miserable if idle; and accordingly, wherever they are, they create occupations for themselves, if there are none to which they seem especially called. Indeed, to every one among us work is in a greater or less degree a necessity of nature. But that activity which results from a mere natural instinct has, of course, nothing of a spiritual character. Perhaps Pascal is right, though his thoughts on the subject are a little sombre and overstrained, when he tells us that this kind of activity is only a relief from the contemplation of self, which we are afraid to be alone with, from an instinctive feeling of discontent with it. As a debtor shuns looking into his accounts, so we shun looking into self, and for the same reason. Self and the accounts are both unsatisfactory, and in frightful disorder.

Again, the better class of men, in whose hearts a supernatural motive has not yet found place, work from the high and elevating motive of duty. This motive exalts the character to the very highest pitch to which a mere natural character can attain. "It is my work," says the man, "and I shall not shrink from it, however much of danger and hardship it may involve." It is a fine mind which so speaks; perhaps we may admit that the owner of such a mind is "not far from the kingdom of God;" but if the intention have no reference to God's appointment, God's Will and service, truth forbids us to say that it is a spiritual or supernatural mind. Cicero and Seneca might have worked from a sense of duty; but Cicero and Seneca knew nothing of the living and loving Lord, who appoints labourers to various parts of His vineyard, endows them with various talents, and rewards them according to their diligence in improving those talents. God must enter the mind, before our motives can be supernaturalized.

Finally, a great mass of human activity is really destitute of any intention at all, and so runs to waste in a spiritual point of view. Multitudes of men work mechanically and by the same instinct of routine which causes a horse to go round in a mill. They throw themselves into their pursuit in the morning, with about as much reflection and thought as the poor dumb animal, when he submits himself afresh to the harness, and thrusts his neck once again into the well-known collar. But man is surely made for something nobler than to work by mere force of habit. Look at him. What powerful and stormy affections, what lively intelligence, what strength of purpose and of moral choice, is latent in that human heart! God did not intend that creature for a piece of clockwork, to run down when it is wound up, without any consciousness of the design which it subserves. He must have meant man surely to act with foresight, with design, with purpose, with intelligence, with affections, even as He Himself works!

Such, then, are the views and motives with which the majority pursue their vocations. And now what is the true motive, the supernatural motive, which lifts up the humblest duties into a higher atmosphere, and refines away their earthliness, and glorifies them? " Whatsoever ye do, do it heartily, as to the Lord, and not unto men; knowing that of the Lord ye shall receive the reward of the inheritance: for ye serve the Lord Christ." It will be seen by consulting the context, that this precept, and the corresponding one in the Ephesians, have a primary reference to the duties of slaves. Now no duties can be imagined lower in the social scale than those of a slave in a heathen family,—a position in which many members of the early Christian community found themselves. The duties of the slave were bound upon him by the most galling necessity; if he neglected or evaded them, he did so at the risk of the lash, the brand, and the treadmill; yet the Apostle intimates that even these duties may be ennobled and sanctified by importing into them a Christian intention. Let the slave look behind and beyond his earthly master, to the gracious and glorious form of the Lord Jesus, who stands in the background, requiring service of him. Let him yield that service heartily, as to the Lord, and not unto men, and it shall be owned, blessed, accepted, rewarded. Now we cannot but think that there is a deep wisdom in this particular arrangement of the Word of God, by which a precept so universal in its character as that of the consecration of secular duties to the Lord, is connected in the first instance with the business of slaves. The *à fortiori* inference is so abundantly evident that, if the humble drudgery of a slave admits of such a consecration, much more does any nobler form of human business. No man after this can say, " My duties are so very commonplace, and so very petty, that they cannot have a religious dignity and value; or so bound upon me by necessity that there can be no spontaneity in rendering them." Your duty, whatever it be, is at least as noble intrinsically as that of the bond-servants of antiquity, whom their masters regarded merely as a species of live stock. And therefore, if the duties of those bond-servants admitted of being done heartily, as to the Lord, much more do yours. Then that you should strive so to do them, is our first practical counsel to you respecting your work. First, before you go forth to your daily task, establish your mind thoroughly in the truth, that all the lawful and necessary pursuits of the world are so many departments of God's great harvest-field, in which He has called Christians to go forth and labour for Him. Let us regard them all as, at least, if nothing more, wheels of the great world-system, whose revolutions are bringing on the Second Advent and Kingdom of Christ. Then, imagining yourself for a moment under no worldly obligation to pursue your particular calling, undertake it with the deliberate and conscious intention of furthering His Work and Will. Choose it with your whole will, as the path in which He would have you to follow Him, and the task to which He has called you. Consecrate it to Him by a few moments of secret prayer, imploring Him to take it up into the great scheme of His service, and to make it, all humble, weak, and sinful as it is, instrumental in furthering His designs. Then put your hand to it bravely, endeavouring to keep before the mind the aim of pleasing Him by diligence and zeal. Imagine Jesus examining your work, as He will do at the last day; and strive that there may be no flaw in it, that it may be thoroughly well executed both in its outer manner and inner spirit.

At the beginning and end of every considerable action, renew the holy intention of the morning.

As to the smaller duties of life,—the mint, anise, and cummin of God's Worship,—there should be an honest attempt to bring them too under the control of the ruling principle. The Scripture exempts *nothing* from the compass of God's Service:—" Whether therefore ye eat or drink, or whatsoever ye do, do all to the glory of God." " Whatsoever ye do, in word or in deed, do *all* in the name of the Lord Jesus." But a word or two of caution is here necessary for weak and scrupulous minds. The Scripture shows its divine perfection by setting up an ideal standard of duty, which was never yet actually reached except by the Lord Jesus Himself. God speaks in the Scripture; and God *must* require perfection,—cannot require any thing less or lower. Perfection, therefore, must be the aim of all, and this in small things as well as great. But eschew, as being particularly adverse to real progress, all little unworthy scrupulosities, such as would be counted absurd by strong common sense. If you are conscious in the main of an intention to serve God in all things, small and great, put foolish scruples and questions of casuistry out of court without an hearing. God will have the service which comes of a sound mind and a joyous heart; and nothing more impedes and impairs soundness of mind and joyousness of heart than petty scruples. The Devil is the author of scruples, both in the mind of the hypocrite and of the Christian. He allows them in the hypocrite, as the one thing having the semblance of religious duty, by which he compounds with him for laxity and licentiousness in the weightier matters of the law. He originates them in the Christian, as being a fertile source of down-heartedness, timidity, and despair. Now the best way to resist the Devil on all occasions is to turn a deaf ear to him. Let us make sure of consecrating to God by prayer, and a good intention, the more considerable duties of the day. Let us strive, at all periods, whether of work or refreshment, to realize His Presence, and the great end for which we are, or ought to be, living. We shall find by degrees that the main business of the day, if done with pure intention, will lead the smaller duties in tow, like long-boats following in the wake of a man-of-war.

For the rest, let us make a wise and holy use of the efficacy of Christ's Blood and Grace. That doctrine, if rightly and deeply received, will give the mind a spring of elasticity, of indomitable cheerfulness, courage, and hope. Nothing which we do will for a moment bear the scrutiny of Almighty God as a judge. Be it so; but Our Lord's Work *will* endure that scrutiny, and come triumphant out of the ordeal; and His Work is by faith ours, as entirely as if we were the doers of it. Our own efforts after sanctity are always breaking down and giving way under us. True; but in Him doth all fulness dwell; and out of that fulness will we look to receive grace for grace, so that more and more visibly, if only our wills be true to Him, the lineaments of His Blessed Image may be reproduced in us by the power of His Spirit.

CHAPTER III.

ON MAINTAINING THE CONSCIOUSNESS OF GOD'S PRESENCE IN THE WORKS OF OUR CALLING.

"The Lord appeared to Abram, and said unto him, I am the Almighty God; walk before Me, and be thou perfect."—GEN. xvii. 1.

IN a certain sense we all *must* walk before God, whether in solitude or among the haunts of men. "He is about our path, and about our bed, and spieth out all our ways." But it is open to us to realize His Presence, or to dismiss it from our minds. And it is the first of these courses which God counsels Abraham to adopt when He says, "Walk before Me, and be thou perfect." The words seem to imply that the realization of the Divine Presence in all things is the great secret of perfection; that is, of course, of such perfection (most imperfect at best) as man can by grace attain unto. Animal and vegetable life both form round a nucleus, or centre, which is at first a mere point or speck undiscernible except by the microscope, but which contains in it the germ of the animal or plant which is to be formed by expansion from it. And in some eminent servants of God the spiritual life has all formed itself from this one centre, developed itself from this one nucleus,—the realization of the Presence of God.

We are still engaged upon the question how the work of our calling may be done devoutly. The first part of the answer was given in the last Chapter: "Do all *for* God." The second part remains to be given: "Do all *in* God" by habitual mindfulness of His Presence.

It is an easy thing to see and to say that men should be mindful of God's Presence while engaged in their daily work. But it is not so easy to see how, with any of the higher forms of work, such advice can really be put in practice. The consideration of this point will serve to bring out in sharper relief the meaning of the precept.

The counsel, then, to be mindful of God's Presence in the midst of our daily secular occupations, might seem to be quite practicable for those who have to work merely with their hands. It might seem as if the peasant who turns up the soil with his spade, the lacewoman who plies her bobbins with busy finger, the boy set in the fields to scare the birds from the crops, could have no difficulty in turning the mind to the Presence of Almighty God, inasmuch as with them the mind has no other engagement. But all work which is not *purely* mechanical, (and even the pursuits I have named can scarcely be called mechanical altogether,) all work which involves attention,—much more all work which involves thought,—seems to preclude the realization of the Divine Presence at the moment of its being done. For the human mind is so constituted that it cannot be given to two subjects simultaneously, any more than the eye can be fixed upon two objects simultaneously. Where men are said to have the gift of attending to two matters at once, this is only a figure of speech, indicating the power of rapid transition from one matter to another. It would seem then that, while engaged in any work which asks for an exercise of mind,—reading, or writing, or computing, or conversing, as the case may be,—men *cannot* think of God's Presence, and that therefore it would be unreal to exhort them to do so.

Before answering this objection, let me call attention (and, as we are giving counsels upon work, it will not be wandering from the point to do so) to the element of truth and reason which there is in it. It is a moral lesson, which quite deserves the rank of a spiritual counsel, that undivided attention to one thing at a time is necessary to do any work well. Such attention is at once a duty to the work, and a duty to the mind engaged in the work. Exclude for the time all thought of other matters, as carefully as if they did not exist. If other business presses, there is no help for it,—it must wait till the first is transacted. Where persons are heavily engaged, there is a certain feverish fidgetiness to take up several tasks at once, which greatly interferes with quietness and thoughtfulness of mind, and so with progress. Let the aim of such persons be to do the thing well, rather than to get through it fast. A saint of old inculcated this precept very well, though very quaintly, when he said that "Christians often need to be reminded that with only one pair of hands they cannot thread two needles at the same time." And a wiser man than he, speaking as the organ of the Spirit of God, said, "Whatsoever thy hand findeth to do, do it with thy might."

But in answer to the objection respecting the impossibility of realizing the Divine Presence, while engaged in any work which calls for mental effort, it is to be observed that what we recommend, and what is surely attainable, is the mere consciousness that God's eye is upon us.

That this consciousness need not interfere with the most active exercise of the powers of the mind, is clear from the following consideration:—

A man's mind is never more actively engaged than when he is making an extempore address. Under such circumstances he must think, remember, judge, imagine, institute comparisons, all within the space of time allotted to his speech; and all not in a disjointed aimless way, but with the view of proving one point and persuading to one conclusion: thought, memory, judgment, imagination, comparison, must all be gathered (if the speech is to be an effective one) like so many rays of the sun into one burning-glass, and made to concentrate their forces on a single point. Probably there is no exercise in the world which so calls out the whole mind simultaneously as that of extempore speech.

Yet, what speaker for a moment forgets, or can forget, that the eyes of his audience are upon him? It is just their intense consciousness of the human presence, of its reality, and of the impossibility of escaping from it, that makes the speaking with many able men so difficult a thing. They might express themselves fluently enough in solitude, but in public their consciousness of the human presence is too much for the mind, paralyzes it for the time being. He who proposes to become a speaker must acquire the habit of so holding under this consciousness, as that free play may be allowed to the exercise of the mind. Of holding it under, I say,—for it is impossible that any speaker should ever entirely suppress it. So far from suppressing it, most men, when speaking, are unusually sensitive of impressions from the upturned countenances which are fixed upon them. The feelings of the audience communicate themselves to the mind of the person addressing them by a curious, almost electric, sympathy: if their features evince interest, he takes heart and goes on swimmingly; if their attention flags, he is discouraged; if they seem perplexed, he feels that he must somewhat expand his matter, and explain himself; if they are very animated, and have fairly embarked with him on the full current of his argument, he feels that he is master of their minds, and can sway them to and fro, as the wind sways the trees of the wood. But any how, consciousness of their presence forms, if I may so say, the very groundwork of his mind.

It is abundantly clear, then, that consciousness of *a* presence need not interfere with the most active operations of mind. And if consciousness of the presence of man need not do so, why need consciousness of the Presence of God? All that the precept, "Walk before Me, and be thou perfect," implies is, that we should acquire and maintain such a consciousness. But how is this done? Our senses give us assurance of the human presence, and the senses are in all of us sufficiently keen and alive. But how shall we obtain an habitual assurance of a truth whereof our senses give us no notice whatever?—how shall we walk before God, as seeing Him who is invisible? In the same way by which all other results in the spiritual life are obtained,—by trustful, expectant, sanguine prayer, and effort. It is obvious that this very grace—mindfulness or consciousness of God's Presence—may be made the subject of special Prayer, an answer to which, as in the case of every spiritual blessing which we petition for, should be looked for with confidence, on the ground of God's promise to Prayer. But then there is, besides this, the doing what in us lies to attain the end. And what in us lies is this,—to call the attention definitely to God's Presence, as occasion offers, at the necessary breaks or periods in our work, and the occasional mingling with the act of recollection two or three words of secret prayer, which may suggest themselves on the moment; such as, "Thou, God, seest me,"— "Have I also here looked after Him that seeth me?" —"Thou art about my path" (in the daytime), "and about my bed" (in the silent watches of the night).

The conception of God's Presence will take different shapes in different minds. We may regard Him as locally present every where, the veil of matter screening Him from our view, just as a king might really be moving up and down in the midst of a company of blind persons; or we may regard Him as having a certain intimate connexion with our own minds, as upholding momentarily in us the powers of life and thought, according to that word of St. Paul's, "In Him we live, and move, and have our being;" or lastly, we may think of Our Lord in human form looking down upon our probation from the Heavenly Throne, just as He appeared at the martyrdom of St. Stephen. All other modes of viewing the subject resolve themselves into the primary ones, in which, as you will see, there is a reference to the three Persons of the Blessed Trinity. Even the most earnest work would not be materially impeded, and certainly it would be done in a brighter and happier, as well as a holier state of mind, if these little efforts of attention were made during its progress. And it will be found, in course of time, that the constant recurrence of the thoughts to God will pass into an instinctive consciousness of His Presence, and that the mind will acquire a tendency to gravitate towards Him at all times, which will operate easily and naturally as soon as it is relieved of the strain which worldly affairs put upon it. An excellent writer on devotion, whom we have quoted previously, speaking on the topic of secular affairs, and showing how they must be despatched with earnestness, and yet without solicitude, says,—" Do as little children do, who with one hand hold fast by their father, and with the other gather hips and haws or blackberries along the hedges; so you, gathering and managing with one hand the things of this world, must with the other always hold fast the hand of your Heavenly Father, turning yourself towards Him from time to time, to see if your actions or occupations be pleasing to Him; but above all things take heed that you never let go His protecting hand, thinking to gather more; for should He forsake you, you will not be able to go a step without falling to the ground. My meaning is, that amidst those ordinary affairs which require not so earnest an attention, you should look more on God than on them; and when they are of such importance as to require your whole attention, that then also you should look from time to time towards God, like mariners of the olden time, who, to arrive at the port to which they were bound, looked more up towards heaven than down on the sea on which they sailed: thus will God work with you, in you, and for you; and all your labours shall be accompanied with consolations."

In cultivating the consciousness of the Divine Presence, we shall find it useful to catch at every help which our circumstances afford. Let us just glance at some of these circumstances, and at the account to which they may be turned.

It is not hard to see how a rural walk, even through the plainest country, may suggest devout musings. As we mark the sprouting leaf, or blossoming flower, we may call to mind that God is silently, but powerfully putting forth His activities in our immediate neighbourhood; as we brush by the hedge, and make the little bird dart up from it in the palpitation of sudden fear, we are on the field of His operations. Why, when standing upon such ground, are we impressed so slightly with awe of His power and His skill? Mechanism of human contrivance generally strikes awe into the mind of the unsophisticated beholder. In the great belltower or clock-tower of a cathedral, where the huge rafters, which form the case of the machinery, cross each other above our heads and under our feet, or in the engine-house of some great manufactory, where cranks and pistons sough, and wheels whirr on all sides of us, and we are warned that, if part of the machinery caught our dress, we should be drawn in and crushed to pieces by one revolution of the engine, with as little power to resist as the mouse who is under the paw of the lion; in such places a nervous shuddering thrills through the frame, and the consciousness of so tremendous a force so near at hand is apt to shake and dismay the mind. How is it that we feel little or no awe when in the neighbourhood of a Power whose operations are irresistible,—a Power who holds our breath in His hand, and by closing His hand upon it at any moment might stop instantaneously that palpitation of the heart, and that circulation of the blood, which we call by the mysterious name "Life?" It is partly because God works so silently, without any display of His machinery,—because the peep of the dawn, and the opening of the blossom are done by the evolution of gentle, but most effectual, influences; God eschewing in His operations that horrid clank and whirr, which announces itself as powerful, and terrifies by the announcement,—partly also because, almost unconsciously to ourselves, we entertain a secret disbelief in the Omnipresence of a Personal God; and cover Him up from our own regards in an abstraction meaningless, powerless, passionless, devotionless, to which we give the chilling name of "Nature."

But does the walk through the streets of the crowded city suggest no thoughts of God's nearness?

Are not the activities of His Providence busy with every one of the individuals whose path intersects ours? If we could know the life of each of them, is there not a providential drama, which is working itself out in their fortunes, gradually developing its catastrophe in the subordinate incidents of their career? And amidst all the many councils, schemes, and devices, which each of them is forming, and in virtue of which they seem to be the ultimate masters of their own destiny, is there not a Power behind the scenes, "directing their steps,"—a Divinity that shapes their ends, rough hew them how they will? Is it not a solemn thing to be in the immediate neighbourhood of a Power, which is unrolling inch by inch the groundplan of many human lives?

But another reflection may usefully come to our aid in our efforts to realize the Presence of God amid the throng and hum of men. The Incarnation of the Son of God, and His covenanted Presence among the two or three gathered together in His Name, leads us to connect the thought of God with human society in a manner, which before the Incarnation would have been impossible. The abstract God we associate in our minds with the lone places of nature; we hear His whisper in the breeze which stirs the leaves of the sequestered glen, His louder utterance in the thunder, the avalanche, and the wild wind which churns the ocean into fury. But the Eternal Wisdom of God, Who for our sakes became incarnate, describes Himself as "rejoicing in the habitable parts of the earth, and having His delights among the sons of men." Christ walked up and down in the midst of us, trode our streets, sat by our hearths, ministered at the sick-beds of men, was the invited Guest at their marriages, and the great Comforter at their funerals, to teach this among other lessons, that we may find the footprints of our God, if we will only look for them, in human society. The human face with all its power of expressiveness, both in sorrow and in joy, is a sort of sacrament of His Presence; and a true faith will enable us

to pierce the veil, under which He conceals Himself
from the bodily eye, and to find Him still mixed up
with the interests and concerns of men, forbearing, forgiving, warning, counselling, comforting. The peculiar
value of this last reflection lies in the fact that, for
reasons connected with the constitution of the mind,
it is far more easy to realize the Presence of God in
solitude than in company. There is something in us
which immediately responds to the words of Christ,
when He counsels privacy for the purpose of devotion,
"Thou, when thou prayest, enter into thy closet, and
when thou hast shut thy door, pray to thy Father
which is in secret." An instinct, deeply implanted in
our spiritual nature, assures us that we must shut out
the world, if we would realize the Divine Presence.
And this is eminently true *as far as our hearts are
concerned.* To disencumber them of earthly cares,
earthly interests, and the debasing, corroding influence
of worldly affairs, is an absolutely essential condition of
our drawing nigh to God. But the mere company of
others need not be a hindrance, nay, may be rather a
help to this detachment, if we learn to connect society
with the thought of Christ, and Christ with the
thought of society. If He condescended to join
Himself to human life, to take an experimental interest
in every stage and in every phase of it, is not that
sufficient to sanctify its every stage and phase? If
He was essentially a man of the city, and not, like His
forerunner, a man of the wilderness, may not men of
the city hope to find His footprints by the side of their
daily life, and take occasion, even from that life, to
think of Him much, and thus spiritualize their earthly
citizenship? Few stars in the firmament of the Church
shine brighter than that of St. Matthew, one of the
twelve Apostles, and the Evangelist of what may be
called the mother Gospel. And what was St. Matthew
originally? A man conversant not with rural, but
with city life,—not with contemplation, but with
business. Not an unsophisticated fisherman, like the
rest of his colleagues, but a collector of taxes for the

Roman Government, one who sat daily at the receipt of custom, driving a trade essentially secular. Yet God Incarnate crossed his path, and singled him out of the throng as one who should draw many souls, minted anew with the image and superscription of the Heavenly King, into the treasury of God, and sat at meat in his house in company with many publicans and sinners, and set him upon one of the twelve thrones, which Apostles shall visibly occupy in the regeneration of all things, and placed around his brow, as a coronet, the Pentecostal tongue of fire. It is a great lesson that, if only our hearts are right and true, we may find Christ,—or rather may be found of Him,—in the traffic of secular affairs. May we so learn this lesson, as to know it, not in theory only, but by experience!

> "There are in this loud stunning tide
>   Of human care and crime,
> With whom the melodies abide
>   Of the everlasting chime;
> Who carry music in their heart,
> Through dusky lane and wrangling mart;
> Plying their daily task with busier feet,
> Because their secret souls a holy strain repeat."

CHAPTER IV.

OF INTERRUPTIONS IN OUR WORK, AND THE WAY TO DEAL WITH THEM.

"We are created in Christ Jesus unto good works, which God hath before ordained that we should walk in them."—EPH. ii. 10.

WE have spoken in the two foregoing Chapters of the work which God has allotted to us, and of the spirit which must be thrown into it, if we would convert it into a sacrifice. He who tries to infuse this spirit into his daily work will do it earnestly. He will throw all his powers of heart and soul into it; and whereas before much of his duty has been done mechanically, his nobler faculties will now be called into exercise in the doing of it. It will all be done thoughtfully and seriously, and mixed with prayer, the highest effort of which the mind is capable.

And the very earnestness with which the work is now done may bring with it a snare. When the mind is intently bent upon one action, and that action is felt to be a serious one, it is greatly embarrassed and annoyed by interruptions. Other things making a claim upon the attention, distract and harass us. Of course it is not so with the man who hangs about upon life with no serious pursuit. Interruptions are to him a pleasing variety; nor can he at all appreciate the trial of which we speak. But in proportion to the seriousness with which the Christian does his work will be, if I may so say, his sensitiveness to interruptions. And as this sensitiveness is very apt to disturb his peace, (and in doing so to retard his progress,) we will in this Chapter show the manner in which interruptions should be met, and the spirit with which they should be encountered.

The great remedy, then, for the sensitiveness to which I have alluded, is a closer study of the mind that was in Christ, as that mind transpires in His recorded conduct. The point in the life of Our Lord to which I wish to call attention, is the apparent want of what may be called method or plan in His life,—I mean method or plan of His own devising, the fact that His good works were not in pursuance of some scheme laid down by Himself, but such as entered into God's scheme for Him, such as the Father had prepared for Him to walk in.

I. And, first, notice His discourses, both in their occasions, and in their contexture.

(1) They most often take their rise from some object which is thrown across His path in nature, from some occurrence which takes place under His eyes, or from some question which is put to Him. For the wonderful discourse in John vi. upon the Living Bread, we are

entirely indebted to the circumstance that after the miracle of the loaves the carnal multitude sought Him, in anxiety to have their natural wants once again satisfied by miracle. It was not that Jesus had previously prepared for them such a discourse; but this was the discourse which their conduct drew from Him.—He meets a Samaritan woman at Jacob's well, and oppressed with the noontide heat, asks her for water from her bucket. Her answer leads on to a close dealing with the woman's conscience, and to the announcement of certain great truths respecting that living Water, whereof whosoever drinketh shall never thirst. But here again the words rise spontaneously from the occasion.—The murmurs of the Pharisees and Scribes, because Jesus received sinners and ate with them, elicited for our everlasting consolation the noble parables of the lost sheep, the lost coin, and the prodigal son.—An observation falling from a guest at table, a mere devout sentiment casually dropped in His hearing, "Blessed is he that shall eat bread in the kingdom of God," drew from His lips the parable of the great Supper.—A certain man asked Him to undertake an arbitration between himself and his brother as to their respective shares of their hereditary property. This suggested to Our Lord the topic of covetousness, and the parable of the rich fool, illustrative of that topic.

All the above are instances in which Scripture itself explicitly *traces* the connexion between certain occasions and the discourses of Our Lord. And divines have recognized many others, where the connexion, though not expressed, is not obscurely implied.

(2) But a similar remark holds good respecting the contexture of these wonderful discourses. Jesus spake as "never man spake," as never wise man after the flesh had any idea of speaking. For Our Lord's great discourses are not constructed upon any such method or plan, as the human intellect recognizes. Pascal somewhere remarks that there are two orders of discourse,—one which he calls the order of the intellect, the other the order of love. The order of the intellect is

to have an exordium, a series of arguments bearing on the matter in hand, a series of illustrations, and what is called a peroration or close. This order does not admit of divergences or digressions; any interruptions of the plan are to the mere intellect impertinences, and the pruning-knife of a merely intellectual critic would cut them unsparingly away. The order of love, on the other hand, says this truly spiritual writer, is to have a heart so penetrated with the subject, as to be impatient of the restraints of intellectual method, and to burst away in pursuit of favourite topics, as the mind within suggests. This, says he, is the only order observed in the writings of St. Augustine and St. Paul, and in the discourses of their Divine Master, Jesus Christ. And the remark is pre-eminently true. Take the Sermon on the Mount, and try to analyze it. You will find that it defies methodical analysis. While no head of Christian precept is left untouched, there is no such systematic arrangement as we can easily put upon paper. There was no doubt an undercurrent of thought in the mind of the Divine Preacher, welding together the different sections of the great Sermon, and leading Him on fluently from topic to topic; but nothing can less wear the aspect of a discourse framed upon a dry preconceived plan. Doubtless it was as the swallow caught His eye, skimming along to its nest with food for its young, and as the lily or blue-bell of Palestine waved before Him on the hill-side, that He took occasion to illustrate His precepts against worldly carefulness by those wonderful sections, beginning, "Behold the fowls of the air," "Consider the lilies of the field." This is the only plan observable in the discourse,—the plan of a loving heart pouring itself out, as occasion serves, for the edification of mankind.

II. But the absence of mere human plan, or rather strict faithfulness to the plan of God, as hourly developed by the movements of His Providence, characterizes the life of Our Lord even more than His discourses. His object throughout is not to carry out schemes preconceived by Himself, but to study God's guidings, and to be true to God's occasions and God's inspirations. Take only that portion of His life recorded in a single chapter,—the ninth of St. Matthew. Jesus is interrupted in the midst of a discourse which He was holding in the house, by the appearance of a couch with a palsied man upon it, lowered into the midst of the court under His eyes. So far from accounting the interruption unseasonable, He first absolves, and then heals the patient, and thus secures glory to God from the multitude. The miracle performed, He passes out into the open air, perhaps for refreshment, and His eye catches Matthew sitting at the receipt of custom. He calls him, and Matthew follows. Matthew invites Our Lord to a meal, and our Lord accepts the invitation; sits down with publicans and sinners, and profits by the occasion to speak of the freeness of His Grace.—In connexion probably with His appearance at a festival, the disciples of John ask Him why *His* disciples did not fast. He explains why. Jairus comes to solicit His merciful interference in behalf of a dying daughter. Jesus follows him forthwith to his house, when, lo and behold, another interruption, which to the feelings of Jairus, all impatient to have the great Healer under his roof, must have been extremely galling. The woman with an issue of blood steals a cure from Him on the road. Jesus stops to draw from her an acknowledgment of the benefit, and to dismiss her with a word of consolation and blessing. Then He resumes His former errand of love, arrives at Jairus' house, and raises the dead maiden.—Coming out, probably on His return to His own abode, the blind men follow Him into the house, and receive their cure.—They have scarcely gone out, when the man possessed with a dumb devil is brought to Him, and restored; and thus ends the detailed portion of the chapter, what follows being a general and summary survey.

This is a good specimen of Our Lord's whole way of life, and of how He went about doing good, not on a rigid, unbending, preconcerted plan, but as the Father, in the course of His Providence, ministered to Him the occasion.

Now, as God ordained beforehand certain good works in which the Son of His Love was to walk, so He deals with each follower of His Son, according to the humble capacity of that follower, on a similar principle. Christian, whoever you are, whatever your sphere, whatever your gifts, whatever your station, God has a plan of life for you. More than this, He has a plan of useful life for you, a plan of doing good, —certain occasions and opportunities of doing good all mapped out for you in His eternal counsels. These occasions and opportunities are to arise day by day upon you, as you pursue your beaten path of life, just as while the globe turns round upon its axis, the sun in course of time rises upon those parts of it which before were dark. Now this, perhaps, is a novel view to some of my readers. They are accustomed to think of the place which Our Lord has prepared for His followers,—of the joys which God has prepared for those who unfeignedly love Him;—but they think comparatively little of the sphere of good works, which is just as much prepared for them to occupy here as is the sphere of glory hereafter. Yet this is a certain and infallible truth. If God have before ordained certain persons to eternal life, He hath also before ordained good works for those individuals to walk in.

Reader, are you a firm believer in the Providence of God? because the whole doctrine which we are setting forth is really wrapped up in God's Providence. Do you believe that the whole of your affairs—trivial as well as great, irregular as well as in the ordinary course—are under His absolute, daily, hourly supervision and control? that nothing can possibly arise to you or any other, which is not foreseen by Him, arranged for by Him, brought by Him within the circle of His great plan? that the little incidents of each day, as well as the solemn crisis of life, are His ordering? Then you virtually concede all that the Apostle asserts in this verse. For you admit that the occurrences of each day, however unlooked for, however contrary to expectation, are God-sent, and those which affect *you* sent specially and with discrimination to yourself.

Now it cannot be thought that God sends events to a living soul, in order that the soul may be simply passive under the events. If God sends you an event, it must have a meaning; it must be a sign to you that you are to do something, to brace yourself up to some action or to some state of feeling. All that God sends to a human spirit must be significant. God has sent us His Word. We know that He designs us not simply to hear it, but to embrace it with a living faith and a loving obedience. We are to meditate upon it, to apply it to our consciences, mould our character and conduct in conformity to it. Now the same God who has sent us His Word equally sends us the daily occurrences of life, the chief difference being that, whereas the Word has a general voice for all, in which each is to find his own case represented, the occurrences are charged with a more specific message to individuals. Now there is many a man who says, " I will conform myself to the general indications of God's Will made to me by His Word;" comparatively few who say, " I will conform myself to the special indications of God's Will made to me by His Providence." But why so few? Does not God come home to us more closely, more searchingly, more personally by His Providence than even by His Word? Does not His finger rest upon each of us more particularly in the government of affairs than even in Revelation? And why are we to imagine, as many seem to imagine, that no other events but such as are afflictive and calamitous have a voice for us? Why not every event? Why is not the ordinary intercourse of life to be regarded as furnishing in God's design and intention opportunities of either doing or receiving good? I say of doing *or* receiving good. Surely either one or the other is a thing greatly to be coveted. In nine cases out of ten we may fail of *doing* good; but if in those cases we have received good, and received it too in the course of His plan for us, and in the way of His Providence, surely the occurrence which has called us off from our ordinary pursuit is not to be regretted.

Here, then, lies the real remedy for the uneasiness of mind which is caused by interruptions. *View them as part of God's loving and wise plan for your day, and try to make out His meaning in sending them.* When in your hour of morning devotion you distribute your time before hand (as it is in every way wise and proper to do), let it always be with the proviso that the said arrangement shall be subject to modifications by God's plan for you, as that plan shall unfold itself hour by hour to your apprehensions. When you have entered upon the day, observe narrowly the quarter in which His finger points, and be true to that direction. There lies thy prepared task. There are the good works, not which thou hast devised, but which God hath before ordained that thou shouldest walk in them. Break not away for an instant from the guidance of His Providence; for remember that thou art a child walking among pitfalls and stumbling-blocks, and no sooner shalt thou release thy grasp than thou shalt be broken, and snared, and taken. A case of distress is flung in your way as you are bound upon your daily occupations. The spirit of the age says, "Dismiss it, —you have no time to spare,—leave it to the Poorhouse or to the Mendicity Society, and pass on." Or it is suggested, in the midst of your avocations, that there is some word of sympathy to be said or to be written to a friend in trouble,—only a cup of cold water in point of intrinsic value, but still a very refreshing one to a man in the furnace of affliction. "But you are too much occupied," says the busy, bustling, hard spirit of the age; "you have no time for sympathies or sentimentalities; you must go forward; if you desire to be successful in life, you cannot afford to stop on the way." Now without denying that in particular cases such counsel may admit of palliation in a greater or less degree, Truth compels us to say that this was not the mind which was in Christ Jesus. His ear was never inaccessible to human suffering, and His mind was never unobservant of God's plans. He does not pass over the woman with the issue of blood. He does not leave her without her lesson and without her consolation, because He is bound on an errand of love to the house of Jairus. He does not make occasions bend to Him; but, knowing that occasions are the Father's call, He addresses Himself to serve occasions. He is constantly (according to the advice which He Himself inspired His Apostle to give us) "*redeeming the opportunity.*"

But supposing that during the day no opportunity occurs of *doing* good. Supposing, for example, that the case of distress into which we have patiently examined turns out, as it very frequently will, to be a gross imposture,—have we therefore lost our labour in a spiritual point of view? Not surely, if we have conformed our will to God's design for us. There is no interruption in the world, however futile and apparently perverse, which we may not address ourselves to meet *with a spirit of patience and condescension borrowed from our Master;* and to have made a step in advance in conforming to the mind of Christ will be quite as great a gain (probably a far greater) than if we had been engaged in our pursuit. For, after all, we may be *too* intent upon our business, or rather intent in a wrong way. The radical fault of our nature, be it remembered, is Self-will; and we little suspect how largely Self-will and Self-pleasing may be at the bottom of plans and pursuits, which still have God's glory and the furtherance of His Service for their professed end.

Reader, the path which we have indicated is the path not of sanctity only, but of peace also. We shall never serve God with a quiet mind, unless we more or less tread in this path. It is a miserable thing to be the sport and prey of interruptions; it wastes the energies of the human spirit, and excites fretfulness, and so leads us into temptation, as it is written, "Fret not thyself; else shalt thou be moved to do evil."

But suppose the mind to be well grounded in the truth that God's foresight and fore-arrangement embraces all which seems to us an interruption,—that in this interruption lies awaiting us a good work in which it is part of His Eternal counsel that we should walk, or a good frame of mind which He wishes us to cultivate; then we are forearmed against surprises and contradictions; we have found an alchemy which converts each unforeseen and untoward occurrence into gold; and the balm of peace distils upon our heart, even though we be disappointed of the end which we had proposed to ourselves. For which is better, safer, sweeter,—to walk in the works which God hath before ordained, or to walk in the way of our own hearts and in the sight of our eyes?

Ah, Reader! let us seek to grasp the true notion of Providence; for in it there is peace and deep repose of soul. Life has often been compared to a Drama. Now in a good drama there is one plot, variously evolved by incidents of different kinds, which until the last act present entanglement and confusion. Vice has its temporary triumphs, virtue its temporary depressions. What of that? You know it will come right in the end. You know there is an organizing mind which unfolds the story, and that the poet will certainly bring the whole to a climax by the ultimate vindication of righteousness and the doing of poetical justice upon malefactors. To this end every shifting of the scene, every movement of the actors, every by-plot and underplot is made to contribute. Wheel within wheel is working together towards this result. Well, Life is God's great Drama. It was thought out and composed in the Eternal mind before the mountains were brought forth, or ever the earth and the world were made. In time God made a theatre for it, called the Earth; and now the great Drama is being acted thereon. It is on a gigantic scale, this Drama. The scenes are shifting every hour. One set of characters drops off the stage, and new ones come on, to play much the same part as the first, only in new dresses. There seem to be entanglements, perplexities, interruptions, confusions, contradictions without end; but you may be sure there is one ruling thought, one master-design, to which all these are subordinate. Every incident, every character, however apparently adverse, contributes to work out that ruling thought. Think you that the Divine Dramatist will leave any thing out of the scope of His plot? Nay, the circumference of that plot embraces within its vast sweep every incident which Time ever brought to birth.

Thou knowest that the mind which organized this Drama is Wisdom. Thou knowest more: thou knowest that it is Love. Then of its ending grandly, wisely, nobly, lovingly, infinitely well for them who love God, there can be no doubt. But remember you are an actor in it; not a puppet worked by wires, but an actor. It is yours to study the plot as it unfolds itself, to throw yourself into it intelligently, warmly, zealously. Be sure to learn your part well, and to recite it manfully. Be not clamorous for another or more dignified character than that which is allotted you,—be it your sole aim to conspire with the Author, and to subserve His grand and wise conception.

Thus shall you cease from your own wisdom. Thus shall you find peace in submitting yourself to the wisdom which is of God. And thus, finally, shall He pronounce you a good and faithful servant, and summon you to enter into the joy of your Lord.

CHAPTER V.

FIGHT WISELY.

"*So fight I, not as one that beateth the air.*"—1 Cor. ix. 26.

THE three elements which enter into the composition of the Spiritual Life, are Acting, Fighting, and Suffering. Of the first of these we have spoken; and now, from the consideration of the Christian in his *duties*, we pass to the consideration of him in his *temptations*, or, in other words, we proceed to consider him as fighting.

Two of the main sources whence temptations arise are the Devil and the flesh; or, in other words, our great spiritual adversary, and the traitorous correspondence which he meets with from the heart of man. Now the heart being, according to the sure testimony of God's Word, deceitful above all things, and Satan's method of operation, too, being by stratagem rather than open violence, the first method, therefore, of meeting temptation aright must be to meet it *wisely*. Policy must be opposed by policy, according to the warning of the Holy Apostle: "Lest Satan should get an advantage over us; for we are not ignorant of his *devices*."

How then shall we fight wisely? This is our question in the present Chapter.

Now to fight wisely is not to fight at a venture, but with a definite aim. "So fight I," says the Apostle, "not as one that beateth the air." In which words he is drawing an image from the boxing-match in the Isthmian games, and declares that in the spiritual combat, he does not wear out his strength by vain flourishes of his hands in the air, but plants each blow certainly and with a telling aim (οὕτω πυκτεύω ὡς οὐκ ἀέρα δέρων).

We read indeed that King Ahab was shot by an arrow sent at a venture, that is, without deliberate aim: but this is told us to magnify the Providence of Almighty God who, in His designs of wrath, can direct the aimless shaft whithersoever it pleases Him; not surely to teach us that aimless shafts are likely on common occasions to be successful. Yet what is the warfare of many earnest and well-intentioned Christians but the sending of shafts at a venture? They have a certain notion that they must resist the evil within and without them; but then this evil presents itself in so many forms, that they are bewildered and confounded, and know not where to begin. And so it often comes to pass that their time and labour is thrown away in repressing symptoms, where they should be applying their whole energy to the seat of the disorder.

On the other hand, the first work of the politic spiritual warrior will be to discover his besetting sin, or sins, and having discovered it, to concentrate all his disposable force before this fortress.

Just as each individual has a certain personal configuration, distinguishing him from all other men at first sight; just as his hair has a certain colour, his limbs a certain make, his features a certain cast; or just as each of us is said to be born into the world with some one defective organ, be it heart, liver, or lungs; so in the moral constitution of each individual there is some sin or sins, which more than others is conformable to his temperament, and therefore more easily developed by his circumstances,—which expresses far more of his character than others. This bosom sin has eminently the attribute which the Apostle ascribes to all sin; it is eminently deceitful. Its especial property is to lurk: sometimes it puts on the mask of a virtue or a grace, not unfrequently that of some other sin; but masked somehow or other it loves to be, and the longer Satan can keep it masked, the better it serves his purpose.

Let us give some examples of a bosom sin thus masking itself. With a very large proportion of mankind, the besetting sin is vanity. Who knows not how this detestable sin frequently apes humility, so as really to impress its possessor with the notion that he is humble? Intensely self-satisfied in his heart of hearts, he depreciates himself, his talents, his successes, his efforts in conversation. What follows? A natural reaction of public sentiment in his favour. Men say to him, as in the Parable, "Go up higher." He has been fishing for compliments, and compliments have risen to the hook. Is it not so? For would he not have bitterly resented it in the inner man, had any of the company taken him at his word, and coolly

O

answered to his self-depreciation, "What you say about the inferiority of your talents, and the paucity of your successes, is no doubt perfectly true?" True the words may have been; but he did not say them because they were true, but because his lust of commendation craved some smooth word which might pamper it. Here is the bosom-adder of vanity coiled up in the violet-tuft of humility. To take another case. It is part of some men's character, as their friends would phrase it for them, that they cannot bear to be second. Whatever they do must be done (I do not say commendably well, for all things that are worth doing ought to be done commendably well), but superlatively well, brilliantly, so as to throw into the shade all competitors. Accordingly, they are disposed to decline or abandon all pursuits in which they feel they can never excel. Now what is this feeling, when we bring it into the court of conscience, and come to examine and scrutinize its ground? The world dignifies it with the name of honourable emulation, and accepts it as a token of a fine character. And thus much is true, and may not be denied, that there is usually some stuff in the characters, whose leading principle is such as I have described. In that singular way in which one principle hangs together with another, like bees clustering on a flower, or limpets on a weedy rock, this emulation, as it is called, is somehow connected and intertwined with that energy and resolve which are the raw material from which earthly greatness is manufactured. But, judged by the mind of Our Lord Jesus, which is the one standard of saintliness, how does the sentiment sound, "Because I cannot be brilliant, so as to outshine all rivals, therefore I will be nothing?" It jars strangely, I think, with the music of those words, "The kings of the Gentiles exercise lordship over them; and they that exercise authority upon them are called benefactors. But ye shall not be so: but he that is greatest among you, let him be as the younger, and he that is chief as he that doth serve." And again with those: "Let nothing be done through strife or vain glory; but in lowliness of mind let each esteem other better than himself." And again with that touching expression of Our Lord's humility, prophetically foreseen and predicted by the Psalmist, long years before His coming in the flesh: "Lord, I am not high-minded; I have no proud looks. I do not exercise myself in great matters which are too high for me; but I refrain my soul, and keep it low, like as a child that is weaned from his mother; yea, my soul is even as a weaned child." Alas! when we apply to this feeling the Ithuriel spear of God's Word and Christ's Example, we find it to be the bosom-adder of vanity again, lurking under the marigold of honourable emulation.

Again; a bosom sin, that it may the more easily escape detection and eradication, will wear to a superficial observer the mask of another sin. Indolence, for example, is a sin which carries with it in its train many omissions of duty, and specially of religious duty. Prayer or Scripture reading is omitted, or thrust away into a corner, and gone through perfunctorily, because we have not risen sufficiently early to give room for it. Things go cross during the day in consequence; irritability of temper not soothed by God's Blessing, or calmed by His Presence, throws our affairs into a tangle. We trace it all up to the omission of Prayer, of which we accuse ourselves. But the fault lies deeper. It was not really an indisposition to Prayer which kept us from it. It was indolence which really caused the mischief.

One of the first properties, then, of the bosom sin with which it behoves us to be well acquainted, as the first step in the management of our spiritual warfare, is its property of concealing itself. In consequence of this property, it often happens that a man, when touched upon his weak point, answers that whatever other faults he may have, this fault at least is no part of his character. This circumstance, then, may furnish one clue to the discovery; of whatever fault you feel that, if accused of it, you would be stung and nettled by the apparent injustice of the charge, suspect yourself of that fault,—in that quarter very probably lies the black spot of the bosom sin. If the skin is in any part sensitive to pressure, there is probably mischief below the surface.

What has been said, however, requires a little modification. In very strong characters, where the bias of the will is very decided, the ruling passion can hardly help disclosing itself to its possessor and to those around him. Sensuality, for example, and an insatiable ambition proclaim themselves aloud in the ears of the conscience, and this is St. Paul's meaning when he says, "Some men's sins are open beforehand, going before to judgment." But the far more usual case is that described in the words which follow, "And some men they follow after." Their sins, their weak points, do not transpire till after a long and familiar acquaintance with them; they are subtle and evasive, and sometimes intertwined with the fibres of what is good in them.

It is to aid in bringing to light these secret sins that we make the following suggestions.

First, then, praying heartily for the light of God's Spirit to know thine own heart, observe and reason upon the results of Self-examination. When this most salutary exercise has been pursued for a certain time, you will observe that the same failures are constantly recurring, just as in Prayer the same wants daily recur; so that though the words of our prayers may be a little varied, (and it is more free and pleasant to vary them a little,) the things that we pray for are always substantially the same. The conclusion is almost inevitable that there is something serious beneath these constantly recurring failures. What is it? In what one direction do all the phenomena point? To selfishness? or to indolence? or to vanity? or to want of sincerity and simplicity of character? or to the fear of man and human respect? or to discontent? or to worldly anxiety? Remember always, that in the symptom, and on the surface, it may look like none of these sins, and yet be really and fundamentally one of them. Say often while engaged in the search, "Blessed Spirit, it is Thy office to convince of sin. Help me to seek the ground of my heart, and to drag into the light of day my hidden corruptions, for Jesus Christ's sake;" and your search, if conducted in this method and spirit, will not long be fruitless.

Another plan may just be mentioned as helpful in the discovery of our bosom sin. Let us have our eye upon the occurrences which specially give us pain or pleasure: they will often be veriest trifles,—an expression of opinion, or sneer, a mere passing breath of human praise or censure, which goeth away, and cometh not again; but yet, be it what it may, if it touches us to the quick, the probabilities are, that by tracing it to its source we shall get to the quick of our character, to that sensitive quarter of it where the bosom-adder lies coiled up. Whence those tears of vexation? whence that pang of annoyance? whence that gleam of sunshine shooting across the heart on an otherwise gusty day? Let us trace them to the principles from which they arose, and we shall have made some advance towards the desired discovery.

When the discovery is made, the path of the spiritual combatant becomes clear, however arduous. Your fighting is to be no longer a flourishing of the arms in the air; it is to assume a definite form, it is to be a combat with the bosom sin. Appropriate mortifications must be adopted, such as common sense will suggest, varying with the nature of the sin, and combined always with a heartfelt acknowledgment of our utter weakness, and with a silent but fervent prayer for the Grace of Almighty God. If indolence be the besetting sin, we must watch against slovenliness in little things, which is the mild form of the complaint; if selfishness, we must lay ourselves out to consider and gratify the wishes of others; if vanity, we must secretly bless God in our heart for all mortifications of it, and particularly avoid the snare of speaking humbly of ourselves; if discontent, we must review, in our seasons of devotion, the many bright points of our position and seek our happiness in our work; if human respect, we must habituate ourselves to look at our actions as we shall look at them when the judgment of God upon them will be the only matter of importance; if sensuality, the discipline of fasting and abstinence from some innocent enjoyments must be used as far as health permits, Our Lord having implied this in the strongest possible manner when He said of a certain kind of evil spirits, "This kind goeth not out but by prayer and fasting."

But the great matter to be attended to in each case is, that the whole forces of the will should be concentrated for a time in that one part of the field in which the besetting sin has intrenched itself. Thus point and definiteness will be given to Christian effort, the importance of which has been already shown; we shall not lose our time, or waste our strength, as those who in fighting beat the air; and we shall find doubtless, that in supplanting the besetting sin, we shall be also weakening the vitality of subordinate faults of character, which cluster together round that one nucleus.

Let me say, finally, that for each one of us, no business can be of more pressing moment, of more urgent importance, than this discovery of our besetting sin. The bosom sin in Grace exactly resembles a strong current in nature, which is setting full upon dangerous shoals and quicksands. If in your spiritual computation you do not calculate upon your besetting sin, upon its force, its ceaseless operation, and its artfulness, it will sweep you on noiselessly, and with every appearance of calm, but surely and effectually, to your ruin. So may we see a gallant ship leave the dock, fairly and bravely rigged, and with all her pennons flying; and the high sea, when she has cleft her way into it, is unwrinkled as the brow of childhood, and seems to laugh with many a twinkling smile; and when night falls, the moonbeam dances upon the wave, and the brightness of the day has left a delicious balminess behind it in the air, and the ship is anchored negligently and feebly, and all is then still save the gentle drowsy gurgling which tells that water is the element in which she floats; but in the dead of the night, the anchor loses its holds, and then the current, deep and powerful, bears her noiselessly whither it will; and in the morning the wail of desperation rises from her decks, for she has fallen on the shoal, and the disconsolateness of the dreary twilight, as the breeze springs with the daybreak, and with rude impact dashes her planks angrily against the rock, contrasts strangely with the comfort and peacefulness of the past evening. Such was the doom of Judas Iscariot. Blessed with the companionship of Our Lord Himself, dignified with the Apostleship, and adorned with all the high graces which that vocation involved, he was blinded to the undercurrent of his character, which set in the direction of the Mammon of unrighteousness, and which eventually ensured for him an irretrievable fall.

In conclusion, he who prays (as we should all do), "Show me myself, Lord," should take good care to add, lest self-knowledge plunge him into despair, "*Show me also Thyself.*" The course recommended in this Chapter, if honestly adopted, will probably lead us to the conclusion that our heart, which showed so fair without, is but a whited sepulchre, an Augean stable, full of corruptions and disorders, which it requires a moral Hercules to cleanse; but, blessed be God, the Love of Christ, and the Blood of Christ, and the Grace of Christ are stronger than ten thousand depravities and corruptions, though riveted down to the soul by the chain of evil habit. And when God exhibits to the soul His Love, as mirrored in those bleeding Wounds and the omnipotence of His free Grace, the energy which is felt there is great enough to crush any and every foe. The gentlest touch of God's finger upon the soul is like the touch of the dawn upon the dark horizon. Birds waken and trill their notes, and leaves flutter in the fresh breeze, and there is an electric thrill of joy and hope through the whole domain of nature. My reader, thy whole soul shall leap up at that touch: holy affections shall lift up their hymn of praise within thee, and thy heart shall flutter with mingled awe and joy, and thou shalt know that thou hast found thy Lord.

CHAPTER VI.

OF THE NATURE OF TEMPTATION.

"*Then was Jesus . . . . tempted of the devil.*"—MATT. iv. 1.

A DEVOTIONAL writer of the present day, in answer to the question, "How are we to overcome temptations?" says, "Cheerfulness is the first thing, cheerfulness is the second, and cheerfulness is the third." It is very true. Faint heart never won any thing that was worth winning,—least of all a spiritual battle; whereas victories have often been won against fearful odds by some news which have raised the spirits of the troops. Lightness and brightness of heart, and an unfailing elasticity of spirit, must characterize the good soldier of Jesus Christ, if he is to break his way to the heavenly country through the serried ranks of his spiritual foes.

Having considered, then, in our last Chapter how we may meet temptation wisely, the question now arises,—an answer to which is scarcely less necessary to success,—how we may meet it cheerfully. And it will be found, I apprehend, that a want of cheerfulness in meeting temptation is due to a misapprehension either of its nature, or of the support which may be expected in it, or of its salutary effects.

We shall speak in this Chapter of its nature.

It has been said of the eagle,—and if natural history will not bear it out, the piety with which the fable has been applied serves to reconcile us to the fiction,—that the parent bird practises the young to fly by dropping them, when half-fledged, from her wings; and that, when the breeze is proving too strong for them, and their little pinions begin to flag and waver amid the resistance of the air, she swoops underneath them, having indeed never lost sight of them for an instant, and receives them again upon her own person, and sails on with them majestically as before. And the circumstance, real or imagined, has been called in to illustrate that exquisite passage in the song of Moses: "As an eagle stirreth up her nest, fluttereth over her young, spreadeth abroad her wings, taketh them, beareth them on her wings; so the Lord alone did lead him, and there was no strange god with him."

At all events, whether the eagle disciplines her young or no in the exact manner described above,—and the text does not go the length of saying this,—we have in the supposed fact a most true representation of the way in which God proves His children, while they are yet spiritually fledgelings, and of the sense of danger, utter dismay, piteous cries for help, which such probation involves. At the beginning of the spiritual life, when the first fervours of conversion are upon a man, when he has fully declared for Christ in his own mind, or, in other words, has realized in his own experience the conditions on which Baptism was granted, he is almost sure to dream of Heaven at once, and to overlook that long period of struggle, discomfort, and uncertainty through which he must pass on this side the grave, before he can attain a meetness for glory. It is just as if an Israelite had dreamed of entering into the land flowing with milk and honey immediately after the Exodus, and had overlooked "the waste, howling wilderness" lying between Egypt and Canaan. That history is wonderfully typical; and beginners in religion will do well to bear in mind the arrangement of its several parts. Egypt is a figure of the world, which lies under the dominion of Satan, the spiritual Pharaoh. The passage of the Red Sea is a figure of Baptism, which stands at the threshold of spiritual life. The passage of Jordan is a figure of death; and the earthly

Canaan is a figure of the heavenly. Of what, then, is the wilderness, with its arid sand, its barren sun-smitten crags, its fiery serpents, a picture? Of the Christian's pilgrimage through the region of manifold temptations,—temptations which for the first time awake in all their power, like winds blowing from all the four quarters of heaven, as soon as he becomes an *earnest* Christian, or, as I have phrased it in other words, as soon as he *realizes* his Baptism. So long as he moved in the groove of formalism, and contented himself with a religion of stated ordinances, opposition was comparatively asleep; but now, when he stirs himself energetically in the right direction, it seems as if God had given His summons to the winds to sweep over the garden of the soul: "Awake, O north wind; and come, thou south; blow upon my garden." We are much distressed, like the eagle's fledgelings, when she drops them. At every step, we discover some new corruption of the heart, some new force of sinful passion, or habit, which baffles and beats us back. One besetting sin! we flattered ourselves we had but one; but, lo! their name is legion. The effort which it is necessary to make, in order to maintain watchfulness for a day, fatigues us,—is quite too much for our strength. A crop of little trials springs up, which there is no sort of dignity in resisting or conquering, resulting perhaps from unevenness of temper in ourselves and those we live with,—teasing trials, though of no magnitude, just as flies tease us in the warm weather; they make us lose our equilibrium, and all for a trifle, which is very humbling. Then we secretly hoped to find a resource in Prayer, and looked perhaps to the evening hour of devotion as a period when we would sound the trumpet, and rally our scattered forces. But alas! we cannot pray without such distractions as render the prayer barren, dry, and apparently profitless. In meditation, we find it impossible to fasten our mind to the point, and seem to waste a great deal of time in making the effort. And then comes the thought, so perfectly familiar to all who have ever sought sincerely

Of the Nature of Temptation.

to give themselves unto Prayer,—a thought suspected, while admitted, like a foreigner upon whose movements the police are charged to have their eye, but still admitted—that if Prayer cannot be offered with fluency and glow of feeling and satisfaction to our own minds, it had better not be offered at all. And when the faldstool is abandoned in a fit of peevishness and disgust, the struggle is over for the day; it is as when the weak pinion of the young bird drops motionless by its side, and a steady descent thenceforth commences. The same feelings of disappointment and despondency, on a larger scale, corresponding to the magnitude of the occasion, beset us frequently after receiving the Holy Communion. We looked for the strengthening and refreshing of our souls, and really wound ourselves up to as much devotion as we were capable of; but, on the contrary, the whole of our inner man seems to collapse with the effort, and to lie open more than ever to the assaults of indolence, softness, levity, and dissipation of mind. In a word, we are made to discover that the harder we struggle against the Devil, and the flesh, the harder they struggle against us; according to that profound word of the Apostle's, " The flesh lusteth against the Spirit, and the Spirit against the flesh."

Now it is not the business of the present Chapter to discuss at length the supports of the tempted soul. These are matters for after consideration. Yet I cannot help so far forestalling this part of the subject, as to remark that the eagle, watching her young with keen eye, and sweeping beneath them with outstretched wing, as she sees them faint with exhaustion,—that Our Lord walking on the waters, and stretching forth His hand to Peter when He saw him sinking,—that these similitudes give the exactly true idea of the relations between Christ and the tempted soul. If thou hast not yet finally abandoned the struggle; if thou hast again picked up thy resolve, and taken heart for a new resistance,—why is it? This recovery, this pause in the downward career, was not of thyself. It was the Divine Eagle, swooping beneath her young, as, drooping and baffled, they commenced a downward course; it was the Lord stretching forth His saving hand, and catching the poor disciple before he was altogether engulfed. The mere fact, than which nothing can be more certain, that He is looking on with keenest interest, while humbling thee, and proving thee, to see what is in thine heart;—that He is near at hand to give succour when He sees the right moment to have arrived, a little above thee in the sky, or close at thy side upon the billow;—that His Omnipotence, His Love, His Wisdom, are all engaged in administering the temptation, in meting it out, in adjusting it to thy strength, in not allowing it to proceed to undue lengths —this of itself should prove a cordial to thy heart, and invigorate thee to pursue the course on which thou hast entered.

But a great deal of the distress, which many persons under temptations experience, arises from their not understanding the nature of temptation. In the early stages of spiritual life, more especially, persons often flounder from having crude and ill-defined notions on the subject. They have a certain vague idea that peace and quietness of mind are essential to a right state; and as temptation, of course, destroys peace and quietness, and makes turbid the waters of the soul, they conclude that temptation indicates a wrong state. Hence they have a feeling of guilt connected with temptation, which adds very much to the ordinary discomforts of it. They need to be instructed that temptation is not sin; and that not until the will consents to it,—not until it is wilfully entertained and cherished, —does temptation become sin. Nay, we may go further. Temptation is not always even a sign of a sinful nature. It is quite possible that its appeal may be made to feelings, which in themselves are perfectly pure and innocent. Our Lord's temptation is a proof of this. We are told, on the one hand, that He was "tempted in all points like as we are;" and we are told, on the other, that He was "without sin;"—not merely without *sins*, but "without *sin*," that is, without the sinful tendency or principle. Yet that His trials, both in the wilderness, at the commencement of His ministry, and in the Garden of Gethsemane at its close, were most agonizing, there can be no question. There was a will in our Blessed Lord, as there is in us, which shrunk from every form of physical and mental suffering. Satan had access to His imagination, and filled it with pictures of the ease, comfort, dignity, power which He might enjoy, if He would only abandon the great project of Human Redemption, sketched out before the world began in the counsels of the Eternal Three. There was an inward voice which seconded Peter's words, when he dissuaded from suffering and death, and counselled softer things. Our Lord knew whose voice it was, and that Peter was only the mouthpiece who gave it articulation; and, accordingly, He turns upon the Apostle with the sternest word of reproof which ever escaped His lips, " Get thee behind Me, Satan; thou art an offence" (snare, stumbling-block) "unto Me; for thou savourest not the things that be of God, but those that be of men."

But is it doubted whether, with sinful men like ourselves, temptations can be addressed to us, which shall not correspond with any corrupt and depraved feeling, but shall fasten only upon some innocent principle? The trial of Abraham's faith is a case in point. He was commanded by God to slay his son. The temptation was severe just in proportion as Abraham's parental affection was strong; it was this affection, a pure and innocent one surely, which was made the instrument of the temptation. And, to come down to our own circumstances, there is no difficulty in imagining the case of a man tempted by hunger to steal food, or pressed to do the same thing by the necessities of those dependent on him; or of another, tempted by his very faith in God's love and goodness to presumption. Temptation then, and our accessibility to it, is not always a proof even of a sinful nature. Sometimes, of course, it does prove this; for such disorders have crept into the human heart with the Fall, that its great original affections have to a great extent lost their character by fastening upon wrong ends;—anger has become irritability and peevishness, fear has degenerated into human respect, forethought has corrupted into anxiety, and generous emulation has soured into discontent; and though anger, fear, forethought, and emulation be *in their raw material* no sins, we cannot say as much of their degeneracies. Still, even where a man is tempted by means of these corrupt and degenerate feelings, though it may be an evidence of that "infection of nature, which doth remain, yea, in them that are regenerated;" yea, though he may be hedged in and sore beset by them on all sides, he still commits no sin, unless his will in some measure consents to or encourages them. And as to the guilt arising from the corruption of our nature, it has been the constant doctrine of the Church, that it is removed by the Sacrament of Baptism, when that Sacrament has been realized, in the individual's experience, by Faith. "There is now no condemnation," says our Ninth Article, "for them that believe and are baptized," though "the Apostle doth confess that concupiscence and lust hath of itself the nature of sin."

See now, tempted soul, whether this consideration applied to thine own case, may not somewhat lighten thy burden. You are beset by distractions in Prayer and Meditation. Well; distractions are no sin; nay, if struggled against patiently and cheerfully, they shall be a jewel in thy crown. Did you go through with the religious exercise as well as you could, not willingly harbouring the distraction or consenting to it? In this case, the prayer was quite as acceptable, as if it had been accompanied with those high-flown feelings of fervour and sensible delight which God sometimes gives, and sometimes, for our better discipline and humiliation, withholds. Nay, may we not say, that it was much more acceptable? Do not the Scriptures give us reason to think that prayer, persevering amidst difficulties and humiliations, prayer clinging close to Christ, despite His rebuffs, *is* more acceptable than the prayer which has its way smooth before it, and whose wings are filled by the favouring gale? What else are we to learn from the acceptance of Bartimæus's petition, who cried so much the more, when the multitude rebuked him that he should hold his peace? What else from the commendation and recompense of the Syrophœnician's faith? Wouldst thou know the avenue to the Saviour's heart, when thou art driven from His footstool by manifold discouragements, by deadness, numbness, insensibility,—and He Himself seems to cover Himself with a cloud, so that thy prayer may not pass through? Confess thyself a dog, and plead for such crumbs as are the dog's allowed and recognized portion. Call to mind the many times when thou hast turned a deaf ear to Christ's expostulations with thee through thy conscience. Reflect that thou hast deserved nothing but repulses, and to have all thy drafts upon Him dishonoured; and yet cling to His Sacred Feet, while thou sinkest thus low before Him, resolving not to let Him go, except He bless thee; and this act of humility and perseverance shall make thy lame and halting Prayer far more acceptable to the Divine Majesty than if it sailed to Heaven, with all the fluency of conscious inspiration, like Balaam's prophecy of old, which was prefaced, unhappy soul! by the assertion of his gifts.

Again; mere feelings of irritability, indolence, impurity, collapse, weariness, partisanship, unkindness, suspiciousness, and so forth, are not in themselves sins. They must be consented to and harboured before they can become so. Just as musicians prelude their pieces by a flourish, so Satan occasionally runs his fingers over the key-board of the mind, awakening all these feelings, in their turn, and confounding us by the consciousness of the amount of evil which there is within. But there is still no sin, so long as we reject and renounce these feelings, and thrust them out by prayer and instant application to some useful work. Our minds may be rendered uncomfortable by them, or, as the Apostle Peter phrases, we may be " in heaviness through manifold temptations;" but heaviness and discomfort are no sins. Nay, heaviness of spirit, resulting from temptation, is the Cross of the Garden laid on us by Him who bore it in Gethsemane; and it is a great honour and privilege to be called upon, like the three chosen ones of the chosen, to come and watch with Him for one short hour.

Yes! multitudinous temptations are, indeed, a great dignity, as helping to assimilate us to the image of Christ; and, if we comport ourselves well under them, a great means of spiritual advancement. When a hard winter sets in, and the earth is covered with a mantle of snow, and each little knot and spray in the hedgerow is encrusted with icicles, vegetation seems to be killed, and every green thing blighted. But it is not so. The genial forces of the earth are driven inward, and working deep in her bosom. The snow mantle is doing for her what the fur mantle does for the human frame,— concentrating and preserving the vital heat within. So it is in Temptation: the time of temptation is a cheerless and dreary hour, when every thing seems at a standstill, and the spiritual pulse can no longer be heard, it beats so faintly to the outward touch; but if the will is faithful and true, and the soul patient, the life is really concentrating itself, and rallying its forces within. The cheerless outward aspect is nothing:— there are hidden agencies at work, which in due time shall bring out the full bloom and redolence of a spiritual spring. There have been moderate Christians, there have been shallow Christians, without very much temptation; but there never yet was a saintly Christian, never yet one who pressed to the higher summits of the spiritual life, never one, whose banner bore the strange device " Excelsior," who was not made the victim of manifold temptations. There are many good men in the world who seem to live in a continual light gaiety and sunshine of heart, and yet whom it would be quite wrong and wide of the mark to reckon irreligious men; they pay a very unfeigned attention to the concerns of Religion, are in high esteem both for kindness and prudence, are counted examples in their social circle, and are in their way devout,—and all this without seeming to find much difficulty and impediment. If they are what they appear to be, they are not deep men; and while we may not for a moment judge them otherwise than charitably, we need not for a moment envy them. When God besets the soul with temptations, He is calling it to something high in spiritual enterprise, and great in spiritual attainment. Let us recognize it as being so, and pray earnestly not to frustrate the vocation by the perversity and sluggishness of our own wills.

"My brethren, count it all joy when ye fall into divers temptations; knowing this, that the trying of your faith worketh patience. But let patience have her perfect work, that ye may be perfect and entire, wanting nothing."

CHAPTER VII.
FIGHT WITH DISTRUST IN SELF AND TRUST IN CHRIST.

"*And in the fourth watch of the night Jesus went unto them, walking on the sea. And when the disciples saw Him walking on the sea they were troubled, saying, It is a spirit: and they cried out for fear. But straightway Jesus spake unto them, saying, Be of good cheer; it is I; be not afraid. And Peter answered Him and said, Lord, if it be Thou, bid me come unto Thee on the water. And He said, Come. And when Peter was come down out of the ship, he walked on the water, to go to Jesus. But when he saw the wind boisterous, he was afraid; and beginning to sink, he cried, saying, Lord, save me. And immediately Jesus stretched forth His hand, and caught him, and said unto him, O thou of little faith, wherefore didst thou doubt?*"—MATT. xiv. 25—31.

THE harmony with themselves of the characters described in Scripture is a proof that these characters really existed,—an internal evidence in favour of the authenticity of the Bible. It would be very difficult for an impostor, for example, to frame two such incidents as St. Peter's failure in his attempt to walk upon the waters, and St. Peter's denial of his Master, both exhibiting precisely the same weak point in the Apostle's character under circumstances totally different. Or, had he framed them, he would not have thrown them out, as St. Matthew has done, far apart from one another in the narrative without any remark to connect them; but would have given his reader some hint that, if compared and set side by side, they would be seen to have, under great diversities, a similarity of principle. As it is, the coincidence is too subtle to have been designed: and we cannot otherwise account for it, than by supposing St. Peter to have been an actually existing man, whose sayings and doings are recorded; and the same points of character are constantly coming out in the same man, whatever the variety of circumstances in which he is placed.

But when pointed out, the coincidence is full of interest. It is interesting to see St. Peter's boast of attachment to Christ, and St. Peter's fall both rehearsed beforehand, as it were, to a private audience, when comparatively little was at stake. The Apostle was enthusiastically attached to his Master, and conscious of the strength of his attachment. He was also bold with all the boldness of chivalry, presumptuous, and self-reliant. These latter qualities procured for him a tremendous fall in the great crisis of the apprehension of Christ; but they had procured for him already a fall in a previous lesser crisis. Then, too, as just before his denial, he had virtually professed his faith in Christ, and his attachment to Christ, and had challenged a trial of that faith and that attachment: "Lord, if it be Thou, bid me come unto Thee on the water." Then, too, he had gone on well, and in pursuance of his professions, up to a certain time, walking on the waters for a few paces, just as on the later occasion he drew his sword and smote a servant of the

High Priest, and cut off his ear. Then, too, he had failed after the expiration of a time, and exposed himself to the remarks of his less enterprising colleagues, as being unable to go through with that which he had begun: when he saw the wind boisterous, his heart failed him, and he was afraid, and began to sink. Thus both his trial, and his shortcoming in trial, had been practised, if I may so say, beforehand.

Now here at once a thought meets us, very necessary to be dwelt upon, in discussing the subject of Temptations. Temptations, then, are not always of the same magnitude, or on the same scale. Occasionally only, in the course of a lifetime, some great crisis comes to approve the stedfastness of our Christian Principle. There are inducements to form a connexion which is doubtful, or to desert a right cause which is becoming unpopular, or to be lenient in condemning evil, or to hazard a crooked policy for a great gain or a high distinction. These great opportunities, however, occur but seldom. Days and days wear away, each of them formative of our character,—each of them leaving upon that character the visible stamp and impress of the way in which it has been spent,—which are unmarked by any momentous trial, and when our conduct is in no sense before Society. These days furnish nothing more than the petty temptations to indolence, vanity, temper, selfishness, loquacity, and so forth, which are never at any time absent from us, and from which no sort of life, whether public or private, can claim exemption. Yet think not, disciple of Christ, that these petty temptations are to be despised. It is in these miniature trials that God rehearses His actors behind the scenes, before He brings them forward on the public stage, thoroughly trained and fitted to play their parts. Peter's part was rehearsed upon the waves, under the eyes of his kind Master and his colleagues, before he was called to play it in the High Priest's palace, under hostile criticism, and amidst the retainers of the party then in power; and had not Peter failed in his rehearsal, he would probably not have failed on the more critical occasion. It is a mark of a shallow or superficial mind to think lightly of little temptations or of little sins. Even judging according to mere magnitude, the stress of many little trials, constantly harassing us day after day, may be as severe an exercise of Christian patience as one tremendous trial, whose duration and intensity are limited. A shower of needle arrows—such as those with which the Lilliputians assailed Gulliver in the fable—steadily poured in upon us day by day would be more trying than one hour's exposure to darts of an ordinary size. And to do battle all day long for years with temper or vanity may argue, in the sight of God, as great stedfastness of principle, as the endurance of the agonies of a martyr, which run their course, and are terminated before sundown. But character transpires in all circumstances, small as well as great: and if, by God's grace, character stake a good shape in the minor circumstances of life, it is likely to retain that shape when it is more keenly sifted. Never yet was a man true to Christian principle in his own little circle, who became untrue to it when placed in a position of trust.

And there is yet one other reason which should make us highly esteem our daily small temptations, and very much study our conduct in them. They are a far better discipline of humility than sublimer trials. We get no credit for meeting them well. No one but those most intimate with us—and not always even they—knows *how* we meet them. It flatters our vanity to demean ourselves well in a great crisis; but there is no dignity in resisting sins of temper or of the tongue. And yet, while there is no dignity in the thing achieved, there is great difficulty in the achievement. Now humility, if genuine, is the sweetest flower which grows in the garden of God; and any opportunities of cultivating it should be highly prized and carefully improved. Welcome, then, little Temptations, if they discipline us in this lovely grace! These, if met in faith and love, are all that is needed to mature our characters for glory,—

> "The trivial round, the common task,
> Will furnish all we ought to ask,
> Room to deny ourselves,—a road
> To bring us daily nearer God."

We have spoken of humility. The incident of St. Peter's history, on which we have been commenting, brings out strongly his want of it, and his failure in consequence. He failed on this as on the later occasion, just because he felt strong in himself. He was conscious of his faith in Christ, and love for Christ, and felt that they were strong enough to carry him through any thing. It is very remarkable too—and we shall miss much of the instruction conveyed by the incident if we fail to remark—that *the grace in which he breaks down is his own characteristic grace.* St. Peter was a bold man, an enterprising man, a chivalrous man, a generous man; it was his boldness, enterprise, chivalry, and generosity, which, sanctified by Grace, were hereafter to carry him through fire and water in the Service of his Master. Yet in both cases, strange to say, his fall exhibits him as timorous and pusillanimous,—characteristics quite opposite to those which he really had. He, a hardy Galilæan fisherman, quails at the bluster of the elements; he is cowed, and lowers his colours at a question from a maid-servant who kept the door. It was the same with other eminent saints and servants of God. Moses, who was very meek above all the men that were upon the face of the earth, was yet debarred from entering Canaan, because on one occasion he lost his equanimity, and spake unadvisedly with his lips. Abraham, the father of the faithful, could not believe that God would protect him at Pharaoh's court, if he took the straightforward path of confessing that Sarah was his wife. St. John, the Apostle of Love, was for calling down fire from heaven upon Samaritans who refused a reception to his Master. All these broke down in their strong points, not in their weak ones.

And the lesson which we derive from the failures of all is one and the same—the extreme brittleness and frailty of the human will, even in those points in which it seemed most to be relied upon. St. Peter was not aware of this brittleness; he had to be instructed in it by very painful and humbling falls. He felt strong in himself, able to walk upon the waves, able to do and dare in his Master's service; and consciousness of our own strength is a sure forerunner of a grievous fall. It was this consciousness which made him desirous to approve his faith and love, by walking upon the waters to meet his Master,—which made him court trial. And to court trial is always a symptom which indicates something unsound in the heart of the person courting it, some self-reliance which mars his faith. We are taught to pray, "Lead us not into temptation,"—a prayer which can only be offered sincerely by those who feel their own utter weakness. But those, who, like St. Peter, long for an opportunity of approving the stedfastness of their faith, virtually pray, "Lead us into temptation." And then, when led into it, and when it pleases God to make experiment of them, they fail.

Then here we come across the first thought, which we desire to impress upon our readers in this Chapter, in connexion with Temptations. Self-trust, in however small a degree, is a sure secret of failure: and if hitherto we have failed again and again in meeting Temptation, if our best resolves hitherto have been baffled and beaten back, it will be well to examine whether there be not some particle of self-reliance lurking at the bottom of our hearts. It may lurk there when we least suspect it. Very often it requires some time and consideration to bring it to light: very often it assumes a specious and plausible shape. For instance, after our falls we find that we are bitterly disappointed with ourselves, disgusted with our own folly and weakness, and thrown out of heart altogether for future efforts. There is something in this which looks well, but it will not bear probing. Why should we be disappointed with self, unless we expected something from self,—thought secretly that self might be in a measure depended upon? God is teaching us by our falls; but oh, how slow we are to learn the lesson that no amount of evil in ourselves ought to surprise us, that we ought to be prepared for any thing in that quarter, for any shortcoming in Grace, for any outbreak of sin! The heart is a running issue of evil; and it is not to be wondered at that the issue bursts forth occasionally. If a man secretly says in himself, "I am not yet as bad as that,"—"I have it not in me to be so untrue to grace, so faithless to Christ as that:"— "Is thy servant a dog, that he should do this great thing?" he still thinks he has a certain reserve or stronghold of virtue in his own bosom, on which he can fall back. This is self-reliance, and he must be beaten out of it before he can succeed against temptation, according to that glorious Christian paradox of the Apostle, "When I am weak" (that is, thoroughly imbued with a sense of my own weakness), "then am I strong;" and it is wonderful how this profound humility connects itself with that elasticity and joyousness of spirit without which a successful warfare against temptation is out of the question. Constant disappointment is very wearying to the mind, and sure to break the energies of a man; but if he has flung himself down so low that he cannot be disappointed, if he has fairly given up his own heart as incorrigible— which indeed it is—and is looking in quite another quarter for the requisite strength, it is surprising with what cheerfulness and alacrity he picks himself up after his falls, wonderful what a bound and buoyancy there is in the spirit which can truly say to Christ, and only to Him, "All my fresh springs are in Thee."

Yes; "all my fresh springs are in Thee!" Self-distrust alone, though we must always fail without it, will never by itself secure victory; the soul which has made the discovery that it has nothing in itself to hang upon, must hang upon Christ. This is strongly and strikingly brought out in the narrative on which we have been commenting. It was not till St. Peter's eye was caught by the fury of the elements, by the raving wind, by the boisterous surge; it was not until his attention was diverted from the Saviour, that he began to sink. Had he steadily kept Christ in sight all through, it might have gone well with him to the end. So long as he was in the ship, his thoughts were engaged with the majesty and power of his Lord, who could even walk on the waves; now that he is in the midst of the trial which he had courted, his mind wanders to his own danger, and his faith is shaken.

Now here comes out another point of holy policy in the combat with temptations. It is wise, especially when they are at their height, never to look them full in the face. To consider their suggestions, to debate with them, to fight it out with them inch by inch in a listed field, is, generally speaking, a sure way to fail. Turn the mind to Christ at the first assault, and keep it fixed there with pertinacity, until this tyranny be overpast. Consider Him, if thou wilt, after the picture here presented to us. Think of Him as One who walked amidst Temptations without ever being submerged by them, as of One who by His Grace can enable His followers to do the same. Think of Him as calm, serene, firm, majestic amidst the most furious agitations and turbulences of nature, and as One who can endue thy heart with a similar stedfastness. Think of Him as interceding for His Church on the Mount of Glory, as watching them while they toil in rowing against the adverse influences which beset them round about upon the sea of life, as descending on the wings of love to their relief. Think of Him as standing close by thee in thy immediate neighbourhood, with a hand outstretched for thy support as soon as ever thou lookest towards Him. Remember that *it is not you who are to conquer, but He who is to conquer in you;* and accordingly, "even as the eyes of servants wait upon the hand of their masters, and as the eyes of a maiden upon the hand of her mistress, even so let your eyes wait upon Him, until He have mercy upon you." No man ever fell in this attitude of expectant faith; he falls because he allows himself to look at the temptation, to be fascinated by its attractiveness, or terrified by its strength. One of the greatest Sermons in our language is on the expulsive power of a new affection, and the principle laid down in that Sermon admits of application to the circumstances of which we are speaking. There can be, of course, no temptation without a certain correspondence of the inner man with the immediate occasion of the trial. Now do you desire to weaken this correspondence, to cut it off, and make it cease? Fill the mind and heart with another affection, and let it be the affection for Christ crucified. Thus will the energies of the soul, which will not suffice for two strong actions at the same time, be drawn off into another quarter; and besides, the great Enemy, seeing that his assaults only provoke you to a continuous exercise of Faith, will soon lay down his arms; and you shall know experimentally the truth of those words, "Above all, taking the shield of faith, wherewith ye shall be able to quench all the fiery darts of the wicked one." There can be no doubt that this counsel of looking only upon Christ in the hour of temptation will be most needed (if our consciousness and mind be spared us to the end) in the critical hour when flesh and heart are failing, and when Satan for the last time is permitted to assault our faith. We can well imagine that in that hour doubts will be busily instilled of Christ's love and power, suggestions of our own unfaithfulness to Him in times past, and questions as to whether He will now receive us. The soul will then possibly be scared by terrors, as the disciples in the boat were scared with the thoughts of a phantom, and will tremble in apprehension of being thrust out from the frail bark of the body into the darkness, uncertainty, insecurity of a new and untried element. If such should be the experience of any one who reads these pages, let him take with him this one counsel of safety, to look only to Christ, and to perish, if he perishes, at His feet; let us refuse to look in any other quarter, let us steadily turn away our eyes from the doubts, the painful recollections, the alarming anticipations which the enemy is instilling. We are not proposing to be saved on the ground of any righteousness in ourselves, or in any other way than by free Grace, as undone sinners; then let those words be the motto of the tempest-tossed soul, "My soul hangeth upon Thee; Thy right hand hath upholden me;" ay, and let it be the motto *now*, in hours when lesser trials assault us. Let us make proof even now of the invincibility of the shield of faith, that we may bring it forth in that hour with greater confidence in its power to shield us. And the hand of an Infinite Love shall uphold us in the last, as it has done in previous ordeals, and the prayer shall be answered, which we have offered so often over the grave of departed friends:

"Thou knowest, Lord, the secrets of our hearts; shut not Thy merciful ears to our prayer; but spare us, Lord most holy, O God most mighty, O holy and merciful Saviour, Thou most worthy Judge eternal, suffer us not, at our last hour, for any pains of death, to fall from Thee." "My flesh and my heart faileth; but God is the strength of my heart, and my portion for ever." "O thou of little faith, wherefore didst thou doubt?"

CHAPTER VIII.

FIGHT WATCHFULLY.

"Keep thy heart with all diligence: for out of it are the issues of life."—PROV. iv. 23.

OUR translators of the Bible, in their attempt to maintain idiom, have sometimes sacrificed vigour. "Keep thy heart *with all diligence*" is a feeble expression in comparison of that which you find in the margin: "Keep thy heart *above all keeping*."— "Above all keeping." If you would keep the apple of the eye from injury, not only as a most sensitive part of the frame and one most liable to derangement, but as the organ of the highest of all the senses, a sense for the loss of which not thousands of gold and silver could compensate; much more keep thy heart, so delicate a thing as it is, so susceptible of complete disorganization from the mere dust of an evil thought, so precious too, as being that organ of the moral nature, by which you discern and apprehend Divine truth. If you would keep in a casket, under lock and key, a jewel fit for a monarch's diadem, on the purchase of which a nation's wealth has been expended; much more keep thy heart, for whose allegiance such an infinite price was paid, whose sympathies and affections the Son of God bled, and agonized, and died to win, and which is destined to be a jewel in His Redemption-crown. If you would keep as a most sacred deposit the last token of a dying parent's love; much more keep thy heart, which Christ, the Everlasting Father, having purchased it with His own Blood, bequeathed to thee for thy custody. If thou wouldst keep some outlying fortress, which is the key of a beleaguered position, placing sentinels at every approach, and bidding them challenge every one who passes in and out; much more keep thy heart, which is the key of the character and conduct, and between which and the outer world a busy correspondence is continually being kept up. Finally,—for our precept is so worded that it might be a medical, as well as a moral one,—if thou wouldst keep thy bodily heart, as the centre of the system of the body, as the source of motion and animation to the whole frame, as the golden bowl which sends forth the living jets of the blood to the extremities, whence with freshening, recreating force they fall again into the basin;—if thou wouldst shield this part in war, covering it with the breastplate, or with hauberk's twisted mail; much more keep thy moral or spiritual heart, which is the source of moral life and whence the impulses, affections, sympathies, desires, go forth towards the objects or persons around thee, and return again with new life into thy bosom. Ay, if there be a thing in this world, which should be kept,—which should be the object of unsleeping, anxious guardianship, it is this heart;—" Keep thy heart *above all keeping;* for out of it are the issues of life."

We are now upon the subject of the resistance which the Christian, in his daily life, has to offer to Temptation. We have seen in previous Chapters that he must meet Temptation wisely, cheerfully, self-distrustfully, and with trust in Christ. And we now come to a counsel no less necessary in order to ensure success, namely, that he must meet it watchfully. "Watch and pray," says our Blessed Lord Himself, " that ye enter not into temptation."

It must be evident, even to Reason, that without this precaution of watchfulness over the heart, every other counsel for resisting temptation must be of no avail. This will be seen in a moment from one of the illustrations which has been already employed. The heart is the key of the entire spiritual position. Carry the heart, and you carry the man. Not however that the dangers of the heart are merely external, like the dangers of a fortress. The world and the Devil would not be such formidable foes, if they had nothing to correspond with from within; but our Saviour teaches us that there are many traitors in the camp, with whom they can and do correspond. " From within, out of the heart of men, proceed evil thoughts, adulteries, fornications, murders, thefts, covetousness, wickedness, deceit, lasciviousness, an evil eye, blasphemy, pride, foolishness: all these evil things come from within, and defile the man."

It is also to be noticed, in forming an estimate of our danger, that the exports and imports of the heart are exceedingly numerous. What a fertility of thought, sentiment, impression, feeling, is there in the heart of a single man! It is like an inn or hostelry;—there are every instant fresh arrivals and fresh departures. There are a thousand doors of access to the heart,—conversation, books, incidents, means of grace, all the five senses; and passengers are busily thronging in and passing out at every door. Some of these passengers are bent on doing mischief, on soiling the chambers, and throwing them into disorder; some on doing good, and setting things to right; some are questionable; some, though much fewer than is generally supposed, indifferent. Now will any precaution, short of watchfulness over the persons allowed to enter, avail to keep such an house in order? No! we must require testimonials that those who claim admittance are respectable. The sentinels must be at their posts in the fortress, and demand the password from all who cross their beat; or the general will lay his schemes in vain, and the garrison will be well victualled in vain, and the poor soldiers will fight and bleed in vain. Bravery, and wisdom, and good supplies, will all be of no avail, unless active steps are taken, to see that traitors are not prowling about the camp, ready to fire the fortress, to open the gates, or to suggest treacherous counsel. As a matter of course, to dismiss the figure, unless we keep a guard and narrow outlook upon our hearts, we may find at any moment that we have "entered into temptation," that is, have entertained it with the will, that we are fairly launched on the slippery incline which leads, it may be, to a very grievous fall. What various and rapid movements take place in our minds in the midst of a warm and animated conversation! Can there be any security for us unless we watch and question them as they arise? This moment our vanity is piqued; at another a desire to say something smart at the expense of charity, or something witty at the expense of reverence, or something entertaining at the expense of truth, or something coarse at the expense of purity, runs away with us, and we are far on our road towards sin,—if indeed we have not already arrived there,—before we can pick up the rein and check the steed. Then we are provoked not to be fair in argument, but factious; then, perhaps, to worldly compliance with the opinion of the great, the popular, the many; then, on the other hand, we are prompted to speak the truth ungraciously, without courtesy or consideration for others, apologizing to ourselves and our friends for it, by saying that "we cannot be hypocrites," that "we always say what we think." How shall we keep our foot free of so many snares?

But is solitude less dangerous, in our spiritual warfare, than company? It might be so, doubtless, if the world were the only source of temptations, if they did not arise equally from self and from the Devil. But it is clear that, from the two latter foes, who beset the Christian no less than the former, we cannot be safe any more in solitude than in company. Self is with us, and the Devil may be with us too, in the closet, as well as in the social gathering. Castle-building, with all its odious train of self-flatteries and self-complacencies; the fretting over any little wound which our vanity may have received, until it begins to fester and look serious; the mental aggravation of a slight or insult, by allowing the thoughts to dwell on it, until it fills the field of view in a manner perfectly absurd; the discomposure about worldly cares, which is always increased by solitary pondering of them; and last, not least, the vain conceit that because prayer has been offered quietly, and temper has been dormant, and the tongue closed, that therefore a great victory has been won over the inner man, or, in other words, that sin has been overcome, because it has been latent: all these, together with many coarser and baser thoughts which I need not mention, are the temptations of solitude; and the moment we pass out of the sight and hearing of men, we enter into this new circle of snares.

The remedy, and, under God's Grace, the only remedy, whether in solitude or company, is to "watch," —to "guard," as far as in us lies, "the first springs of thought and will." Let us pray and strive for the habit of challenging our sentiments, and making them give up their passport; eyeing them wistfully when they apply for admittance, and seeking to unmask those which have a questionable appearance. We shall find it useful to have one or two periods of the day for distinct recollection of the secrets of the inner man, when the question, after seeking light of the Lord, will be, "What have been the derangements of the heart, and what has been the cause of them?" Whatever they may have been, we must not for a moment be discouraged by them, but simply saying to the Lord, that such falls were to be expected from us, and that they would have been much worse, had not His Grace upheld us, we must ask Him once more to do that which belongs to Him,—forgive our sins, and raise us up again, and give us grace no more to offend His Divine Majesty. After which we must begin our course anew, as if we had never fallen, with this anthem in our mouths, "All my fresh springs shall be in Thee." The oftener we can manage to make these retirements into our own hearts, and these renewals of our good intentions, the more spiritually prosperous will our course be. For be it remembered that it is by a constant series of new starts that the spiritual life is carried on within us. The waste of animal life is repaired, not once for all, but continually, by food and sleep; and the spiritual life, a far more delicate thing, must perforce waste and decay under the exposure to many adverse influences, to which it is subjected in the world. It too requires therefore continually to repair its forces. It is not hereby meant that the true Christian is constantly falling into grievous or outward sin. We are speaking of the spiritual, not of the carnal man. And by every spiritual man an attempt is made to bring the region of the heart,—the motives, desires, affections,—under the sceptre of Christ. And he who makes this attempt sincerely, soon finds that where there has been nothing faulty in the conduct, the fine glass of the conscience has either taken a tarnish from the vapours of our natural corruption, or that the blacks of the world have settled down upon it.

The only counsel under such circumstances is, "Rub it bright again with the Blood and Spirit of Christ, and proceed with sanguine energy."

It will be found that all the more grievous falls of the tempted soul come from this,—that the keeping of the heart has been neglected, that the evil has not been nipped in the bud. We have allowed matters to advance to a question of conduct,—"Shall I say this, or not say it?" "Do this, or not do it?" Whereas the stand should have been made higher up, and the ground disputed in the inner man. As if the mere restraint upon outward conduct, without the homage of the heart to God's Law, could avail us aught, or be any thing else than an offensive hypocrisy in the eyes of the Heart-searcher! As if Balaam's refraining from the malediction of the lips, while his heart was going after his covetousness, could be acceptable to the Almighty! Balaam, being an inspired and divinely-commissioned man, *dared* not disobey; for he knew too well what would be the result of such an abuse of his supernatural gifts. But we, if, like Balaam, we have allowed to evil a free range over our hearts, *are sure to disobey when it comes to a question of conduct*, not being restrained by the fear of miraculous punishment, which alone held him back. There is therefore no safety for us except in making our stand at the avenues of the will, and rejecting at once every questionable impulse. And this, it is obvious, cannot be done without watchfulness and self-recollection,—without a continual bearing in mind where, and what we are, and that we have a treasure in our keeping, of which our foes seek to rob us. Endeavour to make your heart a little sanctuary, in which you may continually realize the Presence of God, and from which unhallowed thoughts, and even vain thoughts, must carefully be excluded.

But can our own endeavours, essential though they be to success, bring about of themselves this most desirable consummation? Our Saviour teaches us better. "Watch," says He, "lest ye enter into temptation;" but ends not the precious counsel here.

He gives to His Word on this occasion, that many-sidedness of truth, for which all His words are so remarkably distinguished, and which so contrasts with the one-sidedness of mere human teaching: "Watch *and pray*, that ye enter not into temptation." The sentinel must be at his post, no doubt, and must be wakeful at his post if the city is to be kept; but, nevertheless, "except the Lord keep the city, the watchman waketh but in vain." Man must give his exertion, no doubt; but he must never lean upon it; for that would be leaning upon the staff of a bruised reed. Now Prayer is, or ought to be, the expression of human dependence upon God,—the throwing ourselves upon His protecting Wisdom, and Power, and Love. And therefore, when Our Saviour counsels us to unite prayer with watching, He counsels us to throw ourselves upon God, under a sense of our own weakness and total insufficiency. And surely there is enough in what has been said respecting the difficulty of keeping the heart, to engender such a sense of weakness. This throng of thoughts which is continually passing in and out, how shall we dream of examining, trying, judging them all, except by a special Divine interference in our behalf? Divine power can qualify a man for any thing; but nothing short of Divine Power can qualify him for a task so onerous as this. To God, then, let us commit the keeping of our souls, in the most absolute self-distrust. And if this self-distrust is any thing short of absolute, we may expect that constant falls will attend our best endeavours, whose effect, if God bless them, shall be to beat us thoroughly out of this fault. It is a great attainment to be able honestly to say to the Lord, really and deeply meaning what we say: "Lord, I am quite unable to keep my heart myself, and have proved myself so by many humbling falls, in which my adversary has made me bite the dust; but Thou art able to keep me from falling, and to present me faultless before the presence of Thy Glory with exceeding joy; and to Thee therefore I commit the keeping of my soul, simply watching, as Thou hast bidden me, and leaving all the rest to Thee."

He who can say this shall have Christ dwelling in his heart by faith; and this indwelling shall be a sure preservative against evil thoughts; and in that heart, though agitated on the surface, there shall be a peace which it has never known before.

In the inn of Bethlehem there were many going to and fro, and much hurry and disquietude, while caravans were unlading or making up their complement of passengers, and the divan presented a spectacle of many costumes, and resounded with wrangling, and barter, and merriment. But in a stable hard by there was a tender joy too deep for words, and a stillness of adoration which seemed to shut out the outer world; for Mary had brought forth her Firstborn Son and laid Him in the manger, and her heart and that of Joseph were full to overflowing, and angels were gazing down from above on the mystery of the Holy Incarnation.

The soul of man is a noisy hostelry, full of turmoil and disquietude, and giving entertainment to every vain and passing thought which seeks admittance there. But when Christ comes, and takes up His abode in the heart, He reduces it to order and peace; and though it may move amid the excitements and confusions of life, yet hath it an inner stillness which they cannot disturb or destroy; for the King of Peace is there, and Peace is the purchase of His Cross, and the last legacy of His Love and His ancient promise to His people; for so it is written,—"He hath made peace through the Blood of His Cross;" "Peace I leave with you; My peace I give unto you;"—"Thou wilt keep him in perfect peace, whose mind is stayed on Thee, because he trusteth in Thee."

CHAPTER IX.

THE HIGH PREROGATIVE OF SUFFERING.

"Verily, verily, I say unto thee, When thou wast young, thou girdedst thyself, and walkedst whither thou wouldest: but when thou shalt be old, thou shalt stretch forth thy hands, and another shall gird thee, and carry thee whither thou wouldest not. This spake He, signifying by what death he should glorify God. And when He had spoken this, He saith unto him, Follow Me."—JOHN xxi. 18, 19.

IN these words Our Lord predicts the death of St. Peter. In his old age the Apostle was to be crucified, made to stretch forth his hands upon the transverse beam of the cross, and girded (or lashed round the waist) to the instrument of torture by a cord. Tradition says that he was crucified, at his own request, with his head downwards; in that case, the girding, or tying tightly, to the cross would probably be necessary, by way of keeping the body of the sufferer in its right position. In the ordinary mode of crucifixion, to which Our Blessed Lord was subjected, the body rested, not, as is often erroneously supposed, upon the hands and feet, but upon a seat projecting from the middle of the cross; but when the cross was inverted, the body would have no such rest, and it would then become necessary to fix it in another manner by a tight ligament. This is in all probability the reference of the words, "another shall gird thee," though perhaps some will prefer to see in them nothing more than an allusion to the binding of the Apostle previously to his being led away to execution.

But putting aside their original and literal meaning, the words lend themselves very well to a secondary application. They may be regarded as a striking parable of human life in its two great periods of youth and old age. Youth is full of enterprise, energy, hope, vigour, prompt in forming schemes, and active in carrying them into execution; when emancipated from the restraints of boyhood, it exults in its independence, and feels that it is the master of its own destiny: "When thou wast young, thou girdedst thyself, and walkedst whither thou wouldest." But old age is the season of helplessness and dependence;—"another" is called in to perform the most necessary offices, and to supply our lack of service towards our own failing frames; the very old have to be led, fed, apparelled by others, and the end is, that they are carried whither (according to the flesh) man cannot but shrink from going, and laid, in all the weakness and dishonour of death, in the plot of consecrated earth which lies around the church. "But when thou shalt be old, thou shalt stretch forth thy hands, and another shall gird thee, and carry thee whither thou wouldest not."

We are now considering the Christian life in its practical, as distinct from its devotional aspect; the phases of that aspect of it are, as we have seen, three: —acting, fighting, suffering. We have given some counsels on the Christian's work, and on the Christian's temptations, and our plan now requires that we should say something of those occasions, on which his great duty is to lie passive in the hands of God.

I. We remark, first, that suffering in all its forms *is, and should be looked upon as being, a vocation.* There are many, and these real Christians, persons interested in God's Service, who regard suffering in a shallow, superficial point of view, as *an interference with* their vocations, and consequently miss all the golden opportunities of growth in grace and knowledge which it holds out. Their plan of life is put out of joint, and, as it appears, their usefulness impeded, by some accident or some grievous sickness; their activity is at an end, or at an end for a time,—quietness is imposed upon them as a condition of life, or of recovery; they chafe and fret at the restraint, because, as they themselves put it, they are precluded from actively doing good. Now what does this fretting indicate? What but this, that they love not the Will of God, but merely the satisfaction which accrues in the natural order of things from a consciousness of doing good to others? and to cling to this satisfaction is only a higher form of self-love,—not the love of God. The truth is, that God, in sending them the sickness or the accident, has been pleased in His Wisdom and Love to change their vocation, and, if minded to be really loyal to His Will, they must accommodate and familiarize themselves to the idea, not that their occupation is gone, but simply that it is altered. As an illustration, let us imagine the conduct of a campaign by the commander-in-chief of the forces of an empire. No one but he himself is in full possession of his plans: he has laid his schemes with deep foresight, and with the most correct calculation of contingencies, but communicates the whole of them to no subordinate. Advices from home, and from the generals of detachments are arriving all day long at head-quarters, and despatches are as continually going out; but no one knows any more of the contents than concerns his own position and duties. Many lookers on, who cannot see the whole game, misjudge the commander. There is an outcry that he risked unfairly, in an enterprise almost desperate, the lives of a small party: but the real truth is, as men would see if they could but know the whole, that this risk was absolutely essential to the safety of the entire force, and that by the exposure of a score of men to fearful odds the lives of twenty thousand have been secured. Let us now suppose that suddenly some officer is commanded to hold himself and his troop in readiness to undertake some important manœuvre,—to go up into a breach, or to storm a fortress, or to meet and cut off an enemy's supplies: suppose that this enterprise exactly suits both the capacities and inclination of the man on whom it is devolved; that there is room in it for the display of powers which he is conscious of possessing; that it gives him just the opportunity which he coveted, of achieving distinction. He is making his preparations with all sanguineness, and anticipating the final order to depart, when, lo! the order arrives, but it peremptorily alters his destination; he is not to be of the storming party, he is to go into a secluded dingle with his men, far out of the way of the operations, and there lie still, and send out scouts to make observations of the country, and report. It is a hard trial to one who was girding himself for active service, and longing for an opportunity for displaying prowess and forethought; and it is difficult to bear, just in proportion as there is room to doubt the wisdom of the commander's general arrangements, and his considerateness for the individual officer whose destination he thus arbitrarily changes. But supposing these to be beyond all question: supposing that hitherto the most consummate skill had been shown in every arrangement of the campaign, and that on many previous occasions the general had shown the very kindest, and even the most affectionate regard to the interests of this particular officer? Would it then be found impossible, or even difficult, to reconcile the mind to such a disposition of things? Surely not, when once cool reflection had succeeded to the sting of the disappointment. And when our Heavenly Father changes our whole plan of life by His providential despatches, and virtually sends us the order, "Lie still; and let another gird and carry thee instead of thy girding thyself, and walking on Mine errands 'whither thou wouldest;'" shall we venture even to remonstrate, when we are assured by the testimony of His Word that both His wisdom and His care for us are unbounded? and when our own experience of life, brief as it has been, re-echoes this testimony? Ah! to love God is to embrace His Will when it runs counter to our inclinations, as well as when it jumps with them.

What has been said applies quite as much to those thousand trifling occasions of every-day life on which our little plans are disconcerted, as to the serious interference which sickness makes in larger schemes. We are too much wedded to our plans, whether they

be plans for a life, or plans for a day or an hour;—
too little loyal at heart to the Will of God. And
hence arises great uneasiness and discomposure of
mind, which, from whatever source it arises, cannot
fail to be prejudicial, and a hindrance to the spiritual
life. We have set apart, it may be, such an hour
of the day for the purpose of devotion or study. But
just as we were about to spend it so, some call of
necessity or charity arises in another direction. In
either case, whether it be of necessity or charity,
it is God's call; and not our duty only, but our
happiness, lies in responding to it cheerfully and
lovingly. We must be ready to go out of our way,
if God calls us out of our way, or, in other words,
to have our little plans so modified and corrected,
as to be brought into the scheme of His great and
all-wise plan. It is every way better to do what God
intends for us, than what we intend for ourselves.
Our Blessed Lord on a certain occasion was stedfastly
bent upon raising the dead; but as He was passing to
the house where the deceased maid lay, an interruption
arose. A poor woman with an issue of blood crept
up behind Him, and, touching the hem of His garment,
stole from Him a cure. Willingly and graciously
does Our Lord stop upon His way, and take up the
episode into the marvellous poem of His Life. He
makes the poor woman discover herself, and draws
from her a public acknowledgment of her cure. And
not until He has dismissed her with a gracious word
of encouragement does He pass on to fulfil His
original intention. It is a great lesson as to the
spirit which we should cultivate, when it pleases God
to disconcert or interrupt our designs.

But to recur to the point. Regard suffering, even
in its slighter forms, as a vocation, having its special
duties, and offering its special grace. Say secretly
of it,—" Here for the present lies thy allotted task,
O my soul; consider how much may be made of this
period: how largely it may be improved to God's
Service and thy salvation. It is the post to which

thou art appointed: seek to occupy it faithfully and bravely; and more good shall accrue to thee from it than from what thou didst propose to thyself as the line of service of thine own choosing."

But may we not say something more of suffering than merely that it is a vocation? May we not say of it, that it is the highest of all vocations? We might augur thus much from the fact, that under ordinary circumstances, the close of the Christian life rather than its beginning is characterized by suffering. As a general rule, the sick bed is the scene upon which the curtain falls. And we might naturally expect that God would reserve to the last that dispensation by which the character of His children is to be most highly purified and exalted;— that He would call them to the sublimest and most elevating of trials at the end of their career, when, having been proved in lesser matters, they had been found faithful. We find in our text an intimation that this was the case with St. Peter. If any one ever glorified God by active service, undertaken with love and zeal, surely it was St. Peter and his great colleague, the Apostle of the Gentiles. St. Peter was the chief pillar of the early Church: his energy and his gift of government were the main props of her administration, before St. Paul appeared. He was God's prime agent in the spread of the Gospel among the people of the circumcision. Yet not one word is here said of the glorification of God, *in connexion with St. Peter's active days.* The spread of Christ's Kingdom through his preaching and his rule is passed over in silence. The Evangelist speaks of his crucifixion—when those limbs, once so full of vigour, so prompt to move in the Master's Service, were fettered; and when his body was bound fast to the accursed tree, as *the* period, when God reaped from the Apostle a great harvest of glory;—" this spake He, signifying *by what death* he should glorify God."

During the lifetime of God's people, the graces with which He endows them are always a sweet

savour to Him, through the Intercession of Christ.
But in a holy death there is something specially
acceptable, over and above that which there is in a
holy life; and therefore with a marked emphasis it is
written: "Right dear in the sight of the Lord is *the
death* of His saints." Now what is Death but the
crown and climax of human sufferings? It is the
trial of trials,—the deepest shadow which in this life of
shadows falls athwart the soul. Can a man acquiesce
lovingly in this trial,—cling fast to God when this
most chill of all shadows falls across his heart, and
believe still that he shall be brought out into the
sunlight? Then this is a glorious test of the faith
and of the grace that is in him. God delights to see
grace in us at all times; but He loves not to see it
latent. He desires it to be in exercise. And, in
order to bring it into exercise, He uses the instrumentality of suffering. The leaves of the aromatic plant
shed but a faint odour, as they wave in the air. The
gold shines scarcely at all, as it lies hid in the ore.
The rugged crust of the pebble conceals from the eye
its interior beauty. But let the aromatic leaf be
crushed; let the ore be submitted to the furnace; let
the pebble be cut and polished; and the fragrance, the
splendour, the fair colours are then brought out:—

> "This leaf? This stone? It is thy heart:
> It must be crushed by pain and smart,
> It must be cleansed by sorrow's art—
> Ere it will yield a fragrance sweet,
> Ere it will shine, a jewel meet
> To lay before thy dear Lord's feet."

The same law is observable in spiritual character,
which rules the formation of natural. How often in
a smooth and easy life do men, who have something far
better beneath, appear selfish, effeminate, and trifling!
Suddenly they are thrown into some position of high
trust, great responsibility, or serious danger;—are
called upon to face an enemy, or submit to the
hardships of a campaign;—and lo! the character
shows a stuff and a fibre,—ay, and a tenderness for

others,—which no one ever gave it credit for. Resolute will, dauntless self-sacrifice, considerateness, show themselves, where before we could see nothing but what was pliant and self-indulgent. Trial has unmasked latent graces of character; and although spiritual character is a thing of a higher order than natural, yet it is developed according to the same laws of the mind.

But the chief reason why suffering is the highest of all vocations, is that in suffering so close a conformity may be attained to Him, who is the highest exemplification of human virtue. The heroes of Paganism exemplified the heroism of enterprise. Patriotism, chivalrous deeds of valour, high-souled aspirations after glory, stern justice taking its course in their hands, while natural feeling was held in abeyance,— this was the line in which they shone. Our Blessed Lord illustrated all virtues indeed, but most especially the passive ones. His heroism took its colouring from endurance. Women, though inferior to men in enterprise, usually come out better than men in suffering; and it is always to be remembered that Our Blessed Lord held His Humanity, not of the stronger, but of the weaker sex. The leading idea of Him is the patient sufferer, "the lamb dumb before its shearers;"—not till after His ascension into Heaven is He represented to us as "the Lion of the tribe of Judah." And it is for this among other reasons, that, while the Evangelists notice different parts of Our Lord's History,—while two of them are wholly silent respecting His Infancy and Childhood,— and one almost silent respecting the Ministry in Galilee; they all agree in pourtraying His Death with great minuteness. Not only was this Death the propitiation for the sins of the whole world, and therefore the most important of all events to us, but also, viewing Christ merely as an Example, His Death expresses far more of His Divine Character than His Life. What should we know of Christ comparatively —how very imperfectly should we conceive of Him—

if the narratives of the Cross were torn out of the Book of the Gospels? It was the Cross which (to use an expression we should not dare to use, unless an Apostle had led the way) perfected the human character of Our Lord; for God made the "Captain of our Salvation perfect through sufferings,"—not perfect in the sense of sinless, for that He was from His Infancy upwards, but perfect in the sense in which no one can be perfect, who has not submitted to the discipline of trial. The spotless block of white marble may be perfect, in the sense of being without a flaw; but it acquires a perfection of another sort, when, after being shaped and chiselled, it is converted into a beautiful vase, fit for the palace of a monarch. The Lord, in virtue of His Humanity, had a will which shrunk from and deprecated suffering,—a will which we see in operation, when those words flow from Him in the garden; "Father, if it be possible, let this cup pass from Me." This will, however, was gradually brought round into complete acquiescence with the higher will,—an acquiescence which expresses itself in that second cry, as recorded by St. Matthew: "Father, if this cup may not pass from Me, except I drink it, Thy will be done." It was this acquiescence which gave to the human character of Christ, sinless all along, an exquisitely finished perfection, and a certain beauty of maturity, which it had not before.

It is to conformity with Him in this high acquiescence that He called His disciple, St. Peter, when He said to him, "Follow Me." He had told him that he should have scope to follow, in a suffering similar to His own, (for St. Peter too should stretch forth his hands upon the transverse beam of the cross,) and now He tells him to copy His spirit in suffering,—"Follow Me."

And does He not tell us the same also? If the words "Follow Me" were addressed specifically to St. Peter, are there not words of precisely similar import addressed to all disciples to the end of time? Do we not read, "If any man will come after Me, let him deny himself, and take up his cross daily, and follow Me?"

Ah! there is the word of which we are in search, to express the agency of the sufferer in this matter,—"*take up* his cross." It might not be very clear what the agency of a sufferer, pinned down perhaps to a bed of pain,—upon whom, possibly, silence is imposed,—could be. Such an one can *do* nothing in man's estimation, who looketh only on the outward appearance; but in God's estimation, who looketh on the heart, he can do much. He has a moral choice left him,—a will. This will may affirm God's will, or reject it. While no option is left us as to *bearing* the cross, we may either *take it up*, or strive to push it off. We may, on the one hand, harbour the thought that we are hardly dealt with; or, on the other, we may, by enforcing upon ourselves such considerations as that God is a tender Father, and never chastens but for our profit; that suffering is a medicine, remedial, though bitter; that we have deserved infinitely more than is ever laid upon us; and that there is no real satisfaction for man except in conformity to the Divine Will,—bring round the mind to say sincerely (the highest point of perfection this, which human character can reach):

"O Lord, my God, do Thou Thy holy Will!
   I will lie still:
I will not stir, lest I forsake Thine arm,
   And break the charm,
Which lulls me, clinging to my Father's breast,
   In perfect rest."

Are we striving to bring our minds to this point, when, and as, God calls us to suffer? Are we daily practising resignation as opportunity offers? By a patient and loving endurance of annoyances, are we preparing ourselves gradually for the discipline of trials? Christ comes to us morning by morning to present to us, for the day then opening, divers little crosses, thwartings of our own will, interferences with our plans, disappointments of our little pleasures. Do we kiss them, and take them up, and follow in His rear, like Simon the Cyrenian? Or do we toss them from us scornfully, because they are so little; and wait for some great affliction to approve our patience and our resignation to His Will? Ah, how might we accommodate to the small matters of religion generally those words of the Lord respecting the children, "Take heed that ye despise not one of these little ones!" Despise not little sins; they have ruined many a soul. Despise not little duties; they have been to many a saved man an excellent discipline of humility. Despise not little temptations; rightly met they have often nerved the character for some fiery trial. And despise not little crosses; for when taken up, and lovingly accepted at the Lord's hand, they have made men meet for a great crown, even the crown of righteousness and life, which the Lord hath promised to them that love Him.

CHAPTER X.

OF RECREATION.

"*Whether therefore ye eat, or drink, or whatsoever ye do, do all to the glory of God.*"—1 COR. x. 31.

" ST. JOHN the Evangelist, as Cassian relates, amusing
" himself one day with a tame partridge on his hand,
" was asked by an huntsman, How such a man as he
" could spend his time in so unprofitable a manner?
" to whom St. John replied, Why dost thou not carry
" thy bow always bent? Because, answered the hunts-
" man, if it were always bent, I fear it would lose its
" spring, and become useless. Be not surprised then,
" replied the Apostle, that I should sometimes remit a
" little of my close attention of spirit to enjoy a little
" recreation, that I may afterwards employ myself more
" fervently in Divine contemplation[1]."

[1] S. François de Sales, Vie Dévote.

Some persons might be disposed to think Recreation too light a subject to be treated in a work on Personal Religion. But let it be considered that in the broad sense of the term (in which it embraces every species of refreshment bodily and mental) Recreation must form an integral part of human life. Human life, as a matter of fact, is made up of graver and lighter passages. There is no true portraiture of it which does not present its reliefs and recreations alongside of its burdensome pressure and cares. Man's mind is so constituted, that even in the most afflictive circumstances it cannot be always on the strain; such a strain would ultimately break the mind. So it seeks and finds a safety-valve in the lighter passages of life, through which its natural elasticity (for it is wonderfully elastic) vents itself. But then, if this be the constitution of the human mind, and therefore of human life, which is but the development and expression of the human mind, our reliefs, no less than our burdens, must come within the scope of true religion. For there is no truth more certain than this, that religion is designed to leaven our *whole* life; that no district of life, not a single waking hour, is to be excluded from its sanctifying influences. If Recreation is a constituent part of life, Recreation must be capable of being sanctified.

We do not give Recreation too prominent a place in the religious system, when we say that it is for the mind what sleep is for the body of man. No man's body could long endure the stress and burden of daily life without sleep. And no man's mind could, as I have said, long endure any mental pressure without Recreation. It is wonderful what the body gains in sleep, far more than we are apt to suspect; what gentle healing influences are ministered to the animal functions of this dull and heavy frame by that "soft nurse of nature," as our great poet so beautifully calls it. It is often said of infants and young children, that they grow much faster in an hour of sleep than in several waking hours,—the truth being, I suppose, that sleep is an imbibing of energy, and waking existence a waste or expenditure of it. And surely it is no less wonderful how much the mind, I do not say does, but *may* gain in Recreation,—how rapid a growth in grace it may achieve when the harness of a regular pursuit is for a while lifted from off its neck, and leisure is given to it to unbend itself at will. That Recreation is frequently and cruelly abused, and leisure allowed to degenerate into license, is no argument whatever against its possible utility. Sleep itself is not beneficial, but mischievous, if it be not well regulated. A man may easily have too much of it,— more than is good for him; and the excess is not indifferent,—it is absolutely prejudicial. Recreation, like sleep, must be carefully regulated with a view to the great end which it is designed to subserve. There must be some amount of forethought as to the conduct of it, and of restriction upon its freaks and licenses, if it is to be attended with wholesome effects. Perhaps there are some of my readers who altogether resent the idea of such restriction; who wish altogether to exempt Recreation from the interference of religious principle; who look to the little intervals and interstices of work as so much time which may be freely wasted, trifled away, frittered away, sinned away without compunction, flung recklessly into the great gulf of unredeemed possibilities.

In censuring thoughts of this kind which may arise upon the subject, it is necessary to disentangle what is true and just in them from what is radically false and vicious.

It is absolutely certain, then, that there is no single waking moment of our life which we can afford to lose. Never was truer line written by any poet than that of Young,

"———————————————— the man
Is yet unborn who duly weighs an hour."

Probably there is no such thing as an indifferent moment,—a moment in which our characters are not being secretly shaped by the bias of the will, either for good or evil. It is a great mystery, but so it is, that our Eternity is suspended upon the manner in which we pass through a very short span of time. And, analogously, this very short span of time takes its complexion from the moments which go to make it up. If life itself be of such tremendous import, its constituent hours and minutes cannot be insignificant. All minutes must be made available; not indeed available in one particular form, not available in the way of work, but all available in the Service of God, to which both work and diversion may contribute.

But it is possible that what is meant by resisting the interference of religious principle with Recreation, may be merely this, that Recreation will cease to be Recreation, if too much seriousness of thought be thrown into it. And there is some amount of truth here, which we shall presently notice. Unbending no doubt must be unbending, if it is to answer its object.

Let us first say something of the principle by which alone any Recreation can be sanctified, and then offer some advice on the forms which Recreation may take.

First, then, Recreation, like work, is to be engaged in with a view to God's glory: we are not to separate it even in idea from Him, but to bring it within the great scope of His service. This principle is distinctly enunciated in the words of the Apostle,—" Whether therefore ye eat, or drink, or whatsoever ye do, do all to the glory of God." Eating and drinking, the taking of nourishment, is a species of Recreation, when that word is understood in its widest sense. To take nourishment is to refresh the body, even as to take Recreation is to refresh the mind. If then the taking of nourishment may be made conducive to God's glory, and brought within the scope of His Service, so also, without doubt, may the taking of Recreation. Let it be well settled in the mind then, as the first step, that our periods of relaxation may have a religious significance and a religious value; may be a means of religious improvement and of progress in the spiritual life, whose law is progress; and this apprehension is of itself a point gained, although it be only an apprehension of the understanding, and not as yet the choice of the will.

The great point, however, is that choice of the will, or intention of the heart;—that we should be able to say mentally and cordially these words, or their equivalent:—" I have chosen the Service of Almighty God, in whatever position He pleases to place me, as the one object of my life. To this great object I have determined to devote all my faculties of body and soul. But then neither body nor soul can be sound or healthy without innocent Recreation. Innocent Recreation, therefore, I will have,—I take it as a matter of deliberate choice, not merely because it gratifies me, but chiefly because it is subservient to my end." This is the only principle which can sanctify any action, be it grave or trivial.

As to the different forms of Recreation, the following suggestions may be offered.

1. First, of course, care must be taken that there may be nothing in them contrary to the Will and Word of God,—nothing which His Law condemns. Their being useful (in the ordinary sense of usefulness) is not here the question. It would be absurd to require of every kind of Recreation that it shall do some definite good to the minds and bodies of others. It is quite sufficiently useful, if it refreshes our own minds and bodies, and renders them more efficient instruments of the Divine Service. All besides this that can be required is, that it shall be innocent,—a form of diversion on which Holy Scripture lays no ban.

2. But secondly, it does not follow that because it is abstractedly innocent, and because, therefore, we may not presume to judge others for resorting to it, it is therefore allowable for ourselves. There are many amusements, which to the pure are pure, but which with persons whose imaginations have been fouled by evil, and evil which, it may be, they have not yet thoroughly outgrown, would stimulate bad passions, or

at least throw serious temptations in their way. Let no man or woman for the sake of a paltry amusement venture within arm's length of a temptation. To do so were to turn into a mockery the daily petition which Our Lord puts into our lips,—" Lead us not into temptation." By the slightest experience of the spiritual life, we gain some amount of knowledge of our moral temperament, just as by the experience of physical life we gain a knowledge of the kinds of food wholesome and unwholesome for us. Then this knowledge of our own moral temperament must be called into exercise, and acted upon, in judging what amusements are for ourselves permissible. In the spiritual life, as in the physical, the unwholesome must be avoided. Each Christian must be fully persuaded in his own mind of the innocence of those forms of Recreation in which he indulges, not only to the world at large, but to himself in particular. If the circumstantials of any amusement are such as effectually to preclude secret Prayer, the realization of God's Presence and the thought of Our Lord's Passion, to us such amusement is forbidden, though Scripture may be silent upon it. Yet it is quite possible that our neighbour, whose mind is possessed of more recollectedness and self-control than ours, may partake of it innocently. It is very necessary to remember this, because religious persons are very apt to judge and set at nought their brethren for not being equally strict with themselves in regard to amusements. If God's Word has not spoken on the subject, this is nothing more nor less than sacrificing love to a Pharisaic feeling of self-gratulation that " we are not as other men are."

It may seem a truism to say, and yet it certainly needs to be said, that the more amusing amusements are, the better. Busy lives have not time for many; let such as are taken, then, be thoroughly refreshing. Yet what a perfect burden are many forms of so-called amusement! or how do we turn them into a burden by thoughtlessness, and negligence, and the evil habit of letting amusement shift for itself, as if it were a thing not worth caring for in a religious point of view! The ordinary Recreation of ordinary persons very much resolves itself into conversation with friends or casual acquaintance; and there can be no doubt that by taking a little pains with it, directing it in interesting channels, and by unselfish efforts to make it vivacious, conversation may be made to brighten the mind very considerably, and to relieve the pressure of the burdens of life. "Iron sharpeneth iron; so a man sharpeneth the countenance of his friend." Yet how miserably stale, flat, and unprofitable, how utterly devoid of the salt of wit and wisdom are the conversations which often fill up the interstices of our time! The two minds brought together for half an hour are like two circles, which just touch in one point, and then fly off each in its own orbit; there is no manner of intersection, sympathy, or fellowship; and the result is that what should be a relief becomes instantly a drudgery. What can be done under such circumstances, where the persons across whom we are thrown are hopelessly dull, irresponsive, formal, or, it may be, vain, impertinent, or otherwise actively offensive? Matters perhaps may be somewhat mended by good humour; and if not, this must be taken as one of the petty trials of every-day life, which, like serious trials, gives scope for the exercise of Christ-like patience and sweetness, and so for the elevation of our own spiritual character. That may seem to be a mind wholly inaccessible to our view of things; but it is well to remember that every human mind has somewhere within it a source of sympathy, if we did but know where to look for it, and an interest, if we could but find the clue to it. Possibly, as often happens in our intercourse with foreigners, it may be *our own* peculiarities which chill, and offend, and drive inward those whom we meet with. At all events an attempt to copy the mind of Christ and fulfil the Scriptural precept, "Be patient towards all men," cannot fail of drawing down a blessing upon our own spirit—a far greater relief than that which could be found in the liveliest conversation.

But to return to our immediate topic. How often is foreign travel, one of the best and most intelligent forms of Recreation, turned from a pleasure into a burden by the silly, scrambling way in which it is embarked upon! No forethought is exercised on the subject; there is no attempt at unity of method; and both mind and body are exhausted instead of refreshed, by flying about all day long from cathedrals to cataracts, from museums to mountains, and from picture galleries to pinnacles of temples. Such Recreation to a great extent defeats its own end. Variety is, no doubt, one secret of mental relief; but then even in the variety there should be a sort of method and unity of plan, lest it degenerate into mere distraction. And *all* distraction, that of pleasure as well as of business, is a burden to the mind.

Lastly, although no doubt any thing like severe application of the mind would interfere with the end of Recreation, it is very much to be wished that a good education embraced some superficial and elementary knowledge of those lighter subjects of study, which, as they turn upon Nature, can be taken up and pursued wherever Nature is found. It is easy to speak contemptuously of superficial knowledge, and if such knowledge flatters the owner into a conceit of his own wisdom it *is* contemptible; but a very slight intelligence on natural subjects—flowers, shells, trees, the habits of birds, the habits of animals, the habits of insects,—may be at once a great relief to the mind and a rational interest. One of the saddest conditions of a human creature is to read God's Word with a veil upon the heart, to pass blindfolded through all the wondrous testimonies of Redeeming Love and Grace which the Holy Scriptures contain. And it is sad, also, if not actually censurable, to pass blindfolded through the works of God, to live in a world of flowers, and stars, and sunsets, and a thousand glorious objects of Nature, and never to have a passing interest awakened by any one of them. It is a precept of the Divine Master's, occurring in the Sermon on the Mount, and therefore obligatory upon all His disciples, that we should "consider the lilies of the field." If Christians qualified themselves more for an interest in Nature by that which is essential to such interest, a slight knowledge of Nature, there would be among them much more purity, and therefore much more brightness and joyousness of mind. For Nature is God's pure work, unsullied by sin; and therefore the study of it is a pure delight to those who love Him.

Two obvious counsels may be given in conclusion.

a. All excess in recreations must be avoided. They are not, and must not be, regarded as the earnest business of life. The sign of the Cross,—the mark of self-denial and self-renunciation,—should be made upon each and all of them. Indeed this is as essential to the enjoying them as it is to their sanctification. An amusement indulged too far soon cloys. It has not the spring in it which earnest work has.

b. Secondly; our longer periods of leisure should always be made to pay to God the tax of additional devotion. It is a heavenly thrift, and a great gain in the way of refreshment of mind, to make an hour of leisure an hour of communion with Our Lord. We should see to it that, as our alms are proportioned to our superfluous substance, so our prayers should be proportioned to our superfluous time.

Finally; let none think lightly of the subject we have treated in this Chapter. We have been really dealing with the question how the human mind may be preserved in health, vigour, and efficiency. What careful, discriminating, delicate treatment does this mind require at our hand, seeing that God puts upon it such overwhelming honour! Does He not propose to make it the Temple of His Holy Spirit, a house for His special indwelling, a spiritual sanctuary fragrant with the incense of Prayer? If the constitution which He has given it is never thoughtfully studied, if from neglect or thoughtlessness we violate the laws which He has impressed upon it, may we not seriously injure that which is destined to be an instrument of His Service and glory? Lord, make us to hallow Thy House of Prayer. Make us jealous of the purity, vigour, energy of our own minds. And oh! let Recreation, as well as business, be so ordered, as to further instead of interrupting our communion with Thee. Teach us to turn it into fine gold of the altar by the purity of our intention in taking it, and to offer it unto Thee, (for so only can any work of ours be acceptable,) in the union of Thy Son's Merits and Passion.

PART IV.

SUPPLEMENTAL.

CHAPTER I.

ON THE WISDOM AND COMFORT OF LOOKING NO FURTHER THAN THE PRESENT DAY IN OUR SERVICE OF GOD.

"*He that is faithful in that which is least is faithful also in much.*"—LUKE xvi. 10.

THE principle laid down in these words admits of many applications. One of them will form the subject of the present Chapter.

We had occasion to remark recently that all growth proceeds from one nucleus,—forms round one centre. It is so in Nature, it is so in Grace, and it is so in study and the pursuit of knowledge. The first thing to be done by a person bent upon studying any large subject of human knowledge, such as History, or Jurisprudence, or Philosophy, or Divinity, is to limit the field of his researches, and draw a circle round it. In History, for example, the attacking universal History in all its parts would make us miserable sciolists; we should take any well-defined period, to which we happen to be particularly drawn, and make all our studies gather round that period as their centre. Thence our researches may extend themselves into adjacent periods systematically and on principle; and the knowledge so acquired would be sound, not discursive.

Now in so far as the practical life of Christianity is, or ought to be, the study of all of us, it is subject to the same laws as other studies. Here, too, he who would make a solid progress will do well in a certain sense to limit the field. In a certain sense, of course, it admits of no limitation. The Service of God must be co-extensive with our whole life, and reach over our whole compass of duties, without a single exception. Still, in trying to fill this vast area, we shall do well to begin from a centre, and work outward. In Devotion and in Duty address yourself first to what is manageable, and distract not the mind, whose quietness is essential to progress, with too many calls at once. Collect all your energies in one quarter of the field,—whether it be the conflict with the besetting sin, or the realization of the Presence of God, or of any other religious truth which has taken a strong hold upon the mind; and try to occupy that corner effectively. Be faithful in that which is least; and gradually the area of God's Service shall for thee extend itself, and thou shalt be faithful in much.

Now it shall be the object of the present Chapter to show how this principle is capable of application to our Time.

God has divided for us our Time into periods. Our life has, by His appointment, something like the hands of a clock, or the stroke of a bell, to mark its progress. I am not speaking of *artificial* divisions of Time, like the hour or the week. The hour is an arbitrary division of man's making. The day might be divided into three hours, or four, or nine, as easily as into twelve. The week, or rather the seven-day week, is indeed of Divine appointment; but it too, like the hour, is arbitrary and artificial,—and has nothing in Nature corresponding to it. The Romans had eight-day weeks, and other nations may have divided their month after other fashions, into sets of six days, or four days, or three. But I am speaking now of the natural divisions of Time, marked by the movements of the heavenly bodies,—by the circuit of the earth round the sun, the moon round the earth, and by the earth's revolution on its own axis. The year, the month, and the day are God's divisions of Time, and they are divisions inherent in the constitution of the world,—divisions having an outward visible sign on the face of Nature to mark them.

Now of these periods,—the day, the month, the year, which enter into the composition of every man's lifetime,—the day is the least. The day is the least in point of duration; but it may be also said with truth of the day that it is the rudiment of the whole. The day is a life in little, a miniature life. Let a convex mirror be suspended overhead in a room, so as to form a small angle with the wall; you will see all the whole room in it, wide as it may be, with all the details of the furniture, and all the company. And how is this? Every object is, of course, greatly reduced in size, so that every square yard of space in the room appears as a square inch of space, or less, on the mirror. Still there is nothing which finds its place in the room, which does not also find a proportionate place on the mirror. So it is with the day and the lifetime. The day is the convex mirror of the life. Do you desire a summary estimate of a man's whole character, as it will appear upon a calm review after he is laid in his coffin? Study him for a day only, from his rising to his lying down; and it is enough: the germs of the life are in the day; and that microscopic view, aided by a little effort of imagination, puts you in possession of the whole truth respecting him. Is it not written, "He that is faithful in that which is least is faithful also in much: and he that is unjust in the least is unjust also in much?"

But before I enter more in detail into the miniature character of the day, and the help which we may derive from the due consideration of this character, I will point to those passages of Holy Scripture, which imply that, in God's design, the day is the rudiment of the whole life,—a little life in itself.

First, then, the Christian's store of provisions for his journey is meted out to him day by day; which implies that in God's estimate a day is a complete cycle, a little life in itself. On what principle does Our Lord teach us to pray, "Give us *day by day* our daily bread?" Why are we implicitly directed to come again another morning, and yet another and another, for our supplies? Why not pray compendiously and once for all, Give me bread, Lord, during the term of my life? Why, but because another day is not so much another stage in the pilgrimage, as actually another pilgrimage, in itself complete, without any consideration of what went before, or what is to follow after? I know not whether I may live to see another day. If therefore bread for a whole lifetime were to be given me to-day, it might be superfluous, it might be more than was needed. And to pray for more than we need, would be inconsistent with the sobriety which should characterize prayer.

Again;—as the Christian's provisions are meted out by the day, so his thoughts are to have the same limit,—his anxieties (blessed be God!) are to be bounded by the horizon of nightfall. Sweet and solemn are those words,—I know not whether more sweet, or more solemn,—"Take no thought for the morrow, for the morrow shall take thought for the things of itself; sufficient unto *the day* is the evil thereof." Observe that Our Lord does not tell us to take no thought for *this day;* rather perhaps He implies that we should do so. Certainly it would be well to do so in matters spiritual. It would be well if, in the freshness of the morning hour, we were to arrange our engagements, as far as possible, with a little forethought and discretion, and make up the plan of our day till bed-time. "Such a quarter of an hour in the course of to-day may be gained for the highest of all purposes;—I must work hard beforehand to gain it. I shall have to encounter such and such a temptation,—I must be on the watch for it. This hour I shall be alone,—I must guard my thoughts;

the next I shall be in company,—I must guard my tongue. A little contrivance and arrangement here and there may redeem time,—I must see whether the arrangement cannot be made." All this is consideration beforehand,—is thoughtfulness; but it is not the thoughtfulness which the Lord forbids,—for it lies within the horizon of to-day. What He *does* forbid, and what unhappily it is very hard to check in oneself, is the previous contemplation and adjustment of difficulties, which stretch into that unknown to-morrow, which belong not to the cycle of the present day. We are always for flying off mentally to contingencies, things which are to happen by and by, and may never happen; Christ is always for recalling us to that which lies under our hands.

Again. Our purposes are to be limited by the same horizon, which determines our duties, our provisions, and our anxieties; or rather, if we listen to the literal wording of Scripture, by an horizon still more limited. "Go to now, ye that say, *To-day or to-morrow* we will go into such a city, and continue there a year, and buy, and sell, and get gain: whereas ye know not what shall be on the morrow. For what is your life? It is even a vapour, which appeareth for a little time, and then vanisheth away. For that ye ought to say, If the Lord will, we shall live, and do this or that." A precept than which scarcely any may be more cheaply fulfilled in the letter, while it is perhaps the most arduous of all God's precepts to fulfil in spirit and in truth. Surely it is not to be fulfilled by the mere use of the words, "please God," or of the letters D. V., when we speak of our future projects; but by a deep inner consciousness that the future is wrapped in utter uncertainty,—that we can see no further than to what lies under our hand, —and that even the cycle of the present day embraces more time than we have any right to calculate upon. There may be trials awaiting me in the vista of the future, trials threatening to come to-morrow, or the day after to-morrow, or a week hence, or a month hence,— I have simply nothing to do with them at present.

God requires my services day by day, and will graciously recompense me day by day, if I am true to Him, and lead me on day by day, and give me the support of a day in its day, and the grace of a day in its day. And surely a day is not a long time to endure,—there are not so many hours between rising up and lying down, but that I could manage, if I really prayed and really strove, to be watchful, and pure, and self-denying, and zealous in my work, and punctual in my devotions. Come, now, does not it look very practicable; really a thing that may be done, and done by the humblest? Then why should we not begin to-morrow? Why should we not spend to-morrow better than we have ever spent a day in our life? Why should we not lay our plans for doing so this evening?

Thus it has been shown from Holy Scripture that the day is the divinely-constituted element of the life of man,—the element for which he is furnished, and beyond which he need look no further. In short, a day is, as I said before, a miniature life. And now let us draw out this position in detail.

First; The morning hour is a miniature of youth. We know how much depends on the shape and complexion, which the human character takes in youth,—how comparatively exceptional a case it is that a godless and irreligious youth is succeeded by piety in mature age,—how all-important it is that the influences of Divine Grace should be fused into the character when it is plastic, and before it has crystallized. Nor can the importance of the morning hour be overrated. That the period immediately after rising should be scrupulously consecrated to God,—that the earliest thoughts of the day should be filled with God,—that the homage of self-dedication should be renewed before starting on another pilgrimage,—that we should listen to His small voice of warning and encouragement as it issues from the pages of His written Word,—all this is so essentially bound up with the peace and holiness of the day, that one might almost say the two are inseparable. The tone of sentiment and feeling maintained throughout the day is sure to take its colouring from that morning hour.

Secondly. Youth passes away, and the earnest work of life begins; the profession or trade is entered upon. And, in like manner, the morning prime comes to a close; the *worship* of God is completed, and the *service* of God,—that is, work, the work of our calling,—begins. Do it with all thy might, O man, for it is the business which thy Father hath given thee to do. Do it with all thy might; for thou must work the work of Him that sent thee while it is day; the night cometh when no man can work. Thou art to be in thy work a $\mu\iota\mu\eta\tau\dot\eta\varsigma$ $\Theta\epsilon o\hat{v}$,—copyist, imitator of God. Now whatever God does, He does perfectly. If it be but the creation of a leaf or a flower, it is done in such a manner as that the most minute and microscopic examination only serves to bring out fresh beauties. Strive to do thy work in such a manner. Let it be thy earnest effort, that he who looks into it shall find no flaw. Let the thing not only be done, but be done gracefully and ornamentally, as far as may be. It is a great and precious thought that God may be pleased by service done with the whole soul, and with strict punctuality and conscientiousness.

Thirdly. The age of man passes on, and real trials have to be grappled with, when life is mounting now to its noontide. Narrow circumstances, sickness, bereavement,—the manifold snares of the great world, the lures of ambition, or sensuality, or covetousness,—beset the man on all sides. These great trials of faith and patience find themselves represented in miniature in the little crosses, ruggednesses, unpleasant collisions of one day's walk. Temptations in the heat of conversation to overstate things, or to use acrimonious language, or to throw out (for the sake of amusement) words bordering on the profane,—temptations to lose one's temper,—to indulge appetite in eating,—to resign oneself to calls of ease and sloth, or to harbour thoughts of impurity;—all this is the miniature crucible, in which day by day the faith and patience of God's children are tried and approved. Often the noontide sun waxes hot upon them. The bright promise of the morning is overclouded. There are fightings without, and fears within, oppositions, vexations, annoyances, anxieties, apprehensions. It is painful to thwart natural inclinations, as a Christian must do several times in each day: it is called in Scripture "crucifixion of the flesh;" and crucifixion cannot but be painful. But comfort thee, faithful soul!—the night is coming, when, if thou wilt endure patiently at present, the fever-fit of passion, or excitement, or anxiety shall have worn off, and the Saviour shall fold thee under His wing, and thou shalt sit down under His shadow with great delight.

"Be the day weary, or be the day long,
At length it ringeth to Evensong."

So sang the Fathers of the Reformation in a time of sore distress, when the fires of persecution raged fiercely around them, and God's Truth in their persons was hated, hunted down, and trodden under foot. A sweet strain, and which well may have nerved a Christian man to dare and endure all things. Fierce glows the noontide sun of persecution; but man's power has a limit; and suffering, however protracted, must have a limit, and even martyrdom itself is but light affliction, when set in the balance against "the rest that remaineth for the people of God." And as at the close of the most wearisome day is heard the musical tinkling bell, which calls Christians to Prayer, and the Evensong is poured forth at the Saviour's feet, and He bestows His vesper blessing "ere repose our spirits seal,"—so it shall be yet a little while, and then we shall hear His voice calling us to His Bosom with a "Come, ye blessed," and shall answer in accents of well-grounded hope and lofty praise, and shall share the rest of those who sleep in Jesus.

Well, the prospect of the evening hour of communion with God may equally serve to nerve us to a manful endurance. A holy calm will hover round that evening hour,—light and music will then break out upon the soul, if the testimony of conscience be such, that upon the whole we can rejoice in it. Have I endured to-day in the hour of temptation? have I worshipped God in my closet? served Him in my work? obeyed Him in my trials? If not altogether as might be wished, still perhaps a shade better than yesterday,—at all events, there is His boundless Love in Christ; waiting to bless me without money, and without price, and to blot out all transgressions. So, saith the Lord of the Vineyard, "call the labourer and give him his hire." Let his hire be the peace which passeth understanding, which the world can neither give nor take away. Let him be sealed with the Saviour's Blessing, and sleep under His wing.

Lastly. Death;—It is an old tale, how Death is miniatured in sleep. Both are a lying down shrouded in a darkened chamber, where the stir of life is hushed, and the light of life does not penetrate. And from both there shall be an awaking;—for " I believe in the Resurrection of the Body." I believe that, as the stir in the house begins again with the dawn,—so, when the present Economy shall have run its course, those dreary abodes which the cypress and the yew overshadow, shall be peopled with life, and resound with Hallelujah

Such is the analogy between Human Life and the day, which results from the fact that one is the rudiment of the other. Now let us avail ourselves of this fact in the conduct of our spiritual life. In place of that constant reaching forward into the future of Time which characterizes the natural man, let us devote ourselves to doing in the faith and fear of God the duties which call for immediate discharge, and to meeting in His strength the temptations which to-day are imminent. Let our horizon of forethought and care in things spiritual, as well as in things natural, be nightfall. To coin afresh an old proverb, which is homely to vulgarity,—a coinage, by which it would gain much in moral value, as well as in gracefulness,—"Let us take care of the days; and the years will take care of themselves."

But, alas! in the minds of many readers there rises up the discouraging thought, so paralyzing to effort, that already numerous days have dropped away into the gulf of unreclaimed possibilities, like the autumn leaves of trees which grow on the brink of a deep and dark ravine; and that on each of them, even though they have been spent in secular activities, and in eager running to and fro in quest of worldly wealth or worldly distinction, might be inscribed (like oracles upon the Sibylline leaves) the motto which poor Hugh Grotius deemed appropriate to his whole life: "I have wasted my life in laboriously doing nothing at all." Nothing have we done for God in those days, nothing in the work of our salvation; and all beside that man *can* do is vanity. Be it so. But the Gospel, the Good News from Heaven, is not without hope for us, nor without that which is inseparable from hope, a new spring of energy. Although in the system of the Natural Life of man, Time past can never be recalled, there is such a thing in the Economy of Grace as "redeeming the time." When our works are done with a full faith in the pardoning, restoring Love of Christ, with an ardent enthusiastic desire to please Him, and yield Him all the little miserable tribute that we can,—when consciousness of past falls and neglected opportunities redoubles our energy,—when, like Peter, plunging into the water to meet his Lord, we burn with desire to show Him that we love Him more than those, who have not wounded Him so deeply,—then in those days of vigorous Christian impulse we redeem the time, and God restores to us the years which the locust of self-indulgence or irreligious toil has eaten.

Lift up, then, the hands that hang down, and the feeble knees! God gives us more days still,—gives them surely that they may be redeemed, not that they may follow their predecessors into the dark ravine of unreclaimed opportunities. If He lightens our darkness once again, a fresh dawn to-morrow will suffuse itself

than the Present Day in our Service of God. 257

over the face of Nature. My reader, why should it not be a dawn of spiritual life, and hope, and energy in thy breast,—a dawn which shall shine more and more unto the perfect day,—the day of consummated holiness and endless enjoyment?

CHAPTER II.

ON UNITY OF EFFORT IN THE SERVICE OF GOD.

" Thou art careful and troubled about many things; but one thing is needful."—LUKE x. 41, 42.

WHAT a depth is there, combined with what a simplicity, in the words of Our Blessed Lord! On a very fair and bright day, we sometimes see the sea at the distance of a few boat's-lengths from the shore so perfectly clear, that we can literally count the pebbles at the bottom. If we were to throw ourselves out of the boat, we should find that we were strangely deceived as to the depth of that water. Its crystal clearness has made us think it much shallower than in truth it is, and we should find ourselves, to our surprise, far out of our depth in it. So it is with the maxims of Holy Scripture in general; but specially with those gracious sayings, which fell from the lips of the Incarnate Wisdom. So simple that a child can understand them, they are at the same time so profound, that the intellect of the most highly gifted and highly cultivated philosopher cannot fathom them. The principles asserted in them, while they are perfectly plain and intelligible, admit of an infinite variety of applications to the conduct of life; applications which the spiritual mind is instructed by God to make for itself.

One great secret of success in the Christian warfare is quietness of mind. Without interior peace, there is no such thing as true Religion. The peace, which by simple faith in Christ the conscience obtains, is the first step in Sanctification. All Christian virtue is built upon that foundation,—" Therefore being justified by faith, we have peace with God through our Lord Jesus Christ." And still through our whole course, Christ's Blood of Atonement and His Life of perfect Righteousness are the great fountains of peace which travel with us, just as the stream, which flowed from the smitten Rock, followed Israel in their pilgrimage. But, if we are to have success in the pursuit of holiness and in meeting our spiritual foes, there must be peace not only in the consciousness of our acceptance, but peace also in effort and endeavour. The area of holiness is a very wide area; and by attempting to fill it all at once, we may overtax our resources, waste our strength, and throw ourselves out of heart.

We will, therefore, in this Chapter offer some remarks on the principle of spiritual policy which we should adopt, if we desire successfully to meet that discouragement which results from distraction of mind. The principle is thus given us by Our Blessed Lord,— "One thing is needful." And this, among various other applications of it, all equally wholesome and wise, we interpret to mean,—" Let there be one idea at the foundation of your spiritual character, round which that character forms itself: let one single principle be the foundation of all your obedience to God's commandments. You will never succeed, while you are paying equal attention at one and the same time to every department of the Divine Law." A speculative difficulty will perhaps be felt here, which it is well to encounter at the outset.

Are we not bound, it may be asked, to strive after the fulfilment of all God's commandments? Does not the holy Psalmist say, "Then shall I not be ashamed, when I have respect unto *all* Thy commandments?" If therefore any one should advise us to fasten our attention principally upon one of these commandments, is he not relaxing the stringency of the Divine Law, and imposing upon us a single obligation, where God has imposed upon us many? This reasoning is very plausible, but not really sound.

The heathen philosopher, Aristotle, speaking of mere natural virtues, points out that they are so linked together, that if a man possessed one virtue in absolute perfection, he must perforce possess the rest. And a similar remark may be made respecting the graces of the Christian character. They hang together more or less, and one draws another in its train. We may see an instance of this in St. Paul's inspired panegyric on Charity. Read carefully through all the features of Charity, which he pourtrays in that grand chapter, and you will find yourself often crying out, " Why, this is not charity at all, which he is describing, but some other grace, to which we give a distinct name." For instance, "Charity is not puffed up." This seems rather an attribute of Humility than of Charity. Again; "Charity doth not behave itself unseemly;" i. e. shows taste and tact in finer points of conduct. This sounds rather like Courtesy than like Charity. But yet the inspired Apostle is not wandering from his point. Love has the closest connexion with humility and courtesy, so that perfect love can never exist without either. Every breach of love in the world is due more or less to pride. Whence come all wranglings, jars, and discords, but from a secret feeling that a certain precedence and certain rights are our due, and a determination always to stand upon those rights, and never to waive that precedence? Strike at the root of this feeling in the heart, and you strike at the root of every quarrel; or, in other words, secure humility in any mind of man, and you secure love, at least on its negative side. The case is the same with courtesy. Perfect love would involve perfect courtesy; that is to say, a nice sense of propriety in our intercourse with others, and a delicacy of feeling towards them. So far as any one is defective in this perfect courtesy, he wants one of the finer features of love.

Again; it is the law of the natural characters of all of us that one particular feature or class of features stands out prominently, and gives its complexion to the whole character. We may be quite sure that our spiritual characters will form themselves in the same way. They will have a pervading colour, they will manifest a particular leaning, whether we wish it or not. Our minds are so constituted that each feature of them cannot be equally developed. Nor indeed is it consistent with God's design in regard to His Church that it should be so. That design includes variety of mind. As each stone has its place in an arch, and no one stone will fit into the place of another, so the mind of each Christian, with its various moral and intellectual endowments, has its peculiar place and its appropriate functions in the vast Temple of the Church of Christ.

St. Peter, St. Paul, and St. John, were equally good Christians; but the mind of the first did not adapt itself easily to the evangelization of the Gentiles; that of the second was not contemplative; that of the third had no high gifts of administration and rule, though it was endowed with a marvellous insight. It is the Lord's design now, as it was then, that His different servants should exhibit different graces of the Christian character; and we shall do well in framing our minds to the holiness which He requires, to frame them with reference to His design, and with the eye constantly fixed upon it.

But again; and this has a most important bearing on the question at issue;—all growth proceeds upon the principle which we are recommending. Natural growth means the gathering together of particles of matter round a single nucleus, which nucleus appropriates and assimilates those particles. If we take a small fragment of the blossom of a flower, and examine it with a powerful microscope, we shall see that it consists of a series of colour-cells, ranged in perfect order, (like the cells in a honeycomb, or the stones in a tessellated pavement,) which contain the pigment of the flower. Originally there was but one single cell, containing the vital principle of the whole flower; but as the germ was fed by the dews and rains of heaven, and by the moisture of the earth, it gathered to itself particles from the elements which surrounded it, and gradually formed a daughter cell, and then another, and another, until the whole resulted at length in this magnificent mosaic of cells, so far superior to any pavement which King Solomon had in his palace, or even in his temple. Well, spiritual growth proceeds by the same rule as natural; it is for the most part a development out of one sentiment, an accretion round the nucleus of one idea. It is our part to watch this law of our minds, and to endeavour by prayer and forethought, and wise effort, to turn it to account.

Now, practically, how is this to be?

1. There can be no doubt that the besetting sin or fault, if any one is prominent, should be the first quarter in which the Christian should turn his thoughts, and prayers, and efforts. His particular shortcoming is an indication by God in what part of the field his work lies. Having ascertained, then, his besetting sin (and we gave directions for doing this in a preceding Chapter), let him set himself as his main business, dismissing other matters for the present, however interesting to his curiosity, or attractive to his tastes, to adopt a course of life wholly contrary to it in thought, word, and deed. Let the main tenor of his life be a continual prayer and struggle in God's strength against this one sin. And he will find ere long that other graces are forming in his mind, besides that which he has set himself specially to cultivate. This perhaps may be the explanation of the phenomenon, which puzzles us in many Scripture characters, —that they fail signally in the very grace which they most especially illustrate. The truth may be, that this was originally the very weak point of their character,—that Moses, for example, was by nature impatient and irritable; but that waging special war against this sin, he became by grace the meekest of men, though nature broke out again when he was tried with unusual severity at Meribah.

At all events it is certain that "the one thing needful" for those beset with any moral and spiritual infirmity, is to rid themselves of it, rooting it, as far as possible out of their hearts, with loathing and abhorrence. Until this is achieved, there is no business for them of equal importance.

2. But supposing that, on a survey of our character, it should not appear that any one fault or sin has a greater prominence than another; (though this will rarely be the case,) we may then set ourselves to choose, according to our own inclinations, some broad Scriptural principle which may be made the foundation of our whole spiritual character. We may devote our life, or at all events, some period of it, to the cultivation and illustration of one particular grace. Let me give one or two examples. "Hallowed be Thy Name," is the earliest petition of the Lord's Prayer. We conclude that the hallowing of the Name of God is the object which should lie nearest to the heart of a true Christian. Now let us take this to ourselves as our rule of life,—devote ourselves steadily, for a longer or shorter period, to the fulfilment of this duty as the "one thing needful." Let us set ourselves to hallow God's *Word* by never introducing it lightly in conversation, or using it to point a jest, however innocent, and by always lifting up our heart for divine illumination while we read it, thus practically placing a difference between it and other books. Let us set ourselves to hallow the congregation of Christ's Church, by never joining in *Public Worship* without calling seriously to mind that He is in the midst of us. Let us set ourselves to hallow God's *Temple*, which is our body, by thinking much of the consecration which it (no less than the soul) has received in Baptism, and by carefully separating it, by means of abstinence, if need be, from all approaches to impurity. And finally let us set ourselves to counteract in our own minds the mischief, incident to a controversial age, of discussing religious subjects of the gravest moment with a certain flippant fluency. The practice of interlarding conver-

sation with oaths is now happily almost extinct; but the levity and irreverence which gave rise to it may show itself in other forms, and often does show itself even among religious people. We may bandy the Sacred Name about in a theological argument, and discuss topics into which angels fear to intrude, in the rash and hasty way in which Uzziah handled the ark, and with as little awe upon our spirits. Other details in the application of the principle will suggest themselves, into which I need not enter.

Or we might attempt to make poverty of spirit— the subject of the first Beatitude—the leading thought of our religious character. We might set ourselves to cultivate this grace as the "one thing needful;" by meditating frequently on our misery and wretchedness, on our shameful and numerous falls, on the repeated failure of our resolutions, on the subtle and powerful enemies by which we are surrounded, watched, and opposed, and on the far greater progress in grace which others have made, with advantages much inferior to our own. Also by welcoming humiliations, and mortifications of our vanity, whether great or small, and blessing God for them, as bitter but wholesome medicines suitable to our malady. By frankly confessing to our intimate friends, where it can be done discreetly and without risk of harm to them, the more flagrant evils of our life, with an entire willingness to lie as low in their eyes as we do in God's. By constantly calling to mind and acknowledging before God that as for the gifts which we hold of Him, they are but gifts, and entail responsibilities without giving any cause for glorying; and that the grace which is in us *is* grace, that is, free favour shown to the undeserving, and that our very correspondence to grace comes of this free favour, and not of any good thing which dwelleth in us.

Having chosen our principle, whatever it be, it will be part of the business of every morning to anticipate the occasions on which it may be brought into exercise, and to seek the help of Our Lord, that we may be faithful when those occasions arise; and it will be part of the business of every evening to examine our consciences in reference to this one needful thing, and ascertain by a searching inquiry how the resolution has been kept.

It will be well to say, in conclusion, one word of advice as to the sort of principle which it is desirable to choose for the purpose of building upon it a holy life. Choose not, then, too narrow a principle,—by which I mean one which gives no scope for exercise or trial, except on rare occasions. Suppose, for example, that submission to the will of God under the loss of friends were chosen as the principle. There is not here room enough for every-day practice. Bereavement, much as it behoves us to conduct ourselves well when it does come, is of rare occurrence.

On the other hand, too broad a principle will destroy the unity of aim and endeavour, which is recommended. Too broad a principle is in fact more principles than one, and so defeats the end. For which reason, if the principle fixed upon be very broad, it will be wise to narrow it a little in the earlier stages of the spiritual life, that our attention may not be distracted and our resolve enfeebled, by multiplicity of detail. Not of course that we may excuse ourselves from the obligation of any part of God's Law; but that unity of effort in striving after its observance, the setting before us one thing as for the time supremely needful, is the true secret of keeping it at all.

Finally, choose a principle to which your mind is naturally drawn when in a right frame. We are all attracted by different lines of thought in religion, and no man has a right to impose upon his neighbour his own line. If you read the Scriptures daily with prayer, simplicity, and thoughtfulness, it cannot fail that some of the thoughts which arise upon them will be made to breathe and burn in your heart. So came home the words of Jesus to the disciples on the road to Emmaus, while He talked with them by the way, and while He opened to them the Scriptures. Consider, when you receive these inspirations, whether they may not be given for some special purpose; whether they may not take shape in some definite practical resolve.

We have pointed out one method of obviating those distractions which are so baffling to Christian progress, and we will end by a general counsel to cultivate quietness of mind in all other ways as well as in this. Never shall we attain to holiness, so long as we are careful and troubled about many things. Cares and anxieties, even of a spiritual character, must be thrown upon God; the mind must be absolutely unburdened of them; and we must leave our Father to provide for them, when the need arises. If business presses, one thing must be done at a time, well rather than rapidly, and whatsoever affair is not immediately imminent, must be left to settle itself as best it may. Scruples of conscience, those great foes of progress, must be overcome by taking a healthy and manly view of the duties of religion, by fixing our minds upon its great essentials, and sometimes by communicating the case to a discreet and pious adviser. But sins,—actual and humbling falls,—may not these legitimately distress and harass the mind, and make the hands hang down, and palsy the knees? No; not if the true policy in such cases is rightly understood. Take the fall as another impressive lesson of the utter vanity of self-reliance, and the utter depravity of thy own nature. Go straight to the Good Physician, whose doors are always open, and ask Him to heal thy guilt with His Blood, thy fallen will with His Grace. Never did petitioner apply to Him for bodily healing who failed to obtain it. Is it conceivable that He will be less gracious, when we come to Him to sue for the supply of our spiritual wants? Who put it into our hearts to sue? Who draws us to His footstool? Who but Himself? And will He reject the prayer of His own instigation?

"How shall our Divine Shepherd, who followed after His lost sheep for three and thirty years with loud and bitter cries through that painful and thorny way, wherein He spilt His heart's blood, and laid down His life,—how shall He refuse to turn His quickening glance upon the poor sheep which now follow Him with a desire, though sometimes faint and feeble, to obey Him? If He ceased not to search most diligently for the blind and deaf sinner, the lost piece of money of the Gospel, till He found him; can He abandon one, who, like a lost sheep, cries and calls piteously upon his Shepherd? If the Lord knocks continually at the heart of man, desiring to enter in and sup there, and to communicate to it His gifts, who can believe that when that heart opens and invites Him to enter, He will turn a deaf ear to the invitation, and refuse to come in [1]?"

CHAPTER III.

OF THE WAY IN WHICH WE SHOULD SEEK TO EDIFY OTHERS.

"*Let your light so shine before men, that they may see your good works, and glorify your Father which is in heaven.*"—MATT. v. 16.

NOTHING is a more sure and regular indication of the birth of true religion in the heart, than the presence there of a desire to do good. Desire to do good is "the spot of God's Children,"—the spot which the inward operation of His Grace throws out upon the surface of the moral constitution. No devout man ever lacked altogether this uniform mark of a devout mind. For did not Our Lord go about doing good? And is He not our great Exemplar? And must not Christian men seek in some way or other to do good, if they would at all conform themselves to this Exemplar? Such is the implicit reasoning of every mind, almost on the first moment of its taking up earnestly with Personal Religion. And who shall find a flaw in it, or say it is incorrect?

---

[1] The Spiritual Combat, chap. iii.

Yet this desire, from not being always directed in the right channel, has led good men into mistakes, which have not only laid waste their own spiritual life, and corrupted the fountains of piety within them, but have also rent the seamless vest of Christ, and introduced schism into that Jerusalem, which was originally built as a city that is at unity in itself. Instances of the latter result are unhappily of frequent occurrence among the middle and lower classes of this country. A man hitherto licentious, or at all events utterly thoughtless and godless, receives his first religious impressions from some sermon which he has casually heard, or some startling dispensation of God's Providence. The religious instinct is newly created in him, and operates (partly from its very strangeness to the man's ordinary habits) with wonderful freshness and vigour. Unhappily for him, neither he, nor any one else who has influence with him, perceives that this instinct needs guidance. It is a strong motive power, like steam in the natural world, and like steam it may produce an explosion and do mischief as well as convey passengers along a road or across an ocean. Unguided, and abandoned to its natural operation, it too often does the former. The man feels, (and remember that it is part of the instinct of Grace within him that he should feel,) "I must do good to my neighbours." Then comes in the fallacy,—the fundamental mistake, —that this good can be done in no other way than by preaching, or, in other words, by direct religious admonition, designed and intended to edify. Our Lord preached; and before He ascended, He said, "Go ye and preach:" accordingly the Apostles preached: St. Paul preached; and why, this new convert thinks, should not he? So preach he will; and if his circumstances are such that he cannot preach in the church, he will preach in a meeting-house, and become a little focus at once of spiritual, or I should rather say fanatical, excitements and parochial discontents. So he gets together his knot of disciples, and the plain brick building of studied ugliness is reared, and the good old church, with its solemn and reverend services and unexciting doctrine, is forsaken by some who indeed never yielded to it any rational or intelligent allegiance, and the schismatic begins, as he conceives, to edify. Now it is quite clear that this result is wrong; as clear as that the main motive which led to it is good. We are driven, therefore, to infer that there has been some mistake as to the true method of edifying others, which has vitiated the conclusion.

Let us examine in this Chapter the nature of the duty of edification, and ask how it is to be fulfilled by persons in general.

The fundamental passage, on which the duty of Edification is built, is found in the fifth chapter of St. Matthew,—" Let your light so shine before men, that they may see your good works, and glorify your Father which is in heaven." It should be remarked, in reference to this text, that the Sermon on the Mount, from which it is taken, is a perfect code of Christian Duty; so that nothing can claim to be a general duty, binding on all disciples, but what can find and show you its place in that Sermon. I say binding on *all* disciples; for to the disciples, not exclusively to the Apostles, was it spoken. And we may observe, in passing, that grievous mistakes are occasionally made, by the indiscriminate application to all Christians, of what was said to the Apostles of Christ in their Apostolic character. Thus, the words, " Go ye into all the world, and preach the Gospel to every creature," are often ignorantly quoted, as if they made the literal and direct evangelization of the world the duty of every private Christian. Quite as reasonably might it be maintained that all Christians have the power of remitting and retaining sins, because to the Eleven it was said, " Whose soever sins ye remit, they are remitted; and whose soever sins ye retain, they are retained." Those words were addressed to a particular body of men, raised up to perform a particular work, whose gifts, qualifying them for this work, were peculiar, and died with them, never to revive; while their functions are, in all essential points, continued in the great Office of the Christian Ministry. The glorious Sermon on the Mount is of no such limited scope, but embraces within the compass of its requirements the infant of days who was baptized yesterday, quite as much as the hearers who sat on the windy hillside listening to it, and thrilled with the sweetness and the solemnity of the Divine Discourse. Here, then, we are to seek for, and hence we are to gather, that duty of Edification which is incumbent upon all alike; and thus it runs,—" Let your light shine before men."

It will be seen, by referring to the context, what is the precise force and significance of this precept. The temptation of the primitive disciples, who lived in the days when persecution was abroad, would be to wrap up in their own bosoms their Christian Profession, so that it should not transpire and involve them in trouble. Is it not enough, they would think, to believe in Christ with my heart, without the confession of the lips, without apprising a scornful and malignant world of my convictions? In reply to all which corrupt reasonings, Our Lord tells them that it is unlawful for them in any way to hide or obscure their profession. Freely allow it to transpire, says He,—for such is His sentiment, clothed in a modern dress,—ye are the light of the world, and God hath not kindled this light of grace in the midst of a crooked and perverse generation, in order that it should be covered up or hid. " Men do not light a candle, and put it under a bushel, but on a candlestick, and it giveth light unto all that are in the house. Let *your* light so shine before men, that they may see your good works, and glorify your Father which is in heaven." Now what is there in the passage, thus understood, to prove that Christians generally are under the obligation of giving direct religious admonition to their neighbours? Edification by example, and not by admonition, is what the Lord is speaking of; for He says distinctly, " Let your light so shine before men, that they may,"—not hear your good words,—but, " *see your good works*, and glorify your Father which is in heaven." Nor does He prescribe Edification by example *for the sake of edification*. He does not bid us do any thing, which otherwise we would not have done, for the sole purpose of edifying another man. He does not say, "Strive to fix attention on your good works, and to make them arrest observation;" He does not say, "Wave the light about, and flourish it in the air, and say to all the world, Take notice, brother, here is a light;" but what He says is simply, Λαμψάτω, *Let it shine*. Every light will and must shine as a matter of course, and must enlighten all that are in the chamber, unless there is an intervening obstacle in the way; and what Our Lord forbids, is the placing such an obstacle in the way through moral cowardice and fear of man's censure. Christian, come out and be seen! No slinking there into a dusky corner, in order that your world-opposed ways may escape a sneer. Let men see you evidently conducting yourself on supernatural principles, living above the world, quietly and unostentatiously serving God in your vocation. Be much in Communion with God; strive to adorn your profession with every grace; while at the same time you do not shun the world's eye or make the smallest compromise of principle.

You see that all this falls far short of, or rather is an entirely different thing from, a general exhortation to edify by admonition. Without denying that, under certain circumstances, such admonition may be a part of our duty towards our neighbour, it is certain that (even under such circumstances) it is a delicate and difficult task, and not without certain dangers for both parties concerned.

It may be of use briefly to point out some of the dangers.

First. The religious admonition of others, where we have no definite call to the work, proceeds upon an assumption of superiority in the person admonishing, the acting upon which is likely to develope and strengthen spiritual pride. Surely the assumption that I am better than the man whom I propose to admonish, might prove to be baseless, if I knew more.

We are wholly ignorant of another's inner life; we can never look deeper than the outward appearance. He may be dry, and cold, and hard (to all appearance), and irresponsive to religious appeals; and yet it is possible that that irresponsiveness may come from intensity of reverence, and from the fact that, while mine is a shallow character, his is a deep one. And this is certain, that I am conscious of far more evil in myself, than ever has transpired to my knowledge as existing in him. Of course, the case is wholly different, if I have a commission to instruct him, or if our relative positions in society, as in the case of master and servant, teacher and scholar, make it my duty to do so. The admonition then rests upon the commission, or upon my position in Society, both which are quite independent of my own religious attainments. But when I have nothing but those religious attainments to rest it upon, I should surely be rather chary of admonition than otherwise, unless it is a very clear case that my religious attainments are superior to his.

Secondly. Such admonition is almost always a failure. The feeling that he is to be lectured, and that too by one who cannot found any claim upon his position, generally sets a man's bristles up, and puts him at once into an attitude of hostility to truth, which drives out the little grace that there may be in him. No; if we wish (as every Christian must wish) to do good to others, let us pave the way by little acts of help, kindness, and self-sacrifice shown to our neighbour when in a difficulty. Let us live hard by him in such a manner that the most careless observer cannot help observing that we are conducting ourselves upon Christian principle. A time will come, perhaps, when he will say of us, under distress and convictions, "I believe that his religion is something more than talk; for I have seen his light shining before men; and I shall go to him and ask his advice." Then, acting on the same principle which we have hitherto observed towards him, we may give him all the help we can in the way of advice, but still without parade, or pretence to more than we really know or have felt,—without flashing the light in his eyes.

Thirdly. The diffusion of spiritual feeling—its being allowed to come abroad too freely (and it must more or less come abroad in religious conversation)—is any thing but healthy for this delicate plant. If any man questions this, I say, "Go and try." Take a very intimate and confidential friend; and divulge freely to him, by letter or otherwise, what are called your religious experiences, your feelings in prayer and meditation, your delight in certain parts of the Holy Scriptures, and so forth. Of course, admonition may be given much short of this; but yet such an effusion of the heart is the direction in which admonition is tending, for it always implies, and almost always expresses, something of spiritual feeling in the admonisher. Well; are you any the better for it, when it is done? Is prayer more or less easy, when you have thus unburdened your heart? Has not the odour of devotion lost something of its fragrance and freshness, by being allowed too freely to come abroad? It is sure to transpire any how, if you will simply let it alone; but you cannot force vents for it, without doing it mischief.

We have said enough to counteract the mistaken notion of the way in which the Edification of others should be carried on, and will just exhibit in conclusion the positive side of this duty.

In a word, then, we are not so much to aim at the edification of others, as to set a wholesome example, and to see that there are no obstructions in the way of our edifying.

Resolve to know much of the inward life of Religion. Cultivate in every possible way a spirit of private devotion. Determine to know the power of Prayer, as distinct from its form. Practise more and more in all companies, and under all circumstances, the thought of the Presence of God. Seek more and more to throw a spiritual meaning and significance into your pursuit; to do it more simply and exclusively from the motive of pleasing God, and less from all other motives. Try, by a holy intention, to give even to the more trifling actions of the day a religious value. This will be feeding the light with oil.

Then as to not obstructing it. Never lower your principles to the world's standard. Never let sin, however popular it may be, have any sanction or countenance from you, even by a smile. The manly confession of Christ before men, when His cause is unpopular, is made by Himself the condition of His confessing us before His Father. If people find out that we are earnestly religious, as they soon will, if the light is shining, let us make them heartily welcome to the intelligence, and allow them to talk and criticize as much as they please. And then, again, in order that the light may shine without obstruction, in order that it may easily transpire what we are, we must be simple, and study simplicity. This is by no means so easy as it at first sight appears; for in this highly artificial and pretentious age all Society is overlaid with numerous affectations. Detest affectation, as the contrary of truth, and as hypocrisy on a small scale; and allow yourself freely to be seen by those around you in your true colours. There is an affectation of indifference to all things, and of a lack of general sensibility, which is becoming very prevalent in this age, and which is the sworn foe to all simplicity of character. The persons who labour under this moral disorder pretend to have lost their freshness of interest in every thing; for them, as they would have it believed, there is no surprise and no enthusiasm. Without assuming that they are really the unimpressionable creatures which they would make themselves out to be, we may warn them that the wilful dissembling of a generous emotion is the way to suppress it. As Christians, we must eschew untruth in every form; we must labour to seem just what we are, —neither better nor worse. To be true to God and to the thought of His Presence all day long, and to let self occupy as little as possible of our thoughts; to care much for His approval, and comparatively little for the impression we are making on others;—to feed the inward light with oil, and then freely to allow it to shine,—this is the great secret of Edification. May He indoctrinate us into it, and dispose and enable us to illustrate it in our practice!

CHAPTER IV.

IN WHAT THE SPIRITUAL LIFE CONSISTS.

"*And He opened His mouth, and taught them, saying, Blessed are the poor in spirit: for their's is the kingdom of heaven. Blessed are they that mourn: for they shall be comforted. Blessed are the meek: for they shall inherit the earth. Blessed are they which do hunger and thirst after righteousness: for they shall be filled. Blessed are the merciful: for they shall obtain mercy. Blessed are the pure in heart: for they shall see God. Blessed are the peacemakers: for they shall be called the children of God. Blessed are they which are persecuted for righteousness' sake: for their's is the kingdom of heaven.*"—MATT. v. 2—10.

IT may seem somewhat singular, at or towards the end of a work, which has been devoted to the subject of Personal Religion, to give an answer to the question, "In what does the Spiritual Life consist?" This definition, lying as it does at the foundation of the whole subject, should have been made, it would appear, rather at the outset than the close. To this I can only reply that, if not formally made hitherto, it has all along been presupposed, implied, and often explicitly referred to; and that it is far from useless at the close of any systematic course of teaching to bring out into full prominence the fundamental idea or ideas of the whole course, before finally bidding adieu to the subject. This must be my justification for introducing this question at so late a period.

In what then does the Spiritual Life consist? Unless the answer to this question is very clearly defined in our own minds, we shall assuredly never make any solid attainment, but shall be always building and unbuilding, "ever learning and never able to come to the knowledge of the Truth,"—and all from a fundamental blunder or confusedness of thought.

I. First, then, by way of clearing away popular and prevalent errors, we may broadly assert these negative positions, that the Spiritual Life consists neither in ordinances, nor in actions, nor yet, as some seem to imagine, in activities. Let not the assertion be misunderstood. The Spiritual Life *is closely connected with* ordinances, actions, and activities,—but it no more stands in these things—it is no more ordinance, or action, or activity—than the life of a tree is the fruit of the tree, or the means used for cultivating the tree.

1. *It does not consist in Ordinances, many or few.* It does not stand in many prayers, ejaculatory or stated, nor in hearing many Sermons, nor in studying many chapters of the Bible, nor in many acts of Public Worship, nor even in many Communions. These are means, in God's Hand, of kindling the Spiritual Life in the soul of man, or means of feeding the flame when kindled; but they are not the flame itself, they are not the life. It may be very necessary for a fruit-tree, in order to its bearing fruit, that its roots should be stirred with the spade, overlaid with the manure, moistened with the watering-pot; but nothing can be clearer than that the spade, the manure, and the watering-pot are distinct things from the life of the tree. Yet so apt are we (at least in spiritual subjects) to confound means with ends, and to erect the means into an end,— an intellectual perplexity, indeed, but one which sometimes appears to me to bear a trace of the Fall, and to be due ultimately to the corruption of our nature,— that even religious people often find it hard to conceive of a devout life in the absence of an apparatus of ordi-

nances: whereas it is quite clear that such might exist where, for some reason or other, the ordinances could not be had; in which case God, who is independent of ordinances, would no doubt supply their virtue immediately to the soul. The whole system of Monasticism is an exaggeration of this fundamental error. If a man has once brought himself to believe that vital religion is not only much helped by (which is true), but actually *stands in*, the study and meditation of God's Word, and stated acts of worship, private and public,—of course it is only the logical sequence from such a view that, dismissing secular affairs altogether, and retiring from Society, he should abandon himself wholly to these exercises of Religion. But if, on the other hand, it is perceived and acknowledged that ordinances exist for the sake of living well, that is, devoutly and spiritually, it is then seen to be a mistake and an inversion of the reasonable method of proceeding *to live for Ordinances*, which is precisely the principle of monastic life. It is a very pregnant saying of Our Blessed Lord's, that "the Sabbath was made for man, and not man for the Sabbath." We may apply it not merely to the observance of Sunday, but to all those ordinances which the seventh day of rest represents, and with which it is associated in our minds. These ordinances are made for you, not you for them. They are designed to bless your inner spirit with love, and joy, and peace; not designed to be an iron frame, a Procrustean bed, to the measure of which that inner spirit is painfully to cramp itself. Accordingly, wherever Our Lord and His Apostles touch upon the essence and vitals of true religion, there is an ominous silence as to ordinance, however explicitly ordinances may be recommended in other connexions. The beginning of the Divine Sermon on the Mount goes to the root of the matter, and answers the fundamental question,—"In what does true religion stand?" Our Lord is there describing not the furniture, food, and clothing of the Spiritual Life, but the very life itself, which is more than meat, and the very body itself, which is more than raiment.

And not a single ordinance is mentioned from beginning to end of the Beatitudes. Where St. Paul details the fruits of the Spirit, the same silence is observable. And his compendious and noble description of the kingdom of God in the human soul runs thus: "The kingdom of God is not meat and drink,"—it stands not in outward institutions, but in interior affections,—" but righteousness, and peace, and joy in the Holy Ghost."

2. *The Spiritual Life does not consist in actions.* The actions are the result, the fruit, but they are not the life of the tree. Yet how frequently, in the popular estimate of the subject, are the two confounded. How gladly would many accept this definition as perfectly adequate, and as exhausting the subject—" The life of true religion is a life of usefulness, full of good works and almsdeeds which are done!" There is, of course, no question that where the life of true religion exists, it produces these. "Every good tree," says Our Lord, "bringeth forth good fruit." But though the circulation of the sap secures the production of the fruit, the fruit is not the same thing as the circulation of the sap. Minds which recoil from the idea of a life devoted exclusively to ordinances, are often apt to fall into this opposite error. The sum and substance of true religion in their view is merely the going about doing good. If the good is done, if the hungry are fed, the ignorant educated, the miserable relieved, they look no deeper nor ask any thing more; this they think is true, deep, practical religion. But suppose the case of a man, entirely destitute of resources and abilities, labouring on perseveringly for the good of his fellow-creatures in a very humble sphere, yet blessed with no visible success, because he has none of the instrumentality necessary to secure success,—they might rather hesitate to put him on a level with the supporter, patron, and advocate of many charities, whereas it is quite conceivable that in the eyes of God he stands on a far higher level. The tendency of our English mind, which seeks every where for definite and tangible results, strongly inclines us

to estimate character by outward usefulness. We take instinctively a hard external view of the fruits of the Spirit, looking at the thing done rather than at the mind of the doer. Whereas the Apostle Paul, in his enumeration of those fruits, *does not mention a single action*, but merely a series of tempers,—"love, joy, peace, long-suffering, gentleness, goodness, faith, meekness, temperance."

3. We said, lastly, that the Spiritual Life does not consist in activities, that is, in intensified action. And we think the warning particularly needed in our own Church at the present day. From one cause or another we have a great deal of religious activity among us. This activity, however, is by no means exclusively due to religion; religion, like every thing else, takes its colouring from the spirit of the age. Now the spirit of the age is to be stirring, to hate and abolish sinecures, to let no man rest upon his oars. We all of us catch something of this spirit, which is about in the air just now, and our religion, like every other part of our character, takes a certain tone from it. We discover (what is awfully true) that there is a vast mass of misery and sin lying at our very doors. So we say, "Let us be busy, and mend matters to the best of our ability." The national genius here comes in to swell the tide of practical enthusiasm. Englishmen are always indisposed to speculation, always prompt to action. What an apparatus of philanthropy has been created by the spirit of religious enterprise,—special services, special sermons, schools of all sorts and for all classes, refuges and reformatories, hospitals and houses of mercy, meetings, addresses from platforms,—like a forest of masts crowding upon the eye in some busy, noisy dock! Religious people are working in earnest, and with great zest. And shall I say that the zest is in some cases increased by the miserable controversies of the times on which we have fallen? I do really believe it is so. There are many worthy people, young men entering the Ministry more especially, who have been sickened by controversies of religious doctrines altogether. They

are shocked by the extravagances which they have witnessed on one side and the other; and they cry out with Pilate, "What is truth?" Then follows the mischievous inference, "The less we look into the speculative questions of religion altogether, the less we seek any definiteness of view on doctrinal subjects, the happier will be our minds and the greater our usefulness. Religion has another side, the practical; and to that side we will give our whole minds; we will bury ourselves in our work, and thank God there is enough of it to divert us effectually from speculation." If this tendency should operate much more extensively among us, we shall soon lose all dogma, that is, all precise statements of Christian doctrine,—and *as Christian practice is no separable thing from Christian doctrine*, but dependent upon it for its vitality, it may easily be conceived that we are approximating to a very sad state of things. Positive sceptical tendencies operate in the same direction; the insinuation of modern sceptics being that the duties of Christianity are its only essential part, and that, if the fulfilment of these duties be secured, the end is answered; its facts,—the Incarnation, Crucifixion, and Resurrection,—need not be supposed to be historical events at all, but may be relegated to the domain of allegory, and looked upon as pious and edifying myths. Perplexed by these wicked doubts, seeing that they *are* wicked, and yet unable satisfactorily to resolve them,—there is many an excellent man now-a-days, who is taking refuge in his work, and feels that, while he is doing all the good in his power, his foot is planted upon an impregnable rock, from which it cannot be moved. Hence at this period of the religious history of our country more especially, the people of God need to be warned that the Spiritual Life does not stand in religious activities, however intense and fervent, but in something more internal.

II. In what then,—this is our next point,—*does* it stand? Our Lord and His Apostles give one very unequivocal answer. "The kingdom of God," says Paul, "is righteousness, and peace, and joy in the Holy

Ghost." "Giving all diligence," says Peter, as to the one thing needful, "add to your faith, virtue; and to virtue, knowledge; and to knowledge, temperance; and to temperance, patience; and to patience, godliness; and to godliness, brotherly kindness; and to brotherly kindness, charity." It is the Master, however, who gives the fullest and most methodical description of the graces which constitute the Spiritual Life. And in this description we recognize three points, first, that the Spiritual Life is internal; secondly, that it is supernatural; and, thirdly, that it is developed amid the trials and antagonisms of daily life.

First; it is internal. It consists in a series of dispositions wrought in the heart by the power of the Holy Ghost. Any life, therefore, which is not more or less interior, is certainly not the life of the Spirit. Any life which is so busy as to leave no room for meditation and devout affection, any life which spends all its energies in external work, without ever rallying or recollecting itself at its source, is certainly not the life of the Spirit. Any Martha's life, cumbered about much serving, but neglectful of sitting at the feet of the Divine Master, is certainly not the life of the Spirit. But we must say more. Not even are private religious exercises, independently of the mind with which they are performed, the life of the Spirit. Confession of sin, without a deep and humbling sense of it, is not Spiritual Life. And what must we say of a deep and humbling sense of it which does not literally take the outward form of confession? We must say that with God it is confession, although the mouth may have uttered no sounds, and the mind framed no words. The asking of God certain graces, without a longing to be holier, is not Spiritual Life. And what of the longing to be holier, if it should not find occasion to burst forth in actual prayer? It *is* prayer in God's eyes, and no prayer is so, which does not involve a movement of desire in the heart.

Secondly. *The Spiritual Life is supernatural*. We are accustomed to confine this term merely to the sphere of the senses; we mean by the supernatural such an inversion of the order of nature, as is visible to the eye or ear. But there are miracles of the inner, as well as of the outer man; and the Spiritual Life is such a miracle. There are heathen virtues, which are quite in the order of nature, quite on nature's level, and which nature, with the ordinary assistances of reason and the moral sense, has produced. Aristides was just; and Alexander was generous; and Diogenes was temperate; and Pliny was amiable; and Leonidas was brave. But poverty of spirit, and meekness under insults and oppressions, and the rejoicing under persecutions, and the glorying in tribulation, and the mourning over sin, these things belong to a different system of things altogether,—a system which reverses the order of nature in the heart of man. It is *against* nature to take a slight humbly, or to accept an injury sweetly and gently. And because it is against nature, you might educate a heathen most carefully, and train him most diligently from his childhood upwards in all good habits, and yet never bring him up to this point. The effect is due to a Power above nature, a certain thread let down into the soul from the Risen Humanity of Christ,—" the power," as St. Paul calls it, " which worketh in us," and which, on the day of Pentecost, descended to take up His abode in the Church.

Thirdly. *The Spiritual Life, by the very definition of it, is developed amid trial and antagonism.* We see this in several of the particulars. " Blessed are the meek: for they shall inherit the earth." Who are the meek? When is meekness seen? When is there scope for manifesting it? There is no scope, except in circumstances of irritation or provocation. There is no room for meekness in a hermitage, where the will can never be thwarted, and where there are none of the jars and collisions of daily life. There is no such thing as meekness without antagonism, either from men or circumstances. To feel kindly and philanthropically disposed, when all men speak well of us, and no cross word is thrown in our teeth, and no cross incident harasses us, is not meekness at all, but natural benevolence, or, if you will, natural amiability. " Blessed are the merciful: for they shall obtain mercy." Mercy is not merely goodness; but goodness in the face of demerit. To relieve the deserving poor, or to relieve them without any remarkable indesert on their part, is not necessarily to be merciful. Mercy presupposes wrong done against the agent, of which he *might* take advantage to punish us, but does not. Mercy is towards the unthankful and evil, and can only manifest itself when it comes into collision with such.

We make also one more remark, in casting our eye over these Beatitudes. The first of them is fundamental, and pervades all the graces of the spiritual man. It is always present in his mind, and is more or less matured according to his greater or less growth in grace. "Blessed are the poor in spirit: for their's is the kingdom of heaven." To be beaten utterly out of conceit with one's own strength, goodness, and wisdom, to feel that apart from God's Grace we are nothing, can do nothing,—to be assured that our best resolves are like water or stubble,—to re-echo, with the full and intelligent consent of our hearts, the Apostle's confession, "I know that in me, that is, in my flesh, dwelleth *no good* thing,"—to write upon our old nature "Incorrigible," and to depend with great simplicity upon Christ for all things,—this is the grace which lies at the foundation of every other, and which is matured, and confirmed, and deepened in us at every step in advance.

Apply then, reader, the criteria, which you have just heard, in the examination of your spiritual state. How far is your Christian life internal, a thing hid with Christ in God, and to be manifested when He shall appear,—a thing of spiritual hopes, and fears, and joys, and aspirations? How far is your heart the vineyard of God, fruitful unto Him of holy dispositions, and the diligent cultivation of which is your chief business, your one thing needful? How far is it a little sanctuary of worship, screened from the outer world, where the light of a good and single intention aspires towards God continually, and sheds light upon all that is in the house?

Again; are we deluding ourselves with the imagination of possessing certain graces, simply because we have never been tried? Are we dreaming of a Spiritual Life, without an active manifestation of it? Do we fancy ourselves contented because we are prosperous and happy; or pure, because we are constitutionally cold; or forgiving, because we are never provoked; or peacemakers, because we love our own ease, and keep aloof from the affairs of our fellow-men?

And, lastly, if God indeed vouchsafes to us supernatural assistance, should not our virtues correspond to such aids, and have about them a supernatural cast? Shall we content ourselves with the cheap, easy-going virtues of men of the world,—amiability, integrity, uprightness, generosity? Has not our Judge already asked us in His Holy Word, "What do ye more than others?" And must we not expect Him to repeat the question for each of us individually, when we stand before His judgment-seat at the great Day of Account? Oh, may He stir within us now that spirit of holy emulation, that hunger and thirst after righteousness, which He has promised not to disappoint, that, when He shall appear, we may have confidence, and not be ashamed before Him at His coming!

CHAPTER V.

THAT OUR STUDY OF GOD'S TRUTH MUST BE WITH THE HEART.

"But even unto this day, when Moses is read, the vail is upon their heart Nevertheless when it shall turn to the Lord, the vail shall be taken away."—2 COR. iii. 15, 16.

WE purpose to employ our few remaining Chapters in giving certain detached counsels, not falling under any of the heads which we had marked out for our argument, and yet which seem needed in order to give it completeness.

In the passage which stands at the head of this Chapter, the intellectual blindness of the Jews is traced up to the wrong state of their hearts. And it is distinctly said that, when that state shall become right from having been wrong,—when the nation's heart, which has hitherto been averted from Him, shall "turn to the Lord,"—then the intellectual difficulties connected with the reception of Christ shall vanish altogether,—"the vail shall be taken away." Indeed, even without this statement of the Apostle's, we could have gathered that this was the account to be given of Jewish unbelief. The miracles wrought by Our Lord and His Apostles were so stupendous and overwhelming, and the agreement of His career with the Predictions of Prophecy so close, that the convictions of that generation of Jews must have been carried by force, had there not been a predisposition in the heart not to believe. As soon, therefore, as this predisposition shall be removed, says the Apostle in the passage before us, they shall forthwith be convinced: "when their hearts shall turn to the Lord, the vail shall be taken away."

We shall make this passage the foundation of some remarks which have an important practical bearing on the spiritual life.

Men are well aware, quite independently of Religion, that the understanding is liable to be prejudiced by the heart. They have embodied this truth, taught them by every day's experience, in the old saw, "Love is blind." We are quite conscious of being partial to the faults and weaknesses of those in whom our hearts are deeply interested. We should exclude from the trial of a man's cause both his warm friends and his bitter foes, because we account strong sympathies or antipathies prejudicial to the judgment. And as, for the most part, we love ourselves better than other people, a man of fair mind would exclude himself from any share of an arbitration in which he is personally interested. But the proverb extends to our judgment of things, quite as much as to our judgment of persons. Consider only this very common case in the experience of all of us. A man, in his cool moments, sees some practice which requires a momentary effort,—say, for the sake of illustration, early rising,—to be healthful and expedient for him. While he is not under the temptation, the practice seems to have all arguments in its favour, nothing against it; but as soon as ever the will becomes biassed towards a longer indulgence of sleep on a particular morning, what a number of most ingenious arguments spring up in the mind for this longer sleep! In the raw and chilly morning, the question of early rising seems to wear a wholly new aspect, just as if a case at law, the determination of which, on its being simply stated, seemed a matter of common sense, had been argued before us by a very plausible and specious advocate. In truth, it has been so argued before us, and the advocate has been our own will, propense to indolence, averse to exertion. This is a very humble instance, but, though humble, it is one which may come home to all, of the way in which the bias of the will (or, in other words, the heart) affects the view which the mind takes of any subject. In short, the mind of man,—the faculty by which he discerns Truth,—may be compared to an eye placed above a fuming caldron, which can see nothing clearly, because the vapours intercept the vision. The heart is the caldron, and sends up the vapours which distort the view. Now in seeking to reform Human Nature, the philosophers of antiquity either did not notice this fact, or (which is the more probable hypothesis) did not see how the difficulty which it presents could be surmounted. At all events, by way of persuading men to virtue, they made their appeal to the understanding, and sought to carry their point by convincing the mind. Socrates, the first and greatest of all the ancient philosophers who dealt with moral truth, adopted this method. He saw (and here he was right) that men were not so fallen, that their moral sense made no response to Truth and Reason. And he thought (and here he was grievously mistaken) that Truth and Reason, if forced upon men powerfully and luminously, might hold their own against the strength of passion. He commenced, therefore, by arguing with all those who encountered him, as to the truth and reasonableness of their ways of acting and thinking; he called in question popular sentiments and conduct, and pressed men to defend them, if they could, by sheer argument, from which all superfluous words were to be carefully excluded. If they could not defend their own sentiments and conduct, the implication was, of course, that they must, as reasonable beings, abandon them. As far as the understanding went, nothing could be more conclusive, nothing could more shut a man up to follow virtue, than did this method of Socrates's. But what if men do not, as notoriously they do not, conclude moral questions affecting themselves, on the mere verdict of the understanding? What if they set the will on the judgment-seat? give him the power of summing up, and reviewing the arguments of the understanding, and finally act, not as they see to be right, but as they wish to act, in moments of temptation? Unless you can rectify the will and its prepossessions, you only argue before a corrupted judge, and in the sentence the argument goes for nothing.

Christianity, in seeking to reform mankind, proceeds on a method entirely the reverse of this. It makes its first appeal to the affections, which are the springs of the will, and through them clears and rectifies the understanding.

Historically, Christianity commenced thus. It commenced with the career upon Earth, of Our Lord Jesus Christ,—a career, which, although He taught spiritual Truth, was by no means one of an ordinary teacher. He was the good Shepherd, who came down from Heaven to seek the stray sheep in the wilderness of the world. No tale has so deep a pathos as the tale of this search after the lost sheep. It cost the Shepherd every species of hardship and endurance; it cost Him "strong crying and tears;" it cost Him an agony and blood-sweat; it cost Him a most cruel and shameful death upon the Cross. He went through it all, not willingly only, but with the most joyful alacrity, to serve and to save the sheep. He met with no return from mankind in general, but calumny, vituperation, execration. Often He had no shelter at night, (so inhospitable was the world to Him,) and was obliged to stretch His limbs upon the Mount of Olives, under the canopy of the trees, exposed to the inclemency of the weather. But with infinite forbearance and amazing condescension, He continued His work of self-sacrifice and love, knocking at the door, now of this heart, now of that, and waiting patiently for the response. He endured all things heroically,—became the very impersonation of heroic endurance,—for our sakes, that His voice might win its way to our hearts. And what did this voice communicate? What may be said to have been the main scope of Our Lord's teaching? Is not the summary of it to be found in that verse, "God so loved the world, that He gave His only begotten Son, that whosoever believeth in Him should not perish, but have eternal life?" Did He

not come to reveal "the Father," whose Name was so
perpetually on His lips? Did He not come to declare
the Father's Love, the Father's yearning compassion
over every prodigal child, the Father's infinite willingness to receive such child again to His home? Was
not that Apostolic exhortation only a prolonging of
the echoes of the Saviour's voice: "We pray you, as
though God did beseech you by us, be ye reconciled to
God?" Now we say that these facts, the facts of the
life and sufferings and teaching of Christ, lie at the
foundation of Christianity,—that these are the imple-
ments with which Christianity works,—that this is the
method in which God approached men with the view
of achieving their reformation. He came not with an
argument, though Apostles illustrated the truth by
argument; He came not with a dogma, though the
Christian Creed, when fully developed, embraces many
dogmas; but He came with the pathos of self-devoted,
self-sacrificing Love. The Holy Gospels, which record
the history of this coming, are the first, and in every
way the most important books, in the canon of the
New Testament. Let any one read them with
thorough simplicity for the first time in his life; or if
not for the first time, yet disenchanting himself, if he
can do so, of the effect of familiarity with the contents;
and he cannot fail to be touched by them in a salutary
way, especially by the concluding part of the great
story. Aristotle tells us that Tragedy, presenting as
it does some example of virtue under stress of trial,
purifies the passions, and clears them of their dregs.
There is no such specific for the production of this
effect, as the Tragedy of the Death of Christ. He
who has been drawn by the Spirit of Grace to look on
that Tragedy, (and those who are not so drawn find
nothing in it attractive,) has seen and sympathized
with persecuted Goodness. And we do not believe
that such an one will find any difficulty in the
doctrines of the Gospel,—that of the Atonement, for
example,—when formally propounded. If he assaults
that doctrine with his intellect in the first place, he

will no doubt fall into endless perplexities on the subject. But let him approach it by the avenue of the heart, through the door of the affections and sympathies; and all its difficulty vanishes.

But not only did the history of Christianity commence with an appeal to the hearts of men; but this is the order which Grace observes in its work on each individual soul.

The Scripture says, "*With the heart* man believeth unto righteousness." Justifying faith is certainly not a mere intellectual conviction of the truth. That there may be such a conviction, quite independently of justifying faith, is plain from the fact that the evil spirits confessed Our Lord to be the Son of God, and from the explicit reference which St. James makes to this fact, when he tells us that "the devils believe and tremble." We are driven, then, to the conclusion that justifying faith is an operation of the heart, and by consequence of the will, involving a movement of the affections towards the thing or the person which is the object of faith. If any of God's threatenings be the object, faith takes the shape of fear, which is an affection. If any of His promises be the object, faith takes the shape of hope, which also is an affection; and if Christ be the object of faith, it then takes the shape of trust or love. Any how, it is well for us to understand that the mere satisfaction derived by the mind from external evidence,—the comfort of concluding, after a balance of arguments on either side, that Christianity is of God,—though it may be a very useful auxiliary to vital belief, has nothing to do with the essence of that belief. In all such belief there is a movement of the heart as the fundamental process, although it is quite true that, as the result of this movement, the mind is subsequently enlightened.

All this will be readily admitted, so far as the earliest step in the Christian Life is concerned; but we doubt whether it is sufficiently considered that every forward step in that life must be made on the same principle as the first. We believe that every movement of Grace, as well as the first movement, is an impulse of the heart. It is quite as true to say, "with the heart man is edified," as it is to say, "with the heart man believeth." For there is no true edification without faith; and all growth in grace resolves itself into a growth of faith.

Now let us somewhat expand and practically develope this truth, that edification is through the heart, and not through the mind. Let us mark what bearings it has on the conduct of the spiritual life.

(1) Observe that testimony is borne to it by the universal experience of Christians. What is that impalpable something, which if an inferior Sermon has, it succeeds in doing good, but if a superior Sermon lacks, it fails of doing good? We call it "unction." A Sermon may be very logical without unction, admirably argued, perfect as a composition, original withal, and possessing the great merit of setting old truths in a new light; and yet as a Sermon it shall be indifferent, or at least indifferent in the estimate of spiritual men, because it lacks unction. And what is unction? It is hard to define, no doubt, because it lies more in the manner of saying things than in the things said; and manner is always hard to define. Shall we err if we say that by unction is meant a fervent way of throwing out Divine Truth, corresponding with the fervent character of that truth? Unction would be no merit at all, but the reverse, if the Gospel were to be received by the intellect rather than the affections. In any thing like a scientific demonstration of truth, an appeal to the affections would be absurdly out of place. But the Gospel is primarily and fundamentally an appeal to the affections. And it is naturally felt that for a man to make such an appeal without warmth and fervour in his own spirit, to make it as a by-stander who looks on from without, but is not himself interested, or even to make it in over-studied phraseology; picking and choosing the words which are used, is to adopt a style unsuitable to the subject-matter. Men know that the Gospel is designed to meet their

sympathies; and if it should be presented to them in such a manner as not to do this, they feel that it is wronged and misrepresented.

(2) Owing to our not perceiving, or not remembering, this truth, that edification is through the heart, religious exercises are sometimes taken to be edifying which are not so. Shall I say that much of our ordinary reading of Holy Scripture comes under this head? that it often resolves itself into a mere mental exercitation, and that not of a very high order—an exercitation in which the only faculties evoked are, Attention, Memory, and Comparison? We lodge the points of the chapter in our minds,—we call back one or two texts which convey similar doctrines, or perhaps merely echo back the same phraseology,—we ask ourselves how this or that difficulty is to be explained, and possibly invent some explanation of it; and there we make an end, with a feeling, perhaps, of satisfaction that we have not done amiss. This method of reading may be repeated until we become adepts as textuaries, and have the very words of Holy Writ glibly on our tongue. But oh! what a misuse of terms is there in the phraseology so often applied to things got by rote, of which we say that they are "*learned by heart!*" So far from being learned by heart, such things are often not even learned by mind, for sometimes they are most deficiently understood; and the very utmost that can be said in favour of such learning is that it lodges truth in the memory, which may expand and serve a good purpose at some future time. Has our study of Scripture given any bias to the will in the path of holiness? Has it at all stimulated the affections to the Love of God, or of our neighbour? Has it nerved us against temptation? supported us under trial? opened to us a door of hope, when we were fainting? has it prompted a prayer? or stirred in us a holy ambition? By these and the like questions must its influence upon the heart be tested; and unless it has had some influence upon the heart, there has been no edification in it.

Let the devout man be upon his guard against an
interest in Holy Scripture of a false kind. At first
sight it might seem as if any and every interest in that
Holy Book must be simply good, and deserving of
encouragement. But indeed this is not so. And it is
very necessary to notice this at a period when great
intellectual activity is being attracted towards the
Bible. We cannot wonder at the interest which
attaches to the Sacred Volume even in a literary point
of view. The earlier part of it is the oldest literature
in the world; and, speaking of the Bible as a composition,
there is nothing which can rival it in simplicity,
in grace, in force, in poetry. The very difficulties
which it presents are beyond measure interesting to an
intelligent mind. But even in the critical study of the
Bible, which some are called and bound to pursue, it
should be remembered that the great purport of the
Volume is moral and spiritual,—that it is given " for
doctrine, for reproof, for correction, for instruction in
righteousness." If it be read without any reference to
this, its main object, it must certainly be misconstrued.
But if even the sacred critic must not overlook the
moral design of the Volume, how constantly should it
be kept in mind by him who reads for edification only!
Let such an one hold the mere understanding in check,
and learn to restrain with a very sharp curb his
curiosity. Curiosity is the interest of the mind; and
what is needed for edification is the interest of the
heart. It will be wasting an hour allotted to devotional
reading to spend it on the critical investigation
of a difficult passage. The difficult passages are
not the most instructive; and many of them we believe
to be altogether inexplicable by human research,—to
have been left there purposely, with the view of
proving our humility and faith, and to prevent the
haughty understanding of man from riding proudly
and smoothly over the Word of the Lord.

The plain things of the Word, which "thou hast
known from a child,"—which thou hast received from
thy grandmother Lois, and thy mother Eunice,—are

the really instructive things. The Creed, the Lord's Prayer, the Ten Commandments, and such like rudiments of Faith; all saving truths are wrapped up in these; labour, and pray, and strive to have thy heart affected with them.

(3) Finally; let our studies turn more and more on that which is the core and centre of the Bible. The Bible is a revelation of God; and the core and centre of God's Revelation is Christ crucified. Many other subjects are treated in the Bible besides this; but this is really the pith and marrow of all; this wraps up in itself the whole compass of edification. In the Book of the Revelation we read of " the Tree of Life, which bare twelve manner of fruits, and the very leaves of which were for the healing of the nations." It is the Passion-Tree, or Cross, of the Lord Jesus, which, planted by faith in the hearts of His followers, brings forth there all the fruits of the Spirit, and even the leaves of which,—every slight circumstance of it, which apparently might be detached without injury to the stem,—are medicinal to the soul. Study then the Passion of Christ in all its details—the apprehension, the binding, the buffeting, the spitting, the scourging, the mockery, the gall, the nails, the crown of thorns, the burning thirst, the exceeding great and bitter cry, the Precious Death which crowns the whole. Study it with fervent prayer and longing desire rather than prying curiosity. Study it side by side with thy sins, which made such a sacrifice necessary. So, under the influence of the Spirit of grace and supplications, shalt thou mourn for Him whom thou hast pierced; and this tenderness of spirit thou shalt find to be the principle of growth in Grace,—the greatest of all motive powers in the spiritual life.

CHAPTER VI.

ON LIVING BY RULE.

"*Upon the first day of the week let every one of you lay by him in store as God hath prospered him, that there be no gatherings when I come.*"—1 COR. xvi. 2.

THERE is a discrepancy between this passage and the general tone of New Testament precept, which cannot fail to arrest a thoughtful reader; and we shall endeavour to turn to some account the inquiry, to which this discrepancy might give rise in his mind.

St. Paul, the most disenthralled of all the Apostles from the bondage of Judaism, here gives a rule to his Corinthian converts on the subject of almsgiving. The rule was that on every first day of the week (or Sunday) each member of the Church should lay by a part of his substance, varying with the amount of his earnings during the past week, for the relief of the poor Christians at Jerusalem. The wisdom of such a rule of almsgiving is obvious. A considerable sum would thus be gradually accumulated, which though it might not appear formidable in its separate instalments, a man might hesitate to give in one lump. And then, again, such a rule ensured to the givers a gradual discipline in Christian benevolence, which would be far more beneficial to them, and a far greater test of character, than one great effort of it. A great effort may be made in a moment of excitement; but continual little efforts can only be made on principle. Lastly, by adopting this plan, the collection would be over and done before the Apostle visited them, and their minds would be free of the care and responsibility of it, and ready to receive the spiritual benefits of his counsel and ministry.

There can be no question, then, of the policy of such a rule. Still, a rule it is, and it has all the properties of a rule. It defines the exact method, and the exact period of the duty; the sum is to be proportionate to the weekly earnings; it is to be laid by every Sunday. And it has all the narrowness inherent in the nature of rules; that is, it is not adapted to the circumstances of all men. In the case of incomes not accruing weekly, but yearly, or half-yearly, the rule would require to be recast. The deposit would then have to be made, not on the first day of the week, but whenever the income accrued. And though the Apostolic authority made this precise method of almsgiving binding on the Corinthian Church, there is probably no Christian of modern times who thinks himself bound to the literal observance of the rule in question, however much we may be bound, as of course we all are, to the spirit and principle of it.

But, as I have said, the passage is exceptional; it is not in accordance with the general tone of the precepts of the New Testament. They do not generally enter so much into particulars. They are not commonly rules at all; but great principles of duty; and unless they are apprehended as being such, they will certainly be misconstrued.

It is even surprising, until we come to consider it, when all the difficulty vanishes, what a dearth of rules there is in the New Testament. Who would not have thought, for example, that God would have prescribed to us a certain number of times for prayer daily? How natural that it should have been said, "Pray when you rise in the morning, and when you lie down at night;" and again, "Attend Public Worship on the first day of the week or Lord's Day." Whereas instead of any such rules, we have simply the principles laid down for our guidance, "Pray without ceasing." "Not forsaking the assembling of yourselves together." "Where two or three are gathered together in My Name, there am I in the midst of them."

The fact is, that any prescription of stated times for prayer would not have elasticity enough for a New Testament precept,—it would have too much of the letter, too little of the spirit, to be in harmony with the general tenor of the Volume. . The subject may be regarded in this light. No law of Christ may under any circumstances be violated. His laws, therefore, can never be of such a nature, as that men shall be unable, under certain circumstances, to keep them. Had it been said in the New Testament, "Attend Public Worship every Sunday," the primitive Christians, while under the stress of persecution, might have often found it impossible to fulfil the precept. And modern Christians, engaged in tending sick persons who cannot be left with safety, must, in the case supposed, have broken the command of Christ. Now Christ's commands are no trifles, which may be lightly dispensed with; the very least of them must be magnified and made honourable by the punctual obedience of each disciple. Therefore these commands steer clear of all circumstances, because circumstances are infinitely variable; or, to state the same thing in another shape, they are capable of adaptation to all circumstances, because they prescribe the spirit, and not the letter,— the principle, and not the rule. "Not forsaking the assembling of yourselves together." Should you be really and lawfully hindered by works of necessity and love from attending Public Worship on the Lord's Day, you break no law whatever by absenting yourselves from it; nay, because God sends the hindrance in the order of His Providence, you are doing His Will in absenting yourself, and shall none the less realize His Presence, and receive His Blessing, in the sanctuary of your heart. Whereas, on the other hand, when there is no such hindrance, and when opportunities offer, you do forsake the assembling of yourself together with your brethren, if you do not avail yourself of them. The precept is free enough to give dispensation in circumstances of necessity, while at the same time it is strict enough to secure obedience, where there are no such circumstances.

Notwithstanding what has been said of the absence from Scripture of any specific prescription of stated periods of private and Public Worship, there are very few Christians, it may be presumed, who do not regard morning and evening private prayer, and Public Worship on Sundays, as a sort of law of conscience, to the observance of which they are in all ordinary cases bound. It may be said to be a rule framed out of Scriptural principles by the spiritual instincts and common agreement of Christians, that men shall pray on rising and retiring to rest; and that, as often as the first day of the week comes round, they shall assemble together with their fellow-Christians for united acts of prayer and praise. And these rules have been immensely serviceable;—have secured a large amount of real obedience to the Divine Precepts, which, according to the constitution of the human mind, could not have been secured in any other way. The value and importance of rules, however, is not perceived until we thoroughly understand the relation in which Holy Scripture stands to the spiritual instinct of Christians, and the respective provinces of the two. To this point we will now give our attention.

The field of Nature, then, presents a remarkable resemblance to the field of Scripture; there are many points of comparison between them. One striking resemblance is this, that Nature furnishes materials for all the arts of life, even as Scripture furnishes principles for all rules of holy living. There is stone in the quarries of Nature; there is clay in her soils; there is timber in her forests, and coal in her mines; there is fire in her flints, and the power of steam in her waters; there is food in her grains, clothing in her flocks, and beverage in her vines. The various arts of life develope these resources of Nature for the comfort and well-being of man. And these arts are of the greatest importance to that comfort. Without architecture we must sleep under the canopy of the sky, and cross the mountain stream by springing across from stone to stone; without the weaver's art we should be none the better for the sheep's fleece; and without the industry and ingenuity of man in other forms, corn could not be converted into bread, nor the juice of the grape into wine.

Now just as Nature furnishes all the materials of life, which art developes and makes up, (if I may so say,) for use, so Holy Scripture furnishes the materials for all rules of holy living, which rules the spiritual instinct and experience of the children of God extracts and draws up in form. No rule can be of the least service, whose material, that is, whose fundamental principle, is not found in Scripture. Every rule must be positively vicious and mischievous, whose fundamental principle Scripture contradicts. Thus, if any one should recommend, as a rule of holy living, the dwelling entirely apart from human society, on the ground that such society is often a snare, we should take that man back to Holy Scripture and say, " This is a mischievous and false rule of yours; for it is the will of Our Lord that His disciples should be the antiseptic salt of society, which they cannot be, unless they mix with it. 'I pray not,' said He, 'that Thou shouldest take them out of the world, but that Thou shouldest keep them from the evil.'" The rule, therefore, which shuts men up in the cloister and the hermitage, is as sure to come to a disastrous end, as is the house which has been constructed in entire ignorance of the first principles of mechanics; and whose roof falls in accordingly. You can no more construct a wholesome rule in defiance of a law of Scripture, than you can construct a sound building in defiance of a law of Nature.

From this very simple analogy, then, we learn the great importance, as well as the subordinate position, of rules. It was not the scope of the Christian Scriptures to do any thing beyond furnishing the principles of duty, just as it was not the scope of the Creator in Nature to do any thing beyond furnishing *materials* for the supply of man's various wants. Yet we cannot gather from hence that rules are not absolutely necessary (to some extent at least) for a holy life. Man's wants were surely meant to be regularly and comfortably supplied, though Nature furnishes only the materials for supplying them. The mind of man was endowed with art, in order that he might invent, contrive, plan, and execute the different products of civilization,—bread, raiment, dwellings, bridges, and aqueducts. And one of the great ends for which the Church at large, and her individual members and ministers, have been endowed with the Holy Ghost, is to guide them in framing from the principles of the Inspired Word rules of conduct, which may serve as a material assistance in the attainment of that holiness, without which no man shall see the Lord.

Accordingly, such rules have been, to a certain extent, framed, as we have seen, by the public opinion and general practice of the Church, which may be said to prescribe, at all events, private prayer morning and evening, and Public Worship on Sundays; and which is adopting, if it has not yet universally adopted, family prayer either once or twice in each day. Further rules are given in books of devotion,—where you will find forms of self-examination and preparation for the Holy Communion, and other forms for an annual examination and renewal of our Christian vows. Other suggestions to the same effect are sometimes made from the pulpit, though (as we have before had occasion to remark) more rarely than they ought to be. But we are now speaking more particularly of the individual member of Christ, and of the part he should take in framing, or adopting, such rules, and embodying them in his daily practice. And on this point we desire to speak with all the earnestness and emphasis, which the importance of the subject demands.

Let it be considered, then, how grave is the responsibility with which each of us is charged, of keeping our own souls, and saving them alive. Let it be considered how the issue of our happiness or misery through all eternity is suspended, in the marvellous arrangements of Divine Providence, on the conduct of threescore years and ten,—on the shape which our characters take in that short span of time. Let it be considered again that, putting Christ and His covenanted Grace out of the question, we are utterly unequal to the bearing so great a burden under so sore an opposition, and must in an instant be crushed by it, if we undertook it in our own strength. Be it remembered, too, that this burden cannot possibly be shifted to other shoulders, but must be borne by ourselves alone. And then, from what we know of success, and the means of success in worldly undertakings, let us consider whether we are likely to succeed in administering this all-important affair, and to bring the conduct of it to a happy issue, without some definite plan and method of proceeding, wisely laid and faithfully executed. To some, indeed, it may seem as if the placing ourselves under any rules were for a Christian a sort of return to the bondage of the law, and an interference with the liberty of the new and spiritual dispensation. But be it observed, that the adoption of rules is recommended to Christians not as a bondage but as a help to the will, and as a discipline for bracing and hardening it. What Christian man of these degenerate days can say with truth that he has risen above the necessity of all such rules? What Christian man could safely afford to dispense with the obligation of private prayer morning and evening, and of stated Public Worship, although these obligations are bound upon him, not by the explicit letter of Holy Scripture, but by the godly customs and traditional usages of the Christian Church? The will of the best of us is lamentably weak and vacillating, and needs all the support and strength which can be given to it. This support and strength can only come from the Spirit of Christ; but then this Spirit visits us in the diligent use of the means. Now by general precepts, exacting a perfect and universal obedience, the will is not strengthened. The indefiniteness of such precepts as to time and method renders them easy of evasion, and, when the trial comes, the weak will takes the opening which is left to it by the breadth and spirituality of the law. But when the precept takes the shape of a rule, and condescends to particulars as to time, place, and method, the will, obeying it punctually, finds its power strengthened by such obedience; and submission becomes easier for the future, until at length it is yielded habitually.

How, then, since rules, if discreetly used, are so serviceable, shall we proceed in the formation or adoption of them? Now, just as a little experience of our own physical constitution puts us into possession of the amount and kind of food, the amount and kind of air and exercise which suits us best, so a slight experience of the spiritual life, if it be but an earnest one, soon teaches us what restrictions it is important to lay upon ourselves, what should be our leading resolves, and what form and length of devotion is suitable and expedient for us. Minds are almost infinitely various; and according to the character of our own mind must be the discipline we allot to it. Some persons can profitably go through much longer devotions than others; because some are naturally more recollected, and some more dissipated by external things. Persons in rude health and high spirits will need external mortification in things innocent, to a degree which might be extremely prejudicial to those in whom the tone of animal life is always feeble. Persons called to much active business must study how they may make their devotions very short, very frequent, and very fervent; those who have leisure will be able to consecrate a larger portion of it to direct acts of worship, and will find their account in doing so. Then, as to the desirableness of frequent Communion, this will vary much with the temperament and circumstances of each individual, as well as with his progress in the spiritual life, and the quiet opportunities which he can manage to secure beforehand. Let each man do in this matter as in his conscience he thinks to be best for himself, and, according to the Apostolic rule of love, neither judge his brother as a formalist, because he partakes often of that most blessed Sacrament, nor despise him as irreligious, because he finds a rarer celebration more profitable at present. Again, as to almsgiving, some rule surely must be felt by all of us to be urgently needed; and here, especially, the form and shape which the duty will take will be almost infinitely various. Let each man only make sure of securing by his practice the principle, which is that God has a claim upon a certain fair proportion of our annual income, which portion is literally not ours but His; and that to withhold from Him such a proportion, independently of the dishonour done to Him thereby, is as likely to be prejudicial to our spiritual interests as the withholding from Him a portion of our time for the exercises of devotion. Let this principle be deeply settled in the mind; and then the details adjusted honestly in accordance with it. Though the subject is one which defies, more than any other, all attempts at a general rule, the method prescribed by the Apostle to the Corinthians may perhaps be found serviceable, and in many cases would be quite practicable, that of laying by in reserve a certain portion of money, as our income accrues. The doing this regularly and punctually might very likely free the mind from those perplexing considerations, as to whether we are doing our duty in this matter of almsgiving, which are apt at times to harass all earnest and thoughtful Christians. And to be rid of perplexities is a great point gained towards holy living. It is not easy to grow in grace, while the mind is in a tangle, and the will in a state of hesitation and unsettlement.

Finally, (and passing over without notice many points which might be touched, but which the mind of the reader must supply,) specific resolutions are of the greatest service in the Spiritual Life. They must be framed upon the knowledge of our weak points and besetting sins; and it is well every morning to draw up one or more of them, after a foresight of the temptations to which we are liable to be exposed, and the circumstances by which we are likely to be surrounded. Let it be remembered generally that nothing is so likely to destroy that recollectedness of mind, which is the very atmosphere of the Spiritual Life, as unexpected incidents for which we are in no wise prepared, and which often stir in us sudden impulses of almost uncontrollable feeling. We cannot, of course, foresee all such incidents; but still there are many of them, which, from a survey of the day, we may think likely to arise. Let us arm ourselves for them, when they do come, by a holy resolution, which will take its shape from the peculiar nature of the temptation offered,—a resolution perhaps to busy ourselves in some useful work, and so divert the mind, or to give a soft answer which turns away wrath, or to repeat secretly a verse of some favourite hymn, or only to cast a mental glance on Christ crucified, which indeed is the most sovereign remedy against temptation known in the spiritual world.

In any case let our rules be such as may be easily and cheerfully observed, remembering that we are to serve God in the newness of the spirit, not in the oldness of the letter. Let the object be to make them a help, not to convert them into a penance. And let their inferiority and subserviency to the principle on which they are founded be always kept in mind. Let them not be easily dispensed with when once made; and yet let there be no foolish superstitious scruple about dispensing with them when real necessity arises. Oh, who shall teach the one-sided mind of man the true middle path between the bondage of observances (which is the bondage of Judaism), and that spurious (so-called) freedom, which affects to disdain self-discipline, and refuses to acknowledge itself under the Law to Christ! God will show us the path, if we will not lean to our own understanding, but follow, with the simplicity and docility of children, the guidance of His hand.

CHAPTER VII.

OF THE MISCHIEF AND DANGER OF EXAGGERATIONS
IN RELIGION.

" *Let us prophesy according to the proportion of faith.*"
Rom. xii. 6.

Lord Bacon somewhere compares religion to the sun, which has two contrary effects upon live and dead animal substances. Live animal substances,—the living body of man, for example,—the sun invigorates, and cheers, and promotes the functions of life in them. But in dead animal substances the sun breeds worms, and turns them to corruption. Similarly, he says, religion invigorates a sound mind, and cheers a sound heart, while in a morbid mind it breeds noisome superstitions, and miserable scruples, and grotesque, and even monstrous, fancies; the fault however not being in religion, but in the diseased mind, which is subjected to its influences. Such is the thought of the great philosopher, if these are not the very words in which he has expressed it.

We have only to survey the history of Christianity, to see how eminently just this comparison is. The Gospel, as taught by Our Lord and His Apostles, is holy, pure, divine, transparently clear, radiant alike with the glory of God and the happiness of man—of that there is no doubt; yet what twists has the mind of man contrived to give it, so that in some forms of Christianity you can hardly at all recognize the original draught, as it came from the Divine mind! What follies, fancies, superstitions, licentious doctrines, have founded themselves—not justly, of course, but with a most perverse ingenuity—upon the Scriptures of the Old and New Testament!

This has arisen, not from any fault or shortcoming in the Scriptures themselves (God forbid! His Word is, like Himself, perfect), but from a certain morbid tendency in the human mind to caricature truths presented to it. I believe we cannot express the tendency in question more exactly than by calling it a tendency to caricature. A caricature is the likeness of a person, in which the artist has caught some of the leading points of the countenance, but has so unduly exaggerated them as to make the whole likeness absurd and grotesque. There is always a point of resemblance in a caricature, or persons would not know for whom it was meant; but the point is excessively magnified and thrown out of all proportion to the other lineaments, or people would take it seriously, and it would cease to be a caricature, and become a portrait. Now it would be very interesting to consider every heresy which has hitherto arisen, and see how in each case it has been a caricature of some one point of Christian Truth,—an exaggeration by which the fair proportion of the Faith (of which St. Paul speaks in the Epistle to the Romans) has been distorted, and a single passage of Scripture or a single class of passages, brought into undue prominence. We will take one or more instances from those heresies which are better known. The truth upon which the Quaker founds his whole system, is that the New Dispensation is spiritual. No truth can well be more vital, more important, or more apt, through the subtle encroachments of formalism (a sin which is at all times waylaying us), to be dropt out of sight. It is quite necessary for all of us to turn round every now and then, and ask ourselves whether we are properly awake to it. That the law, under which Christians live, is the law, not of a written table, nor of a written book, but "the law of the Spirit of life in Christ Jesus," written on the fleshy table of the heart; that in place of a code prescribing or forbidding *actions*, our Legislator has given us a code of Beatitudes on certain states of heart and feeling; that in the Gospel morality what we do goes for comparatively little, and what we are— our motives and intentions—for every thing; that each movement of the heart is judged by Him who reads the heart; that God is a Spirit, and therefore to be worshipped in spirit and in truth, and that, accordingly, to approach Him with outward ceremonial, exclusive of the heart, is as much an impossibility in the nature of things, as to endow matter with the properties of mind, and make a stone work a mathematical problem; all this is not only true, but precious truth, of which we require to be reminded continually; and the Quakers would have deserved the warmest thanks of Christendom, if they had done nothing more than brought it forward prominently, and illustrated it strikingly. But, unhappily, having seized this one feature of the Truth as it is in Jesus, they caricatured it. They proceeded on the theory of a spiritual dispensation to such an absurd extent, as to rob the Church of her Sacraments, the repositories and vehicles of that very inward spiritual grace, of which the Quakers themselves were the stoutest maintainers. If religion is spiritual, they argued, we must have nothing material about it; so, notwithstanding the Lord's words, "Go ye, baptizing all nations," and "Do this in remembrance of Me," we will banish from our meetings the water, the bread, and the wine, and be baptized and communicate in the spirit only. It has always been the opinion of pious and judicious divines in the Church, that because, even in the Sacraments, the inward spiritual grace is the chief matter, Christians shut out from communicating sacramentally (by illness or other necessity) may do so spiritually in their closets by uniting their prayers and intercessions with that which is passing in the Church; but the actual renunciation of the outward visible sign, as the Quakers have renounced it, would never have entered into the head of any one, unless his mind had been possessed with some one idea, and he had resolved to make that idea stand for the whole of Christianity.—We offer another and more recent instance of a very serious error, which we fear is fast assuming the proportions of a heresy. It is the delightful announcement of Holy Scripture, which should make every heart bound with joy,—and it may be said to be the very most fundamental truth of our religion, that "God is Love." His Love He has shown by a Sacrifice which must surely have wrung to the utmost His paternal heart, if a similar sacrifice would have proved to a mere human parent the most acutely painful of all trials,—the sacrifice of His dear Son, Who from all eternity had lain in His bosom. Certain divines of our own day have perceived this truth of God's Love clearly. They cannot perceive it too clearly; they cannot proclaim it too loudly,—not if they had a hundred tongues, and the lungs of a Stentor. Down with all teaching, which by real logical inference contradicts this fundamental truth;—it must be false, unscriptural, mischievous. That our God is a hard taskmaster, requiring of us services, which will not ultimately make for our own happiness; that austerities, as austerities, without any spiritual end, are pleasing to Him and propitiate His wrath (a notion utterly and simply heathen); that only the Second Person of the Blessed Trinity smiles upon us with a gracious welcome, and that the brow of the First is always contracted with a gloomy frown towards sinners:—let these sentiments by all means be demolished with axe and hammer, because they contradict God's own testimony respecting Himself. But to go the length of saying that anger is inconsistent with love, (an assertion which the analogy of parental affection surely enables us flatly to contradict,) or to go the further length of saying that justice is inconsistent with compassion, against all experience of human justice; (for over what offender led out to execution, does not the heart of man relent at the last moment, while yet feeling the justice and necessity of the proceeding?) and to acknowledge no relations with God as a Judge, because He stands to us in the relation of a Father, this is a monstrous exaggeration, whereby the Faith once given to the saints is grievously caricatured, and its fair proportions marred. God loves me deeply, purely, intensely; longs to communicate Himself to me;—that is indisputably true, and I may take to myself all the comfort of it without a moment's hesitation. But God hates my sin, detests it, brought Christ to a strict reckoning for it, and will never consent to save me from its guilt without saving me from the power of it too:—that is equally true, and I may take to myself all the warning of it, without a moment's hesitation.

These two instances are enough to show that very serious errors and heresies spring from not maintaining what St. Paul calls "the proportion of the faith,"— that is, from giving to any one doctrine, however true and important, so great a prominence that it throws into the shade all others which counterbalance it.

And be it remembered that, where there is no formal or actual heresy, the one-sided tendency of the human mind is nevertheless operative in religious persons, and may lead to a vast amount of unsuspected mischief and error, which shall corrupt their religion, and breed in it many morbid and fanatical fancies. In many spiritual books, which in the main are excellent,—perhaps I might say in every spiritual book, more or less, which is not the Bible,—a strain is put upon certain precepts of the Gospel, which not only caricatures them, and perhaps sets them at issue with other precepts resting on the same authority, but would have the effect of cramping into an unnatural state the mind which should strive after obedience to them. As nothing illustrates with the same effect as an example, I will give one; and, the better to exhibit the principle, it shall be in an extreme form. A Christian, who had attained a high degree of sanctity, and who died in the most acute suffering, which he bore with exemplary patience, gasped out to the spiritual adviser who attended him, the following words: "Dear friend, God has taught me a great secret, and I will tell it you, if you will put your head closer." His friend did as he desired, anxious to know what this saintly man considered as the crowning lesson of a life of holiness. "He has taught me," said the dying man, the lines of whose countenance were distorted by pain, "to ask nothing, and to refuse nothing."

Now perhaps the first sound of such a sentiment may be to some ears attractive. A sentimental pietism might perhaps whisper, on hearing it, "What beautiful resignation!" But is it beautiful, according to the true canon of beauty in Religion, which is conformity to the Word of God, and the mind of Christ? We admit that to refuse nothing which comes from our Father's hand, however much our lower will, which shuns pain and suffering, may deprecate it, is the state of mind to which every Christian will labour and pray that he may be brought. But *where has God taught His people to ask nothing?* Where has He forbidden them, under suffering, to cry for relief? Did Our Lord, or did He not, pray, "Father, if it be possible, let this cup pass from Me?" If He did, God evidently had not taught His only-begotten Son to "ask for nothing." And His Son's Humanity was spotless in holiness,— He was clearly "void of sin, both in His flesh and in His spirit." Shall we, miserable sinners, presume with a frightful temerity to go further in conformity to the will of God than Jesus Himself went? Forbid it, Lord! We will go to Thee in our troubles with all simplicity, and make known to Thee our request for relief, in submission always to Thy Will; and having preferred our request, we will leave it there in our Father's hands, and account that we have thenceforth nothing more to do with it. But find a vent towards God for our burdened heart we will, because He Himself has opened such a vent when He says: "Ye people, pour out your hearts before Him."

Do you not see now how this holy man erred by exaggeration; how in his dying sentiment he caricatured the grace of resignation? Resignation no doubt is a heavenly and Christ-like grace; but if you will push it to any and every length, regardless of other precepts of God's Word, and even regardless of common sense, (a very valuable aid in religion,) even resignation might become absolutely mischievous. Thus in countries where the weather is sultry, and the people constitutionally indolent, one might conceive a beggar continuing in mendicancy, and doing nothing to raise himself above it, or to improve his condition, on the plea that such was the Will of God, and that mendicancy was the state of life to which he had been called. Resignation is the only precept which such an one recognizes; and he has forgotten that in another corner of God's Word there is a certain maxim, less chivalrous perhaps than resignation, but equally deserving his attention,—that "if any man would not work, neither should he eat." This, of course, is another extreme case. I only adduce it, because it illustrates the fault which we are at present exposing and censuring.

Be it remembered, in pursuing the train of thought which we have thus opened up, that in the lives of the early *Scriptural* saints, who, next to Our Blessed Lord, are our great models, nothing is so remarkable as their perfect naturalness, and freedom from all affected or overstrained spirituality. The great Apostle of the Gentiles, whose name and fame is in all the Churches, immediately after a miraculous escape from shipwreck, bestirs himself to gather a bundle of sticks, and puts them on the fire (for St. Paul was not above feeling cold and wet); and when writing under the afflatus of the Holy Ghost, he bids Timothy bring the cloak which he left at Troas with Carpus, in anticipation of an approaching winter, " and the books, but especially the parchments;" for what studious man—and every minister of Christ must be studious, if his ministry is to be effective—can bear to be without his books and papers? These particulars have seemed to some too frivolous for Inspiration, but they have a real purpose, and subserve a real end, if they show that even Inspiration did not destroy the perfect simplicity and naturalness of those who were the subjects of it. Among the early disciples you would have seen nothing overcharged in character or manner; nay, you would have seen little foibles, (not that these are to be imitated,) of temper, of superstition, of prejudice;— you might have heard sharp words passing between great Apostles, and a rupture taking place in consequence; you might have heard even St. Peter roundly and publicly reproved for clinging to a prejudice; and you might have seen a damsel, recently engaged with others in prayer, which received a miraculous answer, in such a joyful trepidation of nerves when the answer arrived, that she opened not the gate for gladness, but ran in and told "how Peter stood before the gate." Most of us would thankfully acquiesce in being as saintly as the primitive Christians; and surely it is a lesson for us that there is in their sanctity so little over-studied, so little walking on stilts, so little of the forced unnatural attitude, into which modern books of devotion sometimes try to cramp the mind. In ancient piety there was not a particle of asceticism or of Puritanism,—which two things I mention together, because they are the Roman and Protestant sides of the same fault.

How, then, shall the devout man keep his mind free from exaggerations both in doctrine and practice, and hold in check its natural one-sidedness? An impartial study of the *whole* of Scripture is the corrective. Our Church may indicate the remedy. The bulk of the Old Testament is by her read through once, and the bulk of the New Testament three times, in each year. Those who will be at the pains to accompany her in the cycle of the four daily lessons, (a larger portion of Scripture than is read in any schismatical community, Romish or dissenting,) will thus have a fresh current of Scripture always setting in through the mind, and will find that this fresh current has a remarkable tendency to defecate the dregs of the mind, and to clear away those morbid humours which intercept its vision. Adopt either this method, or some other similar to it. Read with real openness of mind, quite willing to renounce any such preconceived views as do not square with the great Canon of Truth. Of set purpose study, and give their fair weight to, those doctrines, or practices, to which your mind is not naturally drawn. Pray for the Bereans' nobleness of mind, in that they brought even the doctrine of Apostles to the test of Inspiration, and searched the Scriptures daily, whether these things were so. How much more, when men are not Apostles, but simply possessors of the mind of Christ, must *their* doctrine be thus searched and sifted! Much irreverent nonsense has been talked of late about a verifying faculty, but, (God be praised!) we have some more certain criterion of Truth in a verifying Book. It is true that there is no error whatever, which may not be bolstered up by an appeal to some part of the Holy Scriptures. Atheism itself, it has been well said, may be proved from the Bible, by simply leaving out the words, "The fool hath said in his heart." But when applied impartially, without favour or prejudice, and in full view of the passages on the other side, Holy Scripture is a thoroughly safe and sound criterion. Do not merely read it, but imbue your minds with it. Do not merely quote it, (a very easy and somewhat poor attainment,) but frame your religious sentiments upon it, and then you shall bear a charmed life against error, and heresy, and all manner of morbid fancies and fanaticisms.

CHAPTER VIII.

OF THE GREAT VARIETY OF MEN'S CHARACTERS IN THE CHURCH OF CHRIST.

"*As the body is one, and hath many members, and all the members of that one body, being many, are one body: so also is Christ.*"—1 COR. xii. 12.

THESE words, and the chapter from which they are taken, teach us that variety in unity is the law of the Church of Christ. The spiritual gifts with which the early believers were endowed were various; some were enabled to work miracles; some to speak with tongues;

some to heal the sick ; some to prophesy ; some had a supernatural insight into character; some interpreted the ecstatic utterances, to which others gave vent. "But all these," says the Apostle, "worketh that one and the self-same Spirit, dividing to every man severally as He will." And it may be added that not only did the gifts come from the same Author; but worked together also to the same end, the service of Christ and the glory of God. This is not explicitly stated by the Apostle, but is quite as strongly implied in the image which he employs, as the former truth. In the passage which stands at the head of this Chapter, the Church is compared to the natural body of man. Now, not only is the life of the body one thing, in whichever of the members it operates; but also the members conspire together to one end. In fetching and reaching any thing, the design is formed by the brain; the object is seen by the eye; the feet are made to walk in that direction; the hands subsequently are raised to grasp the object. Combination *for one purpose* is quite as obvious in the whole procedure, as the interpenetration of the entire body by *one life*.

Now, because we are prepared to expect a resemblance between two children of the same parents, and between two works of the same author, we conclude that God also, in the different departments of His agency, will observe a similar plan and method of working. The organization of the early Church came immediately from God; and, therefore, if variety in unity was the law of this organization, we should expect to find variety in unity in other things also, which God has organized. And if in that which is on all hands admitted to be a work of God, we *do* find variety in unity, this will be an evidence more or less satisfactory to thinking minds that the Church of Christ, which was originally constructed on the same principle, in which even now the same principle of construction is discernible, is from God also.

Now, if we look into Nature, we find that the law

which pervades the whole of it is variety in unity. Not only are the commonest objects by which we are surrounded totally different in species, colour, shape, material,—not only do they offer phenomena totally different to the senses of sight, and touch, and taste,— but even in the same species, and even in the same individuals of the same species, the diversity seems to be endless. It is said that no two leaves of the same tree, though of course of the same general configuration, ever match exactly, so as to lie flat on the table one over another with a perfect correspondence of edges. No two faces, even of twins, so entirely correspond, that an eye familiar with them by constant intercourse cannot in a moment detect the dissimilarity. Indeed, in Nature the variety is far more apparent than the unity. Science, however, is continually bringing to light an unity and simplicity of type in things which on the surface are most different. What objects can present a greater superficial difference than quadrupeds and fishes, both of which however, being vertebrates, are formed on the same general plan? Nor is it merely a resemblance of what may be called ground-plan, but a sameness of agency which we discover in the different works of creation. The same power of gravitation which ties the planets to the sun, and retains them in their orbits, causes the sere and shrivelled autumnal leaf or the over-ripe fruit to fall to the ground. The same power of electricity which rives the strong oak, or shatters the tall spire, attracts light substances towards chafed sealing-wax, and forms the sport of children. The same refraction of the rays of the sun produces the rainbow in the heavens, and makes the tiny dewdrop under our feet to twinkle with the prismatic colours. Finally we can see tolerably clear indications that the various parts of the Universe are working together for one end. This at all events is the case as regards that part of the domain of Nature with which we are immediately surrounded. Very strong forces are at work in and around the earth; forces which, if allowed unlimited sway, might peril the planet's existence; but they play into one another's hands, and hold one another in equipoise. The matter which is discharged from one part of the system reappears in another under a new form, and there serves some other function; so that each atom seems to have its vocation and its place, and to fill that place, and correspond to that vocation.

Such is Nature,—an immense variety, knit together in unity by sameness of plan, sameness of agency, sameness of object. And to step from the realm of Nature into the realm of Grace, the Word of God presents undoubtedly the same phenomenon. The Holy Scriptures are a collection of books written under a great variety of circumstances, and at a great variety of times, the extreme dates between which the different books range being nearly 1600 years asunder. And the Scriptures are as different in kind, as they are in the dates of their publication. In the short volume of the Bible we have histories, biographies, lyrical poems, dramatic poems (the Book of Job belongs to this class), aphorisms, prophecies, rituals, letters. No two compositions in the world can be more widely different in superficial appearance than the Book of Psalms and the Epistle to the Romans, the Prophecy of Isaiah and the Epistle to Philemon, the Book of Ruth and the Book of the Revelation, the Book of Leviticus and the Gospel according to St. Luke. Yet, in addition to minor features of resemblance, which concern only style and method of treatment, such as the thorough simplicity of all the narratives, and the entire absence from them all of exaggeration and rhetorical ornament, those who have studied the Scriptures under the light of faith in Christ Jesus, are well aware that, however dissimilar, they are one organic whole, knit together by a certain plan, and certain principles, which underlie the entire book. The prophecy of the Seed of the woman, which should bruise the serpent's head, is manifestly the nucleus, the single cell (to take an image from the formation of a flower), round which the whole Bible has formed itself, of which the whole is a development, on which the whole is a commentary. The great steps of the plan which runs through the Bible are very easy to trace. A nation of teachers is first reared amidst various fortunes, knit together by the endurance of a common bondage, and impressed with marked national characteristics, in order that they may present a strong front to the prevailing idolatries and wickedness of the world; and in order that they may disseminate amongst other people of the earth the elementary religious notions which they had themselves imbibed from the Divine teaching. As soon as, through God's wonderful dealings with them, they had been thoroughly imbued with these notions, they were dispersed among the nations of the earth, and made to sojourn there. By their instrumentality a class of men called proselytes are raised up in Gentile countries, who, attracted by the elements of truth which there were in the Mosaic religion, adopt it, and become eventually the bridge by which the Gospel passes from the Jewish to the Gentile mind. The way having been thus prepared for Messiah in the hearts of men, the long-promised Deliverer appears at a time of universal peace, and when the union of the civilized world under one empire was favourable to the spread of the tidings of salvation. What remains of the Sacred Volume briefly records the rapid spread of these tidings, gives certain comments upon them, and predicts the complete triumph of the Messiah's cause. Thus there is an uniform plan, running through the whole of Scripture, and cementing together its various books, inasmuch as the entire Old Testament looks forward to Messiah historically,—represents the stages of discipline by which the Jews, and through the Jews the human race, were prepared for His appearance. And we well know that it looks forward to Messiah in another way, typically and prophetically, and that not only all the ritual of the Jews, and all the predictions of their prophets, but also most narratives of the Old Testament, foreshow His appearance in a glass darkly. Thus in the Bible, though its elements are so various, there is a glorious harmony of design, and, as the whole of it emanates from one Spirit, a harmony of agency also.

If then, both in the works of God, and in the Word of God, we find that variety in unity is the prevailing law, shall we not expect to find the same feature in the Church of God, which, quite as much as Nature, quite as much as Scripture, is His workmanship; created anew "in Christ Jesus unto good works?" And this we do find. The members of the Apostolic Church had various gifts, the phenomena of which were different, some consisting in speaking with tongues, some in healing the sick, but all the results of the agency of one Spirit, and all working together for the glory of one Saviour. But it may be said that the Church of modern times is not furnished with the same organization as the early Church: that extraordinary and miraculous endowments have altogether ceased. This is true; but it is true also that all these supernatural gifts rested on a natural basis, had something in the natural endowments of the possessor's mind corresponding to them, and serving as the nucleus of them. Thus, for example, corresponding to the gift of tongues, we find in some persons a great facility of acquiring languages; corresponding to the gift of prophecy, we find in others a natural gift of high and fervid eloquence; some persons even now-a-days, though by no means original or brilliant, have such a wonderful art of imparting what they know, that we can hardly be said to have lost the gift of teaching; others are admirably adapted for government, for the control of other wills and the organization of philanthropic schemes; while even the gift of miracles itself, the most supernatural of all, rests on the power of mind over matter, of which power we have exemplifications in a natural way even now-a-days.

But even putting out of the question the capacities and endowments of the human mind, in which we find a variety as great as in the miraculous gifts, this we may certainly say, that the character and moral temperament of each individual Christian is different from that of his neighbour. So it was of old; and so it is still. In the notices of the Apostles and other early believers, God has sketched for us not only edifying pieces of biography, but prototypes of all Christians to the end of time. Thus St. John represents the contemplative and studious disciple. No single miracle is ever recorded as having been wrought by him; and in the outward spread of the Gospel, although no doubt he did his work, he is not nearly so prominent a figure as St. Peter, and does not for a moment reach the world-wide celebrity of St. Paul. Very thoughtful men who live much with themselves, are by no means so influential with others as those who, vividly apprehending certain simple topics, go forth to proclaim them without any profound reflection upon them. St. Peter governs with a firm hand, and with the now chastened and disciplined will, which belongs to an impetuous temper; he is the great bulwark and rock of the Church, breasting its perils and responsibilities gallantly, before St. Paul appears; Apollos is an eloquent declaimer who blends to the best effect his knowledge of the Greek rhetoric, with that higher knowledge, in respect of which he is said to have been "mighty in the Scriptures;" Barnabas sheds around him, wherever he goes, the quiet healing influence of a man felt to be good, and full of faith;—he has a still small voice of consolation for those upon whom the hand of God is heavy; Timothy has imbibed the lessons of piety with his mother's milk, and, being trained up as a child in the way he should go, has not departed from it as a young man; but he is somewhat timid and pliable, and exceedingly apt to be moulded by a superior will; while Paul, in powers of physical and mental endurance, in the expansiveness of his affections, in his vivid appreciation of his own remarkable experience, is God's chiefest instrument for the diffusion of the glad tidings. These, if I may so express it, are some of the moulds in which Christian character was cast, when Christianity first appeared, and in which we may expect that it will continue to be cast now-a-days. The types are strong types; still, although modern days may show somewhat feebler impressions of them, they are still the same, although less marked.

Now in what has been said there is wrapped up both comfort for ourselves, and a lesson of large charity towards others.

1. Let us not distress ourselves, either that we were not brought to God, or that we are not now serving God, in the same way as some others, who seem to be models of a very exemplary and exalted piety. Certain preachers, and still more certain writers of religious books, construct a sort of Procrustean framework, as a model for all cases of real conversion, and intimate that, if you cannot accommodate your own experience to that stiff frame,—if you have never felt paroxysms of alarm at the threatenings of the law, or paroxysms of ecstasy at the announcements of the Gospel,—your heart is not at this moment right with God. Nothing can be more erroneous philosophically, or more untrue scripturally. God's ways of influencing the human mind for good vary infinitely,—vary first, with the original character of the mind, on which the Holy Ghost has to operate; and, secondly, with the acquired shape which that mind has taken from the circumstances in which it has been thrown, and from its whole history and experience. On the same page of Scripture there is the record of two most remarkable conversions, as different from each other as any two processes of mind, leading to the same result, can by possibility be. Lydia, the purple-seller of Thyatira, became a Christian through the gentle opening of the heart, as by the quiet riverside she attended to the things which were spoken of Paul. The Philippian gaoler is converted, on the other hand, in a manner such as might be expected from the previous habits of ignorance and vice in which, we may reasonably suppose, he had been sunk. He is shaken with strong alarm, as if over the pit of hell, (nothing else would have broken bonds so firmly riveted,) and " he called for a light, and sprang in, and came trembling, and fell down before Paul and Silas, and said, Sirs, what must I do to be saved?" Lydia experienced no such

alarm, but only a gentle opening of the heart, peaceful as the undulations of the river; yet was she none the less a disciple of Our Lord, and none the less dear to Him. The critical, all-important question for all of us is, whether we be indeed Christ's at present, and are following the lead of His Spirit; if so, how we were brought to Him, whether by the quiet drawings of gratitude and love, or by the gradual growth of reflectiveness, and our experience of life's hollowness, or by the trepidations of alarm, is but of little moment.

And then, again, as to our method of serving Him. This must depend on our capacities, our endowments, the position which we providentially occupy, and the opportunities which it gives us. It may not be a high work, or a widely influential work, which we are doing for God, but then it may not be a high work, or a widely influential work, to which He has called us. We *may*, of course, be working *below* the measure of the gift which God has distributed to us, leaving the talent which our Master left with us unimproved, and not putting it out to the exchangers, so that at His coming He may receive His own with usury. That is a point to be looked to, and carefully considered. But the mere brilliancy of the position occupied by another, or the brilliancy of the gifts which qualify him for that position, should never make us indulge in an unquiet longing to be or to do what God has not fitted us for, and which, therefore, He will never require from us. If not called, and not fitted, (and the fitness is the evidence of the call,) we could not undertake such a thing without a most censurable presumption. "I would undertake to govern a hundred empires," said Dr. Payson, "if God called me to it, but I would not undertake to govern a hundred sheep unless He called me."

2. But, again, a lesson of large charity to others is to be learned from what has been said. We ought, if rightly minded, to rejoice in the exuberance and variety of the spiritual gifts possessed by Christians, just as we delight in the rich variety of Nature, or in that of the

Word of God. There are many lines of thought in Religion, many forms which practical and personal piety takes, although, of course, they are all animated by the same essential principles. St. John and St. Paul were both equally devoted to the cause and Person of Our Lord, yet no two men ever existed, who manifested this devotion in shapes more different. Both these members held of the Head by a living union, but they discharged for the Head functions altogether different. Let us not conceive of all genuine religion as moving in one groove of feeling and practice, and refuse to acknowledge any man as a Christian, because he does not run upon our own particular groove. There are several points of view from which Christianity may be surveyed; and although it be one and the same object, from whatever point we look, yet eyes placed on different levels will see it grouped in different perspectives. Our own view of it is at best but partial and fragmentary; let us rejoice in the fact that others see it somewhat differently, and that their view, instead of being contradictory to our own, is in fact the complement of it. It seems to be God's plan and purpose that each individual Christian should exhibit, in the peculiarity of his circumstances, education, moral temperament, and mental endowments, a new specimen of redeeming love and grace. By various discipline here He fits and polishes each living stone for the place which it is destined to occupy in the Spiritual Temple; and when all the stones are made ready, He will build them together each into his place, and exhibit to men and angels their perfect unity. Aaron has been bred under his paternal roof, and inured to Egyptian servitude from childhood. Moses has been lapped in royal luxury from his infancy, educated at a court, and then banished into a wilderness. But the time came when these brothers in blood, so dissimilar in training, so opposite in their experience, so different, possibly, in some of the judgments which they had formed of God's ways, met never again to part in this life. "The Lord said unto Aaron, Go into the wilderness to meet Moses. And he went, and met him in the Mount of God, and kissed him." So shall it be with all true Christians, whose history, discipline, sentiments, have here taken a course which seemed far enough asunder. A meeting and a greeting is reserved for all of them in the mount of God,—let them "see" to it, as Joseph said to his Brethren, "that they fall not out by the way."

CHAPTER IX.

OF THE IDEA OF SACRIFICE, AS PERVADING THE CHRISTIAN'S LIFE.

"*An holy priesthood to offer up spiritual sacrifices, acceptable to God by Jesus Christ.*"—1 PET. ii. 5.

It is a rule all but universal, if we cannot say that it admits of no exception, that all known forms of Religion which have existed upon earth, have involved the idea of sacrifice as a leading and principal feature of them. The Jews, we know, practised sacrifice largely by Divine appointment,—practised it in every shape which the idea of sacrifice can assume. They had their sin-offerings and their trespass-offerings for the expiation of guilt, their thank-offerings in acknowledgment of mercies received, their burnt-offerings and meat-offerings for the acceptance of the worshipper, their free-will offerings for his spontaneous recognition of God out of the fulness of an adoring heart. In short, theirs was a sacrificial system, minute in all its details, and perfect in all its parts. Among the heathen nations of antiquity, we find floating shadows of these various offerings, looking like portions of the Jewish system disintegrated and broken up among the different tribes of Gentiles. Before meals, the ancients would pour out a drink-offering to one of their gods, they would make a votive offering to them after any great escape or deliverance, and, on occasions of public rejoicing or humiliation, they would expose the images of the gods on couches before tables loaded with dainties. Whence came practices so universal in connexion with religion?—a question the more pertinent, because sacrifice does not on the surface approve itself to our minds as a reasonable form of worship. Independently of God's appointment, we cannot say with truth that the slaughter of a poor animal, or the laying a basket of fruit by the side of an altar, seems likely, in the nature of things, to be a form of homage acceptable to the Supreme Being. No doubt, the appearance of sacrifice in all heathen forms of religion is to be accounted for partly by a tradition derived from the first fathers of the human race. The remembrance of Noah's sacrifice after the flood would be carried away by his descendants into the various countries of their dispersion, and there, in lapse of time, degenerate and run wild in a thousand fantastic shapes. Meanwhile the holy seed from Noah to Abraham, from Abraham to Moses, and from Moses onwards, would retain the true idea and the true practice of sacrifice, which was a slip of God's own grafting. We can scarcely, however, think that, even with the help of a primeval tradition, sacrifice would so long have maintained its ground among all the nations of heathendom, had there not been some common sentiment or instinct of the human heart, instigating men to it. And such an instinct there unquestionably is. In the rudest mind which recognizes a God, there exists a desire to give Him some acknowledgment, which may be acceptable to Him, and a feeling that He has a claim upon us for such an acknowledgment, and will require it of us. Mix up this rude feeling with the universal instinct of guilt,—which is to dread a superior power, and to long to propitiate it, and then view the practice of sacrifice as meeting this longing, and on that account readily adopted; and we shall probably find here the explanation of its universal prevalence.

It is a curious fact, as showing the hold which the idea of sacrifice has upon the human mind, that although all literal sacrifices were abolished, or rather superseded, by Christianity, the great corruption of Christianity, which, alas! has prevailed more extensively than its purer forms, still recognizes a literal sacrifice as its centre. The whole system of Romanism revolves, if I may so say, round the Sacrifice of the Mass, which the priest is supposed to offer for the quick and the dead. The doctrine of such a Sacrifice in the Holy Communion is justly stigmatized in our Thirty-first Article as a "blasphemous fable, and a dangerous deceit;"—it is one of the many grievous and frightful perversions of what is called the religious instinct. We adduce it here merely as an evidence how deeply rooted in men's hearts is the notion of sacrifice in connexion with religion,—to show that there is something in us which longs for sacrifice, and will not be content without doing it in some shape or other,—in an idolatrous and corrupt shape, if not in that which God prescribes.

It is vain, utterly vain, to seek to rectify errors of this kind by merely decrying them, or enlisting on a crusade against them. Human nature is too strong for us, and defies the effort we make to undo or suppress any part of its original constitution. Let us seek rather to show in what part of pure and true religion such instincts may find their satisfaction; and then we may hope to draw men off from error effectually, because we shall be filling the void space in their minds which at present error offers to fill.

First, then, it is obvious to remark that the Sacrifice of the Life and Death of Christ (for His Life, no less than His Death, was in a most important sense a Sacrifice) is the very core and centre of the Christian Religion. From this centre the whole system borrows light and vital heat, as the planetary system from the Sun. "He hath given Himself for us," says the Apostle, "an offering and a sacrifice to God for a sweet-smelling savour,"—expressing here, we apprehend, the oblation of the life, thoughts, ways, and sentiments of Christ, which, as being altogether holy, were infinitely acceptable to a holy God. Again; "He gave Himself for our sins;"—"He was made sin for us, who knew no sin;"—"this man after He had offered one sacrifice for sins;"—"He Himself bare our sins in His own body on the tree;"—passages which refer to the Sacrifice of Christ's Death, the only real expiatory sacrifice, which has been, or can be, ever offered. By way of explaining this distinction, which is of great importance, but which may not be familiar to all minds, it should be observed, that the offerings prescribed by the Levitical Law fell into two entirely distinct classes. The one class were called sweet-savour offerings, and were for the acceptance of the worshipper; the thought in them was, man giving to God something which God views with complacency. The second class consisted of the sin and trespass offerings, and are never said to be of a sweet savour: in them the thought was man, as a transgressor, enduring the curse which sin has entailed. Our Blessed Lord endured this curse, when, upon the Cross, He poured out His soul unto death; as it is said: "Christ hath redeemed us from the curse of the Law, being made a curse for us; for it is written, Cursed is every one that hangeth on a tree." But before He became our sin and trespass offering, He had been our sweet-savour offering, presenting to the Father a human heart all aflame, as no human heart but His ever yet was, with heavenly love and zeal, a life wholly devoted to the service of God and man, and the only pure worship which since the days of Eden had ever ascended from the Earth. (I step aside for a moment to remark how utterly without foundation in Scripture are all such incautious expressions as that the Father viewed with complacency the Sufferings and Death of His dear Son; a totally different position from the undoubtedly true one, that those Sufferings and that Death were demanded by the Divine Justice. Christ in dying was offering the sin-offering, *which was not of a sweet savour*, and the idea of which was *not* man, as a worshipper, giving to God that with which God is well pleased, but man, as a sinner, bearing God's curse. Justice must be had upon malefactors; but even among men the execution of the death-sentence is never viewed with complacency or satisfaction. How shall it be supposed that the infinitely loving Father of all finds satisfaction in the course of Justice? But to return.) This sacrifice of the life and death of Christ is the essential foundation of every acceptable offering which can be made to God; so that we may call Christ in a figurative sense the only true Altar, apart from which our poor miserable gifts and services can find no acceptance.

Observe, however, that it is the certain doctrine of Scripture that God requires from Christians,—not indeed a sin or trespass offering, which we could never render,—but offerings of sweet savour, as a testimony of their love and gratitude. I say emphatically, *not* a sin-offering. As far as Christ's work was propitiatory, it stands absolutely alone. "He offered *one* sacrifice for sins;" "He was *once* offered, to bear the sins of many." But although no sufferings, no works, no worship of ours can in the least degree propitiate, though we are effectually precluded from joining in the expiatory part of Christ's Sacrifice, God still requires from us offerings of another character. These are generally described as "spiritual sacrifices," which we are ordained to offer,—"an holy priesthood, to offer up spiritual sacrifices, acceptable to God by Jesus Christ." Christ is said in the Revelation to have made Christians "priests to God and His Father;" and, if priests, it is of necessity that they should have somewhat to offer. More particularly, we are exhorted to the sacrifice of *our bodies*, the thought being that the various members of the body should be yielded as instruments of righteousness unto God,—the mouth to proclaim His word, the eyes to gaze on His works, the hands to do Him service, the feet to walk on His errands. "I beseech you therefore, brethren, by the mercies of God, that ye present *your bodies a living sacrifice*, holy, acceptable unto God, which is your reasonable service." Again. *Praise* is specified as a sacrifice;—"By Him therefore let us offer *the sacrifice of praise* to God continually, that is, the fruit of our lips, giving thanks to His Name." And as the surrender of what we have will naturally follow, and be the just expression of self-surrender, it is added,—" But to do good, and to communicate, forget not; for *with such sacrifices God is well pleased.*" And the same thought appears in the Epistle to the Philippians, where the sweet-savour offerings are expressly referred to, and shown to be competent to Christians : " I am full, having received of Epaphroditus the things which were sent from you, *an odour of a sweet smell, a sacrifice* acceptable, well-pleasing to God."

It is extremely interesting to remark how, while carefully stripping the second Sacrament of the false plumage of an expiation, with which mediæval superstition had tricked it out, our Reformers have maintained the doctrine of a threefold sacrifice in the Holy Communion, or culminating act of Christian Worship,—a *sacrifice of alms* made in the Offertory, and referred to in one of the passages just quoted,—a *sacrifice of praise*, adverted to in the words, " we entirely desire Thy fatherly goodness mercifully to accept this our sacrifice of praise and thanksgiving ;" and *a sacrifice of self,* referred to in a subsequent part of the same prayer ; —" And here we offer and present unto Thee, O Lord, *ourselves, our souls and bodies*, to be a reasonable, holy, and lively *sacrifice* unto Thee."

Now out of the many forms in which a devout life may present itself to the mind, there is none perhaps more attractive than that of a constant oblation to God of all that we are, all that we have, and all that we do. Let the thought of Sacrifice be woven into the texture of our lives, let us study to turn not our prayers alone, but our whole daily course and conversation into an offering ; surely the thought that God will accept it, if offered to Him in Union with the merits of His Son, is in the greatest degree encouraging, —a wonderful stimulus to exertion. Some divines so cruelly strain the undoubtedly true and precious doctrine, that man can do nothing propitiatory, or intrinsically meritorious, as to leave their readers or hearers under the conclusion that they can do nothing to please God. Because we are not competent to a sin-offering, they would have us believe, forsooth, that no sweet-savour offerings are open to us. A blank prospect, and very depressing to energy; for what can be more depressing than the belief, which is sometimes practically instilled, that by no frame of mind, or course of conduct, can the believer secure the loving approbation of his Heavenly Father?—a tenet in flat opposition to those words: "We beseech you, brethren, and exhort you by the Lord Jesus, that as ye have received of us how ye ought to walk and to *please God*, so ye would abound more and more."

"To please God,"—what a privilege to lie open to us day by day, and every hour of the day! What a condescension in our Heavenly Father, when we consider the strictness of His justice, the impurity of our hearts, and our many and degrading falls, to allow us to please Him! That we are suffered to bring a tribute to Him, which, when laid upon the one true Altar, and united with the one true Sacrifice, will be received by Him with complacency and satisfaction, what a dignity for sinful flesh and blood to be heir to! Now if we truly appreciate this dignity, let us show that we do so, by availing ourselves of the many opportunities offered to us of pleasing God, by an acceptable tribute. An act of self-oblation, (couched, perhaps, in the very words already quoted from the Communion Service, or in others equivalent,) may usefully form part of every Morning's Devotion, and remind us of the great thought which should run through the day. Then as to our devotional exercises themselves; the thought that Prayer is an incense, kindled in the censer of the heart by the Holy Spirit, and most fragrant and acceptable to God, if offered through the intercession of Christ, and with faith in His Sacrifice, may surely be a great help to us in offering Prayer. But it is the uniform scope and tendency of Grace, as it acquires a greater mastery over the will, to amalgamate the spirit of devotion with our common actions, and more and more to transfuse Prayer into our daily employments, so that these too may become a sacrifice. We need not go far to seek the materials of an acceptable offering; they lie all around us, in the work of our callings, in the little calls which Divine Providence daily makes to us, in the little crosses which God requires us to take up, nay, in our very recreations. The great point is to have the mind set upon seeing and seeking in all things the service of Christ and the glory of God, and, lo! every trifling incident which that mind touches, every piece of work which it handles, every dispensation to which it submits, becomes at once a sacrifice.

> If in our daily course our mind
> Be set to hallow all we find,
> New treasures still of countless price,
> God will provide for sacrifice.
> We need not bid, for cloister'd cell,
> Our neighbour and our work farewell,
> Nor strive to wind ourselves too high
> For sinful man beneath the sky:
> The trivial round, the common task
> Would furnish all we ought to ask,
> Room to deny ourselves—a road
> To bring us daily nearer God."

If we allow the beauties of Nature to raise our heart to God, we turn them into a sacrifice. If cross incidents, which could not be avoided or averted, are taken sweetly and lovingly, out of homage to the loving will of God, this too is a sacrifice. If work be done in the full view of God's assignment of our several tasks and spheres of labour, and under the consciousness of His Presence, however secular in its character, it immediately becomes fit for presentation on the Altar. If refreshments and amusements are so moderated, as to help the spirit instead of dissipating it, if they are seasoned with the wholesome salt of self-denial, (for every sacrifice must be seasoned with salt,) they, too, become an holy oblation. If we study even perverse characters, with a loving hope and belief that we shall find something of God and of Christ in them, which may be made the nucleus of better things, and, instead of shutting ourselves up in a narrow sphere of sympathy, seek out, and try to develope, the good points of a generally uncongenial spirit; if we treat men as Christ treated them, accounting that somewhere in every one there is a better mind, and a trace of God's finger in Creation, we may thus possibly sanctify an hour which else would be one of irksome constraint, and after which we might have been oppressed with the heavy feeling that it had been a wasted one. If a small trifle, destined to purchase some personal luxury or comfort, be diverted to a charitable and religious end, this is the regular and standing sacrifice of alms, recognized by Scripture and the Liturgy. And, finally, if we regard our Time as, next to Christ and the Holy Spirit, the most precious gift of God; if we gather up the fragments and interstices of it in a thrifty and religious manner, and employ them in some exercise of devotion, or some good and useful work, this too becomes a tribute which God will surely accept with complacency, if laid upon His Altar, and united by faith and a devout intention with the one Sacrifice of our dear Lord.

Yes; if laid upon His Altar: let us never forget or drop out of sight that proviso. It is the Altar, and the Altar alone, which sanctifieth the gift. Apart from Christ and His perfect Sacrifice, an acceptable gift is an impossibility for man. For at best our gifts have in them the sinfulness of our nature; they are miserably flawed by defectiveness of motive, duplicity of aim, infirmity of will. "The prayers of all saints," what force of impetration must they have with God, if, as we are assured, "the effectual fervent prayer of a" (single) "righteous man availeth much!" Yet when St. John saw in a vision "the prayers of all saints" offered by an angel "upon the golden altar which was before the throne," it was in union with that which alone can perfume the tainted offerings of even regenerate man; "There was given unto him much incense, that he should offer it *with* the prayers of all saints upon the golden altar which was before the throne."

The incense is the Intercession of Jesus. Place your offering,—be it prayer, or almsdeed, or work, or submission,—in His hands for presentation; pray Him, as your only Priest, to transact for you with God, and He will do so. And the sun of God's favour shall shine out upon that offering, and the dew of His blessing shall descend upon it, and you shall be gladdened with your Father's smile.

CHAPTER X.

OF ALLOWING IN OUR MINDS A PREPONDERANCE TO TRIFLES.

"*Woe unto you, Scribes and Pharisees, hypocrites! for ye pay tithe of mint and anise and cummin, and have omitted the weightier matters of the law, judgment, mercy, and faith: these ought ye to have done, and not to leave the other undone.*"—MATT. xxiii. 23.

IN the course of our thoughts on Personal Religion, attention to what may be called little duties, if not always urged explicitly, has been the under-current of our thoughts throughout. Our regular daily life is not marked by noticeable incidents or great crises; the fluctuations of interest in it are homely and trivial. It is of this average common-place life that we have been endeavouring to show how it furnishes all the materials, out of which, under God's Grace, sanctity may be wrought; and it is therefore quite in accordance with the genius of our subject to consider little duties, little sins, little trials, little self-denials, little cares. For of these little things ordinary life is made up; the trials of our normal state are merely annoyances, not serious trials; its sins are failures of temper, or of the tongue, or omissions of devotion; its duties are often little details of business, or little acts of kindness, or a routine of correspondence almost mechanically performed; its pleasures, when the first freshness of youth has worn off, are a smile, or an old association, or a quiet evening at home, or a genial meeting with a genial friend; its cares and responsibilities, though they may press pretty heavily upon ourselves, are such as a prime minister or a grand vizier would think beneath contempt. If Christian principle is to be shown at all by the majority of men, it must be shown in a common-place sphere of this sort; and it is exactly by showing it on these common-place occasions that we shall, under God's blessing, and by His grace, brace ourselves for the heavier trials and more arduous responsibilities, which He may see fit at any moment to lay upon any one of us. What a dignity does it give to our daily life to remember that by consistent quiet maintenance of Christian principle on these trivial occasions, we may lay in a stock of oil, in other words, nurse, and cherish, and educate a faith and love, which shall burn brightly in the hour of real trial! Whereas he who despises these small occasions, and waits for a grand opportunity to exhibit Christian principle, as one waits for a gala night to let off a blaze of fireworks, is certain to break down when the stress of trial arrives. And it is because we think, as I have before expressed, that the pulpit too little addresses itself to small duties and homely trials; that it soars too exclusively among doctrines and the principles of conduct; that it speaks too exclusively the language of Tragedy, and too little that of common life, that we have been anxious to press home upon our readers, in this little treatise, the cultivation of Personal Religion in that sphere which lies immediately under their hands. And now, in sounding this note for the last time, we still feel how deeply important it is that it should be made to vibrate long and loud in the memory of the reader; how it is almost impossible that we can attach too much importance to such particulars of duty as improvement of time, control of temper, watchfulness in conversation, restraint of appetite, even on occasions where it might innocently be indulged, and gentle bearing of disappointments.

And we may say with truth that duties even lower in the scale than these, duties not moral at all, or not moral in their primary aspect, have yet their importance, and, according to Our Lord's admonition in the text, must not be left undone. It is the last touches of the pencil,—the fine finishing strokes,—which give to a drawing its completeness. And the Christian, remembering his Lord's words, that "whosoever shall break one of these least commandments and teach men so, the same shall be called least in the Kingdom of Heaven," will labour to give to his obedience this finish and completeness by not neglecting even the finer traits of duty. He will eschew, for example, in every thing that pertains to God, the smallest approach to slovenliness. Slovenliness is irreverence in little things; and not the smallest approach to irreverence will the Christian tolerate. Thus, for instance, he will pay attention to postures in prayer, whether private or public. If Daniel kneeled upon his knees in his chamber three times a day and prayed; if St. Paul and the Tyrian Christians kneeled down on the shore to pray; if Our Blessed Lord kneeled when offering prayer in the garden; the Christian will feel that neither in his closet nor in the house of God is he at liberty to adopt any attitude, which betokens indolence, carelessness, or levity. And of another kindred point he will be observant,—a point trifling in itself, and yet having far more influence upon the general heartiness and effect of Public Worship than many a one which is intrinsically more important. In the services of the House of God he will join audibly in the prescribed responses, not contented without expressing aloud his assent to what is there proceeding. It is one characteristic glory of the Church of England, distinguishing her alike from Roman and schismatical communions, that the public prayers which she prescribes are *really* common prayers, in which the people no less than the minister have a share as well as an interest,—so that the sacerdotal character of *all* Christians is recognized by our Liturgy, inasmuch as all are directed on occasions to join in it. Every right-minded Churchman will love by his practice to bring out this feature of our Prayer Book, and will feel that in doing so he is not merely complying with an ecclesiastical rule, but also doing something to kindle fervour of spirit in others by expressing the fervour of his own spirit. Be it remembered of all these lesser duties, that negligence of them is, to say the least, an extremely bad augury of fidelity in higher things; for he who is careless about the little items of obedience is usually reckless also about its large sums; and our Master spoke with His usual profound insight into human character, when He said: "He that is faithful in that which is least, is faithful also in much; and he that is unjust in the least, is unjust also in much."

It is however quite possible that, through the morbid action of the human mind, which seems to corrupt and deprave every good principle which it touches, respectful attention to little things may degenerate into a punctiliousness and a wretched scrupulosity which shall drain off the energies of the soul from the larger and more spiritual duties of religion.

This was the case of the Pharisees. While they paid tithe with unfailing accuracy of their smallest garden herbs, they did not seek judgment, or relieve the oppressed,—their sentences were unrighteous, their practices extortionate, and their hearts insensible to the sufferings of others. Men bring with them into religion their natural character; and in natural character, as in religious, you will find two extremes in regard to little things,—that of those who pay too little attention to them, and that of those who allow their minds to be wholly taken up with them. On the one hand, we have the old proverb already adverted to, warning those, who are careless of small items, that they may sacrifice thereby large sums; and there are notoriously men who need the warning,—who are quite heedless of small expenditures, and care only for considerable amounts. On the other hand, there is to be seen every day this very common phenomenon, persons of wealth, who will stickle and haggle at every little expense incidental to daily life, and yet be comparatively careless about money when it is to be given on a large scale; miserly in small things, and spendthrifts in great; their whole care about property being apparently that it shall not go off in drops and driblets, though for the great drains upon it they are not solicitous. These opposite habits of mind are imported into religion. Some men's religion is all general, and, if I may say so, panoramic; they love large views of doctrine, broad principles of duty; like to have a distant spectacle of religion opened to them from the pulpit, but do not much relish admonitions on the minute and humble duties of daily life. Such are not, and cannot be, growing Christians; life is made up of particulars; and with particulars these men will not condescend to deal. Some, on the other hand, are punctilious about little things, and forgetful of the great spirit of the law. It seems as if the account to be given of such characters was as follows;—that we have all only a certain amount of conscientiousness, and that, if this be all expended upon the more ceremonial and formal duties of religion, we have none left for its great moral claims. Let us glance at one or two of the forms in which this Pharisaic habit of mind, so strongly reprobated by Our Blessed Redeemer, shows itself now-a-days.

1. The late revival of a stricter and better discipline in the Church, and of a more reverent feeling towards ecclesiastical antiquity and the arrangements of our own Book of Common Prayer, though a thing to be very thankful for in the main, has given rise to a crop of petty discussions on points purely ritual or antiquarian, which may easily draw off the mind from subjects of graver import, and with many have actually that effect. We have not any of us too much religious zeal; it is a great pity to spend any of it on such questions as the make of a robe, the shape of a chalice, and whether one

or two collects should be said in the case of a concurrence of Festivals. Generally speaking, such points are hardly worth the energy spent in the discussion of them. If indeed they are regarded simply as questions of antiquarianism or good taste, let them be left to antiquarians, and men of virtu. And if it can be clearly made out that there is a right and wrong, or even a tasteful and untasteful in such matters, let us adopt in Public Worship the right and the tasteful and eschew the wrong and untasteful; but let not such matters, under the insidious pretence of being matters of Religion, occupy any space whatever in our minds. In matters of Religion we want all our available space for the dear Lord who has bought us with His Blood, and really cannot afford any lodging for rubrics, however ancient, or ornaments, however decorous. Let our Churches be all fitted up in a style suitable to the wealth of the district in which they stand; and, as far as possible, to the majesty of Him, whose Houses of Prayer they are; but, that being done, let us think no more about the building, but turn our whole attention to the living stones, ourselves amongst the rest, who congregate in it. Those living stones will outlast the fires of the Judgment Day. Not so the pomp of our architecture, the marble shaft, the porphyry column, the chiselled capital. On all these is written the inexorable sentence of God's Word, "The earth also, *and the works that are therein*, shall be burned up."

2. Persons of a very different order of mind from those described above often are, in their way, as great sticklers for formalities. There is no such mistake as to suppose that those who inveigh against forms are themselves free from the power of them. The Quakers, who discard the sacred Forms of Jesus Christ's appointment, are themselves the most formal of mankind in their dress and in their language. None of us are free from the influence of forms, nor can we be so; our only care should be to see that we allow not our own favourite forms to degenerate into formality,

which they will begin to do as soon as ever our minds are overmuch occupied with them. Catalogues of forbidden amusements, or precise rules as to the method of spending Sunday, are to some people what rubrics and church ornaments are to others; that is, they are the mint, anise, and cummin, which take up in the mind the space due to the weightier matters of the law. With the best intentions, (and good intentions are always worthy of respect,) they lay down certain regulations as safeguards, in their own case, against the sins of dissipation, gossip, vanity, display, and artificial excitements of feeling :—restrictions most excellent and helpful, if regarded in their true light as forms which are only valuable for the spirit which they enshrine, and, like all forms, capable of modification, adjustment, or even repeal, as circumstances shall dictate. Too often, however, it seems to be assumed that so long as the form is secured the spirit is certainly safe, a fallacy than which there can be none more patent. Because a man has said his prayers, it by no means follows that he has prayed. And on similar principles, because a man has conscientiously avoided some public place of entertainment, and confined himself to the society of what is called a few religious friends, it does not follow that he has escaped the snare of dissipation in that society, still less that the few religious friends have bridled their tongues, and avoided all tattle, unreal profession, and censoriousness. You may sin by rash judgment at a tea-table as freely as in the gayest and most brilliant circle which can be gathered in a rich metropolis; and it may be a question whether there is more of artificial stimulant to the feelings in a theatre than in a certain class of novels. We are apt to smile at Romanists on fast-days, when, observing an abstinence from flesh, they are ready to gratify the appetite with every other viand, however delicate and dainty; but are we not ourselves guilty of exactly the same absurdity, whenever we maintain the letter of a restriction, while we allow its spirit to evaporate? Are our Sundays well spent, merely because they are quietly spent,—because we have given as little trouble as possible on that day (a most just and admirable rule) to our dependents, and have confined our reading and that of our children to sacred books? Alas! these restrictions are excellent; but even they will not infallibly secure the right observance of the Lord's Day. Has the day been a delight to us,—a real refreshment of the inner man? Or have its sacred hours brought with them a sense of monotony and dulness, which has led us virtually to say to ourselves, if we have not ventured to put the thought in express words,—" When will the Sabbath be gone?" If so, despite of all outward formalities, must there not have been something wrong somewhere?

It has been our part in the foregoing pages to suggest to the reader several practices of devotion and several rules of life, which, under God's Blessing, and if used with discretion, may be serviceable to him. And we cannot more appropriately close them than by reminding him that even rules of holy living may be a snare, and prove burdensome and entangling rather than helpful, if, in administering them to ourselves, we do not continually keep our eye fixed on the spirit and principle of them. "The end of the commandment is Love," a growing and ever deepening recognition of God as our tender Father through Christ, and of men as our brethren. To establish this filial and fraternal relation, the Lord Jesus came into the world; and to maintain, and extend, and consolidate it, His Spirit is now abroad in the hearts of His people. So far as rules of holy living help to form in our minds this view of God and our neighbour, they are estimable and precious; so far as they neither help nor hinder it, they are useless; so far as they obscure and perplex it, they are positively mischievous. Let our whole question in Religion be, how we can most grow in the love of Christ and of our neighbour, and in the perception (closely associated with this love) of the importance and value of the human soul. Let us measure that soul by its true gauge, by its likeness to God, in respect of intrinsic worth; by Eternity; in respect of its duration; and by the Blood of Christ, in respect of the price which has been paid for it; and we shall then have no mind for toys and trifles in religion. If we view a painted scene from too near a point, the objects represented are massed together incoherently with one another, and the eye confounds the distance with the foreground. But retire to the proper point of view, and all things fall into their places; the distance drops back and seems to lie beyond the figures, instead of towering over their head. So if, in our survey of Religion, we forget the two cardinal relations of man, which are its principal features, we shall lose the perspective of the picture altogether, and may mistake a remote point for an object in the foreground. But let us, as it were, fall back ever and anon, and view religion under those grand relations. God, Christ, and the human soul will then appear as the very front and centre of our contemplations; and every other object will be scanned in the relative proportions which it bears to these three chief actors on the scene.

CHAPTER XI.

OF IMPROVING OUR TALENTS.

"*For the kingdom of heaven is as a man travelling into a far country, who called his own servants, and delivered unto them his goods. And unto one he gave five talents, to another two, and to another one; to every man according to his several ability; and straightway took his journey.*
"*Then he which had received the one talent came and said, Lord, I knew thee that thou art an hard man, reaping where thou hast not sown, and gathering where thou hast not strawed: and I was afraid, and went and hid thy talent in the earth: lo, there thou hast that is thine. His lord answered and said unto him, Thou wicked and slothful servant, thou knewest that I reap where I sowed not, and gather where I have not strawed: thou oughtest therefore to have put my money to the exchangers, and then at my coming I should have received mine own with usury.*"
—MATT. xxv. 14, 15—24. 25, 26, 27.

Two Parables lie side by side in Matt. xxv. which are the counterpoise of one another. The false deductions, which, by the perversity of the human mind, might be drawn from either of them, are corrected by the other. The Parable of the Virgins, which we shall presently consider, teaches the necessity of a hidden and interior life, (the oil being *concealed* in the lamp,) and that no amount of outward activity in the service of God,—no display of gifts, however brilliant, no profession, however strict and high, will, without such an interior life, last out for the required period. Shall the Christian, then, it might be asked, live in and for himself, communing with God in his own heart, and allowing the outer world to go its own way and take care of itself, as if there were nothing real but his own consciousness? Such is the principle of the monastic life; and it is a false principle. It ignores the existence of a neighbour, to whom, as well as to God, we have duties; and it ignores the gift, by which God qualifies us for outward service towards His cause in the world. To correct such misapprehensions, the Parable of the Talents follows close upon that of the Virgins, and supplies one of the many instances with which the Gospels abound, of the perfectness of our Saviour's discourses. It is as if He had said: "I have told you that you must not *lose yourselves* in the activities of Religion; but now I tell you, with equal emphasis, that those activities must not be suffered to collapse. Without secret Prayer, you can do nothing; but you must not shut yourself up from Service, under the pretext of giving yourself wholly to secret Prayer."

The great point and warning of this Parable lies in the history of the slothful servant; and it is his character, therefore, which we will strive to bring before ourselves as a living reality. Let us ask what sort of person Our Lord in the first instance contemplated; and then we shall gain a clearer view how the Parable may be applied to our own circumstances.

It is quite possible that, even now-a-days, a man whom God's Providence had really called to the ministry of the Church, and more or less qualified for it, might shrink from undertaking the arduous responsibilities attaching to such an office. The thought of the account which must be rendered by the pastor of the souls for which he watches, might terrify him; and natural indolence might conspire, as it often does, with pusillanimous fear, to make him decline a life which, to a conscientious Christian, can, less than any other in the world, be a sinecure. A man in this state of mind would be very likely to magnify, or rather to aggravate unduly, the obligations laid upon him, and to represent God to himself as a hard taskmaster, requiring from us more than He gives us strength to fulfil. But in the Early Church, when persons viewed the work of the ministry less as a profession, and more as a very responsible and extremely arduous calling, the case which I have supposed to occur in modern times was of constant occurrence. It was no unfrequent thing for men, who, by the general suffrage of the congregation, were pronounced to be admirably qualified for the government of the Church and the Episcopal Office, to run away and hide themselves, when it was proposed to confer it upon them. Discovered in their hiding-place, they were dragged out, and consecrated by constraint,—made to serve God and their neighbour in the onerous and honourable position of a Bishop against their wills. Was any such grudgingly rendered service in the thoughts of St. Peter when he wrote: "Feed the flock of God which is among you, taking the oversight thereof, *not by constraint, but willingly;* not for filthy lucre, but of a ready mind?" At all events it is in the highest degree probable, if not certain, that such reluctance was often manifested in the Apostolic age, when the emoluments and dignities of the Pastoral Office were little or none, and when it did little else for the holders of it, than set them up on high as a mark for the arrows of persecution. Under such circumstances as those, one can quite understand that a slothful servant of the Lord would be disposed to hide his talent in a napkin, and to use with his own conscience every ingenious and plausible argument, which might seem to excuse such a course. And one argument, which would readily suggest itself, would be, that he was, after all, meanly endowed for the service of the Ministry; and that but one talent—"is it not," he would think, "a little one?"—had fallen to his share.

And here, perhaps, some explanation may be fitly introduced of a clause in our Parable, which causes at first a little difficulty to a thoughtful reader. In distributing the talents, the master is said to have given "to every man *according to his ability.*" We are to understand from this, probably, that the spiritual gifts of the early Church, of which, primarily, Our Lord is speaking, were distributed with a certain reference to what we should call the natural capacity of the holders, —that natural capacity, however, being itself from God. In the foremost Apostles, who had the greatest spiritual gifts,—in Peter, in Paul, in John,—there were remarkable attributes of natural character, which presented a nucleus, if I may use the expression, for those gifts. They were all men of strong and well-defined character, and would no doubt have been men of mark any where, independently of their vocation to the Apostleship. That strength of character constituted their ability; and their gifts were the talents dealt out to them "according to their ability."—St. Paul was a wonderfully endowed man, even in respect of natural qualifications and circumstances. If any member of the Christian Church ever had great ability, it was he. He had a heart comprehensive enough to embrace mankind, and yet full of an ardent patriotism. His affections were diffusive; and yet we find them concentrated with great pathos upon his Corinthian and Philippian converts, upon Timotheus, his own son in the faith, upon Onesimus, whom he had begotten in his bonds. He was as hard as adamant to all the toils and persecutions of the Apostleship, "ready, not to be bound only, but also to die for the name of the Lord Jesus;" and yet he was full of sensibility to others, and a man of many tears. As regards intellectual endowments, he was a most acute reasoner; and though the fervour of his beautiful spirit, which always kindled with his great theme, sometimes is allowed to interrupt the thread of his argument, it is speedily resumed, and prosecuted to its just conclusion. He had been highly educated, and was familiar with the learning and poetry of the Gentiles, as Moses with the wisdom of the Egyptians. In oratory he had that happy gift, which enabled him to take his audience on their own ground, to accommodate himself to their sympathies, and to make their very prejudices the basis of his appeal to them. And as the crown of all his endowments, he had that courtesy and grace of manner, and that fineness of tact, which is partly native in some characters, but partly the result of good breeding, and a generous and wise discipline in youth. And yet this courtesy was not in the least degree alloyed with affectation, and consisted with the utmost plainness of speech towards pretenders and hypocrites. In these features of moral and intellectual character stood the ability of St. Paul—itself, be it remarked, like all natural ability, the gift of Almighty God. And in proportion to this ability he was richly dowered with spiritual gifts, and held ten talents of the Master, and made them ten talents more. His Corinthian converts were very proud of their gift of speaking with tongues; "but," says St. Paul, "I thank my God *I speak with tongues more than you all.*" He cast out a spirit of Python from a poor crazed girl, the slave and tool of mercenary masters. He shook off from his hand a venomous serpent which had fastened there, and felt no harm. Inspired with a sudden memory of a similar act done by the prophet Elijah, he embraced a corpse; and the corpse, under his embrace, became warm with life. He struck a sorcerer with blindness. He restored instantaneously to the use of his limbs one who had been a cripple from his mother's womb. Nay, even a handkerchief, which had touched his person, chased away diseases and evil spirits from those who laboured under them at Ephesus. He prophesied with such effect that profligates, like Felix, trembled, and could not endure it; and pious women, like Lydia, seemed to find in his words the dawn of a new light, and the inspirations of a new life. He was familiar with sacred ecstasy; and was caught up into the third heaven, where he heard unspeakable words, which it is not lawful for a man to utter. And, finally, "he being dead yet speaketh." He wrote, under Inspiration, with such power, that his writings have been from the earliest days the cordial of every believer's heart, and in the sixteenth century became the alarum, which awoke the Church out of the lethargy of mediæval formalism and superstition. And still, wherever the New Testament is read, his perhaps is the strongest influence which emanates from the Holy Book. Such were the ten talents entrusted to the great Apostle "according to his ability."—By his side was another Apostle, endowed much less wonderfully,—having perchance only one talent entrusted to him;—but equally dear, and equally faithful to their common Lord. St. Barnabas was termed by his colleagues a son of Consolation. He was qualified, doubtless, by natural ability to console. He was deeply attached to his relations; a soft and amiable trait of character, which sometimes, however, as it probably did in his case, indisposes us to listen to the stern voice of principle. He loved to promote unity between those who had a common object at heart; and he appears, accordingly, as the peacemaker between Paul and the original Apostles, who at first, from his antecedents, felt for him some amount of estrangement. He was a retiring man; and liked to put others forward, and see them filling the post for which God had qualified them. It is a gentle, unobtrusive character, such as this, which has a capacity for comforting; and according to Barnabas' capacity, so was his gift. None can really and spiritually comfort others, however naturally qualified for it, except by the gift of the Comforter. Then,

> "Warm'd underneath the Comforter's safe wing,
>   They spread th' endearing warmth around:
> Mourners, speed here your broken hearts to bring,
>   Here healing dews and balms abound:
> Here are soft hands that cannot bless in vain,
>   By trial taught your pain:
> Here loving hearts that daily know
> The heavenly consolation they on you bestow."

The Spirit, then, with which Barnabas was endowed became in him, according to his ability, a spirit of consolation. It might seem to some as if this were but a humble gift: only one talent out of the many, wherewith the chiefest Apostles were endowed. Suppose Barnabas himself had thought so, and reasoned thus: "I am not myself alone fit for any great enterprise;

on such an enterprise I can be only second; all I am suited for is to whisper a word of encouragement to better men, when their hearts are failing, and to raise the drooping spirit of a Christian brother. My gift, if gift it can be called, is a quiet one, and will never make any stir in the world." And suppose that, reasoning thus, Barnabas had resolved to make no use of his talent, because it was a little one,—to decline all Apostolic journeys and enterprises, on the plea that he could be but of little use, and that the responsibilities of an Apostle made his heart quake with apprehension; —his would then have been exactly the case of the wicked and slothful servant in the Parable, who hid his talent in the earth, instead of putting it out to the exchangers, because he falsely reckoned that his lord was a hard taskmaster, who would exact a return for which he had never furnished his servants.

What has been said paves the way for the application of the Parable to our own circumstances.

The counterpart of the wicked and slothful servant is to be sought among persons slenderly, not brilliantly, endowed. It is comparatively seldom that you find a man of splendid gifts, and remarkable powers of influence, not displaying such gifts, or putting forth such powers; for vanity is a strong motive force in the human heart, and generally urges a man to put out what there is in him, if he can at all gain credit thereby. Whence it comes to pass that those men who stand much above the heads of the crowd are generally not chargeable with indolence, however serious may be their other faults. But when we are entirely on a level with the crowd in point of endowments, then the temptations to bury our talent in the earth arise in their full force. And this must always be the case of the many. The majority of men, (at least in countries where civilization has long prevailed, and the system of Society has long been running in a regular groove,) will always be mediocre,—mediocre in intelligence, in information, in position, in fortune, in strength of character, in short, in all those points which qualify us for usefulness to others. And the consciousness that they are so, will always be a plea with such persons for being nothing and doing nothing, for hanging about indolently upon life, without any special aim, and therefore without any special energy. There are many elements of feeling which lead to this result. Vanity here, as elsewhere, is on the alert; if we cannot be in the foremost rank, we will be nothing. Indolence is the next trait; a very subtle sin, as well as an extensively prevalent one, hiding itself often under the garb of modesty, and sometimes under the still more specious garb of love for a devout, studious, and contemplative life. Then, also, there is a cowardly shrinking from being pushed to greater lengths in Religion than we are prepared to go; a dread that, if we once put ourselves by our own act into the harness of responsibility, we shall be driven to a greater distance than we bargained for. Then, last, comes the wickedness which, together with the indolence, the master in the Parable stigmatizes,—the ungrateful, unfilial, impious aspersion of God, as one who requires from us more than He furnishes us for. And so it comes to pass that we have a vast number of professing Christians, church-goers and communicants,—men perfectly blameless as far as moral character and fair reputation goes,—who have never even seriously inquired what the one talent entrusted to them may be, much less whether they are putting it out to interest, and securing a return from it.

Reader, if this most important question has never yet been asked, let it form the subject of your next Self-examination. Rest assured of this, that *one* talent you have, if not many, however deep it may have been buried by your thoughtlessness and indolence, however much, by long want of use and currency, it may have gathered a rust which has eaten away the metal. What is it? Is there any one to whom you may be useful in the way of influence, and who is continually thrown across you, but for whose good you have never yet made a single effort? Are you surrendering for objects of Religion and Charity such a proportion of your worldly goods, as a conscience, enlightened by God's Word and Spirit, dictates? Have you any, and what mental endowments? And if so, are you cultivating them with an ultimate view, though it may be a distant one, to the Service and Glory of God? All advance of human knowledge is good and acceptable, if the Father of lights have the glory of it, but contemptible, nay, mischievous, if it terminates upon the gratification of curiosity or of intellectual pride. Have you any leisure hours? and if so, are they turned to good account? A little time spent upon benevolent objects may be of more avail in promoting them than much money. Do we ever spend our spare time so? Does your position and state of life give you any opportunity of usefulness to others? And if so, do you avail yourself of such opportunity? If you can do nothing else for your fellow-men, may you not perhaps console them by your presence with them, and by the mere common-place intimation of your sympathy? May you not say a word of kindness or encouragement, or bring together estranged friends, or persuade able men to the course to which God seems to be calling them? The trumpeter who stirs the spirit of the troops by a well-timed blast, contributes almost as much to the victory as those whom he animates.

Generally, in what direction is your natural ability (itself God's gift) pointing you? Look narrowly in that direction, and you shall soon see the talent with which God has furnished you. Having discovered it, you are to increase by putting it out to interest. The question must be, not simply how you may use it, but how you may use it in the most profitable manner in which it is capable of being used. Without being too ambitious—ambitious (to pursue Our Lord's own figure a little more into detail) of a higher interest than can be had with security—how may the money be made to fructify most largely? If there are two good uses which be made of leisure hours, of superfluous money and redundant luxuries, of natural parts, which of those two good uses is the best? That is generally speaking the best, which has the nearest reference to the spiritual interests of men, which most immediately subserves the good of souls. This is God's end of ends, and this therefore should be ours.

Remark, finally, how hard thoughts of God, such as the slothful servant entertained, lie at the root of all unfruitfulness in Religion. No soul was ever yet, or ever will be, generous in its dealings with God, which has not first formed a large estimate of God's generosity. We must perforce be niggards towards Him, so long as we think Him a niggard either of pardon or grace. O for a juster conception of the intensity of His love and tenderness for us, of His unspeakable willingness to give us day by day, and hour by hour, all things which are requisite for the spiritual life!

If we have ever so little sincere desire to serve Him and to be His, is it not absolutely certain, from the whole tenor of His words and deeds, that He will meet us more than half-way, and bring us on in the right path with more than a mother's tenderness? He requires from us a very arduous standard of sentiment and duty;—granted. We have not for a moment in the course of these Lectures blinked its arduousness; rather, we have striven to cry aloud in the ears of all hearers, "Excelsior!" But does He demand any thing which He is not ready out of His Son's fulness to supply? Is He a Pharaoh, who, while He requires us to build a Pyramid, bids us go get straw where we can find it? Avaunt the wicked and derogatory thought! For every responsibility which we have to meet, He offers to qualify us. For every height which we have to climb, He furnishes an inward strength. So that, whatever be our faithless forecastings before we fairly come up with our burdens, it is extremely questionable whether, while we are bearing them, the heavier seems more oppressive than the lighter. For the feeling of a burden's oppressiveness must of course be proportioned to our strength. And if with a double burden the Lord supplies a double strength, it is exactly the same to our experience as if with half the burden He left us half the strength. Isaac leads a quiet life; and it is not recorded that any great revelation was made to him. Jacob is tossed with troubles, and in the midst of them, he dreams of the great bright ladder which spanned the distance between heaven and earth, and shadowed forth the one Mediator between God and men,—the man Christ Jesus. The same is the law of the Christian's life; an easy pilgrimage, and no extraordinary support; a tempest-tost career, and a strong consolation. We need not faint then at any prospect before us. Progress in grace may be arduous, difficult, impossible to flesh and blood,—out of the question, it may be said, while living in the world; but to all alleged difficulties there is one simple answer, " HE GIVETH MORE GRACE." The cruse of Grace abounds, like the widow of Sarepta's cruse, in time of dearth. And so we will march bravely onwards, assured that, if the last failure of all should begin to overtake us, there will be a proportionably large inflowing from that cruse into the inner man.

"My flesh and my heart faileth; but God is the strength of my heart, and my portion for ever." "For which cause we faint not; but though our outward man perish, yet the inward man is renewed day by day."

CHAPTER XII.

OF THE INTERIOR LIFE.

"*Then shall the kingdom of heaven be likened unto ten virgins, which took their lamps, and went forth to meet the bridegroom. And five of them were wise, and five were foolish. They that were foolish took their lamps, and took no oil with them; but the wise took oil in their vessels with their lamps. While the bridegroom tarried, they all slumbered and slept. And at midnight there was a cry made, Behold, the bridegroom cometh: go ye out to meet him. Then all those virgins arose, and trimmed their lamps. And the foolish said unto the wise, Give us of your oil: for our lamps are gone out. But the wise answered, saying, Not so; lest there be not enough for us and you: but go ye rather to them that sell, and buy for yourselves. And while they went to buy, the bridegroom came: and they that were ready went in with him to the marriage; and the door was shut. Afterwards came also the other virgins, saying, Lord, Lord, open to us. But he answered and said, Verily I say unto you, I know you not. Watch therefore, for ye know neither the day nor the hour wherein the Son of man cometh.*"—MATT. xxv. 1—13.

IN music, the key-note, which rules the strain, also closes it. It should be the same with compositions. Every discourse, every systematic series of discourses, should, after running its round through a variety of propositions and illustrations, at length return to the chord originally struck, or, in other words, gather itself up again into its fundamental idea. We will endeavour to give our Thoughts on Personal Religion this completeness, by setting before the reader, in rather a different aspect, at their close, the thoughts which originally gave rise to them.

The 24th and 25th chapters of St. Matthew form

but one Prophetic Discourse, (grievously disjointed by the division into Chapters, to the great prejudice of the sense,) which may be called the Prophecy on the Mount; and which corresponds to the great Preceptive Discourse of Christ, called the Sermon on the Mount, which is to be found in the fifth and two following chapters of the same Gospel. This Prophecy was delivered at a most solemn period of Our Lord's career. He had closed His public Ministry amongst that "evil and adulterous generation," with eight solemn woes denounced in wrath against them,—but a wrath chastened, toned down, beautified with all the tenderness of that parting plaint; "O Jerusalem, Jerusalem, thou that killest the prophets, and stonest them that are sent unto thee, how often would I have gathered thy children together, even as a hen gathereth her chickens under her wings, and ye would not!" Then, calling it *their* house, to show that it was no longer God's, He suits the action to the word, and passes out of the Temple, as He utters that sentence: "Behold, your house is left unto you desolate." He then ascends the Mount of Olives, from thence to take a parting view of the City and Temple, and, sitting there, pronounces the Prophecy which is before us; and which, springing from summit to summit in the long perspective of the future, carries us down to that division of the sheep from the goats, which will form the concluding scene of Human History. Our Blessed Lord had always loved to teach by Parables; and He continues this method in the discourse before us. The ancient Greek dramatists used to mass together four dramatic pieces in one series, called a tetralogy,—each piece being often connected with the foregoing, and presenting a fresh development of the fortunes of some royal house. Our Blessed Lord here utters, at the close of His Prophecy, a tetralogy of Parables, that of the evil servant in authority, that of the ten virgins, that of the talents, and that of the separation between the sheep and the goats,—all representing the awful crisis of judgment, as it will be gradually unfolded,—judgment beginning with the house of God or Christian Church,—taking effect, first, upon "the ministers and stewards of God's mysteries," who are the servants in authority; next upon Christians considered in regard of the interior and spiritual life, who are the virgins; next upon Christians considered in regard of their exterior life in God's Service, who are the servants entrusted with the talents; and, finally, passing on to the non-Christian world, all "the nations," or Gentiles, who shall be judged by the only law which they have had,—the law of kindness to fellow-men, which is written on the human heart.

The connexion in which this Parable of the Virgins occurs having thus been exhibited, we will now point out the chief lessons which it conveys.

The persons here warned, then, are those who have received genuine religious impressions, and have corresponded with fervour to the grace originally bestowed upon them. Such were the majority of Christians, in the times when the Gospel was first preached with the Holy Ghost sent down from Heaven. All were then earnest in some measure; for the mere profession of Christianity carried with it persecution, and so involved a test of sincerity,—all were animated in some degree not by faith only, but by zeal and love. A flame of joyful hope and earnest aspiration was kindled upon every heart,—the flame this of the lamp of the virgins. The question was, of course, how long such a state of mind would hold out,—how long such a flame would burn. An expectation prevailed among the members of the Early Church, and even the Apostles seem to have been more or less partakers of it, that the flame would not have to burn very long. From such expressions as, "We which are alive, and remain unto the coming of the Lord!" "The Judge standeth before the door;" "Little children, it is the last time;" "Yet a little while, and he that shall come will come, and will not tarry;" "This same Jesus, which is taken up from you into heaven, shall so come in like manner as ye have seen Him go into heaven," they had gathered, not unnaturally, the impression that "the day of Christ was at hand." The Bridegroom would soon return to bring them in from the cold outlying stations of the world to the joyous light and genial warmth of the Wedding Festival;—the Lord Jesus would come again, as He had promised, and receive His own unto Himself. But if He tarried, as we know that eventually He did, what then? Why, this tarrying would give great scope for discrimination of character. It would show clearly who could, and who could not persevere in His absence. Hitherto religion had been very much a matter of impression with Christians; Heaven had seemed, at their conversion, to open to them all its treasures; the Holy Spirit had seemed, when their Baptism was consummated by imposition of hands, to descend upon them, if not in the likeness of fiery tongues, yet in a flame of zeal and love. But this tarrying of the Bridegroom would considerably alter the aspect of religion;—would reduce it from a matter of impression to a matter of principle. It was easy enough to kindle into faith, and hope, and love, when the fervid eloquence of Apostles broke upon their ear, and the elevating example of Apostles was under their eyes; but when their Apostle left them to visit other regions, when he died in cruel torments, witnessing of his Lord, and the tidings reached them of his death; and yet the Bridegroom gave no signal, and they were left still exposed to all the inclemency and dangers of the dark night, the faith, and hope, and love, then began to burn a little low in the socket. And then would come out the distinction of character between Christian and Christian. Passive impressions are designed to be the foundation of active habits, and some would try to make them so. Others would allow their impressions to collapse, without providing for the renewal of them. Instead of regarding them as something to begin and go on upon, they would let them terminate on themselves, and wear out, as it were, their stock of grace, before the day of reckoning came, without an attempt to replenish it.

IV.]   *Of the Interior Life.*   355

And are there no Christians, now-a-days, of exactly the same order? None who remain satisfied with the stock of grace which they received, when they were first brought under religious impressions? Oh, how brightly would their light have been found shining, had they been called away by death, or, in other words, had the Bridegroom come to them, when the first fervour of those impressions was upon them! How zealous were they then! how strict were their lives! how faithful was their protest against the world, and its corrupt works and ways! They even talked of being assured of their own salvation, not at all ostentatiously or boastfully, but merely because in those days God's Spirit did so powerfully bear witness with their spirits that they were the children of God. But alas! their original impressions were not secured, and (if I may so say) stereotyped by activity in the interior life of faith. They did not make the resistance of bosom sins, and the formation of the mind of Christ within them, their one study and pursuit. The indolent, evil thought would still insinuate itself, until it leavened their entire character: "I have been religious once; the oil of grace was poured into the vessel of my heart; and I can quite afford to go on upon my old stock." Unhappily the ministry of God's Word, as it has been carried on in this Church of England for the last half-century, tended to foster this miserable delusion. Almost all the good preaching was directed to awaken the conscience, not to guide it; to make lively impressions, not to render them permanent. If men went away from the sermon pricked to the heart, with the arrow of conviction rankling in their conscience, impressed once for all with the value of the soul, the danger of sin, the preciousness of Christ, that was all which, for the most part, either preacher or hearers looked for; the next Sunday it was sought to do the same work over again upon fresh minds. There being unhappily little or no intercourse on spiritual subjects between the minister and the people, there was nothing but his own religious experience to force upon his notice the fact that the human conscience, after being quickened, urgently needs direction, or, in other words, that Christians need gradual edification, as well as that primary work upon the heart, by which they are turned from darkness to light, and from the power of Satan unto God. And, accordingly, it came to be regarded as the whole business of the ministry to impress; and the pulpit being unquestionably the great means of doing this, public prayers and Sacraments (the means of edification rather than conversion) were, to the great detriment of true religion, postponed to the pulpit; and the hearer, having been worked up to a certain state of feeling on elementary religious truths, (reiterated oftentimes every Sunday, whatever might be the text,) was thenceforth left to fare for himself. If he had made a genuine earnest commencement in religion, if he had lit his lamp of Christian profession with the oil of Divine grace, that was enough; no pains was taken to have a reserve of oil in the oil-vessel.

We shall further expand the lesson of the Parable, if we look somewhat more deeply into the emblems of the light and the oil, and consider the relation which exists between them. Observe, then, that the flame of a lamp is continually burning away the oil. Also, that the flame is visible; and the oil hidden in the vessel. The oil, according to an emblem very usual in Scripture, signifies the Holy Spirit, or divine grace in the inner man of the heart. The light, or flame of the lamp, shall take its interpretation from Our Lord's own words; " Let your light so shine before men, that they may see your good works, and glorify your Father which is in heaven,"—a reference which gives considerable insight into the consistency of Scripture with Scripture. The flame is, in the broadest sense of those words, that confession of Christ before men which is the external condition of salvation,—the confession which is made for each of us by our representatives in Baptism, renewed in our own persons at Confirmation, virtually repeated whenever we join in an act of

Christian worship, repeated more emphatically still whenever we receive the Holy Communion. But the burning of the flame implies something more than the mere nominal profession, which, under the present condition of things, all Christians make. When Our Lord bids us let our light shine before men, He means something much more than this merely nominal profession. He expresses the entire example of the Christian life, given both by its external activities, and by its quiet influence. The kind actions, the benevolent philanthropic schemes, the usefulness to others, whether below us or around us,—all these are parts of the flame; n proportion as these are prominent in any man's life, the flame of his lamp burns brightly. But note, now, that *it is in the nature of flame to burn away the oil by which it is fed.* Christian, if you have spent a busy day in God's Service and in works of love,—if you have stood in the breach, and made a manful protest against worldly sentiments, practices, maxims,—if you have run hither and thither on the errand of mercy to the poor, the sick, the dying,—if your hands have been busy on some work whereby the truth of God may be maintained, and His glory and the interests of His Church subserved; this is all good, so far as it goes, and a subject of devout thankfulness; but still it is external work, and as being external, *it necessarily makes a demand upon, and consumes the powers of, the inner life.* It is all an outgoing of oil; and, if there be no incomings thereof, the flame will not burn long. This good work, this kind word of admonition, this act of beneficence, takes up so much grace,—so much grace spends itself in the production of it; and, accordingly, when it has been produced, more grace will be wanted. Now the question is, are you taking measures to have more? And this question carries us beyond the external life altogether into the hidden man of the heart,—it leads us away from the flame into the oil-vessels. "Your life," says St. Paul (i. e. the springs and sources of it,) " is hid with Christ in

God." What of this hidden life? How is it thriving? "When Christ, who is our life, shall appear," will this hidden life, which you have been leading, leap to light, and be made abundantly manifest? Would you know what is the method of nourishing the springs of this hidden life,—of securing a reserve of oil? One word, understood in a broad and spiritual sense, represents the entire method,—Prayer. Man of profession, are you a man of prayer? Man of work, are you a man of prayer? Man of activity, are you a man of prayer? If your light is shining before men, are you giving all diligence to have a supply of oil that you may keep it so?

And yet, because of the sad tendency of the human mind to formalize spiritual things, and to reduce spiritual exercises into an "opus operatum," (as the Romanists reduce the grace of repentance to the imaginary Sacrament of Penance,) it is quite possible that the term Prayer, when it is said that Prayer is the method of feeding the lamp with oil, may need some explanation. By Prayer, then, we mean not the mere quarter of an hour, or half an hour, which a man spends on his knees daily, but rather the spirit and temper of mind, in which the Christian aims at going through his day. There may be stated prayer, recurring every morning and evening, without the hidden life. And, conversely, there may be the hidden life under circumstances, which render stated prayer an impossibility. The prayer we speak of is that which mixes itself up with all our actions and recreations, as a lump of some solid substance, whose nature is to melt in liquid, gives a taste to every drop of the liquid in which it is allowed to stand awhile. But it too often happens that the prayer of stated periods, though attentively and devoutly said, stands isolated and alone, and never manages to transfuse its sweetness into our ways, character, and conduct. Such prayer is not for a moment to be identified with the hidden life. And, on the other hand, although we have said that the external life of service and profession consumes the grace which is ministered inwardly, this is only true so far as the external life *is* external. The life of active service *may* be so conducted as to secure fresh supplies of grace. If in every part of his active work for God the Christian sets God before him; if he is very jealous of the purity of his motives and the rectitude of his intentions, and very self-searching on these points; if he pauses awhile amidst his occupations, to realize the Presence of God; if he offers up all the works of his calling to God in the union of Our Lord's Death and Passion; if he is diligent in ejaculatory prayer; if, even in the little crosses and annoyances of the day, he regards the will of God who sends them, and takes them accordingly with sweetness and buoyancy of spirit; if he cultivates the habit of allowing the objects of Nature, and passing events, to remind him of spiritual truth, and lead his mind upward; if, in short, he turns each incident of life into a spiritual exercise, and extracts from each a spiritual good,—then he is cultivating the internal life, while he engages in the external; and while, on the one hand, he is expending the oil of grace, he is, on the other, laying in a fresh stock of it in his oil-vessels.

The main lesson, then, taught by our Parable, may be said to be that of perseverance unto the end. In other Scriptures, the doctrine is brought out that God Himself *secures* the perseverance of those who are truly His own people,—as, for example, to quote only the words of Our Lord Himself: "My sheep shall never perish, neither shall any man pluck them out of My hand." Here the equally necessary lesson is adverted to, that perseverance there can be none without spiritual industry. The wise virgins had taken pains to lay in a reserve of oil; the foolish ones had taken no such pains. The warning, then, is for those, in whose hearts the flame of the spiritual life has been once kindled, but who, forgetting the law of our moral nature, that the best impressions consume the energies of the soul, and require to be secured in their results by the active cultivation of Christian graces, give no diligence to make their calling and election sure, and so eventually frustrate their calling and election. We believe there are very many such. We believe that where conversion is considered every thing, and edification nothing; where quiet instruction in the lessons of holiness is sacrificed to exciting addresses, which stimulate the understanding, and arouse the feelings; and where religion is apt to resolve itself into a religious emotion every Sunday, just stirring the torpor of a worldly life with a pleasurable sensation,— there will be many such. And we have devoted this little work, upon which, as we close it, we implore God's Blessing, through Our Lord Jesus Christ, to an exposure of the hollowness of such a form of piety, and to a protest in favour of that interior life (or, in other words, that Personal Religion), for the lack of which no brilliancy of active service done to God can by possibility compensate.

THE END.

www.ingramcontent.com/pod-product-compliance
Lightning Source LLC
Chambersburg PA
CBHW032019220426
43664CB00006B/300